SUICIDE PREVENTION
IN
SCHOOLS

SERIES IN DEATH EDUCATION, AGING, AND HEALTH CARE

HANNELORE WASS, CONSULTING EDITOR

ADVISORY BOARD

Herman Feifel, Ph.D.
Jeanne Quint Benoliel, R.N., Ph.D.
Balfour Mount, M.D.

SUICIDE PREVENTION
IN
SCHOOLS

Edited by
Antoon A. Leenaars
and
Susanne Wenckstern
Windsor, Ontario

◉HEMISPHERE PUBLISHING CORPORATION
A member of the Taylor & Francis Group

New York   Washington   Philadelphia   London

SUICIDE PREVENTION IN SCHOOLS

1 2 3 4 5 6 7 8 9 0   E B E B   9 8 7 6 5 4 3 2 1 0

This book was set in Times Roman by Hemisphere Publishing Corporation. The editors were Amy Lyles Wilson and Kathleen Porta; the production supervisor was Peggy M. Rote; and the typesetter was Phoebe Carter. Cover design by Renée E. Winfield.
Printing and binding by Edwards Brothers, Inc.

A CIP catalog record for this book is available from the British Library.

Library of Congress Cataloging-in-Publication Data

Suicide prevention in schools / edited by Antoon A. Leenaars and
  Susanne Wenckstern.
      p.   cm.—(Series in death education, aging, and health
  care.)
    Includes bibliographical references.
    Includes index.
    1. Students—United States—Suicidal behavior.   2. Teenagers—
  United States—Suicidal behavior.   3. Suicide—United States—
  Prevention.   I. Leenaars, Antoon A.   II. Wenckstern, Susanne.
  III. Series.
  HV6545.8.S85   1990
  362.2' 87' 088375—dc20   90-36063
                                                                                              CIP

ISBN 0-89116-954-7 (cloth)
ISBN 1-56032-081-8 (paper)
ISSN 0275-3510

To Lindsey, Heather, and Kristen

Contents

I
INTRODUCTION

II
SUICIDE PREVENTION IN SCHOOLS

Preface

Both children and adolescents do commit suicide. Although suicide is rare in children under 12, it occurs with greater frequency than most people imagine. Suicide is all too frequent in adolescents. The United States and other countries—such as Canada—saw a striking rise in suicide in this age group between the 1950s and the late 1970s. The rates in the 1980s and 1990 are of considerable concern. An even greater number of our youth attempt suicide and/or think seriously about suicide as the solution to their life's difficulties. Then, of course, there are those who are engaged in other forms of self-destructive behavior, and there are the survivors.

These observations are frightening. Yet, something can be done. Schools especially can make major contributions toward saving lives and assisting before, during, and/or after such a dire event occurs.

We believe that suicidology has an important role in schools. Staff in schools must act as "reasonably prudent persons." The decision of the Ninth Circuit Court in *Kelson vs. the City of Springfield*, 1985, supports this view. In that case, we understand, the court held that a person may bring action against a school for nonprudent behavior. We (A. A. Leenaars) have consulted on a case in the United States where school administrators allowed a special "Nerd Day," resulting in significant abuse of a few individuals and we believe a significant traumatic reaction in one individual—within, of course, the context of that person's life—that contributed to his suicidal solution. Suicidologists and staff at schools together need to provide sound guidance to our youth.

Caplan in his book, *Principles of Preventive Psychiatry* (New York: Basic Books, 1964) outlined the now widely accepted approach to the prevention of mental and public health problems. He distinguished the concepts of primary prevention, secondary prevention and tertiary prevention. In relation to any event (e.g., suicide) one can act before, during, and after. The concepts that are used today to differentiate these three types of prevention are: *prevention, intervention,* and *postvention.*

Prevention relates to the principle of good mental hygiene in general. It consists of strategies to ameliorate the conditions that lead to suicide. "To do," *venire,* something before the dire event occurs. Preventing suicide is best accomplished through primary prevention. In schools, prevention is education. This is in keeping with the general aim of schools, namely to educate young people. We need to educate our young people (and staff at schools) about suicide. Such education, given that suicide is a multidimensional malaise, is enormously complicated, almost tantamount to preventing human misery.

Intervention relates to the treatment and care of a suicidal crisis or suicidal problem. Secondary prevention is doing something during the event. Suicide is defined as an event with biological (including biochemical), neuropsychological, sociocultural, interpersonal, psychological, and personal philosophical/existential aspects. Obviously suicide is not solely a medical problem and many persons including those in schools can serve as lifesaving agents. Nonetheless, professionally trained people, psychologists, psychiatrists, social workers, and psychiatric nurses continue to play the primary roles in intervention. A great deal has been learned about how to intervene—in crisis intervention and therapy—with suicidal young people.

Postvention, a term introduced by E. Shneidman in 1971, refers to those things done after the dire event has occurred. Postvention deals with the traumatic aftereffects in the survivors of a person who has committed, or attempted, suicide. It is offering psychological services to the bereaved survivors. It includes working with all survivors who are in need—children, parents, teachers, friends, and so on. School systems are an especially critical force in these endeavors.

Prevention, intervention, postvention (or prevention as a generic term) in our schools are all important in addressing our problem of suicide in youth. We would go even further and say that they are mandatory responses of a caring, humanistic institution. Yet, critical reflection and research are urgently needed to provide the most sound response possible.

In this volume, we attempt to outline the state of the art of prevention in schools. To do this, we have managed to obtain the cooperation of a highly competent group of contributors. We know them personally and learned about their work mainly over the years through the conferences of the American Association of Suicidology and the Canadian Association for Suicide Prevention. They are *the* suicidologists in our schools.

Here are a few notes (in the order of which their paper appears in the text) about our contributors:

JUDIE SMITH, M.A., is a Suicidologist with the Dallas Independent School District, Texas. She is Cochairperson of the National School Committee of the American Association of Suicidology (AAS).

DAVID LESTER, Ph.D., is Professor of the Department of Psychology, Stockton State College, Pomona, New Jersey. Known as a researcher, he is currently Vice President of the International Association for Suicide Prevention (IASP).

GEORGE DOMINO, Ph.D., is Professor of the Department of Psychology, The University of Arizona, Tucson, Arizona. He is known for his research on attitudes toward suicide.

RONALD DYCK, Ph.D., is the Provincial Suicidologist in Alberta, Canada. He is active in assisting in the establishment of comprehensive prevention programs.

CATHIE STIVERS, Ph.D., is Assistant Professor of Health Education at the University of New Mexico, Albuquerque. She is an expert in the development of self-esteem in youth.

LINDA SATTEM, M.A., is Executive Director of the Suicide Prevention

Center, Inc., Dayton, Ohio. She and her staff have developed a number of
school-related prevention programs.

ROGER TIERNEY, Ph.D., is Head of Counselling at Mount Royal College in
Calgary, Alberta. He is Chairperson of the School Committee of the Canadian
Association for Suicide Prevention (CASP). *RICHARD RAMSAY*, M.S.W., is
Associate Professor of Psychiatry at the University of Calgary. *BRYAN TANNEY*,
M.D., FRCP(C), is Associate Professor of Psychiatry at the University of
Calgary. *WILLIAM LANG*, Ph.D., is Head of Counselling at the Banff Centre for
the Arts.

DIANE RYERSON, M.S., A.C.S.W., is President of the Peake/Ryerson
Consulting Group Incorporated, Englewood, New Jersey. She is Cochairperson of
the National School Committee of AAS.

JAMES OVERHOLSER, Ph.D., is Assistant Professor of the Department of
Psychology at Case Western Reserve University, Cleveland, Ohio. He is known
for his work on evaluation of school-based programs. *STEVEN EVANS*, Ph.D., is a
clinician at Western Psychiatric Institute, Cleveland. *ANTHONY SPIRITO*, Ph.D.,
is Assistant Director of Psychology at Rhode Island Hospital, Providence.

LEE ANN HOFF, Ph.D., is Director of the Life Crisis Institute for Research,
Education/Training, and Services, Boston, Massachusetts. She is author of the
now classic book on crisis intervention, *People in Crisis*.

KIM SMITH, Ph.D., is Director of the Menninger Clinic in Albuquerque, New
Mexico. He is known for his research and clinical endeavors on teen suicide.

JAMES EYMAN, Ph.D., is a staff psychologist and Director of the Suicide
Research Program at the Menninger Clinic, Topeka, Kansas. He is known for his
work on assessment and therapy with suicidal patients.

JOSEPH RICHMAN, Ph.D., is Professor Emeritus at Albert Einstein College
of Medicine, New York, New York. Dr. Richman has specialized in crisis
intervention and family therapy.

ANTOON A. LEENAARS, Ph.D., C.Psych., is a Psychologist in private
practice in Windsor, Ontario. He is President of the Canadian Association for
Suicide Prevention (CASP) and Board Member of the American Association of
Suicidology (AAS), being active in both these associations' School Committees.

SUSANNE WENCKSTERN, M.A., is a Psychology Consultant with The
Windsor Board of Education, Ontario. She is a member of the Canadian
Association for Suicide Prevention's (CASP) School Committee.

BONNIE FRANK CARTER, Ph.D., is Director of Research and Program for
Youth Suicide Prevention Services, Department of Psychiatry, Albert Einstein
Medical Centre, Philadelphia, Pennsylvania. She is active clinically addressing
suicide in youth. *ALLAN BROOKS*, M.D., is Director of Child Psychiatry and
Program Medical Director for Youth Suicide Prevention Services at that same
institution.

FREDERICK LAMB, M.S., is a clinician at the University of Medicine and
Dentistry of New Jersey, Piscataway. He is known for his extensive work on
postvention in schools. *KAREN DUNNE-MAXIM*, R.N., M.S., a survivor, is
Coordinator of the Survivor Support Program at that same institution. *MAUREEN
UNDERWOOD*, A.C.S.W., is Project Director of the New Jersey Youth Suicide
Prevention Project, Trenton. *CHARLESETTA SUTTON*, A.C.S.W., is Cocoordinator
of the Suicide Prevention Project at the University of Medicine and Dentistry of
New Jersey.

JOHN KALAFAT, Ph.D., is Director of the Department of Education at St. Clares Riverside Medical Center, Denville, New Jersey. He is known for his work on evaluation of prevention programs. *MAURICE ELIAS,* Ph.D., is Associate Professor of Psychology at Rutgers University.

ALAN BERMAN, Ph.D., is Professor in the Department of Psychology at American University, Washington, DC. He is an expert on youth suicide.

We believe that these suicidologists have an important contribution to make in our schools. Addressing suicide in schools has a pivotal place in preventing suicide in youth. We hope that this book can be used to assist before, during, and/or after such dire events occur.

Antoon A. Leenaars
Susanne Wenckstern

Acknowledgments

First and foremost we need to make explicit our debt to the contributors—the authorities in the field. We wish, with deepest gratitude, to thank them for their contributions. Without them this volume would not exist. On the same note we would like to thank the American Association for Suicidology and the Canadian Association for Suicide Prevention for providing the opportunity to network with these school suicidologists. Discussions with E. Shneidman, especially regarding prevention, intervention, and postvention, were extremely helpful. The word processing services of Sherry and Maria (Word Creations, Inc.) were invaluable to this volume. We are also extremely appreciative of the editorial guidance of Ron Wilder and Hannelore Wass and their excellent staff at Hemisphere.

I

INTRODUCTION

Both children and adolescents commit suicide. An even greater number of our youth attempt suicide or think seriously about suicide as *the* solution to their life's difficulties. And then there are the survivors: Something can be done. Schools especially can make major contributions toward saving lives and assisting before, during, and/or after such a dire event occurs. Part I is an introduction to suicide prevention in schools. It consists of three chapters: general considerations about suicide prevention in schools, a cross-cultural look at the suicide rates of children and teenagers, and an overview of our young people's attitudes toward suicide. Part I, then, contains some comments that are preliminary to our discussion of prevention, intervention, and postvention.

1

Suicide Intervention in Schools: General Considerations

Judie Smith
Psychological/Social Services, Dallas Independent School District, Texas

The schools provide a logical forum for the integration of suicide intervention efforts. Students are in school 7 to 8 hours each day for approximately 180 days each year. School personnel interact daily with young people and have the opportunity to observe their changes in behavior, understand the stressful situations they encounter, and respond to their direct or subtle cries for help. School suicide programs are built on the premise that it is possible to predict and avert the self-destructive behavior of students. Few would argue that the tragedy of teen suicide cannot be prevented. If it were otherwise there would be little hope for those in despair. There would be little meaning for the mushrooming number of school and community programs whose objectives include seeking options with students who see no way out of their pain and turmoil.

Suicide is a needless end to suffering for the thousands of young people who consider or actually kill themselves each year. It is needless because it kills not only the suffering but all possibilities of future joy and happiness as well. Because most of those who are suicidal do not want it to happen, suicide does not have to happen. This paradox is the fundamental concept of ambivalence. Ambivalence allows support from friends and assistance from counselors or therapists to lessen the intensity of the crisis or lighten the depth of the depression. If a suicidal person were fully determined to die there would be few warning signs and few nonlethal suicide attempts. Instead, the desires to end the pain of living and to go on living are found in the ambivalent suicidal person at the same time. This conflict is communicated through verbal statements and behavior changes by 80% of suicidal young people (1). If the warning signs are recognized by school personnel, family, and peers, the self-destructive act may be prevented.

THE ROLE OF THE SCHOOLS

Why should the responsibility for the prevention of suicide fall to the schools? All too many of society's problems are either blamed on the failure of the schools or delegated to the schools to correct. Three considerations justify the schools' involvement: (a) Schools have the responsibility of helping students develop into productive citizens who can contribute positively to society, (b) Schools have the responsibility to identify and attempt to resolve problems that interfere with the educational process, and (c) Schools have the opportunity and resources to identify and offer assistance to at-risk children (2). Perhaps the most potent argument for the development of school suicide prevention programs is that *education is the key to prevention,* and education is the mission of schools.

Planning

The school district can take the lead and coordinate a task force or advisory council composed of community mental health representatives, school counselors, psychologists, social workers, and nurses. Some communities may chose to rely on private consultants or public mental health agencies for direction if the school district itself lacks the expertise. In any case, the schools must take at least a coleadership role if the program is to be successful. School counselors, psychologists, nurses, or specially trained teachers can provide the consistency and will have already established a trusting relationship with the teens. These are the people who know the students, parents, and neighborhood and they must be incorporated into the program. The planning task force should begin by conducting a needs assessment to understand the problem faced by its particular community. The second order of business is to share this information to establish support from parents, administration, and the school board. Because the school setting is the most logical place for the focus of a community's teenage suicide prevention program, it is vital that support for the program be fostered before it is implemented. All schools contemplating their role in suicide prevention need to have a clearly-written policy that has been accepted by their school boards and the understanding and support of the administration. Preparation for training can be undertaken by the advisory council/task force or delegated to the coordinator of the program. A review of training materials and available workshops is helpful. Excellent regional and national conferences that describe successful programs are held each year. Sometimes, the state will provide training material and seminars led by professional suicidologists. Careful planning can anticipate problems and draw on previous successes to avoid the pitfalls that others have faced. Here is an outline of planning steps:

1. Form community task force or advisory council.
2. Conduct needs assessment.
3. Identify goals.
4. Foster support of school board and administration.
5. Select coordinator(s) or hire consultant(s).
6. Write school policy.
7. Plan program components with short-term and long-term goals.
8. Train crisis team and/or crisis counselors (or identify them in community).
9. Implement project.
10. Evaluate program.
11. Revise based on evaluation.

OBJECTIVES

Specific objectives are tailor-made for each community and will include changes in attitude, knowledge, and behavior of the program participants: students, school personnel, and parents. Virtually all school programs' major objective is to relay the warning signs of suicide to teachers, counselors, and support personnel. A comprehensive program would include parents and the students themselves in this effort. A general goal for a school suicide prevention program would be to *reduce the risk for suicide* among the students. Once suicidal students have been identified the necessary intervention can take place.

The most effective comprehensive school programs include additional objectives in their planning. A good analogy is the danger of a house fire. Once the house is burning an all-out effort must be made to put out the fire and protect the people in the house from harm. Once a young person is headed down the dangerous path toward suicide, the first step is to learn how to recognize the danger and how to intervene effectively. *Intervention* is the beginning objective for school programs. If the fire is detected too late and the house burns down, care must be given to those who have survived in order to assist them with the long process of healing and rebuilding. After a teenager or child has committed suicide, *postvention* procedures will help return the school to its normal routine, comfort those who are grieving, and hopefully, prevent additional suicides. Perhaps the most important part of the house fire analogy for the reduction of the incidence of suicide is *prevention*. Taking a proactive stance in developing fire retardant materials for houses and teaching fire prevention safety rules will lessen the likelihood that the house will catch fire in the first place. Lessening the risk for suicide in children means early prevention; even as early as the elementary school years. Teaching life skills of decision-making, dealing with losses, communicating feelings, and building self-esteem to elementary school children will help young people choose positive alternatives to suicide when they face a serious crisis or suffer from depression. A school climate of support and encouragement creates an environment where children can make the transition into adulthood feeling good about themselves. Secondary school suicide prevention will take a different form. Its components will be more direct in addressing the issues of suicide. A school may choose to implement a peer helper program, teach from a suicide prevention curriculum in a classroom, or plan suicide awareness sessions. Every middle school and high school must have someone on the staff who is trained in suicidology and crisis intervention and who has access to community resources for suicidal students. Emergency care and long-term therapy are not the roles of the school. The planning of a school suicide prevention program must incorporate these available resources in planning a program to fit the characteristics and needs of its own community.

A CASE STUDY

When Mrs. White saw Ed's face in the waiting room of the counselor's office, she expected the worse. She knew Ed and Scott were best friends and she had been concerned about Scott since the beginning of the fall semester 3 months ago. Scott had spent the summer with his father in New York City, over 1,000 miles and a world apart from Scott's southwestern community. Scott's parents separated when he was in the third grade. His mom had custody of Scott and his two younger brothers. It was not easy for the family, and all three children understood the financial hardship. The mother had a live-in boyfriend who was harsh and abusive to the boys. Scott's home life was not pleasant. Scott had always enjoyed the short visits with his father and now that he was 17 he told both parents he wanted to live in New York with his dad. It turned out to be nothing like he imagined. Supervising a teenage boy did not fit his dad's lifestyle. The father had little time for or interest in his son. After 3 months Scott's father sent Scott back to his mother.

When Scott handed in his journal in his English class his teacher alerted the school counselor, who had been specially trained by the suicide crisis team. The teacher had attended a suicide awareness session during an inservice day. She realized that the repeated themes of despair and death might indicate that Scott was considering suicide. The counselor conducted a risk assessment and called Scott's mother for a conference. They both agreed that Scott needed outside professional help. An appointment was made with a counseling agency for later that afternoon.

Scott kept his appointments regularly for about 1 month before he stopped going. He checked in with Mrs. White at school every week and things seemed to be going well on the surface. But she sensed an undercurrent of apathy and non-chalance that was not like Scott. When she expressed her concern to Scott's mother she was told that Scott did not need counseling anymore and that they could not afford the "luxury." She said she appreciated Mrs. White's concern, but she was sure that Scott was going to be fine.

Ed knew otherwise. Scott had confided in him last night that he and his girlfriend had made a suicide pact. Ed had learned about suicide in health class. His teacher had emphasized how important it was to take such comments seriously. He was torn between loyalty to Ed to keep the secret and fear that there would soon be a double suicide if he did not take action. When Mrs. White sent for Scott she discovered that he had not come to school that day. His girlfriend also was absent.

Mrs. White called the school psychologist for assistance. The counselor and psychologist called Scott's mother at work and drove to their home. Their intervention prevented Scott and the young girl from dying. They were found in the garage with the doors closed and the car engine running.

Several people were credited with preventing a tragedy. The teacher had memorized the suicide warning signs. The counselor followed written policy by conducting a risk assessment, notifying the parent, and referring her to a community mental health agency for further treatment. The friend knew not to keep his information a secret even though he struggled with the necessity of betraying Scott's confidence. This was a dramatic scenario that exemplified a successful intervention because this community had invested in a school-based suicide program. The players knew their roles and played them well enough to save the lives of Scott and his girlfriend.

CONCERNS AND BENEFITS

The Dallas Independent School District begins its suicide prevention training sessions for school counselors (primary caregivers) with an exercise entitled "Concerns and Benefits." The old myths and fears of suicide linger and must be addressed before those involved in school programs can be effective in making the program successful. Two questions are asked of the participants: What are your concerns of this program? and What do you think its benefits will be? The concerns and benefits are listed on large sheets of paper and taped to the walls of the training room (Table 1). They are reviewed periodically and discussed again after completion of the course. If concerns are not anticipated and addressed openly, they will jeopardize the success of the program.

Table 1 Sample concerns of counselors

Concerns	Benefits
Taking over parental responsibilities	Saves lives
Parents see school replacing experts	Communicates caring to students
Need continuing training	Parents increase confidence in counselors
Liability	Reduces fear of helping suicidal students
May err in assessing risk	Can respond quickly when have procedure
May inadvertently encourage suicide	Personal satisfaction
Parents' failure to accept referral	Faculty becomes more sensitive to problem
Difficulty in initiating any new program	Safer, supportive environment for kids
Attitudes of teachers, administrators	Increases competence
Will miss some who need help	Organizes efforts
Additional paperwork	Moves school counseling in right direction
Interfacing with other faculty	Become better informed
Comfort level	Institutes a systematic reporting procedure
Longevity of program	More involvement of staff
Lack of administrative support	Builds cohesiveness in faculty
Personal stress	Increases resources for students
Additional time required	Forms support system among caregivers

HISTORICAL PERSPECTIVE

The field of suicidology is a newcomer in the ranks of scientific study. The word was coined by Edwin Shneidman, the founder of the American Association of Suicidology (AAS), and was included in the *Oxford English Dictionary* for the first time in 1989 (3). As the understanding of the suicide phenomenon increased, ways to prevent its occurrence were developed. Crisis intervention became a legitimate and vital counseling method. Some major universities now offer graduate counseling courses in crisis intervention. Counseling educators realize how often a school counselor is called on to aid a student in crisis. They also realize the importance of being prepared for this future responsibility.

Organized school suicide prevention programs were introduced in the late 1970s. One of the first efforts was developed by Tom Barrett in the Cherry Creek (Denver, Colorado) School District (4). The first statewide program was adopted in California. Charlotte Ross was instrumental in the drafting of a bill that provided for pilot projects in San Mateo and Los Angeles County. These have served as guidelines and the impetus for the multitude of school prevention projects now in progress. The idea of using the resources of a school to prevent the occurrence of suicide met with occasional resistance. In response to these initial pilot programs, some educators feared they might plant seeds in the minds of their students or increase their own liability. According to a study by the Center for Policy Studies at East Texas State University in 1983, principals were much more open to accepting suicide prevention programs if there had been a suicide attempt or completion in their schools (5). The impact and reality of the danger became real for them. As experience from around the country proved these fears of doing harm to be unfounded, school administrators began to seek assistance in developing programs for their districts. However, a continuing controversy regarding one component of school programs remains. Teaching from a suicide prevention curriculum in the classroom is questioned by Shaffer, Gould, and Whittle's unpublished research (6). They point out the possibility of upsetting some teens who may realize they have lost the opportunity to help a friend who has been suicidal. There is no evidence that a suicide prevention curriculum induces suicidal behavior. In general, Shaffer et al. believe these programs are beneficial. This research is yet to be replicated but it indicates a need to be cautious and to always make sure the teacher or curriculum presenter is properly trained and qualified to handle serious concerns or make professional referrals when necessary.

There has been an increased awareness of the problem of teenage suicide with the abundant media coverage of the too frequent suicide epidemics, beginning with Plano, Texas in 1983 (7). Professional suicidologists have been alarmed about the frightening increase of teenage suicides in the last three decades (8). But it took continuing headlines and prime-time television programs to capture the attention of the public. Communities formed task forces and held town meetings to explore the best ways to keep their young people from killing themselves. Parent organizations, teacher workshops, and school assemblies scheduled speakers to talk about suicide. Teenage suicide became a popular subject for authors and journalists. Epidemiologists and suicidologists willingly shared information on risk factors and warning signs. People are more sophisticated about suicide today as a result of this public concern. With the increase in knowledge has come a more accepting attitude toward school-based suicide prevention programs.

Two recent national conferences focused on the role of the schools in suicide prevention. In April 1987 the Wingspread Conference, sponsored by the American Association of Suicidology with support from the Coors Foundation, the Johnson Foundation, and the National Education Association, brought researchers and educators together to begin the development of guidelines for school programs. A theoretical framework was sketched out and the conclusion was reached to emphasize primary prevention beginning in elementary school (8). The Orlando Conference in October 1987 targeted educators and suicidologists who were planning and implementing school programs. Each year many well-attended sessions at the annual meeting and conference of the American Association of Suicidology are devoted to suicide prevention in the schools. The last three conferences have featured plenary sessions to examine the "tough" issues and exemplary programs. Interest is high among professionals to offer safe and effective means of educating students, school personnel, and parents about suicide and suicide prevention.

The American Association of Suicidology

The AAS has taken an active leadership role in providing for school prevention programs. This role fits comfortably in its mission, which was adopted in 1982 (10). "The mission of the American Association of Suicidology is to understand and prevent suicidal behaviors. It will accomplish this mission by directing efforts to:

I. Advance suicidology as a science; encouraging, developing, and disseminating scholarly work in suicidology.

II. Encourage the development and application of technologies which reduce the incidence and prevalence of suicidal behaviors.

III. Compile, develop, critique, and disseminate accurate information about suicidal behaviors to the public.

IV. Encourage the highest possible quality of suicide prevention services to the public.

V. To identify, assess, arrive at positions, and publicize official AAS positions on issues of public policy effecting study and prevention of suicide.

VI. Encourage training in the study and prevention of suicide."

As interest in school programs increased, a standing committee of AAS was formed in 1986 to establish standards and encourage the exchange of ideas. It is an advocacy committee for the implementation of school/community-based suicide awareness programs. The membership was divided into six subcommittees: legislative, training materials, standards and guidelines, evaluation, communication, and grants. Each subcommittee has produced practical documents to assist those who plan and implement school programs. Examples of available documents include a list of available resources for funding programs and a training workshop in grant writing (available from the Division of Psychology in Education at Arizona State University); an annotated list of audiovisual materials (available from the Suicide and Information Center in Calgary, Albert); and postvention guidelines (available from AAS Central Office, Denver, Colorado).

As the number of school programs continually increased, the need to document and compare the various types of programs, the content they emphasized, and how they approached the task of evaluation became apparent. At the request of the AAS School Programs Committee, a questionnaire was distributed and analyzed by Smith, Eyman, Dyck, and Ryerson (11). One-hundred-and-fourteen programs were identified in 33 states in the United States and 5 Canadian provinces. These programs reach more than 2 million students and adults annually. Most of the programs are based either in schools or crisis centers and funded by the schools or public money. Emphasis in the classroom is placed on teaching crisis intervention facts and skills. A third of the participants used a printed curriculum and 72% developed their own materials. A quarter of the survey participants reported having a peer support component and three-fourths had some form of crisis intervention team procedure. The report encouraged AAS to continue its leadership in developing minimum standards for content, supervision, and program evaluation.

Legal Concerns

A lawsuit in Oregon prompted many communities to consider implementing a suicide prevention program in their schools. In *Kelson v. the City of Springfield* (1985) the parents of a 14-year-old boy sued the school district for negligence after the boy committed suicide while at school. The complaint contained allegations that the school had a duty to provide suicide training to their employees and that they had failed to do so. The case was admitted to court because the boy's death allegedly resulted from inadequate staff training. An out-of-court settlement was reached in this case.

There are two prior legal cases in which a school district has been sued following the suicide of a student. In *Bogust v. State of Wisconsin* (1960) parents sued the director of student personal services at Stout State College when their daughter committed suicide 6 months after the counselor terminated their sessions. The parents held that the counselor did not secure emergency psychiatric treatment, tell the parents that the girl was suicidal, or give proper guidance. The courts ruled that there was no liability because, with his background and training, the average school counselor would not know that the student was going to commit suicide and thus could not be expected to advise the parents or provide corrective guidance. He had no duty to perform in any such manner. Thus failure to do so was not actionable in court. Another factor in this case was the lapse of 6 months. If the student had demonstrated agitation when she was told of the termination it might have been different (12).

Action was brought to recover against the Greece Central School District (1976) in Buffalo, New York, for mental and emotional distress suffered by the sister by reason of her brother's suicide and to recover medical expenses incurred by the mother for her daughter. The complaint was that the district's employees, teachers, and administrators carelessly, recklessly, and negligently allowed the brother to commit suicide. The court did not rule in favor of the mother and the complaint was dismissed (12). This case does not have as much bearing on the current concern for legal implications of school suicide programs as other cases.

While the case of *Bogust v. State of Wisconsin* bodes well for schools, another case is more troubling even though the public schools were not involved. A young teenager who was thought to have emotional and behavioral problems was placed in a reform school in New York State. He committed suicide after he exposed himself to a female attendant in the boys dormitory and was disciplined with a slap by a male employee. He was left unattended in a bathroom where he hanged himself. Because he was in a reform school the state had assumed "quasiparental power" over the child and was responsible for protecting him from injury. The court ruled that the suicide should have been predicted after such upsetting events, knowing the boy had a history of emotional and behavioral problems, and that the reform school "had a duty to prevent it." Farren cautions that this quasiparental power may put school districts at risk. "If you somehow accept responsibility for someone, you become more responsible for what happens to them" (12).

Although student suicides have not brought many school districts into the courtroom, Farren thinks that the problem of student suicide is a "time bomb." He warns that training teachers to identify students who may commit suicide could increase the likelihood that a school district may be sued if a child kills himself or herself. Ironically, "by educating your people, you're making them more vulnerable for failing to conduct themselves properly."

There are unanswered legal questions to be tested in the courtroom. It is highly recommended that an attorney's advise be sought before implementing a school suicide prevention program. The school attorney for the Dallas Independent School District believes there is no real protection from the possibility of being sued. If a school employee follows school policy there is little likelihood that the suit would be successful. Legal issues do not deter a district from its obligation to provide suicide prevention programs. The attorney for the Johnston, Colorado, School District states that "Employees and officials of school districts which have had completed suicides or suicide threats and/or recognize or should recognize that they have a problem have the responsibility under threat of liability to perform as would a 'reasonably prudent person under similar circumstances,' which would require as a minimum that the district provide services and/or programs dealing with suicide prevention. In other words, identify, evaluate, and provide or cause others to provide to students who are in jeopardy" (13).

Legislation

Encouragement for teen suicide prevention efforts has come from state legislatures. The lawmakers have responded to citizen input with public hearings, community task forces, and testimony of suicide prevention experts. Based on the growing concern of the continuing loss of young people from suicide, 11 states have passed legislation calling for state plans to establish programs involving the public education system. The following summary describes the basic intent of these state bills (14):

California, 1983

This bill provided for the development of a statewide youth suicide prevention program through the establishment of state-mandated demonstration programs in two designated counties. Existing suicide prevention and crisis centers located within those counties served as coordination centers for the planning and development of the statewide program. The Department of Education was required to report annually to the Legislature regarding the status and effectiveness of the programs. $300,000 was appropriated from the 1984 budget.

Connecticut, 1987

A task force was established to study teenage suicide. It addressed classroom instruction, community-based programs, teacher and parent training programs, and available counseling services. It developed an identification and prevention model for utilization by governmental, community, and educational organizations. Public hearings were held throughout the state.

Florida, 1984

Under the provision of this law the Department of Health and Rehabilitative Services developed a state plan for the prevention of youth suicide. The Department of Education and appropriate public and private local agencies and organizations were provided an opportunity to participate in the development of the state plan. The plan provided for instruction of school staffs; law enforcement personnel; and education of the public. It included the development of school curriculum and training materials. Each service district developed a specific plan for its local area.

Maryland, 1986

A youth suicide prevention school program was established, administered by the Department of Education in cooperation with local education and appropriate community agencies. The department was required to establish a school demonstration program, allocate funds, and assure that youth services bureaus provided certain services to address youth suicide prevention.

New Jersey, 1985

A youth suicide prevention program was established by the State Department of Human Services and administered by community mental health service providers in cooperation with local boards of education. The objectives were to develop classroom materials, training programs for teachers and counselors, and other community-based programs. Guidelines were prepared in consultation with the

Commissioner of Education. Proposals were solicited for suicide prevention projects from community mental health service providers interested in participating in the program. These proposals were to include procedures for evaluation. A Youth Suicide Prevention Advisory Council was established within the Department of Human Services. $300,000 was allocated for the purposes of this act.

New York, 1987

The Office of Mental Health was authorized to establish, in consultation with the Council on Children and Families, a special program to provide grants to organizations or schools to educate the general population (in particular, parents, teachers, clergy, health and mental health professionals, and adolescents themselves) of the positive actions that can be taken to identify and treat adolescents who are at high risk for suicide.

North Carolina, 1987

A Youth Suicide Study Commission was created to study the issues and causal factors associated with youth suicide. The Commission was to study the relationship of youth suicide to drug addiction and child abuse, an effective monitoring system, treatment and intervention programs, coordination of existing services, and funding resources. $25,000 was allocated to fund the Commission.

Rhode Island, 1986

The Department of Education was instructed to develop and prescribe a suicide prevention awareness program for public school students. Local school committees were to provide for the incorporation of this program into existing health education courses. The Samaritans provided workshops for the training of teachers. $35,000 was appropriated to the Samaritans for this purpose.

Texas, 1989

Material for inservice programs will be developed and distributed by the Texas Education Agency (TEA) to train teachers, counselors, school nurses, and administrators in the prevention of and response to suicide or attempted suicide by public school students. School districts will repeat the training each year and evaluate the effectiveness of their suicide prevention and response procedures during that year. The TEA will also provide guidelines to promote cooperation among schools and local agencies in suicide prevention. The legislation also formed a state Youth Suicide Prevention Advisory Committee.

Virginia, 1987

A joint subcommittee was established to study the causes of suicide among children and youth and to develop strategies to implement effective youth suicide prevention programs. Local and state officials, as well as the public and educators, were to participate in its study so as to emphasize a partnership between government and the public. The cost of the subcommittee's work was estimated to be $19,800.

Wisconsin, 1985

The Department of Education, in conjunction with the Department of Health and Social Services, was instructed to develop and conduct training programs in suicide prevention for the professional staff of public and private schools and county departments of public welfare or social services. These programs included: information on development of positive emotional mental health, detection of suicidal tendencies, intervention techniques, and coordination of school suicide-prevention programs and other state and local agencies.

The U.S. Congress has considered pieces of legislation that would create federal support for research, education, and training programs dealing with suicide prevention. Bills introduced by Representative Gary Ackerman and Senator Frank Lautenberg would award grants to "private, nonprofit organizations" to establish "youth suicide prevention programs." The American Association of Suicidology passed a resolution endorsing both bills. Money is now available through the National Institute of Mental Health, authorized by the 1990 Public Health Act to fund two to four research demonstration projects.

FUTURE DIRECTIONS

School suicide prevention programs are fledgling enterprises. They have not had the experience or long-term evaluation necessary to prove their effectiveness. The need is apparent for educational involvement in the movement for youth suicide prevention. Local resources dictate which components are included in these educational projects. Raising the awareness of common warning signs for all those who come into contact with children and teenagers should be included in school-based suicide awareness sessions. Once suicidal individuals have been identified, their friends, parents, teachers, counselors, and other support staff need to be taught how to respond and what professional resources are available in their community. It is desirable to have a professional crisis team intervene with these suicidal students, if possible. In the future, crisis teams will likely broaden their services and become involved with other crisis management problems in addition to suicide. The homicide rate is often as high as the suicide rate. Headlines capture the national attention when a sniper opens fire on a playground full of children or a disgruntled person takes hostages from a classroom. Drug abuse erodes the values and motivation of young people. Cult involvement and gang violence are spreading. These frightening trends pose a threat to future generations and our society.

The causes of suicide and other destructive behaviors are interwoven. It is logical for those who design suicide prevention programs to combine efforts with other school projects to help protect at-risk students from self-destructive behavior. Bob Yufit, the 1989 president of the American Association of Suicidology (AAS), stated that AAS needs to "develop school prevention programs, not only to promote more effective identification and intervention of suicidal and self-harmful behaviours, but to teach youngsters how to cope more effectively with stress, loss, rejection, and isolation" (15). Teaching life skills to elementary school children and improving the nebulous school climate will probably have a tremendous effect on preventing suicides by helping young people develop sound mental health. Funding and grants for substance abuse programs already share some aspects of suicide prevention, such as peer facilitating or peer counseling. Mentoring projects, peer tutoring, and support groups are becoming part of efforts to reduce dropout rates. Obviously, these kinds of efforts by the schools will also reduce the risk for suicide.

Yufit also called for AAS members and those interested in preventing suicide to "become more visible to legislators and educators to increase our impact." Eleven states have passed legislation mandating teen suicide-prevention studies, advisory councils, guidelines, training workshops, and grants to fund model school programs. If the incidence of teen suicide continues to be a concern to the public, additional states will consider adding legislative support to preventive efforts.

Comprehensive school-based programs now emphasize postvention procedures. All large school districts, and many small districts, have had a student commit suicide. Even small districts sometimes have several suicides in quick succession, suggesting a contagion phenomenon. Postvention requires expertise in grief counseling and knowledge of the dangerous effects that a suicide can have on survivors. Much has been learned by those who are called to assist a school in returning to its normal routine after the devastation of a suicide. These guidelines and other aspects of school programs need to be collected in a central location for distribution to educational institutions and others who are interested in reviewing them. Training seminars and workshops will assist in the preparation of professional for this role.

As additional school programs appear each year it is logical to be concerned about their standards and understanding of the critical issues. The AAS School Programs Committee is in the process of compiling standards for school policies and classroom curriculum. A review of standards and guidelines for other aspects such as peer helper classes, counselor crisis intervention training, and faculty suicide awareness sessions can be added to the data bank.

One of the goals proposed by the Strategic Planning Committee to the AAS Board of Directors in April 1989 is to "develop guidelines for program evaluation/program components for schools by 1991" (16). Large scale valuation of school programs has yet to be undertaken. There is precious little available funding for research and little has been initiated. The existing programs and guidelines were developed from few years of experience, and recommendations were based more on impressions than acceptable data. It is yet to be determined what effect school programs have on changing the behavior of suicidal students. Nonetheless, a beginning has been established and acceptable headway is visible. Future vital statistics of mortality will tell us if we are moving in the right direction.

REFERENCES

1. Smith, J. (1986). *Coping with suicide.* New York: Rosen.
2. Smith, J., & Garza, L. (1989). Project SOAR: Suicide; options, awareness, and relief. Dallas, TX: Dallas Independent School District.
3. *Oxford English Dictionary.* (1989). 2nd edition. England.
4. Barrett, T. (1985). *Youth in crisis; Seeking solutions to self-destructive behavior.* Longmont, CO: Sopris West.
5. Harris, M. B., & Crawford, R. W. (1987). Youth suicide: the identification of effective concepts and practices in policies and procedures for Texas schools. Center for Policy Studies and Research Monograph, No. 3. Commerce, TX: East Texas State University.
6. Shaffer, D., Garland, A., & Whittle, B. (1988). An evaluation of youth suicide prevention programs; executive summary. In a report to the Governor's Advisory Council from the New Jersey Youth Suicide Prevention Project.
7. Coleman, L. (1987). *Suicide clusters.* Boston: Faber and Faber.
8. Poland, S. (1989). *Suicide intervention in the schools.* New York: Guilford Press.

9. *Report of the Wingspread Meeting.* (1988). American Association of Suicidology Task Force on School Suicide Prevention Efforts.
10. American Association of Suicidology Mission Statement. (Adopted April, 1982).
11. Smith, K., Eyman, J., Dyck, R., & Ryerson, D. (1987). *Report of the School Suicide Programs Questionnaire.* In a report made to the American Association of Suicidology Board of Directors.
12. *Nation's Schools Report.* February 29, 1988.
13. Ruof, S., & Harris, J. (1988). Q. and A. on legal issues related to suicide. *Communique: National Association of School Psychologists, 16.*
14. Smith, J., & Ryerson, D. (1989). The school corner: States with teen suicide prevention legislation. *Newslink, 15.*
15. Yufit, R. (1989). Message from the new president. *Newslink, 14.*
16. American Association of Suicidology five year strategic plan. (1989). *Newslink, 14.*

2

A Cross-Cultural Look at the Suicide Rates of Children and Teenagers

David Lester
Richard Stockton State College, Pomona, New Jersey

As Maris (1) has noted, teenage suicide is probably *the* issue in suicidology right now. Many books have appeared on the topic (2), and the media give major attention to suicidal deaths among teenagers. Indeed, in the United States teenage suicide rates have risen 287% between 1960 and 1980 (1). In contrast, the suicide rate among those aged 45 and older has decreased during this same time period. The concern for teenage suicide is clearly merited.

This chapter seeks to provide some understanding of the teenage suicide epidemic in America by looking at teenage suicide from a cross-cultural perspective. For example, it is pertinent to ask whether all nations of the world are experiencing this rise in teenage suicide. And if the rise is not universal, to discover which nations are experiencing a rise in teenage suicide. Furthermore, is this rise in teenage suicide part of a general trend of rising suicide rates in the world or are teenagers the only age group showing this increasing suicide rate?

The data for this chapter were obtained for 1970 and 1980 from suicide rates published for those aged 5–14 and 15–24 by the World Health Organization (3). Nations with populations of at least one million in 1980 and at least 250 suicides overall were included (so that the suicide rates would be reasonably reliable estimates).

SUICIDE IN THOSE AGED 15–24

The nations in the sample and their suicide rates in 1970 and 1980, both for the total population and for those aged 15–24, are shown in Tables 1 and 2. It can be seen that there is great variation among the nations of the world in the change in youth suicide rates.

Nations with the highest increases in youth suicide rates are Norway (+224%), Spain (+93%), Switzerland (+80%), and Thailand (+78%). In addition, New Zealand, Israel, Finland, Canada, and the Netherlands have experienced large increases in their youth suicide rate from 1970 to 1980.

In contrast, several nations have witnessed decreases in the youth suicide rate, including Chile (−32%), Venezuela (−28%), and Sweden (−13%). West Germany and Japan also experienced decreases during this period.

More detailed examination shows that many nations have experienced increasing suicide rates in general from 1970 to 1980. This, it perhaps makes more sense

Table 1 Suicide rates (per 100,000, per year) in 1970 and changes by 1980 for the total population
and for those aged 15–24 and 5–14

Country	Total population		Youths 15–24		Children 5–14	
	1970	% Change by 1980	1970	% Change by 1980	1970	% Change by 1980
Australia	12.4	−11.2	8.6	+30.2	0.3	−33.3
Austria	24.2	+6.2	16.5	+9.1	0.3	+666.7
Bulgaria	11.9	+14.3	6.9	+34.8	0.9	0.0
Canada	11.3	+23.9	10.2	+50.0	0.4	+50.0
Chile	6.0	−18.3	10.1	−31.7	0.8	−75.0
Denmark	21.5	+47.0	8.5	+42.4	0.3	0.0
Finland	21.3	+20.7	14.7	+60.5	0.8	−37.5
France	15.4	+26.0	7.0	+52.9	0.4	0.0
Germany (West)	21.3	−1.9	13.4	−6.7	0.9	+11.1
Greece	3.2	+3.1	1.5	+20.0	0.1	+300.0
Hong Kong	13.6	−0.7	7.7	+1.3	0.5	−60.0
Hungary	34.8	+29.0	18.9	+5.8	1.2	+91.7
Italy	5.8	+25.9	2.9	+34.5	0.3	−33.3
Japan	15.2	+15.8	13.0	−3.8	0.3	0.0
Netherlands	8.1	+24.7	4.0	+50.0	0.4	−75.0
New Zealand	9.6	+12.5	8.0	+73.7	0.5	−40.0
Norway	8.4	+47.6	3.7	+224.3	0.2	+300.0
Portugal	7.5	−1.3	4.5	+2.2	0.1	+400.0
Singapore	8.9	+25.8	7.8	+32.1	0.5	+80.0
Spain	4.2	+4.8	1.4	+92.9	0.1	0.0
Sweden	22.3	−13.0	13.3	−13.5	0.5	−40.0
Switzerland	18.6	+38.2	13.0	+80.0	0.4	+150.0
Thailand	4.2	+76.2	7.2	+77.8	0.3	+200.0
United Kingdom: England and Wales	8.0	+10.0	6.0	+6.7	0.0	0.0
United Kingdom: Scotland	7.6	+31.6	5.8	+65.5	0.0	0.0
United States	11.5	+2.6	8.8	+39.8	0.3	+33.3
Venezuela	6.8	−23.5	14.5	−28.3	0.7	−42.9

to compare the increase in youth suicide rates with those of the total population.
Furthermore, the rise varies with sex.

Using a criterion that the percentage increase in the youth suicide rate must be
10% or greater than the percentage increase in the overall suicide rates, the following nations had a rising youth suicide rate in both males and females: Finland,
the Netherlands, New Zealand, Norway, Scotland, Spain, and Switzerland. Nations with a rising youth suicide rate in males only were: Australia, Canada,
France, Greece, Israel, Italy, Thailand, and the United States. Nations with a
rising youth suicide rate in females only were: Austria, Bulgaria, England and
Wales, and Singapore.

It is clear that there is no universal pattern. Different nations are experiencing
very different changes in the rates of male and female youth suicides as compared
to the suicide rate of the total population.

Lester (4) has shown that nations with a higher quality of life have higher
suicide rates. He explained this phenomenon by using a theory of suicide and
homicide proposed by Henry and Short (5). Henry and Short argued that when

Table 2 Suicide rates by age in countries of the world in 1970 and 1980

Sex and year	5–14	15–24	25–34	35–44	45–54	55–64	65–74	75+
				Australia				
Male								
1970	0.3	12.4	20.1	26.1	33.6	30.9	31.9	38.5
1980	0.3	17.6	22.9	23.4	22.3	24.0	22.4	31.9
Female								
1970	0.3	4.7	7.8	11.8	14.6	17.0	14.4	9.5
1980	0.2	4.5	6.9	9.8	9.2	7.9	7.1	9.1
				Austria				
Male								
1970	0.7	27.0	31.7	46.6	58.5	64.6	72.7	77.7
1980	3.9	28.8	36.3	43.9	59.3	56.3	72.6	85.7
Female								
1970	0.0	5.7	8.2	16.4	22.3	25.7	27.6	29.4
1980	0.7	6.7	11.1	14.3	20.7	23.0	29.1	33.9
				Bulgaria				
Male								
1970	1.1	9.0	11.6	11.3	19.3	27.1	53.2	108.3
1980	1.1	11.1	12.9	16.3	21.9	26.8	52.2	108.7
Female								
1970	0.8	4.8	4.9	5.3	9.8	15.9	18.4	34.5
1980	0.6	7.4	5.8	5.7	8.2	14.4	17.0	31.9
				Canada				
Male								
1970	0.6	15.6	20.1	26.6	27.9	31.9	28.0	24.6
1980	0.8	24.8	29.5	25.1	30.7	28.5	26.9	38.1
Female								
1970	0.1	4.8	8.6	10.6	14.5	11.4	9.5	4.6
1980	0.3	5.4	8.1	8.8	13.7	12.1	9.5	5.9
				Chile				
Male								
1970	1.1	14.3	17.7	14.9	16.6	13.9	22.1	19.9
1980	0.3	10.8	12.1	13.9	12.5	15.3	10.6	21.2
Female								
1970	0.5	6.1	3.4	1.6	3.2	2.9	3.0	3.5
1980	0.1	2.9	1.9	0.9	1.7	2.9	1.3	2.4
				Denmark				
Male								
1970	0.5	11.1	25.4	39.5	55.9	48.8	45.7	55.0
1980	0.3	16.3	42.7	61.8	70.7	71.8	60.4	81.3
Female								
1970	0.0	5.7	10.6	22.6	30.2	34.1	26.7	19.1
1980	0.3	7.7	16.7	35.8	42.8	39.3	32.9	31.6

(*Table continues on next page*)

Table 2 Suicide rates by age in countries of the world in 1970 and 1980 (*Continued*)

Sex and year	5–14	15–24	25–34	35–44	45–54	55–64	65–74	75+
				Age				
				Finland				
Male								
1970	1.3	22.5	41.5	55.8	60.9	62.6	66.5	50.5
1980	0.6	37.5	55.7	55.0	60.3	54.9	62.1	60.1
Female								
1970	0.3	6.7	9.4	11.2	20.6	15.9	12.2	7.4
1980	0.3	9.1	9.5	11.4	16.8	16.2	22.8	9.7
				France				
Male								
1970	0.7	9.4	17.1	25.5	36.2	51.1	55.3	74.4
1980	0.7	15.7	27.4	32.7	39.7	41.2	57.1	99.6
Female								
1970	0.0	4.4	7.4	8.0	11.3	16.3	17.9	18.6
1980	0.2	5.4	9.6	13.2	14.9	17.2	22.6	24.4
				Greece				
Male								
1970	0.0	1.7	3.9	6.1	6.7	10.6	10.7	11.6
1980	0.7	3.0	5.4	5.6	5.2	5.4	10.1	16.6
Female								
1970	0.1	1.4	1.7	1.0	3.2	4.3	1.7	5.6
1980	0.1	0.6	1.1	1.9	2.8	2.9	4.5	6.1
				Hong Kong				
Male								
1970	0.6	7.2	27.3	23.8	33.8	41.5	50.5	88.7
1980	0.0	7.9	18.7	17.2	27.6	31.4	53.8	63.0
Female								
1970	0.4	8.2	11.1	18.9	13.2	26.8	46.4	89.1
1980	0.5	7.6	12.4	11.8	14.3	21.4	44.4	64.6
				Hungary				
Male								
1970	1.9	27.8	48.6	63.6	78.4	85.1	104.9	146.4
1980	3.6	31.5	58.3	86.8	106.4	96.7	116.3	202.2
Female								
1970	0.4	9.6	11.0	17.5	23.8	33.8	46.2	76.4
1980	0.8	8.0	16.4	26.7	36.2	42.2	52.9	90.6
				Italy				
Male								
1970	0.3	3.5	5.9	7.4	11.4	18.3	24.3	33.3
1980	0.3	5.3	8.3	9.1	14.0	17.3	26.5	37.4
Female								
1970	0.2	2.3	2.7	3.5	5.2	7.0	7.5	7.8
1980	0.1	2.4	3.3	4.2	6.8	8.2	10.2	10.2

Table 2 (*Continued*)

Sex and year	5–14	15–24	25–34	35–44	45–54	55–64	65–74	75+
				Age				
				Japan				
Male								
1970	0.5	14.0	20.1	17.8	20.1	32.3	50.4	82.1
1980	0.4	16.6	24.9	28.9	33.3	32.2	40.9	73.3
Female								
1970	0.2	11.9	13.8	10.0	13.5	20.6	40.5	66.3
1980	0.2	8.2	11.4	12.5	15.1	17.8	35.5	60.2
				Netherlands				
Male								
1970	0.7	5.8	6.4	11.1	15.7	24.0	25.4	42.5
1980	0.2	8.3	14.9	15.1	17.1	22.3	26.1	41.1
Female								
1970	0.1	2.1	5.5	7.5	11.0	12.6	14.9	17.5
1980	0.0	3.7	8.0	8.9	12.4	14.1	14.3	12.0
				New Zealand				
Male								
1970	1.0	12.1	10.4	23.1	24.5	16.8	34.6	31.2
1980	0.7	19.5	17.8	17.4	17.3	22.2	24.4	35.6
Female								
1970	0.0	3.8	2.9	8.5	12.1	21.1	19.2	11.1
1980	0.0	8.1	9.3	6.8	15.6	4.4	13.1	17.8
				Norway				
Male								
1970	0.3	5.4	15.0	17.4	19.2	24.7	19.6	13.3
1980	1.2	20.4	18.2	20.6	28.6	31.8	25.5	24.0
Female								
1970	0.0	2.0	4.5	10.1	10.4	8.9	6.9	1.9
1980	0.3	3.3	9.0	6.7	14.2	12.1	9.6	4.7
				Portugal				
Male								
1970	0.1	5.6	6.2	17.5	14.5	27.6	43.4	72.2
1980	0.2	5.2	7.9	14.7	18.6	24.1	31.0	53.7
Female								
1970	0.1	3.6	2.1	3.0	3.8	6.7	9.2	11.7
1980	0.8	4.1	5.4	3.8	4.2	5.4	5.6	11.0
				Singapore				
Male								
1970	0.3	9.1	8.1	13.3	23.2	39.0	56.5	137.9
1980	1.3	9.0	17.7	8.1	17.5	32.9	40.9	107.4
Female								
1970	0.7	6.3	15.7	0.0	14.1	14.5	39.9	53.6
1980	0.4	11.7	10.1	8.3	12.3	17.1	34.5	57.3

(*Table continues on next page*)

Table 2 Suicide rates by age in countries of the world in 1970 and 1980 (*Continued*)

Sex and year	Age							
	5–14	15–24	25–34	35–44	45–54	55–64	65–74	75+
Spain								
Male								
1970	0.1	2.0	4.1	7.0	9.6	15.7	21.9	29.0
1980	0.2	4.3	6.2	6.6	9.7	12.4	18.6	28.5
Female								
1970	0.1	0.9	1.4	1.6	3.8	5.4	5.7	6.9
1980	0.0	1.1	1.3	2.1	3.3	4.9	4.7	6.4
Sweden								
Male								
1970	0.5	18.5	27.9	44.9	52.5	54.6	46.3	48.8
1980	0.5	16.9	33.3	37.6	43.9	35.3	39.3	48.9
Female								
1970	0.6	7.9	15.3	19.3	26.0	17.8	15.6	13.0
1980	0.0	5.8	11.3	16.2	17.8	21.2	14.5	11.4
Switzerland								
Male								
1970	0.8	21.3	27.6	31.2	46.2	49.0	49.5	74.1
1980	1.5	34.2	36.5	42.2	46.1	63.4	58.9	80.7
Female								
1970	0.0	4.7	10.2	8.8	19.5	19.1	21.7	16.0
1980	0.7	12.3	14.8	17.6	21.7	20.8	26.8	23.2
Thailand								
Male								
1970	0.3	7.2	5.7	9.0	8.5	11.7	9.5	10.7
1980	0.7	12.8	11.1	11.6	13.8	12.9	12.6	*a*
Female								
1970	0.3	9.9	3.4	3.8	3.0	2.8	2.2	1.1
1980	1.2	19.6	8.6	7.4	7.1	4.8	3.3	*a*
United Kingdom: England and Wales								
Male								
1970	0.0	6.0	9.1	11.3	14.1	17.5	20.7	23.9
1980	0.1	6.4	13.0	15.5	15.4	17.9	18.2	21.6
Female								
1970	0.1	2.6	4.4	7.4	10.3	12.9	15.3	9.7
1980	0.0	3.0	4.2	8.1	10.9	11.8	13.3	11.0
United Kingdom: Scotland								
Male								
1970	0.0	5.8	8.6	15.6	13.1	24.0	12.9	21.7
1980	0.0	9.6	15.2	19.1	23.4	17.8	18.8	23.2
Female								
1970	0.0	1.8	5.8	8.2	15.1	12.7	5.7	5.6
1980	0.0	3.1	7.0	9.6	14.3	14.3	10.9	8.1

Table 2   (Continued)

Sex and year	5–14	15–24	25–34	35–44	45–54	55–64	65–74	75+
				Age				
			United States					
Male								
1970	0.5	13.5	19.6	22.2	27.8	32.8	36.5	41.8
1980	0.7	20.2	24.8	22.3	23.0	24.4	30.2	43.5
Female								
1970	0.1	4.2	8.6	12.1	12.5	11.4	9.3	6.7
1980	0.2	4.3	7.0	8.4	9.4	8.4	6.5	5.4
			Venezuela					
Male								
1970	0.3	14.5	12.6	17.8	19.0	28.8	42.5	47.5
1980	0.3	10.4	13.9	13.1	18.5	20.6	24.9	46.8
Female								
1970	1.1	11.3	5.6	4.1	4.1	3.0	7.6	5.3
1980	0.4	3.5	3.2	3.3	2.8	2.4	1.8	2.8
			West Germany					
Male								
1970	1.4	19.6	27.0	35.1	43.2	51.6	53.9	75.2
1980	1.6	19.0	26.9	33.0	42.0	38.9	54.0	72.8
Female								
1970	0.5	6.9	11.5	15.9	25.4	27.2	26.1	27.0
1980	0.3	5.6	9.9	14.0	20.4	23.6	27.1	25.9

[a]Data reported for those 65+ in 1980.

people have a clear external source to blame for their misfortune, they are more likely to be angry and assaultive and less likely to be depressed and suicidal. A high quality of life means that there are fewer external events to blame one's misery on, and so suicide should become more common.

For the nations listed in Table 1 the suicide rates were significantly correlated with an index of the quality of life provided by Richard Estes (6) ($r = 0.54, p = 0.002$) and the gross national product per capita ($r = 0.57, p = 0.001$). Youth suicide rates were positively correlated with the same two indices, but not significantly ($r = 0.25$ and 0.27 respectively). Thus, youth suicide rates were less strongly related to these variables.

The change in the overall suicide rate from 1970 to 1980 was significantly related to the suicide rates in 1970 ($r = 0.53, p = 0.001$). Thus, nations with the higher suicide rates in 1970 experienced a greater absolute increase in the suicide rates from 1970 to 1980. For youth suicide rates, the analogous association was not significant ($r = -0.03$).

SUICIDE IN THOSE AGED 5–14

Tables 1 and 2 show that the suicide rates of those aged 5–14 were much lower than the rates of those aged 15–24. This is probably a result of the fact that they do have lower suicide rates, but it is also a result of the fact that many agencies responsible for certifying death do not accept the fact that children commit suicide.

For example, the zero rates in England and Wales and in Scotland are clearly a result of the decision not to certify the deaths of children as suicide.

The low rates of suicide make them relatively unreliable. However, the rates for those aged 5–14 were positively correlated with the rates of those aged 15–24 ($r = 0.65$), though the changes in the rates during the 1970s for those aged 5–14 and those aged 15–24 were not significantly associated ($r = 0.17$). Thus, nations with a higher rate of suicide in those aged 15–24 also had a higher rate of suicide in those aged 5–14.

Barraclough (7) found that a small number of nations reported suicide rates for those aged 5–14 that were higher for females than for males, whereas all of the nations had higher overall rates of suicide (for the total nation) in men than women. Most of these nations were in Asia or South America. However, it is impossible to determine the extent to which reporting bias accounts for this result, because we know that many suicides of children are misclassified. For the nations for which data are reported in this chapter, the suicide rates for those aged 5–14 were higher in boys than in girls in 1970 for 17 nations, equal in 5, and higher in girls than in boys in 5. The five tied nations were Australia, Portugal, Spain, Thailand, and Scotland. The five nations with higher suicide rates for girls were England and Wales, Greece, Singapore, Sweden, and Venezuela. In contrast, only Hong Kong and Thailand had higher rates in women than in men among those aged 15–24.

SUICIDAL ATTEMPTS AND IDEATION

Those who kill themselves are, in a sense, our failures. They are the children and adolescents we could not help. The major mental health problem we face, however, is presented by those who contemplate suicide and those who survive suicide attempts.

We have known for many years that more people attempt suicide than complete suicide. In the 1950s the most common estimate for the relative frequency was eight attempts for every completed suicide. Today, estimates are much higher. Maris (1) estimated that the attempted suicide rate in American youth is at least 10 times the completed suicide rate, but may be as high as 100 times.

Epidemiological studies of the prevalence of suicidal ideation and suicidal attempts are not common, and certainly cannot be found for many nations of the world. For the United States, surveys of high school students have reported 34% of students to have had suicidal ideation in the previous year (8) and 63% to have had suicidal ideation at some point in their lives (9). Smith and Crawford (9) found that 8% of high school students had made a suicide attempt at some point.

It is evident that suicidal preoccupation is a common occurrence in children and adolescents and may indeed be a problem at some point for the majority of adolescents. It is these adolescents that school counselors and teachers must expect to help on a regular basis.

The lack of data on the incidence of suicidal ideation and attempts points to a need for both longitudinal and comparative studies (1). How is the incidence changing over time? Is it increasing or decreasing? We presently have no data with which to answer this question (2). How does this incidence vary among nations? Do the differences between nations mirror the differences in completed suicides?

Epidemiologists must broaden their concern with suicide to initiate such studies of suicidal preoccupation.

DISCUSSION

This chapter has documented that the rising youth suicide rate is not found in every nation of the world. Some nations are experiencing a decrease in youth suicide rates, while others are witnessing a rise in the youth suicide rates for only one sex.

A search for correlates of the youth suicide rates showed the variables that correlate with the overall suicide rates in nations (such as the quality of life and the change in the suicide rate) are not significantly related to the youth suicide rates. This failure to find significant correlates of the youth suicide rates suggests that different factors and different theories will be needed to account for the youth suicide rates in nations of the world.

Reported suicide rates are quite low in children aged 5–14, but this is probably a result of their suicides being misclassified because tradition has been that those younger than 14 years of age cannot commit suicide. Among children it is much more likely that reported suicide rates will be higher in girls than in boys, whereas adult women in all of the nations discussed here have lower suicide rates than adult men.

REFERENCES

1. Maris, R. (1985). The adolescent suicide problem. *Suicide & Life-Threatening Behavior, 15,* 91–109.
2. Sudak, H. S., Ford, A. B., & Rushforth, N. B. (1984). *Suicide in the young.* Boston: John Wright.
3. World Health Organization. (1973, 1983). *World Health Statistics Annual, 1970 & 1983.* Geneva: Author.
4. Lester, D. (1984). The association between the quality of life and suicide and homicide rates. *Journal of Social Psychology, 24,* 247–248.
5. Henry, A. F., & Short, J. F. (1954). *Suicide and homicide.* New York: Free Press.
6. Lester, D. (1988). Youth suicide in a cross-cultural perspective. *Adolescence, 23,* 955–958.
7. Barraclough, B. M. (1987). Sex ratio of juvenile suicide. *Journal of the American Academy of Child & Adolescent Psychiatry, 26,* 434–435.
8. Ferguson, W. W. (1981). Gifted adolescents, stress and life changes. *Adolescence, 16,* 973–985.
9. Smith, K., & Crawford, S. (1986). Suicidal behavior among "normal" high school students. *Suicide & Life-Threatening Behavior, 16,* 313–325.

3

Attitudes of High School Students Toward Suicide

George Domino
University of Arizona, Tucson

This chapter reports the attitudes toward suicide held by a sample of 327 Tucson, Arizona high school students. From a common sense point of view, attitudes toward suicide would appear to be of central importance to the understanding of suicide and to any preventive actions. Indeed, social scientists have devoted considerable attention to the study of attitudes in general, typically defined as relatively lasting predispositions to respond in particular ways to certain objects (ideas, persons, groups, etc.). Extensive questions have been asked and complex answers have been generated, with the result that the study of attitudes is fraught with arguments, different theoretical stances, and lack of agreement on even some of the basic points. What are attitudes? How do they differ from opinions, beliefs, values? How are attitudes related to behavior?

In the area of suicide, the study of attitudes was almost completely disregarded until the late 1970s when my students and I began a series of studies designed to elucidate the nature and prevalence of attitudes toward suicide in a variety of samples (1-14). The impetus and vehicle for such a series of studies was the construction of the Suicide Opinion Questionnaire (SOQ) (2).

THE SUICIDE OPINION QUESTIONNAIRE (SOQ)

The SOQ contains 100 items that the respondent answers on a five-point scale of strongly agree, agree, undecided, disagree, and strongly disagree. These items are the result of both logical and statistical analyses applied to an initial pool of approximately 3,000 items derived from a comprehensive survey of the suicide literature (2). The items were purposely selected to reflect a wide range of concerns regarding suicide and suicidal behavior. Representative items are given in Table 1. As can be seen from that table, some of the items are purely attitudinal in nature (e.g., No. 9), while others are more factual (e.g., No. 17).

The SOQ has now been used in a substantial number of studies, with a wide variety of samples, from children (10) to mental health professionals (8-9), and used to explore a variety of suicide related variables such a ethnicity, religious beliefs, and cross-cultural status (1-14).

In addition to the 100 attitudinal and factual items, the SOQ contains 7 additional items of a more demographic nature.

Table 1   Representative SOQ items

---

1. Most persons who attempt suicide are lonely and depressed.
5. Suicide prevention centers actually infringe on a person's right to take his life.
9. I would feel ashamed if a member of my family committed suicide.
17. Suicide is a leading cause of death in the U.S.
23. I feel sorry for people who commit suicide.
31. Most people who try to kill themselves don't really want to die.
56. Once a person survives a suicide attempt, the probability of his trying again is minimal.
57. In general, suicide is an evil act not to be condoned.

Analysis of the SOQ

Because the SOQ yields a substantial amount of data, the user is faced with a number of choices as to how to best organize such data. One possibility is to let a statistical technique such as factor analysis dictate which SOQ items are to be considered and how these items interrelate to each other (i.e., as factors). That approach has been used successfully (2) and the results suggest that there are 15 meaningful factors that account for most (about 75%) of the SOQ variance. Thus attitudes toward suicide are quite complex and are interrelated with attitudes toward religion, mental illness, impulsivity, the right to die, normality, morality, and other variables.

Another possibility is to consider clusters of items from a more clinical point of view (i.e., to form scales of items whose similarity reflects clinical judgment rather than statistical properties); for example, to identify all of the SOQ items that are related to religious beliefs, whether or not they form a statistical cluster, and to assign each respondent a total "religiosity" score based on his or her response to these items. Such an approach was used in a recent study comparing SOQ protocols of New Zealand and U.S. college students (11), where a set of eight meaningful clinical scales was developed.

Still a third approach, and the one taken here, is to consider the items as items— that is, to consider directly the information obtained, without transforming it into the hypothetical constructs of psychometric scales, whether clinically or factor-analytically based. Because, however, there are 100 items to be considered, a useful approach is to organize these items into thematic clusters, following the outline of a prior study of attitudes toward suicide among college students (1).

Subjects of This Study

The subjects of this study were 327 high school students drawn from four Tucson area high schools. All students were asked by their classroom teachers to cooperate in an anonymous survey of students' attitudes toward suicide by completing the SOQ. All protocols were completed in group settings, such as classrooms, libraries, and study halls, and cooperation was elicited in homerooms and widely required courses such as English writing, so as to obtain a heterogeneous and hopefully representative sample of high school students. All settings were monitored by school personnel. It was made clear that participation was voluntary, and protocols were returned by placing them in a large locked box. A total of 450 protocols were distributed. Of these, 41 were retained by their recipients, 55 were returned blank, 16 were completed with the instruction that they should be disregarded, 9 were incomplete, and 2 yielded invalid response patterns (e.g., all items marked "I don't know"). This left 327 seemingly valid protocols, a return rate of 73%. Of these, 171 were from males and 156 from females, with ethnic status as follows: 230 Anglo, 41 Hispanic, 18 black, 13 Native-American, 8 "other," and 17 no indication.

The students were almost evenly divided among the four high school years with 76 ninth-graders, 82 tenth-graders, 80 eleventh-graders, 81 twelfth-graders, and 8 no information given.

The four Tucson high schools were selected both for practical reasons (i.e., administrative cooperation), as well as for sampling reasons (i.e., all four serve primarily middle class neighborhoods with a heterogeneity of ethnic and social class backgrounds). None of these schools had special designations, such as magnet schools or schools for the musically gifted, but they represented schools in relatively stable neighborhoods. Nevertheless, it should be kept in mind that the respondents of this study were primarily white, middle-class students attending schools where, according to their counseling staff, suicide is a rare phenomenon, and suicide ideation highly infrequent as a presenting problem.

Any assessment reflects in large part the manner in which the assessment is undertaken and the instruments or procedures used. In collecting the SOQ protocols every effort was made to project an image of seriousness and confidentiality, and one that implied that honest responses would be of value to all concerned. Because high school students can often be less than mature about such undertakings, a variety of steps, in addition to those mentioned above, were taken to increase the validity of the responses. Students were asked to sit away from each other (if possible); given explicit instructions about the confidentiality of the project and about respecting each other's privacy; and asked to cooperate both by well-liked teachers and selected student leaders. In addition, all participating classes were given feedback on the results and on suicide as a general concern.

RESULTS

For this presentation only overall results are presented. No gender, ethnic, or grade differences are considered here. Although responses to the SOQ are given using a five-point scale, the results collapse the five-point scale into a three-point scale, consisting of agree, undecided, and disagree. Thus in the following discussion, agreement includes both strongly agree and agree responses, and disagreement includes both strongly disagree and disagree.

Certainty and Uncertainty: Consensus

One of the first questions we can ask is what opinions do these adolescents express as a group that represent a mean consensus? First of all there is no unanimous agreement or disagreement on the responses to the SOQ. For all 100 SOQ items, some respondents express agreement, others express disagreement, and still others endorse uncertainty. From a psychometric point of view this variation of response is a plus for the SOQ, because validity is based on variability. From an educational and counseling point of view, however, it is legitimate to wish to know those attitudinal aspects that characterize the majority of teenagers. If we define consensus then, as at least 75% or more selecting the same response options, we find that 20 SOQ items reflect such consensus. These are listed in Table 2.

These items cover a wide variety of attitudinal concerns. Thus the fictional "typical" adolescent believes that suicide attempters are lonely and depressed, but that suicide ideation is a fairly common phenomenon. He or she believes that suicide prevention centers are not infringing on one's rights, and that suicide attempters are indeed responsible for their own actions. These adolescents are aware that suicide does not occur unannounced, and that a "friendly ear" may represent an important preventive action. They are rather sophisticated in their attitudes in that they understand that improvement following a crisis does not indicate that the potential for suicide is over, and that simply because a person survives an attempt does not mean that the person will not try again. They see loneliness, depression, and hopelessness as highly related to suicide, and do not have a moralistic punitive stance toward the victims of suicide.

Table 2 SOQ items reflecting 75% or more consensual response

Item number	Item	%	Modal response
1.	Most persons who attempt suicide are lonely and depressed.	89	Agree
2.	Almost everyone has at one time or another thought about suicide.	74	Agree
5.	Suicide prevention centers actually infringe on a person's right to take his/her life.	81	Disagree
20.	Some people commit suicide as an act of self-punishment.	75	Disagree
32.	Suicide happens without warning.	76	Disagree
35.	A person who tried to commit suicide is not really responsible for those actions.	74	Disagree
37.	It's rare for someone who is thinking about suicide to be dissuaded by a "friendly ear".	73	Disagree
39.	The method used in a given suicide probably reflects whether the action was impulsive or carefully and rationally planned.	77	Agree
44.	The probability of committing suicide is greater for older people (those 60 and over) than for younger people (20 to 30).	75	Disagree
48.	Once a person is suicidal, he/she is suicidal forever.	79	Disagree
52.	Improvement following a suicidal crisis indicates that the risk is over.	74	Disagree
54.	Prisoners in jail who attempt suicide are simply trying to get better living conditions.	78	Disagree
56.	Once a person survives a suicide attempt, the probability of his/her trying again is minimal.	74	Disagree
59.	Suicide is a normal behavior.	79	Disagree
71.	A suicide attempt is essentially a "cry for help."	85	Agree
74.	The most frequent message in suicide notes is of loneliness.	82	Agree
77.	Suicide attempts are typically preceded by feelings that life is no longer worth living.	93	Agree
85.	Potentially, every one of us can be a suicide victim.	86	Agree
87.	People who die by suicide should not be buried in the same cemetery as those who die naturally.	89	Disagree
98.	Individuals who are depressed are more likely to commit suicide.	89	Agree

Lack of Consensus

On what aspects of suicide do adolescents disagree most among themselves? To answer this question, we can identify two types of SOQ group response patterns: In one there is a tripartite split of response, such that approximately one-third agree, one-third disagree, and one-third are undecided; in the second, we can disregard the undecided responses, and look for those items where the agree-disagree show an almost equal response split, with not more than a 10% difference between the agrees and the disagrees. These two patterns yield a total of 11 SOQ items, presented in Table 3.

These items are also quite varied and reflect first, strong attitudinal differences and second, lack of knowledge, to be sure, about minor aspects of suicide. Perhaps what is more important may be the behavioral corollaries that these items imply. For example, 36% believe that those who threaten to commit suicide rarely do so. Might not such an attitude lead to indifference when faced with a peer's suicide ideation? A substantial number (42%) see suicide as an acceptable means to end an incurable illness. What are the implications of such a view toward moral and legal questions regarding the cessation of life, euthanasia, and other related issues?

Undecided Responses

A third question that can be asked is on which aspects of suicide do adolescents as a group express uncertainty and indecision? One would expect the undecided response to be selected infrequently and that is indeed the case. There are only 10 SOQ items on which the undecided response is selected with a frequency of less than 9%, so that for each of the other 90 SOQ items, a fair amount of uncertainty is expressed. That is to be expected. After all, at least as an intellectual topic, suicide is something the typical adolescent does not experience except in a most superficial way when mentioned in the daily news or English Literature class. On the other hand, the highest percentage of uncertainty does not exceed 54%. Table 4 presents the 10 SOQ items where the undecided response was selected by 40% or more of the respondents.

Most of these items might be described as factual-demographic items. Is suicide related to age, family background, family size, ethnicity, religious beliefs, and parental suicide? These items suggest quite strongly the need for some education, if one agrees that knowledge about such matters is important.

Mental Illness

Let us turn now to specific themes. The first to be considered is mental illness.

The notion that suicide and mental illness are related is a common one, both in the popular press as well as in the scientific literature. There are 12 SOQ items that cover this area, presented in Table 5.

Neuringer (15) argues that myths or false beliefs about suicide develop as a way of protecting oneself against the psychological perturbation experienced when one faces behaviors that question the worth of life. One such myth is that "you have to be crazy to kill yourself." But in fact, only a small percentage of suicides would be considered psychotic at the time of their deaths. Whether such a myth, and others

Table 3 SOQ items showing lack of response consensus

Item number	Item	Response % Agree	Undecided	Disagree
14.	Those who threaten to commit suicide rarely do so.	36	21	43
18.	Suicide is an acceptable means to end an incurable illness.	42	21	37
26.	The suicide rate among physicians is substantially greater than for other occupational groups.	36	37	27
29.	Suicide is clear evidence that man has a basically aggressive and destructive nature.	41	18	41
47.	Suicide attempters are typically trying to get even with someone.	35	25	40
51.	The suicide rate is higher for minority groups such as Chicano, American Indians, and Puerto Ricans than for whites.	30	39	31
64.	A person whose parent has committed suicide is a greater risk for suicide.	25	44	31
66.	Suicide rates are a good indicator of the stability of a nation; that is, the more suicides the more problems a nation is facing.	35	33	32
81.	People who commit suicide lack solid religious convictions.	28	37	41
92.	Some people are better of dead.	40	15	45
93.	People who attempt suicide are, as a group, less religious.	33	34	33

about suicide, is in fact popular is a debatable issue. For this sample of adolescents, 31% agree that people who commit suicide are usually mentally ill, but a full 89% agree that depression is causally related. Thus, as with college students (1), these adolescents distinguish between depression and mental illness, and ascribe depression much more as a factor in suicide.

Table 4 SOQ items on which the undecided response was selected by 40% or more

Item number	Item	% Undecided
34.	Most suicide victims are older persons with little to live for.	54
94.	As a group, people who commit suicide experienced disturbed family relationships when they were young.	54
41.	A large percentage of suicide victims come from broken homes.	53
89.	Children from larger families (i.e., three or more children) are less likely to commit suicide as adults than single or only children.	52
3.	The suicide rate is higher for blacks than for whites.	49
90.	Suicide attempters are, as individuals, more rigid and less flexible than non-attempters.	49
99.	Suicide is much more frequent in our world today than it was in early cultures such as Egypt, Greece, and the Roman Empire.	47
45.	Most people who commit suicide do not believe in an afterlife.	45
64.	A person whose parent has committed suicide is a greater risk for suicide.	44
96.	Most people who attempt suicide fail in their attempts.	42

Table 5 SOQ items related to mental illness

Item number	Item	Agree	Undecided	Disagree
			Response %	
1.	Most persons who attempt suicide are lonely and depressed.	89	6	5
19.	People who commit suicide are usually mentally ill.	31	11	58
35.	A person who tried to commit suicide is not really responsible for those actions.	74	17	9
38.	People who commit suicide must have a weak personality structure.	27	10	63
41.	A large percentage of suicide victims come from broken homes.	34	53	13
43.	People who set themselves on fire to call attention to some political or religious issue are mentally unbalanced.	53	11	36
58.	People who attempt suicide and live should be required to undertake therapy to understand their inner motivation.	68	12	20
74.	The most frequent message in suicide notes is of loneliness.	82	12	6
82.	People with no roots or family ties are more likely to attempt suicide.	50	30	20
90.	Suicide attempters are, as individuals, more rigid and less flexible than non-attempters.	34	49	17
94.	As a group, people who commit suicide experienced disturbed family relationships when they were young.	28	54	18
98.	Individuals who are depressed are more likely to commit suicide.	89	4	7

Cry for Help

A second major thematic concern is that suicide represents a "cry for help," that the suicidal individual is in fact sending out a rather desperate plea for assistance. There is a corollary that follows from this, namely that if suicide attempts are ways of eliciting help from others, then in fact they are not designed to terminate one's life and are therefore, in the majority of cases, not significantly lethal. The items in this thematic cluster are presented in Table 6.

Thus a full 85% of these adolescents agree that suicide represents a cry for help, but only 48% agree that suicide attempts are designed to elicit sympathy from others, unless that attempt is carried out in a public place like a bridge or tall building: here the percentage of agreement goes up to 64%. A substantial number (68%) agree that suicide is a leading cause of death in the United States, and that most who try to kill themselves don't really want to die (65% agree).

Religion

In most cultures the beginning of life, its major milestones such as puberty, marriage, and the cessation of life have been inextricably woven with the fabric of religion. Thus suicide is linked to religious values and proscriptions, and the attitudes of adolescents reflect this. On the SOQ there are seven items that are related to religion, and these are presented in Table 7.

Perhaps more than with any other cluster of items, there seems to be substantial heterogeneity of opinion as to the interconnections between religion and suicide. A majority of adolescents (57%) believe that the despair reflected in suicide attempts is contrary to religious precepts and to the laws of God and nature (54%), but only approximately one-third see a direct relationship between suicidal behavior and religious beliefs.

Incurable Disease

One of the more visible developments in the area of suicide, at least as far as the layperson is concerned, is the media coverage of elderly couples, often faced with incurable disease and lack of financial and emotional support, who carry out a murder-suicide or double-suicide pact. The termination of life, whether related to hospice settings (where the incurably ill can meet death with dignity and loving care), abortion, cessation of life-support medical systems, or the rights of the individual, has become a much more publicized and discussed issue in our country. There are eight items on the SOQ related to this concern, given in Table 8. One of the themes found in the items in Table 8 concerns the acceptability of suicide. Almost half (47% and 42%) agree that suicide is an acceptable solution to the challenge of incurable illness, but a smaller number (21%) see suicide as accept-

Table 6   SOQ items related to a "cry for help"

Item number	Item	Response %		
		Agree	Undecided	Disagree
14.	Those who threaten to commit suicide rarely do so.	36	21	43
17.	Suicide is a leading cause of death in the U.S.	60	10	22
31.	Most people who try to kill themselves don't really want to die.	65	19	16
37.	It's rare for someone who is thinking about suicide to be dissuaded by a "friendly ear."	12	15	73
54.	Prisoners in jail who attempt suicide are simply trying to get better living conditions.	78	13	9
56.	Once a person survives a suicide attempt, the probability of his trying again is minimal.	8	18	74
63.	Suicide attempters who use public places (such as a bridge or tall building) are more interested in getting attention.	64	22	14
71.	A suicide attempt is essentially a "cry for help."	85	8	7
80.	Those people who attempt suicide are usually trying to get sympathy from others.	48	26	26
83.	People who bungle suicide attempts really did not intend to die in the first place.	55	26	19
91.	The large majority of suicide attempts result in death.	25	23	52
96.	Most people who attempt suicide fail in their attempts.	12	42	46

Table 7 SOQ items related to religion

Item number	Item	Response %		
		Agree	Undecided	Disagree
7.	The higher incidence of suicide is due to the lesser influence of religion.	18	39	43
21.	The feelings of despair reflected in the act of suicide is contrary to the teachings of most major religions.	57	31	12
45.	Most people who commit suicide do not believe in an afterlife.	20	45	35
78.	Suicide goes against the laws of God and/or of nature.	54	21	25
81.	People who commit suicide lack solid religious convictions.	28	37	41
88.	Most people who commit suicide do not believe in God.	14	31	55
93.	People who attempt suicide are, as a group, less religious.	33	34	33

able for the elderly and infirm, and agree with the idea of "suicide clinics" where people could die in a painless and private manner. These findings are in agreement with those of Deluty (16) who, in a sample of college students, found that suicide was judged more acceptable when it occurred as a response to terminal physical illness and less acceptable in relation to chronic, nonterminal physical illness.

Miscellaneous Concerns

Space limitations preclude the consideration of other thematic concerns, but we can briefly look at some interesting attitudinal questions.

Table 8 SOQ items related to the termination of life

Item number	Item	Response %		
		Agree	Undecided	Disagree
5.	Suicide prevention centers actually infringe on a person's right to take his/her life.	9	10	81
13.	People with incurable diseases should be allowed to commit suicide in a dignified manner.	47	25	28
18.	Suicide is an acceptable means to end an incurable illness.	42	21	37
25.	Suicide is acceptable for aged and infirm persons.	21	12	67
50.	People should be prevented from committing suicide since most are not acting rationally at the time.	65	19	16
70.	If someone wants to commit suicide, it is their business and we should not interfere.	12	14	74
79.	We should have "suicide clinics" where people who want to die could do so in a painless and private manner.	19	14	67
95.	People do not have the right to take their own lives.	25	29	45

Is it possible that there may be situations where the only reasonable resolution is suicide? For this sample, 16% agree and 19% are undecided, but the majority (65%) disagree.

What about suicides among young people? From the vantage point of the adult, the thought is often expressed that young suicides are particularly puzzling because the young have everything to live for. This seems to be the majority opinion among adolescents also, with 61% agreeing, 30% disagreeing, and only 9% undecided.

Sometimes the opinion is expressed that a specific person is "better off dead." How prevalent is this opinion among adolescents? Approximately 40% agree, 45% disagree, and 15% are not sure.

Demographic Aspects

Earlier in this chapter it was indicated that the SOQ contains a number of demographic items. The interested reader may well wonder abut some of those items. How many in our sample indicated that they had seriously considered suicide? A full 92 (28%) out of the 327 said yes. Even if one argues that perhaps adolescents tend to be somewhat dramatic in their expressions of affect and that the meaning of "serious consideration" is neither clear nor precise, the high incidence of suicidal ideation, no matter how mild that ideation may be, is of substantial concern. At the very least, all of us ought to be concerned that in an anonymous survey the incidence of ideation is fairly high, although the faculty at each of these schools clearly indicated that suicidal behavior of any kind was a very rare phenomenon in their experience. Clearly there are breaks in the communication process between student and adult. What about actual suicide attempts? Twenty-six respondents (8%) out of the 327 indicated that they had attempted suicide. Both of these frequencies are somewhat higher than those reported for samples of college students; for example, Limbacher and Domino (6) reported a frequency of 20% for suicide ideation and 5% for actual attempts in a sample of 649 University of Arizona students.

That suicide is no stranger to today's adolescent is reflected by the fact that 40% indicate that they have known someone who committed suicide. Of these, 8% report that it was a member of their immediate family, 20% a relative, 18% a close friend, and 54% an acquaintance.

These findings suggest that adolescents have some strong attitudes about suicide coupled with a fair degree of uncertainty, and that there is indeed a need for education, preventive action, and guidance; but above all, a sensitive awareness that suicidal concerns are no strangers to today's high school students is mandatory.

REFERENCES

1. Domino, G., Gibson, L., Poling, S., & Westlake, L. (1980). Students' attitudes toward suicide. *Social Psychiatry, 15,* 127–130.
2. Domino, G., Moore, D., Westlake, L., & Gibson, L. (1982). Attitudes toward suicide: A factor analytic approach. *Journal of Clinical Psychology, 38,* 257–262.
3. Domino, G. (1980). Altering attitudes toward suicide in an abnormal psychology course. *Teaching of Psychology, 7,* 239–340.
4. Domino, G., Cohen, A., & Gonzales, R. (1981). Jewish and Christian attitudes on suicide. *Journal of Religion and Health, 20,* 201–207.

5. Domino, G. (1981). Attitudes toward suicide among Mexican-American and Anglo youth. *Hispanic Journal of Behavioral Sciences, 3,* 385–395.
6. Limbacher, M., & Domino, G. (1985). Attitudes toward suicide among attempters, contemplators, and non-attempters. *Omega, 16,* 319–328.
7. Domino, G. (1985). Clergy's attitudes toward suicide and recognition of suicide lethality. *Death Studies, 9,* 187–199.
8. Domino, G., & Swain, B. (1985). Recognition of suicide lethality and attitudes toward suicide in mental health professionals. *Omega, 16,* 301–308.
9. Swain, B., & Domino, G. (1985). Attitudes toward suicide among mental health professionals. *Death Studies, 9,* 455–480.
10. Domino, G., Domino, V., & Berry T. (1986). Children's attitudes toward suicide. *Omega, 17,* 279–287.
11. Domino, G., MacGregor, J. C., & Hannah, M. T. (1988–89). Collegiate attitudes toward suicide: New Zealand and United States. *Omega, 19,* 351–364.
12. Domino, G. (in press). Popular misconceptions about suicide: How popular are they? *Omega.*
13. Domino, G. (1988). Attitudes toward suicide among highly creative college students. *The Creativity Research Journal, 1,* 92–105.
14. Domino, G., & Leenaars, A. (1989). Attitudes toward suicide: A comparison of Canadian and United States college students. *Suicide and Life-Threatening Behavior, 19,* 160–172.
15. Neuringer, C. (1987–1988). The meaning behind popular myths about suicide. *Omega, 18,* 155–162.
16. Deluty, R. H. (1988–1989). Physical illness, psychiatric illness, and the acceptability of suicide. *Omega, 19,* 79–91.

II

SUICIDE PREVENTION
IN SCHOOLS

Prevention relates to the principles of good mental hygiene in general. Preventing suicide is best done before an attempt occurs. In schools, prevention is education. This is in keeping with the general aim of schools, namely to educate young people. In Part II, strategies for prevention are outlined. Part II consists of six chapters: system-entry issues, the promotion of self-esteem (as *preprevention*), suicide prevention in elementary schools, a comprehensive school program, the development of a program with modifications for special populations or institutions, and some observations about the relevance of sex differences for such programs.

4

System-Entry Issues in School Suicide Prevention Education Programs

Ronald J. Dyck
Department of Health, Government of Alberta, Alberta, Canada

Suicide and its aftermath are receiving more and more attention from a variety of sectors. Government agencies, mental health professionals, educators, and the general public are just some who are voicing concerns about the prevalence of various forms of suicidal behavior, especially among the young. Furthermore, the print and electronic media, through movies, music, and news reports, are drawing increasing attention to suicide as a personal, community, and social problem. Much of this increased attention and expressed concern derives from reports that indicate that approximately 8%–10% of high school students have attempted suicide at some time in their life (1, 2). This finding is particularly alarming when compared with the lifetime prevalence rate for attempted suicide among adults (18 years of age and older), which has been found to range from 1.1%–4.6% (3). Furthermore, in a recent survey 29.1% of junior high school and 45.8% of senior high school students reported having known someone who committed suicide (4).

Because teens are increasingly exposed to suicide and are themselves engaging in suicidal behavior at a rate exceeding the adult population (5), it is readily apparent that strategies that will interrupt this trend are needed. One approach receiving considerable attention involves suicide prevention education. It is assumed that by making persons more knowledgeable of the facts about suicide and more aware of the helping resources available during times of crisis, as well as providing them with basic intervention skills, potentially suicidal persons will be identified sooner and the necessary help initiated. Because most adolescents attend school, it would appear that introducing suicide prevention education into the school setting could be a rather efficient approach for enhancing lifesaving measures. Introducing such an education program, however, has often met with varying degrees of resistance. Indeed, school administrators, educators and teachers, and even parents erect barriers to the introduction of suicide prevention education in the schools, some of which are based more on myth than reality. The purpose of this chapter, therefore, is to identify and discuss the more common of these obstacles and to suggest several approaches that can be used to overcome them.

BARRIERS TO SCHOOL ACCESS

Many of the obstacles to school-based suicide prevention programs derive from a lack of information and knowledge about suicide and its prevention, as well as from the realities found in educational and community systems. Ten of the more common barriers are discussed in the following sections.

Belief That Talking About Suicide Increases the Likelihood of Suicidal Behavior

A major barrier to introducing suicide awareness education into the school system is the notion held by many that suicidal behavior will increase if it is talked about openly. Support for this idea comes from several sources of evidence. Phillips and his colleagues have shown that the frequency of completed suicide increases following newspaper and television news stories about suicide (6, 7). Gould and Shaffer (8) found that suicides also increased following the showing of suicide-related fictional films. Thus, the role of suggestion facilitating suicide, particularly among already vulnerable individuals (9), requires attention.

In addition to the possible suggestion effects, talking about suicide may also promote the use of suicidal threats or gestures as a means of gaining attention or obtaining a desired goal. Many, if not all, suicide awareness education programs emphasize that suicidal messages be taken seriously. Students, therefore, who may wish to manipulate others may use suicidal gestures not so much to indicate despair or a need for help but rather as a means to affect the environment in some specific way.

Last, repeatedly talking about suicide may in fact change listeners' attitude from one of abhorrence to one that is more positive. Social psychology has provided evidence that suggests that familiarity with an object based on repetition increases liking or attraction (10). Moreover, evidence from clinical psychology suggests that persons can become desensitized to fearful and repulsive events through exposure to them (11). Thus, the more openly suicide is discussed, the more likely it is that people will become familiar with and desensitized to the subject. Consequently, greater desensitization may result, such that inhibitions toward suicide will decrease and suicidal behavior will increase.

It can be argued, on the other hand, that as many young persons are already in contact with the subject of suicide through movies, news reports, and music, it is necessary to discuss the subject openly. Furthermore, as modeling of suicide by members of one's own social network has an even greater influence than models in the media (12), and many adolescents know someone who has attempted or committed suicide, it is timely to ensure that all young persons know how to recognize someone who is suicidal and are aware of the available resources to which they can turn for assistance.

Ross (13) has suggested, however, that *how* information about suicide is presented is of critical importance. Research showing the imitative effects of electronic and print media coverage of a suicide have used stories that were sensationalized and that sometimes portrayed suicide in glamorous and romantic ways. Perhaps educational programs that provide facts—rather than make suicide appear glamorous and romantic—and that paint it as a very real tragedy for family, friends, school, and community would minimize contagion and enhance the prevention of suicides. Unfortunately, there is little research as yet that can be used to guide this development.

Denial of Youth Suicide

It is not unusual to hear comments from school administrators and classroom teachers such as "suicide does not happen in my school" or "suicide is not a problem here." Although on the one hand such statements may reflect the state of affairs within a particular school, on the other hand they may reflect a major gap between the facts and administrator's and teacher's perceptions of the problem. Hendrickson and Cameron (14) have provided some supportive evidence for the latter notion. Surveying the deans of students in 90 colleges and universities regarding their perception of suicide, the researchers found that the deans seriously underrated their campus suicide rate. Moreover, even though the deans were able to indicate what kinds of measures were needed to deal with suicide, few had actually implemented any programs.

Such reluctance to confront the problem of teen suicide may stem from a legitimate lack of awareness about the magnitude of the problem (14), or it may derive from an inability to comprehend the fact that some adolescents actually experience such distress that self-destruction is perceived as the only possible solution (13). Thus, denial of the problem on the part of educators inhibits school entry to suicide prevention programs.

Role of the Educator

Another barrier to gaining entry into the school system has to do with the increasing curriculum demands being placed on teachers. At one level, the general public, school boards, and governments are demanding greater emphasis be given to teaching the basics: reading, writing, and arithmetic. At another level, teachers are being asked to teach any number of education programs dealing with such social issues as human sexuality, AIDS, substance abuse, drinking and driving, and family violence. With all these demands, it is not surprising that teachers feel they do not have the time or the physical and emotional energy to incorporate yet one more program into their work. Related to increasing curricular demands is the lack of opportunity for teachers to prepare adequately to teach the content of these social problem programs. How can teachers become "experts" in all these areas when they do not have the time to become better informed themselves? Where are they to find the time within the constraints of the curriculum to deal with both the academic subjects and the social problem programs? In other words, teachers' resistance to suicide prevention education programs may have more to do with a sense of helplessness and general fear that comes from a lack of information about suicide and its prevention than with unwillingness or indifference (15). In fact, de Heus and colleagues (16, 17) found that although teachers care for students who are emotionally disturbed as part of their accepted role, they nonetheless feel ill equipped for the task.

Teacher Attitude toward Suicide

Attitudes not only consist of feelings and emotions toward and beliefs about a particular attitude object but also serve to motivate a wide range of behaviors (18). Resistance to school-based suicide awareness programs, therefore, may stem from the attitudes that teachers and school administrators bring to their work. That is, teachers' feelings of anxiety, panic, or frustration, generated by the topic of suicide, together with their beliefs that they must get on with the curriculum, that they will be held responsible should anything happen, or that the suicide-related behaviors are manipulative render them unable to assist students in need. Moreover, such teacher feelings and beliefs may create perceptual barriers to the acquisition of suicide prevention and intervention skills that would be useful in creating greater student awareness about suicide through classroom instruction.

Insufficient Helping Resources

As suggested earlier, one of the assumptions underlying suicide awareness education is that knowledge about the signs and symptoms will assist in the early identification of a potential suicide. If this assumption is true it is likely that more students will be identified as potentially suicidal, and more helping resources will be required to deal with this increase. When the resources are limited to begin with, however, school administrators have little choice but to resist the introduction of these types of programs. Indeed, the inability to obtain the necessary help for at-risk students will only enhance feelings of helplessness, frustration, anger, and guilt. This is especially true of small, rural communities that are remote and do not have many of the mental health and social services found in major centers. This very real problem of insufficient resources can play a major role in inhibiting the access of suicide prevention education programs to schools.

Potential Values Conflict

In a multicultural and multireligious society, different values about human life and attitudes toward suicide are held and expressed. School administrators must ensure that the values and attitudes expressed by teachers to students are based on facts and fit, more or less, with community expectations, values, and attitudes. It is understandable, therefore, that without sufficient information about the context within which suicide will be discussed and the values and attitudes that will be espoused, school administrators would erect barriers to suicide prevention education programs. For example, some programs may present suicide as an acceptable option under certain circumstances. Others may view the act of suicide even more benignly and suggest that it is each individual's right to commit suicide should he or she choose to do so. At present, such attitudes remain relatively unacceptable to the community, and therefore school personnel remain wary of suicide prevention education programs.

Potential Concern from Parents Regarding Suicide Prevention

As with sex education in the schools, school administrators leave themselves open to criticism from parents for providing information about suicide to their children. Some parents feel that their children should not be provided with information about social problems, especially suicide. In addition, some parents are concerned about the context within which these programs are set, especially in terms of the attitudes that will be expressed regarding the "rightness" or "wrongness" of suicide. If the program provides information that views suicide as acceptable under certain circumstances, parents may not want their children to participate. Without the necessary information, therefore, parents will tend to resist the introduction of a suicide awareness program and put pressure on the school administration to do likewise.

In addition to having similar concerns, school administrators need to decide on how much parent involvement there should be in the program. Is parental consent necessary? Should parents be given an information session first? Should parents and students be involved together in the class? From the point of view of some administrators, obtaining the answers to these and other questions or concerns are more bother than they are worth. Thus, program introduction into the school is denied.

Adolescent Feelings of Responsibility

As part of most suicide prevention education programs, adolescents are given information about how to help a person in a suicidal crisis. Generally, this involves encouraging students to be a friend to the person in need, listening to and talking with the person, with a view toward getting expert help. Some administrators, teachers, and parents feel that adolescents should not be given such a responsibility as many students themselves do not yet have the necessary coping skills or sufficient life experiences that would be helpful to them in providing assistance. Moreover, adolescents may have a great deal of difficulty in remaining objective in the helping situation. Consequently, should a friend go on to commit suicide, how would the adolescent helper cope? These concerns have been expressed with such forcefulness that schools resist suicide prevention programs.

Common versus Suicidogenic Antecedents

Because of the proliferation of social problem education programs for schools, some educators have suggested that health programs that emphasize personal and social skill development may be far more effective in preventing youth suicidal behaviors than any awareness programs could hope to be. This argument is based on the assumption that there are several common causes underlying the different social problems. If these causes were dealt with by providing good life-skills education, then the incidence of such behaviors as suicide would be reduced. Thus, there would be no need for a program to address the specific problem of suicide.

Proof of Program Effectiveness

Many school administrators, teachers, and parents would like to ensure that the curriculum or program delivered to students is effective in reaching its stated goals and objectives. Unfortunately, although there are many suicide prevention education programs in existence and each is trying to gain greater acceptance, very few in-depth evaluations have actually been conducted (15). Consequently, school administrators may not allow the introduction of a suicide prevention education program into their institutions as this method of preventing youth suicide is untested. This is a valid point, and, indeed, schools are no place for untested programs that deal with serious issues such as life and death.

STRATEGIES FOR SCHOOL ENTRY

To introduce a suicide prevention program into schools, several different entry points should be given consideration. First, entry through the Department of Education of the provincial of state government will provide access to all schools as the department's mandate is to set educational curriculum requirements for the province or state. Thus, suicide awareness can be required as part of a health curriculum that is taught to all students of a certain grade.

Second, a suicide prevention program can be introduced to schools of a particular district through the local school board. Although the board does not set curriculum content requirements, it does have the authority to establish programs that are felt to benefit the students in the particular district.

A third point of entry is through the administration of a local school. The principal must ensure that all curriculum demands of the Department of Education are followed and the policies and guidelines established by the local school board are adhered to. However, in most schools, principals have the freedom to establish a program, such as a suicide prevention program, that can benefit the students and the community. The fourth entry point is through an individual classroom teacher. For example, an English teacher who has just taught a novel or play that deals with suicide, or a health teacher who may want to cover such social problems as suicide, may invite a suicide prevention specialist to talk with the students about the issue. Of course, the comprehensiveness of the suicide prevention program will determine, in part, which specific entry point is attempted.

In the Province of Alberta, Canada, entry into the school system has been gained at each of these four levels. More specifically, the Department of Education has included suicide awareness education as a part of the recently revised health curriculum for junior high school students. Individual school boards throughout the province have been diligently working at developing policies and guidelines for dealing with not only the potentially suicidal student but also the aftermath of suicide. Within specific school districts, school principals have invited suicide prevention persons to conduct in-service education workshops for staff, parents, and students, and they have asked these experts to assist in working out the details of a more comprehensive approach to suicide prevention. Throughout the province, many classroom teachers have invited experts in suicide prevention to come into the classroom to discuss the subject in more detail.

The question of how to gain entry into the system can and must be asked, especially in light of the many issues (discussed earlier) that create resistance. Given the existence of many different kinds of school programs, it is difficult, if not impossible, to give detailed steps to follow that will result in the desired goal. Nonetheless, there are four areas that must be emphasized in gaining entry into the educational system, regardless of entry point. These include credibility, suicide prevention training, participation in educational conferences, and research.

Credibility

According to Hovland and Weiss (19), a credible communicator is one who is both trustworthy and an expert. To gain entry into the educational system with a suicide prevention program, the program initiator must be perceived as an expert in suicide prevention and must be knowledgeable about educational systems.

Credibility is also based on having a well-prepared and well-documented program. Thus, the written proposal should include the following:

1. *Rationale for the program.* This should include the underlying values and beliefs of the program: A clear statement regarding the attitudes about suicide to be presented should be included, as well as statements about why the proposed approach is being suggested rather than another.

2. *Goals and objectives.* Not only should these be given for the overall program, but goals and objectives should be specified for each component of the program as well. These statements must be clear and precise and made in measurable terms so that evaluation is possible.

3. *Content and format.* The proposal should identify the target groups to be reached (e.g., students, parents, teachers, administrators) and specify what particular topics will be covered. Samples of handouts, questionnaires, and even audiovisual aids should be included. It may be advantageous to include a summary of and a review or evaluation for any film that will be used, as well as a sample of discussion questions to be used.

4. *Protocol for referral.* It is very important not only to identify potential resources for managing a student who is suicidal but also to have a well-developed plan that can be used in referring a student for help. Some initial contacts with community agencies are probably necessary in order to obtain their commitment to be available for the management of suicidal students.

5. *In-service education.* If teachers are to be the primary providers of the suicide awareness program, then an intensive in-service program should be designed to assist them. In addition to providing these teachers with lesson plans, materials, and practice, the in-service should provide them with an opportunity to explore their own attitudes toward suicide. Even if teachers will not be the providers of the program, in-service education is necessary to increase awareness of the magnitude of the problem, provide information about how to recognize a student who may be potentially suicidal, and give suggestions as to how to help, as well as information about the local resources.

6. *Postvention strategy.* In gaining entry into the school system, considerable attention should be given to dealing with the aftermath of suicide in the event that it should occur. Confronting this issue at the beginning and, together with the educators, developing a plan of action for postvention, will enhance the program's credibility.

7. *Program evaluation strategy.* Because there is so little evaluation data available in terms of what kind of school program is most effective for what types of students (15), and because every program can benefit from on-going evaluation, the suicide prevention program proposal must include an evaluation component. Demonstration of a good youth suicide prevention school program evaluation design (see 20–22) can serve to increase the program's credibility: Specifically, decision-makers will see the commitment to on-going improvement in the overall program.

Suicide Prevention Training

To improve school staff's skill level in dealing with an immediate suicidal crisis, more intensive suicide prevention training for at least selected staff (e.g.,

school counselors, health teachers, and other teachers in whom students confide) is
essential. This is also relevant to mental health or social service staff and other
natural caregivers in the community who may be called on to provide assistance to
the school in time of crisis.

Participation in Educator's Conferences

Some of the most significant opportunities for introducing school-based suicide
prevention programs have come from conducting workshops or giving keynote
addresses at conferences, especially those for school administrators or for school
counselors. These presentations which give people ideas about the role of schools
in suicide prevention and challenge what exists within their individual school,
school district, or province, can open significant opportunities for further dialogue
and program development.

Research

Although at first research may not appear to be very important for decreasing
school resistance, it can serve several important functions. First, research can
provide information about the magnitude of suicidal behaviors (suicide ideation,
planning, and attempts) in a given location or even in a specific school. Moreover,
it can ascertain the level of training and competence in suicide intervention and
treatment within school personnel and community agencies. Research can also
serve to uncover the most beneficial training methods for improving knowledge
about the practical skills in suicide prevention, as well as to examine the benefits
of one type of program over another. All these data can serve to gain entry into a
school system with a suicide prevention education program.

CONCLUSION

School suicide prevention education programs have been designed to effect an
overall reduction in the prevalence of suicidal behaviors among young persons
through early recognition and immediate help. Some Departments of Education,
school boards, and even individual school administrators have resisted the introduction of these programs in schools for a variety of reasons, some based more on
myth than fact and others that are legitimate and should be given serious and
careful consideration. At times, however, some people are so committed, focused,
and excited in their efforts in suicide prevention that they expect others, including
school personnel, parents, and lawmakers, to respond affirmatively and immediately to their agenda without question. It should be remembered that for educators
to do so would be irresponsible. Because they, too, are concerned about the lives
of children, every program introduced to their students must be carefully examined, weighed, and considered in light of the overall impact on the students. Thus,
suicide prevention specialists and educators must strive together to provide life-
enhancing and lifesaving opportunities to students. It behooves everyone in the
area of suicide prevention to answer the questions and legitimate concerns of
educators and parents in the best way possible. It is my sincere belief that through
such on-going debate, better approaches to suicide prevention in schools will be
conceived, nurtured, and implemented.

REFERENCES

1. Smith, K., & Crawford, S. (1986). Suicidal behavior among "normal" high school students. *Suicide and Life-Threatening Behavior, 16*(3), 313–324.
2. Friedman, J. M. H., Anis, G. M., Boeck, M., & Difore, J. (1987). Prevalence of specific suicidal behaviors in a high school sample. *American Journal of Psychiatry, 144,* 1203–1206.
3. Dyck, R. J., Bland, R. C., Newman, S. C., & Orn, H. (1988). Suicide attempts and psychiatric disorders in Edmonton. *Acta Psychiatrica Scandinavica, 77*(suppl. 338), 64–71.
4. Frigo, L. N., Dyck, R. J., & Wright, J. (1989). *Suicides among junior and senior high school students.* Unpublished manuscript.
5. Dyck, R. J. (1988). Suicide in the young: Implications for policy and programming. Paper presented at the 20th Annual Behavioral Sciences Conference, Banff, Alberta, Canada.
6. Phillips, D. (1984). Teenage and adult temporal fluctuations in suicide and auto fatalities. In H. S. Sudak, A. B. Ford, & N. B. Rushforth (Eds.), *Suicide in the young* (pp. 69–80). Boston: John Wright.
7. Phillips, D. P., & Carstensen, L. L. (1986). Clustering of teenage suicides after television news stories about suicide. *The New England Journal of Medicine, 315*(11), 685–689.
8. Gould, M. S., & Shaffer, D. (1986). The impact of suicide in television movies: Evidence of imitation. *The New England Journal of Medicine, 315*(11), 609–694.
9. Lester, D. (1987). *Suicide as a learned behavior.* Springfield, IL: Charles C Thomas:
10. Zajonc, R. B. (1968). Attitudinal effects of mere exposure. *Journal of Personality and Social Psychology* (Monograph Suppl. Pt. 2), 1–29.
11. Marks, I. M. (1978). Exposure treatment: Conceptual issues. In W. S. Agras (Ed.), *Behavior modification: Principles and clinical application* (2d ed.). Boston: Little, Brown.
12. Hafner, H., & Schmidtke, A. (1986). *Effects of the mass media on suicidal behavior and deliberate self-harm.* Paper presented at the Working Group on Preventive Practices in Suicide and Attempted Suicide Conference, York, United Kingdom.
13. Ross, C. P. (1981). Teaching suicide prevention in schools. In *Depression et Suicide* (pp. 632–637). CA: Pergamon Press.
14. Hendrickson, S., & Cameron, C. A. (1975). Student suicide and college administrators: A perceptual gap. *Journal of Higher Education, 46*(3), 349–354.
15. Mulder, A. M., Methorst, G. J., & Diekstra, R. F. W. (1989). Prevention of suicidal behavior in adolescents: The role and training of teachers. *Crisis, 10*(1), 36–51.
16. de Heus, P., Diekstra, R. F. W., & van der Leeden, B. I. (1986a). Suicidaal gedrag van leerlingen in het Voortgezet Onderwijs. 1.: Hoe gaat de school om met suicidaal gedrag? (Suicidal behavior among secondary school children. 1.: How does the school cope with suicidal behavior?). *Pedagogische Studien, 63,* 218–227.
17. de Heus, P., Diekstra, R. F. W., & van der Leeden, B. I. (1986b). Suicidaal gedrag van leerlingen in het Voortgezet Onderwijs. 2.: Wat voor taken heeft de school volgens de leraren? (Suicidal behavior among secondary school children. 2.: Which tasks belong to the school according to the teachers?) *Pedagogische Studien, 63,* 252–261.
18. Worchel, S., Cooper, J., & Goethals, G. R. (1988). *Understanding social psychology* (4th ed.). Chicago: Dorsey Press.
19. Hovland, C. I., & Weiss, W. (1952). The influence of source credibility on communication effectiveness. *Public Opinion Quarterly, 15,* 635–650.
20. Nelson, F. L. (1987). Evaluation of a youth suicide prevention school program. *Adolescence, 22*(88), 813–825.
21. Shaffer, D., Garland, A., & Whittle, B. (1988). *An evaluation of three youth suicide prevention programs in New Jersey* (final project report). Trenton, NJ: New Jersey Dept. of Health.
22. Tierney, R. J. (1988). *Comprehensive evaluation for suicide intervention training.* (Doctoral dissertation). University of Calgary, Alberta, Canada.

5

Promotion of Self-Esteem in the Prevention of Suicide

Cathie Stivers
University of New Mexico, Albuquerque

In the light of the uncertainty of the effectiveness of formal suicide prevention services and suicide prevention centers nationwide (1), I propose that the most effective way of preventing youth suicide is to guarantee each child an upbringing that is conducive to the development of a positive self-esteem. By doing so, the "host" will become "immune" to the "disease" of depression and all the other symptomatology of suicide ideation. This will ultimately lead to a decrease in the number of times suicide is even considered as a solution to a bleak situation.

I begin with the definitions of self-esteem and related terms, followed by a discussion of the importance of self-esteem in a child's development. A brief review of literature is then provided, which points to the link between self-concept and health behavior, and more specifically to the relation of self-concept to suicidal personality or intent. In conclusion, I provide practical information on fostering a positive self-concept in youth, including a partial listing of resources and current programs that focus on the promotion of a positive self-concept.

DEFINITIONS AND CONCEPTS

Although the terms *self-concept* and *self-esteem* are often used interchangeably, they are not the same. *Self-concept* is the way a person feels about him- or herself: the image of self in one's own mind. Obviously, one's self-concept is affected by many people and things, as is discussed later. It is important to distinguish, at this point, between self-concept and self-esteem. Self-concept is actually made up of two separate components: self-esteem and self-acceptance. Self-esteem is feeling good about one's self on the basis of perceived strengths, whereas self-acceptance is valuing one's self regardless of perceived weaknesses (2). Self-concept, then, literally means taking the bad with the good.

Related to self-concept and self-esteem is *self-efficacy,* which is one's belief in the ability to do a specific behavior (3). *Empowerment* is the development of a high sense of self-efficacy (2), a capability that health educators and counselors encourage and promote in their clients. Strecher et al. (4) described the relation between self-esteem and self-efficacy as follows:

> *Self-esteem is concerned with an evaluation of self-worth, while self-efficacy relates to an evaluation of specific capabilities in specific situations. People often try to develop self-efficacy*

in activities that give them a sense of self-worth, so that the two concepts are frequently inter-twined. (p. 77)

Long (5, p. 16) identified four interrelated and interactive components that contribute to a positive self-concept:

1. Competency—"the development of skills and abilities which allow one to take charge" of one's life, work, relationships, and self;
2. Self-esteem—"feeling good about yourself, and the time spent alone";
3. Congruency—giving yourself permission to appear and behave in ways that are consistent with how you feel; "taking off the 'mask' made up of the 'shoulds' from others and worn to get the approval of others, and simply being one's self to get one's own approval"; and
4. Control—self-responsibility and self-approval of one's beliefs, values, and behaviors.

Promoting a self-concept, then, would include fostering both self-esteem and self-acceptance. Although both are important, the major focus of this article is on self-esteem.

IMPORTANCE OF SELF-ESTEEM
IN CHILD DEVELOPMENT

How important is the development of a positive self-esteem early in one's life? "If your child has high self-esteem, he has it made. Mounting research shows that the full-functioning child (or adult) is different from the person who flounders through life" (6, p. 3). Educational psychologist Erik Erikson claimed that an adult's self-esteem is largely dependent on childhood experiences, and the resolution of three basic tensions during early childhood: trust versus mistrust, autonomy versus shame and doubt, and initiative versus guilt. Erikson further stated that these tensions are sequential; that is, resolution of one tension prepares the child for the next one. Additionally, the earlier these three tensions are addressed and resolved, the more equipped the child will be in coping with recurring problem situations throughout life (7). Problem-solving is not the only area in which one will have success as a result of early self-esteem development: "Your child's judgement of himself influences the kinds of friends he chooses, . . . and how productive he will be. It affects his creativity, integrity, stability. . . . In fact, self-esteem is the mainspring that slates every child for success or failure as a human being" (6, p. 3)

Convincing evidence exists that points out the relation between self-esteem and academic success or failure (8–14), drug use (9, 10), premarital intercourse (15), running away (16), adult psychopathology (17), and adolescent deviant activity (18). Indeed, the adoption of various negative health behaviors may be partially due to faulty self-concept (12, 19).

DEPRESSION AND SUICIDE

When children are not successful in attaining and maintaining high self-esteem, they may erect defenses (such as sublimation, denial, or projection); they may submit and begin a vicious cycle of self-defeat, leading to self-effacing and even self-destructive behavior; or they may withdraw, hiding their true feelings (6). Any one of these avenues can lead to major mental health problems.

Certainly, depression is a common result (20). Depression is often considered to be the single best predictor of suicide, particularly among teenagers. "One of the greatest determinants of depression is low self-esteem. A depressed adolescent looks at himself as lacking such attributes as ability, performance, intelligence, health, strength, . . . popularity. . . . The adolescent becomes convinced that he is totally worthless, inept, inadequate, and impoverished. . . . a total failure and a burden to those around him" (21, pp. 95–96). Individuals with such a poor self-image may come to depend on external signs of their worth. This creates a dangerous set-up, for a period of failure in work or relationships can further perpetuate their feelings of self-disgust (22). These events and feelings, coupled with poor communication with family, a sense of isolation, and feelings of rejection can culminate in self-destruction (22, 23).

Psychological abuse, intentional or not, is significantly higher in families of suicidal youngsters (24). The family situation of suicidal youngsters reveals difficulties in the parent–child relationship, beginning early in the child's life. The parents are often frustrating, rejecting, and unkind, and seem to want the child's physical presence but are unwilling to make emotional investments. "They want him or her to be there and not there at the same time—to be under their control and to fulfill parental expectations, though as parents they have given the child little incentive to do so" (25, p. 158). The child strives to fulfill his/her parents' expectations, yet derives no pleasure in doing so. "At the same time they do not feel free to act in ways that would separate them from their parents. Such youngsters may make few emotional demands, but become instead withdrawn, depressed, and quietly preoccupied with death and suicide" (25, p. 158).

Cases have even been noted where the parents have expressed outright their feelings that they did not really want the child, or that they would be happier if the child were dead. Although this is not the typical pattern of child neglect, it is obviously very demeaning. The children then see themselves as an unnecessary burden, and recognize that they are treated coldly by their parents, constantly being criticized or told that they are not wanted around. The children's natural reaction to this is the conclusion that they can only please their parents by killing themselves, fulfilling their wishes for their absence (20).

Supporting literature has identified core factors contributing to adolescent suicidal behavior, including a perceived loss of parental love and intimacy, followed by a resulting loss of identity and self-worth, and possibly even by a death bond with the parents (26–29). In addition, numerous studies have revealed a significant direct relation between low self-esteem and suicidal tendencies (30–37).

HOW TO FOSTER POSITIVE SELF-CONCEPT IN YOUTH

Because children view themselves in the way they think their significant others feel about them, parents and teachers must strive to do everything possible to foster positive self-concept in children. A variety of techniques may be practiced:

1. Treat children with respect and expect the same behavior from them.

2. Help children find their strengths and encourage them in both their strengths and weaknesses.

3. Avoid comparing one child with another; respect individuality and uniqueness.

4. Actively listen to children and try to understand their points of view.

5. Encourage children to express both good and bad feelings without fear of losing your love.

6. Discipline a child for a specific behavior he or she exhibits, *not* because he or she is a bad person.

7. Help children to discover acceptable ways to behave in areas where they are having difficulty.

8. Provide opportunities for children to experience success and independence.

9. When in doubt, hug and praise the child.

10. Build your own self-esteem, in addition to the child's. Children notice how you feel about yourself and will model many adult behaviors.

The Center for Self-Esteem provides these reminders for teachers, who influence children's development of self-esteem (38, pp. 1–2):

1. "Conditional acceptance, the withholding of affection until academic or other tasks are completed, should be used with discretion";

2. Similarly children need to be accepted and/or loved unconditionally by the significant adults in their lives, including teachers and parents;

3. The self-esteem reflected by teachers will be recognized and absorbed by their developing students; and

4. "Children enhance their identity and self-concept when they learn to express themselves in socially acceptable ways."

Briggs (6) has also pointed out some considerations to be made when practical applications and methods of building self-esteem are being developed and implemented:

1. Consider nonverbal communication of judgments (body language) as well as verbal communication.

2. Accentuate and provide for positive life experiences that will help create a positive identity in the youngster. Successful past experiences increase the chance for future successes and increased self-confidence.

3. "Low self-esteem is tied to impossible demands on self. Underachievers most frequently come from homes where there is constant pressure to do more and better" (pp. 39, 48).

4. It is not enough for the adults to say they love the child; the child must feel loved. There is a big difference between "being" loved and "feeling" loved.

5. Children should not only be *accepted* for who they are, but also *cherished* for who they are. They must feel special just because they exist.

6. Where sympathy impedes self-esteem, empathy fosters it because judgment is set aside.

7. Autonomy and mastery are building blocks in the development of a positive self-esteem during the early years.

8. Accomplishment of self-esteem during the middle years (8–12 years of age) is dependent on the development of physical, social, and academic competence.

9. For high self-esteem, the teenager needs to "establish final independence from family and agemates; be able to relate to the opposite sex; prepare for an occupation for self-support; and establish workable and meaningful philosophy of life" (p. 155).

10. "A basic rule about human behavior is that negative feelings exist before negative acts" (p. 197). If the negative feelings are allowed to be expressed, and are dealt with in an empathetic fashion, the negative behavior can be prevented.

11. Avoid comparisons between or among individuals; someone always falls short with this type of competition. The ensuing jealousy will only reduce self-respect.

Examples of application of self-esteem-building techniques in schools and similar settings can be found in the literature. One such application focuses on accentuating the positive instead of the negative, a practice recommended by Chandler and Kolander (39). Because self-concept can be directly affected by beliefs or thoughts that children hold in their mind, consciously or subconsciously, Chandler and Kolander suggested that negative self-thoughts ("I'm so stupid" or "I don't have what it takes") should and can be converted to positive self-thoughts ("I'm smart and I can do it" or "I have the courage to give it my best shot"). They provide examples of such positive affirmations for a variety of health topics: decision making, personality theories, stress management, death and dying, aging, goal achievement, drugs, tobacco, and alcohol. Examples of positive affirmation statements under the topic of depression and suicide include "I am a unique and creative being," "Being me makes me special," and "I am a beautiful and worthwhile person" (p. 296). The practice of accentuating the positive through affirmation can not only contribute to a positive self-esteem, but can also facilitate behavior change if necessary or desired.

In Wisconsin, a teaching unit was designed to build a positive self-concept in K–2 children to help them feel good about themselves by being aware of and discussing their feelings. An additional purpose was to guide the students into desired behavior changes that maintained positive self-concept. The unit, called "I Am Great," focused on small group interaction, self-identity, decision making, feelings, positive reinforcement, and individuality. Evaluation of the implementation of the unit revealed a positive significant difference in self-concept, as evidenced by pretest and posttest comparisons between experimental and control groups over a 2-week period (19).

A similar unit was devised for middle school students in a New Mexico public school district (40) so that students could

> explore who they are, how to communicate with others effectively, and to overcome fears of developing self-esteem. [The unit] promotes the sharing of ideas, encourages individuality, and develops an understanding of how we all control our own lives and destinies. (p. iii)

The long-term goal of this teaching unit is to "raise self concepts in individuals to a level where the students feel confident and capable of learning in other areas" (p. iii).

The daily lesson plans are entitled, "What is my Self-Concept?" "Self-

Concept: Past, Present, and Future," "Physical Self," "Choosing How We Feel," and "Assertive Training." Each lesson combines content and minimal lecture with student-centered activities that are designed to disclose to the student his or her own level of self-esteem, the positive and negative influences on self-esteem, and methods of increasing self-esteem. Evaluation components are written in for each lesson. Although the entire unit has not yet been used and evaluated, feedback following the presentation of one of the lesson plans in the middle school setting was positive.

ADDITIONAL RESOURCES
FOR SELF-ESTEEM CURRICULUMS
AND MATERIALS

Examples of other programs and curriculum materials nationwide include "I Can" in Dallas, Texas; "Personality Fitness Training" in Tulare, California; "Positive Action Self-Concept Curriculum" in Twin Falls, Idaho, "PLUS: Promoting Learning and Understanding of Self" in Irvine, California; "Quest: Skills for Adolescents" in Columbus, Ohio; and "Unlocking Your Potential" in Bend, Oregon. Information on these programs and many others can be obtained from the Center for Self-Esteem, P.O. Box 1532, Santa Cruz, California 95061 (41). A list of speakers and their topics from the 1986 Conference on Self-Esteem and a list of self-esteem classroom activities resources and materials can also be obtained from the center.

The Center for Self-Esteem is a nonprofit corporation that was established in 1982 with several purposes in mind:

1. To alert educators to the importance of student and staff self-esteem as one of the essential components of an effective school
2. To disseminate information about self-esteem programs, materials, consultants, and schools with exemplary programs
3. To conduct research related to self-esteem
4. To seek and support grants to individuals and groups with programs designed to build self-esteem
5. To provide speakers and consultants to schools, districts, and groups interested in learning more about self-esteem (personal correspondence, Ragnar Gilberts).

A similar organization, The National Council for Self-Esteem, has recently been formed to "increase national awareness of self-esteem; empower people to enhance their academic, personal, social, and vocational excellence through the development of self-esteem; and foster communication and cooperation between people and agencies which promote the development of self-esteem" (42, p. 3). More information can be obtained by writing to 6641 Leyland Park Drive, San Jose, California 95120.

CONCLUSION

It is a well-documented fact that low self-esteem is a significant contributor to the onset of depression and other mental illness, and that it can ultimately lead to self-destruction. Inarguably, suicide is a multicausal phenomenon. Many of the risk factors, however, may well be traced back to failure to develop a positive self-concept. Suicide crisis intervention efforts may be unsuccessful because the efforts are directed only at the symptoms of the original problem, which occurred long before the symptoms appeared. Prevention of such symptoms is possible through the development, nurturing, and maintenance of a high self-esteem. The fostering of self-esteem, and therefore of self-concept, is not only possible, it is critical to the survival of youth.

(Additional examples of self-concept curriculums and activities are provided in the lists of references. Additionally, a self-concept teaching unit for fourth graders has been provided as an appendix.)

REFERENCES

1. Dew, M. A., Bromet, E. J., Brent, D., & Greenhouse, J. R. (1987). A quantitative literature review of the effectiveness of suicide prevention centers. *Journal of Consulting and Clinical Psychology, 55,* 239–244.
2. Long, V. O. (1988). [Unpublished material]. Albuquerque: University of New Mexico, Department of Counselor Education.
3. Lawrance, L., & McLeroy, K. R. (1986). Self-efficacy and health education. *Journal of School Health, 56,* 317–321.
4. Strecher, V. J., DeVellis, B. M., Becher, M. H., & Rosenstock, I. M. (1986). The role of self-efficacy in achieving health behavior change. *Health Education Quarterly, 13,* 73–91.
5. Long, V. O. (1987). The pursuit of happiness: Feeling good about yourself, problems and prescriptions. *Counseling Interview, 19,* 15–17.
6. Briggs, D. C. (1970). *Your child's self-esteem.* Garden City, NY: Doubleday.
7. *I need to be me: The emergence of self.* Madison, WI: Wisconsin Clearinghouse. (Original work published 1917)
8. U.S. Department of Health & Human Services. (1981). *Adolescent peer pressure: Theory, correlates, and program implications for drug abuse prevention* (U.S. DHHS Publication No. (ADM)84-1152).
9. Norem-Hebeisen, A. A., & Martin, F. B. (1980). *Parental support as an approach to primary prevention of chemical abuse* (final project report submitted to St. Paul Companies). St. Paul, MN: The Companies.
10. Smith, G. M. (1975). Teenage drug use: A search for causes and consequences. In D. J. Lettreri (Ed.), *Predicting adolescent drug use: A review of the issues, methods, and correlates* (DHEW Publication No. ADM 76-299). Washington, DC: U.S. Government Printing Office.
11. Ahlgren, A., Norem-Hebeisen, A. A., Hochhauser, M., & Garvin, J. (1980). *Antecedents of smoking among pre-adolescents.* Unpublished manuscript.
12. Bachman, J. G., O'Malley, P. M., & Johnston, J. (1978). *Adolescence to adulthood: Change and stability in the lives of young men.* Ann Arbor, MI: Survey Research Center.
13. Beier, B. (1988). *Self concept.* Unpublished manuscript, University of New Mexico, Albuquerque, Health Promotion Program.
14. Leonardson, G. R. (1986). The relationship between self-concept and selected academic and personal factors. *Adolescence, 21,* 467–474.
15. Cvetkovich, G., & Grote, B. (1976, May). *Psychological factors associated with adolescent premarital coitus.* Paper presented at the National Institute of Child Health and Human Development, Bethesda, MD.
16. Brennan, T. (1980). Mapping the diversity among runaways: A descriptive multivariate analysis of selected social psychological background conditions. *Journal of Family Issues, 1,* 189–209.
17. Kohlberg, L., LaCrosse, J., & Ricks, D. (1970). The predictability of adult mental health from childhood behavior. In B. Wolman (Ed.), *Handbook of child psychopathology.* New York: McGraw-Hill.
18. Eskilson, A., Wiley, M. G., Muehlbauer, G., & Dodder, L. (1986) Parental pressure, self-esteem and adolescent reported deviance: Bending the twig too far. *Adolescence, 21,* 501–515.
19. Papenfuss, R. L., Curtis, J. D., Beier, B. J., & Menze, J. D. (1983). Teaching positive self-concepts in the classroom. *Journal of School Health, 53,* 618–620.
20. Wagman, S. P. (1978). Adolescent suicide: A review. *The Osteopathic Physician, 52–53,* 10–15.

21. Hafen, B. Q., & Frandsen, K. J. (1986). *Youth suicide: Depression and loneliness.* Evergreen, Colorado: Cordillera Press.
22. _____. (1981). Recognizing and helping others who may be suicidal. *The Harvard Medical School Health Letter, 6*(12), 3–4.
23. Barry, R. J. (1986, April). Teenage suicide. An American tragedy. *FBI Law Enforcement Bulletin,* pp. 17–21.
24. Holden, C. (1986). Youth suicide: New research focuses on a growing social problem. *Science, 233,* 839–841.
25. Hendin, H. (1987). Youth suicide: A psychosocial perspective. *Suicide and Life-Threatening Behavior, 17,* 151–165.
26. Hendin, H. (1975). Student suicide. Death as a lifestyle. *Journal of Nervous and Mental Disorders, 160,* 204–219.
27. Sabbath, J. C. (1969). The suicidal adolescent—The expendable child. *Journal of the American Academy of Child Psychiatry, 8,* 272–289.
28. Peck, M., & Litman, R. (1975). Current trends in youthful suicide. *Tribuna Media.*
29. Tuckman, J., & Connon, H. E. (1962). Attempted suicide in adolescents. *American Journal of Psychiatry, 119,* 228–232.
30. Wetzel, R. D. (1975). Self-concept of suicide intent. *Psychological Reports, 35,* 279–282.
31. Farberow, N. L., & McEvoy, T. L. (1966). Suicide among patients in general medical and surgical hospitals with diagnoses of anxiety reaction or depressive reaction. *Journal of Abnormal Psychology, 71,* 287.
32. Kamano, D. K., & Crawford, C. S. (1966). Self-evaluations of suicidal mental health patients. *Journal of Clinical Psychology, 22,* 278–279.
33. Lester, D. (1972). *Why people kill themselves: A summary of research findings.* Springfield, IL: Charles C Thomas.
34. Neuringer, C. (1973). Attitude toward self in suicidal individuals. *Life-Threatening Behavior, 4,* 96–106.
35. Neuringer, C. (1974). Self- and other-appraisals by suicidal, psychosomatic, and normal hospitalized patients. *Journal of Consulting and Clinical Psychology, 42,* 306.
36. Spalt, L., & Weisbuch, J. B. (1972). Suicide: An epidemiological study. *Disorders of the Nervous System, 33,* 23–29.
37. Wilson, L. T., Braucht, G. N., & Miskimins, R. W. (1971). The severe suicide attempter and self-concept. *Journal of Clinical Psychology, 27,* 307–309.
38. Gilberts, R. (1986, October). Teachers build self-esteem. *Self-Esteem Newsletter,* pp. 1–2.
39. Chandler, C. K., & Kolander, C. A. (1988). Stop the negative, accentuate the positive. *Journal of School Health, 58,* 295–297.
40. Magadini, B. (1988). *Self-concept curriculum submitted to APS curriculum coordinator for middle schools.* Unpublished manuscript.
41. Reasoner, R. W. (1988). Self-esteem curriculum resources. Santa Cruz, CA: Center for Self-Esteem.
42. *Self-Esteem Newsletter* (1988, May). pp. 1–4.
43. Fontecchio, J. (1984). [Self concept teaching unit for fourth graders.]. Unpublished material, University of New Mexico.

APPENDIX: SELF-CONCEPT TEACHING UNIT FOR FOURTH GRADERS

THE MAN IN THE GLASS

When you get what you want in your struggle for self,
And the world makes you king for a day,
Just go to a mirror and look at yourself,
And see what that man has to say.
For it isn't your father or mother or wife,
Whose judgment upon you must pass,
The fellow whose verdict counts most in your life
Is the one staring back in the glass.

Author Unknown

OVERVIEW

This is a self-concept unit designed for fourth graders. Students have had some brief instruction on self-concept in previous grades; however, this is their first exposure to planned consecutive lessons on this subject.

The unit is divided into seven individual lessons, all less than 1 hr long. The unit will be taught over 6–8 weeks during the health science period. This unit should be used within the first 3 months of the school year.

The overall purpose of the unit is to help children become aware of their self-concept and some of the ways it is developed and maintained throughout a lifetime. Comments will be greatly appreciated.

Table 1

Content	Outcome	Student experiences	Methods	Evaluations
		Lesson 1 (40) min: Mind-clearing; introduction to self-concept		
Mind-clearing activity (10 min)	Students will clear their minds and be able to grasp something new.	Students will sit relaxed, comfortably, with eyes open or closed, and take a few deep breaths. They will allow thoughts to come and go but not study or dwell on them. Students will continue to be aware of the thoughts until they stop coming and their mind is more clear (2–4 min).	Chairs or carpeted floor Reference 4, p. 33	Teacher will determine if students' breathing is more relaxed. Teacher will observe if there is a pleasant sense of well-being among class members. Teacher will see if students appear generally more relaxed and ready for learning.
Introduction to self-concept theory Written pretest and discussion (30 min)	Students will become more aware of the meaning of self-concept.	Students will spend time thinking and talking about self-concept with their classmates and teacher.	Pencils, ruled paper Reference 3, p. 11–13	Teacher will evaluate the discussion orally through student answers to the following questions: (a) Do you know what I mean when I say self-concept? (b) How do you think we get self-concept? (c) Do you think a person can change their self-concept? How? (d) If self-concept is the idea or picture one has of himself, do you think a person's self-concept may influence the way he does his schoolwork? the way he plays? whether he tries out new things? Teacher will further evaluate unit by reviewing written response of individual students.

Lesson 2 (60 min, possibly divided into two 30-min sessions): Development of a sense of belonging; increase acquaintance between members of the class

Develop a sense of belonging: I am somebody, guess who I am? game. (15 min)	Students will be able to identify own and other class members' belongingness, through biographical data.	Students will write at least five (not too obvious) items describing themselves. This may include hobbies, talents, major trips, awards, or unusual things about their family. (Teacher should include a card!) Students will then guess who other students are by description on card.	Pencils, blank 5 × 7 cards Reference 1, p. 35	Teacher will collect cards and reach descriptions orally. She will determine students' interest by their participation.
Identify connectiveness with family (10 min).	Students will be able to trace their family heritage (belonging).	Students will draw family tree. This will include the student, parents, grandparents, etc. Students will take this drawing home to have parents help them complete tracing.	Construction paper Magic Markers Reference 1, p. 219	Teacher will walk around room checking that students complete drawing correctly.
Increasing acquaintance of class members. Developing a sense of belonging with the class group (15 min)	Students will become better acquainted with members of the class. Students will begin to develop a sense of belongingness with other members of the class.	Students will be given 10 min to talk to as many members of the class as possible. Through this communication the students will attempt to fill out the clue sheet given to them.	Handout 1 Reference 2, p. 30–31	Teacher will discuss the findings and note individual reactions as students raise their hand to be identified.

(Table continues on next page)

61

Table 1

Content	Outcome	Student experiences	Methods	Evaluations
Increase awareness of group belonging (20 min)	Students will be able to describe group connectiveness.	Students will divide into groups of five. They will tape-record 1-min descriptions of different groups to which they belong (one group per student). This may include group characteristics or feelings about how they like the group. Students may listen to each other's recordings or their own at various times throughout the week.	5 tape recorders 5 tapes 5 microphones Reference 3, p. 81–83	The teacher will evaluate the students' sense of group belonging through an oral discussion at the end of 1 week. Discussion questions may include the following: Did you hear about any groups that sounded appealing to you? Would you like to belong to any groups other than the ones to which you now belong? Did people report on similar or different kinds of groups?

Lesson 3 (60 min): Development of a sense of uniqueness; think about and describe oneself—increase a sense of accomplishment and self-worth

Content	Outcome	Student experiences	Methods	Evaluations
Develop a sense of uniqueness. One-of-a-kind art activity (15 min)	Students will be able to verbally identify how they are different and unique.	Students will observe teacher as she creates an art design. Tears various colors of crepe paper into different forms and mounts them on drawing paper (an abstract expression)	Art paper Crepe paper Construction paper	Teacher will evaluate the students' knowledge by their verbal response to discussion question.
		Students will create their own unique design within 5-min limit.	Reference 1, p. 137	Can the ideas we've talked about be applied to human beings?

Activity	Objectives	Procedures	Materials	Evaluation
		Students will compare their artwork and discover uniqueness.		
		Students will discuss how this "one-of-a-kind" art piece may be applied to human beings. Each person is different, unique, irreplaceable, and impossible to duplicate.		
Think about and describe oneself. Who Am I Today? activity (15 min)	Students will be able to identify some of their unique characteristics.	Students will complete Who Am I Today worksheet. Students will divide into small groups and compare their answers.	Handout 2 Pencils Reference 2, p. 16–17	Teacher will evaluate students' knowledge through their verbal response of identifying individual characteristics.
Emphasize student's strengths. What I Can Do Book (30 min)	Students will be more aware of their strengths in their own areas of interest.	Students will make books that emphasize what they can already do. Cut out two large circles for cover and several circles from writing paper for inside pages.	Construction paper Ruled paper Scissors, pencils Paper punch, yarn Glue Handout 3 Reference 5, p. 32	Teacher will walk around room pointing out strengths of individual students she has observed. Teacher will evaluate students' perception of themselves through writings in book.

(Table continues on next page)

Table 1

Content	Outcome	Student experiences	Methods	Evaluations
		Lesson 4 (30 min): Development of a sense of models		
Choosing an ideal model (15 min)	The students will identify qualities that they feel make up the ideal role model. Students will write five qualities they have identified.	The student will imagine some of the qualities he would like to have or ways he would like to appear to other people. Student will consider different models, different relationships, and how he may try to be like them. Students will write down qualities visualized. Students will discuss various qualities necessary to help them accomplish what they would like to become.	Pencils Ruled paper Reference 1, p. 183–185	Teacher will evaluate student's knowledge through written qualifications of models and through verbal discussion.
Picture oneself as competent and successful (15 min)	Students will be able to recognize themselves as great persons (as they view their ideal role-model).	Students will bring a picture of themselves from home. Students will imagine themselves as a famous star, anyone they would like to be. Students will cut a design depicting what is famous or idealistic about their model (example: football).	Photo of self Handout 4 Glue Construction paper Reference 2, p. 28	Teacher will evaluate students' knowledge by asking them to describe qualities of their famous persons and relate those qualities to themselves. Teacher will display artwork around room to initiate future discussion.

Lesson 5 (45 min): Development of a sense of power; assessing wants and realizing alternatives

Activity	Objectives	Activities	Materials	Assessment
		Students will glue their picture to the design and art paper.		
Develop a sense of power: If I Were God of the Universe exercise (30 min)	Students will be able to imagine themselves as all-powerful.	Students will imagine themselves as all-powerful all-knowing gods of the universe.	Pencils Handout 5 Reference 1, p. 182	The teacher will evaluate the students' knowledge by written expressions. Teacher will have students justify orally their rank ordering.
	Students will express in writing their feelings of control.	Students will complete the phrases of the written exercise.		
		Students will divide into groups of five to share completion of their exercise and rank order what they feel is most important to least important.		
Addressing wants and realizing alternatives (15 mins)	Students will understand that there are always alternatives available.	Students will think of how they want to act, feel, or think.	Pencils Ruled paper	Teacher will evaluate students' knowledge by oral responses.
	Students will realize they have the power of choice—choosing what they want and seeking it.	Students will list all of these ideas. Students divide the alternatives into possible and impossible ones, then choose which one they like the best out of the *possible* alternatives.	Reference 7, p. 97–99	Questioning: which of the possible alternatives did you choose and *why?*

(Table continues on next page)

Table 1

Content	Outcome	Student experiences	Methods	Evaluations
		Lesson 6 (40 min): Enhancing another's self-esteem aids oneself; positive self-messages		
Enhancing self-esteem of others—enhances self-esteem of oneself (20 min)	Students will be able to identify positive attributes of class members	Students will sit in a circle and have one student move to the center of the circle. Five other students around the circle will compliment, praise, or give positive feedback to the student in the center. Students will give specific feedback on behavior they like or appreciate about the centered person, excluding praise about a person's outward appearance.	Chairs Reference 3, p. 59–60	Teacher will evaluate activity by asking centered students to share their feelings as peers praised them. Teacher will ensure that all students have time in center at some point during following week, and provide opportunity for sharing.
	Students will experience feelings as related to them by peers and teacher.			
Positive self-messages (30 min)	Students will be able to recognize positive messages.	Students will select a message from the choices teacher reads to them: I will relax when I am feeling nervous. I will love myself. I will be a fast runner. I will take better care of myself. I will be good-looking to others. I can do what I decide to do. I am strong and wise.	Carpeted floor Chairs Reference 4, p. 78–82	The teacher will evaluate the students' experience through their verbal response as they share reactions. The teacher will continue to encourage students to choose to behave in a positive way, and to listen to their choices.
	Students will try to internalize these selected messages.			The teacher will observe future choices students make and possible increase of self-image.

I can control myself.
I will act responsibly.
I am a good person and a good friend.
I will think before I act.

Students will sit relaxed with eyes closed and repeat the selected message to themselves silently and slowly.
Students will imagine what their lives would be like if they believed messages they selected.

Students will experience a period of silence in which to assimilate their messages.

Students will share reactions to their experience.

Lesson 7 (50 min): Development of self-responsibility; choices and responsibility—accepting responsibility

Developing self-responsibility (20)	Students will gain the meaning of responsibility.	Students will listen as teacher shares ideas on self-responsibility.	Pencils Handouts 7, 8, & 9	The teacher will evaluate students' understanding by written feedback and drawings from handouts.
		Students will complete handout on the meaning of self-responsibility.		
	Students will be able to write the meaning of	Students will draw pictures concerning their feelings about responsibilities in	Reference 6	The teacher will evaluate students' understanding by written feedback and drawings from handouts.

(Table continues on next page)

Table 1

Content	Outcome	Student experiences	Methods	Evaluations
	responsibility and list at least three responsibilities at home and at school.	various situations—themselves, families, others, and environment.		The teacher will evaluate students' knowledge by verbal questioning on the alternatives listed and the choices made, and also, *why* students made these decisions.
Choices and responsibility (10 min)	Students will realize they make choices about what to do and are responsible for these choices.	Students will form groups of five and mark from their list the things they *have* to do. Students will then practice saying "I choose to . . ." There are very few things we really *have* to do.	Pencils Reference 7, p. 94–96	
		Students will return to large group to discuss consequences of not doing things on their list and also to discuss what alternatives they may have, to help them realize they do have a choice but are responsible for the choice they make.		
Accepting responsibility: pet care (20 mins)	Students will develop a feeling of importance and sense of responsibility by caring for a pet.	Students will put together a fish aquarium, decorate it, and fill it with fish.	Fish Fish food Fish care booklet	Teacher will spend time with the class helping them to build aquarium and devise list of responsibilities to pet care.
		Students will make up a list of daily and weekly duties necessary to care properly for the fish.		Teacher will evaluate the students' sense of accepted responsibility by observing their consistent care throughout the year.

REFERENCES

1. Canfield, J., & Wells, H. (1976). *100 ways to enhance self-concept in the classroom: A handbook for teachers and parents.* Englewood Cliffs, NJ: Prentice-Hall.
2. Cihak, M., & Heron, B. (1980). *Games children should play: Sequential lessons for teaching communication skills in Grades K–6.* Goodyear.
3. Gram, R., & Guest, P. (1977). *Activities for developing positive self awareness 4–6.* Milliken.
4. Harmin, M., & Sax, S. (1977). *A peaceable classroom: Activities to calm and free students energies.* Winston Press.
5. Harris, A. (1983). *Albuquerque public schools (APS) guidance/counseling activity book.* Albuquerque, NM: APS North Area Office.
6. Harris, A. (1981). *Albuquerque public schools (APS) guidance/counseling life planning—career domain book.* Albuquerque, NM: APS North Area Office.
7. Hendricks, G., & Roberts, T. (1977). *The second centering book: More awareness activities for children, parents and teachers.* Englewood Cliffs, NJ: Prentice-Hall.

6

Suicide Prevention in Elementary Schools

Linda Sattem
Suicide Prevention Center, Inc., Dayton, Ohio

There is a general consensus that caregivers would prefer to identify those individuals at risk early, and to teach coping, mental health skills, and other preventive measures as opposed to "picking up the pieces."

Through the years there has been an interest in children, and in how to incorporate both preventive and early warning systems into a child's life circle. Several factors inhibit these efforts, including miscommunication between children and adults (whether because of language, lack of time, disinterest, etc.), inability or unwillingness to recognize various manifestations of trouble (e.g., symptoms of child abuse), and a lack of research and knowledge about the current experiences of children.

Self-destructive acts among children are of particular concern, especially what these acts mean, how to prevent them, what causes them, and how to reach both the children and the adults around them.

The program described here is a youth-system-based prevention and early identification process that uses puppets. The basic concepts are developed from the experiences of young children and concern their exposure to and understanding of death, loss, grief, and sharing feelings.

ORGANIZATION

The Suicide Prevention Center, Inc., in Dayton, Ohio, is a multifaceted mental health organization that has specifically targeted suicide and self-destructive behaviors since its inception in 1965.

One of the center's most interesting prevention programs uses puppets in working with elementary school children, Grades kindergarten through 6. This focus is primarily through educational systems, but is also used in scouting, latchkey, and religious organizations.

The program was developed from 1982 to 1983 in response to two factors. First, very young children, beginning at age 7, were calling the center's 24-hr crisis lines. Most of them were suicidal and self-destructive, but at the same time they did not understand death's finality. Second, the center was being asked to speak to groups of young children. A member of the Speakers Team approached with the idea of using puppets.

During this development period, several avenues were pursued. Extensive research was conducted into childhood suicide, children's concepts of death, prevention programs with elementary-school-aged children (e.g., dental care, bicycle safety), and the use of puppets as a teaching modality. Consultation, script writing, and training was developed with a local puppeteer troupe, Quality Puppet Players. Finally, a small pilot program was conducted in several schools. This included debriefing the teachers involved over a period of time to determine the program's impact on the children.

Currently, volunteer Puppeteer Team members are recruited and trained twice a year. The number of team members averages 15; each offers 1–3 programs per month during the academic year.

RATIONALE

Gradually, educational and other youth systems have been expected to train young people in living and social skills. The center has seen youth systems, such as schools, church youth groups, group homes, juvenile detention centers, day-care centers, and scouts, become a focal point for adolescent suicide prevention.

Unfortunately, this expectation has not been accompanied with the resources needed or the processes to mobilize other parties, particularly parents. Schools have floundered under this expectation. If a young person under their care attempts or completes suicide, they are often held uniquely and solely responsible by the community.

As the center's programs with adolescents developed, it was asked to help elementary schools on two fronts: first, with actual case intervention and consultation; second, with prevention programs.

The center's intervention, training, and consultation efforts are described elsewhere (1). I focus here on the development of the prevention program (2).

A multitude of prevention programs have been designed around health and wellness issues for elementary school children. Many of these focus on current behavior, such as oral hygiene, which is expected to be carried into adulthood. Other programs, such as those on alcohol and tobacco use, target developing attitudes that will carry into later years in the form of abstinence. Through the years, these programs have gradually reflected more complex issues, such as teen pregnancy and sexual assault prevention. This change has been coupled with a growing awareness of the extensive mental health needs of youth, including elementary-school-aged children.

Goodwin et al. (3) surveyed 500 elementary school personnel on the mental health needs of the children in their care. The highest-ranked item in the Self-Image subscale was children's having a poor image or making negative self-statements. Many other high-ranking items were depressive reactions or "masked" depression modalities. This research also highlighted the imbalance of causes being identified as non-school based, whereas the solutions are expected to be school based (3).

Other research has clearly documented the perception of depression in children as seen by adults and in actuality (4, 5). The research found most helpful for this program is Pfeffer's work with depressed and suicidal children (6, 7).

Little has been documented about children's attitudes toward suicide. One exception is Domino, Domino, and Berry (8) who studied 116 junior high school students (Grades 6–8). This research was descriptive, but offered little help from a prevention focus. Domino et al. offered this reflection in their conclusion:

. . . what is needed is not only the replication of these findings but empirical data on such questions as the developmental aspects of such attitudes, the relationship of attitudes to actual behavior, and the delineation of the role of family, and television on the formation of such attitudes. (8, p. 285)

There has been considerable study and documentation of children's understanding of and attitudes toward death (9).

Using these theoretical frameworks, the center set out to develop a prevention program that would both enable identifying currently at-risk children and have an impact on future behavior, ultimately preventing suicides from both angles.

The use of puppets for therapeutic intervention with children has been documented since the early 1930s. An experiment using puppets with maladjusted or neurotic children performed by Woltman in 1935 has become a model for many other avenues (10).

Woltman found that the children discussed their problems very freely with the puppeteer. Woltman felt that the puppet show entered the children's world and spoke their language—a major factor in therapeutic interventions.

Researchers have reported that puppets offer an intimate link not found with television and film. The complete absorption with the action on stage leads to spontaneous participation (11). The puppets have qualities apart from an actor; they affect audiences differently, whether the program targets mass education or dramatizes the advantages of reading, writing, brushing teeth, and cleanliness (12).

Puppets have been used in a wide variety of learning settings, including libraries (13). Preschool children were the focus of a puppet program by a guidance unit to facilitate the growth of feeling-words vocabulary, to help them verbally express what they were experiencing internally (14). Kindergarten teachers have used puppets to deal with difficult subjects such as death, war, going to a new grade, and new siblings (15).

The use of puppets with elementary and secondary school students has also been pronounced. They are used to teach new skills (e.g., use of the Dewey decimal system), and to review and reinforce. In a school setting, a major unique factor is that the puppet is not seen as a teacher. It is seen not as an adult disciplinarian, but rather as an equal, an understanding friend (16).

A specific puppet program for third graders, focusing on substance abuse, incorporates the elements of teaching children to listen to their friends, and then to seek out adult assistance. The teachers are trained, offering follow-up in the classroom with a visit by a resource person within 1 week. The students have reported that the program is successful (17).

Specific support for the rationale of the use of puppets comes from a number of sources. In a guidance setting, puppets (a) offer a chance for expression, (b) are accessible, (c) are nonthreatening, and (d) heighten the child's receptiveness (18). Several counselors see puppets as their right (or left) arm (19).

An investigation into children's responses to puppets over several years found that most children strongly identify with the hero, who expresses their own wishes and desires. Although the situation onstage can be very threatening, the puppet carries reassurance that this is make-believe. This does not detract from the realness, as the children follow the action, identify with characters, and project their wishes into the show. This mix of fantasy and reality makes it easier for children to enter into the spirit of the problem (20).

Additionally, research with the DUSO (developing an understanding of self and others)-1 Program found the use of puppets, fantasy activities, colorful pictures, and stories resulted in significant gains in the self-concept of the children. Children exposed to programs designed by teachers, not including these elements, did not have any gain in their self-concept scores (21).

How critical is the early development of resources and problem-solving skills, particularly as they relate to suicide? Research with college students has noted that those with serious suicidal ideas do not experience more serious stressful life events than nonsuicidal students. However, they have fewer resources to deal with these stressors. The students with suicidal thoughts were less likely to have received training in how to deal with emotions and problems (22).

PROGRAM RESEARCH

The center's puppet program was part of a formal research process in 1985–1986: Project Lifesaver. Project Lifesaver is a multiyear study of the needs of educational systems. The first effort was to document both the need for, and the impact of, suicide prevention programs within two school systems (adults, $N = 323$; elementary school children, $N = 1,460$; secondary school children, $N = 2,104$).

The second effort was to prepare a comprehensive resource manual for educational systems. The third, and current, effort is to develop, pilot, and then publish a college-level curriculum to prepare schoolteachers, counselors, administrators, nurses, and social workers on three levels (undergraduate, graduate, and postgraduate).

The research with elementary school students focused on three areas: expression of feelings, utilization of resources, and death education. *Expression of feelings* centered on eliciting information about the acceptability of openly expressing those feelings frequently found during times of loss. A critical message of the puppet show is that when a person has experienced a loss (through death, divorce, separation, or a pet's running away), there are many new feelings and emotions with which to deal. All of these are natural and normal. What a person does with these feelings is important.

In general, the results indicated that girls were more willing to express and accept feelings than were boys on all grade levels. On several grade levels, the acceptance increased significantly postprogram (although all increased), and environmental and developmental factors were found.

Mother was the overwhelming choice of resource for all grades but sixth. *Friends,* slowly but surely, became more influential, finally edging out *mother* and *father.* School resources (particularly teachers) declined as the age of the children increased. A change was found in the preassessment–postassessment: the teacher increased as a resource for boys in Grades K–2.

Formal death education is an uncommon situation for most children. The overwhelming response from children (preassessment and postassessment) in Grades 3–6 to the item "sometimes I have questions about death and dying" was *yes* (67%–79%). Little change in children's understanding the permanence of death was expected, due to maturation and developmental issues. The various stages of understanding death were verified by the research.

Several individual cases were brought to the attention of the researchers. These ranged from a second grader whose mother had committed suicide to a principal's reporting a suicidal fourth grader to a school nurse concerned about a number of students wishing they were dead.

The elementary school teachers' inservice focus was on four areas:

1. Recognition of depression and suicidal indicators
2. Short-term crisis intervention
3. School and community resources
4. Factual information about suicide

Of the elementary school teachers, 92% reported that they would recommend the inservice training to other schools.

Teacher–client satisfaction and how well the program objectives were met were assessed. Eighty-four percent would recommend the program for their respective grade level. Concerning the objectives, the following results were determined:

1. The children were able to identify and discuss feelings that are common responses to crisis, grief, and loss: 80%–100% successful, 58% of respondents; 60%–70% successful, 24% of respondents (total—82% of respondents).

2. The children received information to help them fully comprehend the permanence and finality of death: 80%–100% successful, 42% of respondents; 60%–70% successful, 24% of respondents (total—66% of respondents).

3. The children had an opportunity to share and learn information about adult resource people to talk to in time of crisis: 80%–100% successful, 53% of respondents; 60%–70% successful, 26% of respondents (total—79% of respondents).

PUPPET PREVENTION PROGRAM

Puppeteer Team members complete a rigorous application, reference, screening, and training process before they are accepted into the program. The center's puppeteering program includes a wide range of needed skills and knowledge:

Knowledge	Skills
Children's concept of death	Puppeteering
Developmental issues	Public speaking
Suicide and self-destructive behavior	Interviewing children
Emotions, feelings	Leading groups
Dynamics of groups	Crisis intervention
Crisis intervention	Suicide prevention
Educational systems	Stress management
Community and school resources	Communication
Communication	

Additionally, the center looks for specific attitudes and values in the person. For example, a person who believes that children should be seen and not heard would not function well in the program.

Through the years, 10 skits have been developed in three basic categories. Category 1 helps to identify feelings; Category 2 includes death loss, talking about and listening to feelings, and who is available to talk to; and Category 3 explores other losses and reemphasizes talking and listening.

The teachers are consulted to determine what experiences the students have had or are having. For instance, when presenting to a class who has lost a child to death, the puppeteers would select one skit over another.

The children are aware that there will be a puppet program, and no one is required to stay. The puppeteers introduce themselves, the puppet characters, and the topic(s), and then perform the first skit. Following this and each subsequent skit (the total is usually three skits), the puppeteers lead a discussion of the topics and feelings that were illustrated. It is not unusual for younger children to ask questions directly of the puppet character.

A favorite first skit is "Jaws." This skit is a good introduction to both puppetry and the issue of death and loss. (Sally and David are playing tag. Sally says, "You're it!" as she runs on stage. David follows, saying, "I'll catch you." Sally and David chase each other around the stage a few times, taking turns being "it," then get tired and sit to rest. They breath heavily as if winded from running around. Then Sally says to David . . .)

Sally:	Hey! I've got an idea. Let's go fishing.
David:	Nah . . . I don't feel so good—I don't wanna go today.
Sally:	Why not? You look fine to me, and besides that you were playing just a minute ago!
David:	Well, I may look fine, but I don't feel fine! (Pause) To tell you the truth, going fishing makes me think about my goldfish, Jaws. Remember him? Well, he died.
Sally:	(Laughing) You feel bad about a goldfish? That's silly!
David:	Come on. I really loved Jaws and I miss him too!
Sally:	Oh, I'm sorry. How did he die?
David:	He drowned!
Sally:	(Loud laughter) A fish that drowned! Now that's funny! (More laughter)
David:	No, really. I put him in the toilet to change his water, and my brother didn't see him and flushed him down! (Starts to cry)
Sally:	Oh—I'm sorry, David. I didn't mean to make you cry. I never knew Jaws meant so much to you. Guess I should know better, 'cause boy did I cry when my dog died. (Slight pause) But you know what? My Mom said it was OK to cry when something you love dies.
David:	(Still crying a little) Really? My Mom said "Now, David, don't cry. We'll get you another goldfish." (Slight pause) She just doesn't understand how special Jaws was. He loved me. No other goldfish will be like Jaws!
Sally:	You're right. Jaws was special. I think you'll always remember him and the way he loved you. C'mon. Let's take a walk.

Although there is often laughter and fun with this skit (and others like it), it does not preclude the basic process of reaching and identifying young children who have suffered a loss.

On one occasion, a youngster began crying. One puppeteer continued the discussion while the other approached the child. The puppeteer, comforting the child, stated that it seemed that she was feeling sad. The little girl, through tears, replied that her goldfish had died the past summer, and that she did not think that anyone would understand how she felt. Others had ridiculed her loss. Now she knew that what she felt (and was still feeling) was normal: she was not "crazy."

A frequently used second skit is "Forever is for Always." This skit presents the loss of a person. (Uncle Harry is sitting on stage reading a newspaper. David comes on stage playing with a toy car, making a lot of noise as he plays. After David has played around a little while, he runs the car over to where Uncle Harry is sitting and appears to have seen Uncle Harry for the first time since he entered the room. David says . . .)

David:	Oh! Hi, Uncle Harry. Whatcha doing?
Harry:	Well, I was trying to read the newspaper before it got too noisy in here. No . . . just

	kidding. Actually, I'm glad you're here. I want to ask you something. I read where it says a Mr. Jones who lived on Maple Street died. Don't you know his son, Bobby?
David:	*Bobby's daddy died!!? I just saw him the other day and he seemed fine to me! (Pause) Uncle Harry, is dying scary? Is it really bad?*
Harry:	*No, David. I don't think dying is supposed to be scary. It's just that no one really knows what happens to us when we die.*
David:	*Why does it have to happen? How come all the things we have have to die? I don't want them to die!*
Harry:	*I know you don't—neither do I. If there's one thing I've learned in all my years, it's that no two people are alike, and each person is very special. Life is so precious, because a person can never be replaced. But we also have to realize that death is a natural part of life.*
David:	*Yeah, I know that, but I still have trouble understanding. When somebody dies . . . isn't that bad?*
Harry:	*What do you mean by* bad?
David:	*Well, when someone dies, everyone around them gets sad and cries. Nobody feels good, and sometimes they even get angry.*
Harry:	*All those things are OK to feel when someone dies. Feeling sad hurts. It hurts bad! But, after awhile, the hurt can go away.*
David:	*How will it go away? Right now, I feel awful! Poor Mrs. Jones! Poor Bobby! (Slight pause as if thinking about things) Oh no!! What will I say to him if I see him when school starts?*
Harry:	*Just be your usual self. Be a good listener if he wants to talk about it. That will help him more than anything.*
David:	*It will? (Slight pause) And do you think it would be OK if I reminded Bobby about the time his dad helped me when I fell off my bike in front of his house? His dad was so nice.*
Harry:	*Now I think you're getting the idea. (Puts arm around David) Let's go get some lunch.*

There was an opportunity to videotape a classroom program, which then became part of a presentation at the American Association of Suicidology Conference in Toronto, Canada. The following edited transcript was taken from this film. The discussion followed the second skit ("Forever is for Always"), lasted 7 min, and took place in a fourth-grade class. At times, general discussion is summarized to enable highlighting the six children who spoke of specific death losses and the puppeteer's responses.

Puppeteer 1:	*In this play we talked about someone dying: who died?*
Children:	*Bobby's father; Mr. Jones; Bobby's dad, etc. (Lots of hands and responses spontaneously)*
Puppeteer 1:	*In our first play we talked abut animals dying, and that happens a lot when we are growing up. This is probably very common, for each of us to have that experience. But not everyone has the experience of someone in their family dying. That's not an easy experience. Have any of you lost a grandma, or grandpa, or uncle, or aunt, or had someone die in your family?* *(Lots of hands)* *Several of you have. Would anyone share that experience with us? Tell us about it?*
Child 1:	*My mom and dad got a divorce, and I spent the weekend with my mom and my dad called up at 2:00 in the morning. We didn't know what was going on.* *(Continues to report that his grandfather died, how he couldn't sleep for three days, he didn't want to eat, he couldn't understand, he had dreams; he begins to bury his face in his chest, and cannot continue)* *(All the children are silent during this and other times when a child is telling their experience)*
Puppeteer 1:	*You feel pretty upset about it.*
Child 1:	*Yeah. (Silence)*
Puppeteer 2:	*Were you able to talk to anyone about your feelings?*
Child 1:	*Yeah. My mom. (Silence)*

Figure 1   The puppeteer knows that a one-on-one relationship is effective.

Puppeteer 2:	*Was she able to help? I bet she was upset also.*
Child 1:	*Yeah. It was hard.*
	(Continues to report doing some special thing with his mom after the death)
Puppeteer 1:	*Do you have special memories of your grandpa?*
Child 1:	*Yeah. (Reports going fishing a lot)*
Puppeteer 1:	*That's a special memory for you. Anyone else care to share with us?*
Child 2:	*Um, yeah. We were going to visit my uncle in the summertime, but I never got to see him before, and he died when we were in Minnesota.*
Puppeteer 1:	*Before you got there (Yes), so you never had a chance. I'm sure your family was very sad. If it was an uncle then it was one of your parents' brothers; that can be very hard. A very hard experience. Do you want to say something?*
Child 3:	*My grandfather, he died last year. I spent the night with him and I went to get him some breakfast and when I came back he'd had a heart attack. And he was on the ground when the ambulance came, and my mom came and took me home and then I had to stay by myself.*
Puppeteer 1:	*While your mom went to the hospital? (Yeah) That must have been a very hard time. It's hard to be there when someone dies. It's not easy for us to understand that. Do you still remember him? (Yeah, silence) What ceremony do we have when someone dies?*
	(Funeral, etc.; show of hands; Figure 1)
Child 3:	*I went to the showing, but couldn't go to the funeral. (Continues with some description)*
	(General discussion of who's been to a funeral, show of most hands)
Child 4:	*About 3 years ago, my cousin Amber, she lives with us now, because her father, he got drunk and shot her mother. Then he got sad about it so he shot himself. I went to the funeral, I couldn't even go up to look at him because I was so sad. (Continues to describe the funeral, persons there, people crying)*
Puppeteer 1:	*They cried. It's important for people to be together at times like that, a sad time.*

	To be together to help each other; talking to each other helps; crying helps. A funeral is a way to say goodbye to someone.
Child 5:	*My cousin died this weekend. I was so sad I couldn't go to the funeral.*
Puppeteer 1:	*Couldn't go to the funeral.*
Child 5:	*No, I was so sad. My mother and my sister did. (Silence)*
Puppeteer 2:	*That happens sometimes. I remember when my grandmother died. My grandmother was a favorite person and I didn't feel like going. I saw her after she died but I couldn't go into the funeral. I hurt so bad. I had never hurt like that before. I talked to a man, a friend, about it outside. Then I felt better so I went to the cemetery.*
Child 6:	*My grandma died. She was real, real sick. I tried to wake her up, but she wouldn't, she was dead. We went to her funeral but I couldn't look at her. (Silence)*
Puppeteer 1:	*That happens.*
Puppeteer 2:	*Those are hard times. But don't those feelings have to come out? (Chorus of yes, yeah) That's the important thing about feelings, some day it has to come out. (Continued with an illustration about a bottle of pop that is shook up, lots of cutting up and laughter; then puppeteer relates this grief and sadness, finishing with a transition into the third skit)*

Although suicide is not one of the losses included in any of the skits, approximately 20% of the time children talk about a suicide or a homicide–suicide loss.

The formal part of the program ends with the puppeteer's talking individually to each child (Figure 2). The puppeteers continue to carry their last puppet character. This character is part of their "goodbye" and hugs, kisses, or licks the face of each child (Figures 3 and 4). The reactions of the children are amazing. They love

Figure 2 The puppeteer listens intently as the child expresses her feelings.

Figure 3   Attentive listeners raise their hands to answer the puppeteers' questions.

this, often asking for second or third hugs. The children thank the puppets, talking to them and telling them secrets.

The puppeteers provide immediate feedback and consultation to the teacher, scout leader, or youth leader, who is required to be present the entire time. This consultation includes discussing those children who said or did things that concerned the puppeteers. On occasions, children have revealed significant losses not known to the adult in the setting.

The transcript offered earlier illustrates how frequently death losses are revealed. Examples of other cases include the following:

> A young boy who spoke about how his father never married his mother. His father had left, so he never had a chance to know him. The teacher (latchkey program) commented to the puppeteers that they "really got the kids to open up."
> A young girl began to talk, but could not continue, tears welling up in her eyes. The puppeteers reassured her that she did not have to talk now about what was hurting her, but what was important was that she talk with someone.
> During the discussion of whom a person could talk to, a young boy reported that his dad was in jail and that he missed him, but he hoped to be able to talk to him once he got out. (Again the teacher had no idea of the situation.)

Resource materials are left with the adults. Agency staff debrief the puppeteers, and cases are discussed as a group on a monthly basis. Staff also continue to offer consultation and on-site intervention.

On-site intervention has been used repeatedly in kindergarten through 6th grades.

An example of how these components work together is a recent case with a girl in kindergarten. The teacher had received training and noticed that the girl was displaying a number of significant behavioral changes, appeared depressed, and had lost her mother recently, although she refused to talk of this death to anyone. The mother's death was suspicious.

The school asked for an assessment and intervention. During the lengthy initial session, the child revealed that her mother had been murdered by her father. The child had been in the next room, heard the murder, and ran in to find her mother's body. The father had threatened to kill a pet if she told anyone.

Although the child continued to discuss this openly with the interventionist, she continued to refuse to speak to anyone else. Even after a variety of situational changes had been made (e.g., removal from the home), she did not openly talk of her loss until the puppet program occurred in her class. In fairly rapid succession she began verbalizing to the teacher ("My mommy died. I'm so sad and scared.") and to others in the school and child welfare systems.

SUMMARY

The puppet program offered by the center is the prevention component of an integrated system of responding to the needs of suicidal children and the systems that work with them.

It focuses on teaching children about feelings, how to share them, and the feelings that accompany a loss, and that losses come in all types.

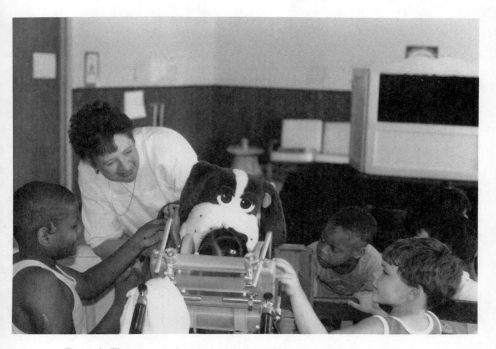

Figure 4 The puppeteer knows that special children need special attention.

The persons offering the program are extensively trained and supervised. The puppeteers have been instrumental in uncovering young children at risk, who are then assisted by other components of the center.

The program is designed with the developmental and maturational stages of children in mind, balanced with the issues that are found with suicidal children: overwhelming feelings of grief and loss.

Not only is the puppet prevention program viable in working with young children, but as any puppeteer will tell you, it is tremendously rewarding—and fun!

REFERENCES

1. Suicide Prevention Center, Inc. (1988). *Lifesaver program manual*. Dayton, OH: Author.
2. Bernhardt, G., & Praeger, S. (1985). Preventing child suicide; the elementary school death education puppet show. *Journal of Counseling and Development, 63*, 311–312.
3. Goodwin, L., Goodwin, W., and Cantrill, J. (1988). The mental health needs of elementary school children. *Journal of School Health, 58*, 7.
4. Korup, U. (1986). Parent and teacher perception of depression in children. *Journal of School Health, 55*, 9.
5. Epstein, M. S., & Cullinan, D. (1986). Depression in children. *Journal of School Health, 56*, 1.
6. Pfeffer, C. (1981). Suicidal behavior of children: A review with implications for research and practice. *American Journal of Psychiatry, 138*, 154–159.
7. Pfeffer, C. (1986). *The suicidal child*. New York: Guilford Press.
8. Domino, G., Domino, V., & Berry, T. (1986–1987). Children's attitudes toward suicide. *Omega, 4*, 17.
9. Piaget, J., & Inhelder, B. (1969). *The psychology of the child*. New York: Basic Books.
10. Wall, L. V., (Ed.). (1965). *The puppet book*. Boston: Plays, Inc.
11. Batchelder, M. (1967). The creative values of puppet theatre. In M. Niculescu (Ed.), *The puppet theatre of the modern world* (pp. 40–41). Boston: Plays, Inc.
12. Batchelder, M. (1947). *The puppet theatre handbook*. New York: Harper & Brothers.
13. West, L. (1982). The magic of puppets. *School Library Journal, 29*, 29–33.
14. Maurer, C. (1977). Of puppets, feelings and children. *Elementary School Guidance and Counseling, 12*, 26–32.
15. Martin, A. (1987). Encouraging youngsters to discuss their feelings. *Learning, 16*, 80–81.
16. Fleming, C. (1983). Puppets put learning center stage. *Learning, 11*, 94–98.
17. Robin, M. (1985). No happy ending. *Early Years, 16*, 51–57.
18. Egge, D., Marks, L., & McEver, A. (1987). Puppets and adolescents: A group guidance workshop approach. *Elementary School Guidance and Counseling, 21*, 183, 192.
19. James, R., & Myer, R. (1987). Puppets: The elementary school counselor's right or left arm. *Elementary School Guidance and Counseling, 21*, 292–299.
20. Wolman, A. (1964). Psychological rational of puppetry. In M. Haworth (Ed.), *Child psychotherapy* (pp. 395–399). New York: Basic Books.
21. Stacey, S., & Rust, J. (1985). Evaluating the effectiveness of the DUSO-1 (revised) program. *Elementary School Guidance and Counseling, 20*, 84–90.
22. Carson, N., & Johnson, R. (1985). Suicidal thoughts and problem solving preparation among college students. *Journal of College Student Personnel, 26*, 484–487.

7

Comprehensive School Suicide Prevention Programs

Roger Tierney
Mount Royal College, Calgary, Alberta, Canada

Richard Ramsay and Bryan Tanney
University of Calgary, Alberta, Canada

William Lang
Banff Centre for the Arts, Banff, Alberta, Canada

Other articles have documented concerns about the increased incidence of suicidal ideation and behaviors among North American youth, including suicide, attempted suicide, and parasuicide. This article addresses responses to these concerns by school systems responsible for providing elementary, middle, and high school education, and discusses the development of comprehensive suicide prevention programs in the context of a few selected school jurisdictions.

Several types of suicide prevention programs can be found in North American school systems. Although most are laudable in intent, they are generally small scale and school-specific in scope. Comprehensive programs, tied to large-scale, system-wide implementation policy, are few in number. Comprehensive programs deal with all aspects of suicide prevention and are broad in scope and content. In a school context, this means that a suicide prevention program must be based on system-wide policy (scope) and must address all aspects of suicide prevention: prevention, intervention, and postvention (content). Comprehensive programs require coordination and networking components, along with implementation commitments from every major stakeholder group in the school system: board members, administrators, professional staff, support staff, parents, and students. We discuss the background development, major components, and evaluation of comprehensive suicide prevention programs in schools.

DEVELOPMENT

The inclusion of prevention, intervention, and postvention as required elements in a comprehensive approach to suicide prevention is a recent development in the field of suicidology (1, 2). The inclusion of these components has come from convergent developments in mental health and education that advocated (a) the acceptance of broad models of prevention (3), (b) the involvement of non-mental health professionals and paraprofessionals in suicide prevention (4, 5), and (c) the concept of schools' having a role in emotional development or affective education (6–9).

Earlier in this century, suicide prevention was largely seen as the exclusive preserve of mental health professionals. Prevention was synonymous with treatment. Suicide was viewed as a form of psychopathology that had to be treated with psychotherapeutic processes in mental treatment facilities. Shneidman and Farberow's book, *Clues to Suicide* (10), contained three articles on intervention. All three dealt with specialized psychotherapy of the suicidal patient. The concluding chapter provided suggestions for preventing suicide, and dealt exclusively with psychiatric intervention. Mid-century literature as a whole dealt only with professional treatment for those who had already attempted suicide, or who were experiencing severe ideation, generally as a concomitant to other psychiatric disorders, largely depression and alcoholism.

A major shift in suicidologists' view of suicide became apparent in the early 1960s. This shift was reflected in Farberow and Shneidman's next book, *The Cry for Help* (11). It emphasized the communicative nature of suicide and stressed the need to respond to the distress reflected in such "cry-for-help" communications. General public awareness of the potential communication of suicide through the recognition of warning signs was promoted as a preventive measure. Prevention was no longer synonymous with intervention or treatment of an incident that had already happened; it was now expanded to include the prevention of incidents from happening in the first place.

The shift away from suicide prevention as being the exclusive preserve of mental illness professionals continued throughout the 1960s, owing to the development of the community mental health model and the concept of multidisciplinary mental health teams (3), the emergence of mutual support and self-help concepts, and the accepted use of paraprofessionals and volunteers. Fewer than 10 years after *The Cry for Help,* Shneidman, Farberow, and Litman's book, *The Psychology of Suicide* (4), clearly reflected the shift toward the use of paraprofessionals, multiprofessional teams, and crisis services. They emphasized treatment as being only a part of the much broader concept of intervention, and advocated expanded roles for many occupational and volunteer groups under the intervention concept.

Besides expanded roles for various lay and professional groups, Gerald Caplan's community mental health model delineated broader concepts of prevention (3). Although his work was not specifically directed to the field of suicidology, it was closely related. His formulations regarding primary, secondary, and tertiary prevention paralleled Shneidman's (1) formulations of prevention, intervention, and postvention. These three facets, regardless of which terms are used, are considered central to comprehensive school suicide prevention efforts (6, 12–14).

The impetus for development of suicide prevention programs in schools has come from a variety of persons and organizations concerned about youth suicidal behavior. Individual teachers have often tried to develop or find materials and programs or, more frequently, have turned to community agencies for assistance. In the United States, these agencies are usually local crisis centers or county mental health services. In Canada, they are preventive social services agencies or nongovernment mental health organizations.

In some jurisdictions, local community mental health or crisis line agencies have initiated contact with local school systems to offer inservice or classroom

instruction services. Community-based suicide prevention–crisis centers
mental health agencies have an obvious mandate to provide direct s
suicidal people. Many have also viewed indirect services as part of thei
and have developed suicide prevention–education programs, classroom presentations, and other services for schools (15–20). The American Association of Suicidology (21) also developed a curriculum for use in schools. In some areas, school
district personnel, either alone or in cooperation with mental health authorities,
have taken on the responsibility for program development.

Early efforts in this regard focused less on the development of prevention and
awareness programs and more on preparing staff to deal directly with the student
at risk of suicide and with individual and institutional responses to suicide deaths.
These early efforts were marked by the publication of reference manuals with
information and suggestions for recognition and intervention (22–24). More elabo-
rate training presentations intended to improve the skill competencies of school
personnel in suicidal situations (18, 25–28) came later.

In some jurisdictions, concerns about the rising incidence of youth suicide have
resulted in the establishment of government- or community-based task forces to
study the problem and make recommendations. Some of the more prominent ones
include the national task force of the U.S. Department of Health and Human
Services (29). Canada published the results of a task force on suicide in 1987 (30).
Alberta reported the results of a major study, the Boldt Report, mandated by its
government in 1976. California did the same in 1977 (C. P. Ross, personal communication, December 1983), and again in 1986 (31); New York in 1984 (24);
Vermont in 1988 (13); and Virginia in 1989 (32).

The recommendations of task forces and the influence of other lobbying efforts
by concerned citizens have produced youth suicide prevention legislation in five
states: Alabama, California, Florida, Wisconsin, and New Jersey (12). Legislative
developments in Canada have been limited to cabinet approval for expenditure of
funds relating to suicide prevention in one province. The development of school-
based curriculums and increased training of school personnel are the common
threads that run through all of these legislative responses. In addition, the particu-
lars of each piece of legislation encourage cooperative approaches between
community-based services and school systems. Education and mental health services are encouraged to work together in the development of health promotion and
youth suicide prevention programs. School systems, however, have traditionally
had considerable difficulty in deciding whether they wish to be involved in such
programming (12, 25). Although there is recognition of the importance of community involvement (33), the commitment of school systems to the development of
comprehensive suicide prevention programs has been more difficult to obtain. In a
recent survey of prevention and intervention programs for suicidal adolescents,
Simmons, Comstock, and Franklin (34) noted that although a number of agencies
feel that school programming is important, schools in general remain reluctant to
have suicide-specific educational programs. This is largely because of four factors:
(a) perceived financial costs, (b) stigma surrounding the issue of suicide, (c) logis-
tics and complexities of the task, and (d) differences in approach and philosophy
between education and mental health fields.

In 1985, a literature review of the documents held by the Suicide Information
and Education Center in Calgary revealed that most school suicide prevention

programs focused on suicide awareness instruction aimed at students in classroom settings. This instruction ranged from single-session presentations to three- or four-lesson modules provided either by classroom teachers or by visiting resource people from community mental health or crisis center organizations. There was little evidence of any comprehensive programs in actual operation, although several were listed as being under development. A more recent review of post-1985 literature indicates that a number of comprehensive programs have now been or are in the process of being implemented. Unfortunately, the actual number and nature of these programs is hard to determine because of the limited number of public domain publications available (35). Most of the available information is found in unpublished handbooks, policy statements, and handouts. Thus, information tends to be incomplete. Also, there is no widely known central clearinghouse for information on school programs (33). Celotta et al. have estimated that up to 100 suicide prevention programs are currently operating in North American school systems, although this is likely an underestimate.

We have found limited information on five school districts and one state educational system that have developed and are implementing model programs that reflect a commitment to the principles of comprehensive school suicide prevention programs. It should be noted that although we recognize that there are other comprehensive programs in existence, there is no written literature on them. Programs discussed here are only those definitely known to be in use in specific school systems. The five school programs were developed by the Calgary Board of Education (36), the Dallas Independent School District (37), Fairfax County Public Schools (38), the Los Angeles Unified School District (39), and the Worcester County Board of Education (33, 40). The one state system is that of Wisconsin (41), which legislated a mandatory comprehensive program for all schools. This program is still in the process of implementation (W. Berkan, personal communication, November 29, 1989).

COMPONENTS

This section focuses on the major components of comprehensive suicide prevention programs in schools, using illustrations from some of the model programs.

System-Wide Policy

The commitment to a system-wide policy that includes the basic premises on which a comprehensive school-based suicide prevention program may be based is nicely illustrated in the policy of the Calgary Board of Education (36, p. 2):

1. Youth suicide is a multifaceted societal problem involving social, psychological, and biological factors. It is not a "school problem." However, as schools represent the first major experience with society beyond the family, as they provide students with daily professional contact, and as they have educational expertise, they are in an ideal position to assist students in learning about and effectively dealing with the problems of suicidal ideation and behavior.

2. Effective school policies must encompass prevention, intervention, and postvention. Prevention involves curricular inputs that educate students regarding coping and problem-solving strategies for living, and that educate students regarding the specific topic of suicide at appropriate points in their education. Interven-

tion involves the early recognition of suicide potential, direct contact with the student involved, and referral to system and outside resources, as necessary for assessment and care. Postvention involves dealing with students and staff after a suicide has occurred.

3. All staff have responsibilities (albeit different ones) for dealing with suicide potential. Teachers and administrators may be forgiven for feeling frustrated and overwhelmed by the demands placed on the schools for dealing with "social problems." However, the nature of this concern makes the assistance of all staff necessary.

4. Doing nothing places the schools in more jeopardy than doing something. Suicidal ideation and behavior can be effectively dealt with in many cases if proper efforts are initiated and carried out.

5. Dealing with suicide in a sensitive educational context does not lead to, or cause, further suicidal behaviors. Contagion does not occur when effective programs and services are in place.

System-wide policy indicates a formal recognition that the school district has an important role in, and commitment to, suicide prevention (33, 42). System-wide policy provides for the input, commitment, and participation of all stakeholder groups. This increases the likelihood that a program will meet the needs of various constituents and that it will be accepted and used. System-wide policy provides for clear mandates for action and distinct procedures or protocols for dealing with the issues within the framework of prevention, intervention, and postvention. This allows for a more effective organization and utilization of district and nonsystem resources beyond the individual school. Last, system-wide policy increases the chances that students will receive the required support and assistance for dealing with suicidal issues in themselves and others.

Prevention (Primary Prevention)

Primary prevention refers to program efforts that aim to prevent or inhibit the development of the problem of concern. In essence, this means the promotion of principles of good physical or mental health. When applied to suicide, primary prevention may refer either to the removal of "hazardous event" factors (mental disorder; stress; failed developmental tasks that might be direct, predisposing, or contributing "causes" of suicide) or to the promotion of life-enhancement factors that allow people to cope with the stresses and problems in their lives without resorting to the option of suicide. When applied to schools, primary prevention refers to (a) school climate or psychological atmosphere (6), (b) programs that address the emotional development and well-being of students (8), and (c) programs that specifically address suicide awareness (6, 25, 28).

School Climate

Schools already do a great deal in the area of primary prevention. In fact, this needs to be emphasized so that schools themselves, as well as the public at large, can learn to appreciate the preventive climate in most schools. Although education systems are a common target for complaint, much of this is unfair. Schools are generally quite successful in promoting the development and well-being of children and youth by providing structured and guided opportunities for their intellectual, social, emotional, and physical development. Courses, school-based activities, and teacher–student relations are designed to prepare young people for various aspects of life, and to foster a sense of self-worth. The intent is to teach pupils how to learn, how to compete, and how to cooperate in society. The interaction of school climate with individual and collective units of students contributes in a significant way to the realization of these intentions. As Berkovitz (6) pointed out, school climate or atmosphere can contribute to positive growth enhancement, and is a matter that each school and school district must consider.

Affective–Emotional Development

Programs aimed at the affective educational development of young people are often included within health and life-adjustment curriculums. Curriculums that assist in the development of coping–problem-solving skills for dealing with stress, depression, anxiety, developmental tasks, and the variety of human problems that students may encounter have been developed and implemented to some extent in most school jurisdictions. In addition to curriculums, the availability of identified helping resources to assist those in difficulty is important in fostering growth and reducing the effects of the difficulties. These resources include counseling, psychological, and health services, as well as student assistance programs provided to assist those students experiencing problems.

Suicide Awareness and Education for Students

Programs with specific, suicide-related content have been developed in many areas to inform students about suicide. These awareness- or consciousness-raising activities are generally offered in the latter years of junior high or middle school, and in high school. These programs often combine emotional development content that deals with life factors such as depression, loss, and substance abuse, and suicide content that is significantly related to these other problems. Programs developed by Ross (18, 25), Ryerson and King (28), the Department of Education in California (43), Kalafat and Underwood (42), and the state of Wisconsin (44) are notable examples. The specific focus on suicide helps to create a greater understanding of the topic by assisting students to deal with both their own feelings and those of others concerning the many manifestations of suicide ideation and behaviors.

Awareness programs in schools accomplish this aim with different levels of attention to the students' attitudes, knowledge, and skills concerning suicide and its management as a problem behavior. Areas of focus in the skills area include identifying the warning signs of suicide and such intervention components as how to talk with a friend, what to do, and the resources that may be called on for assistance. This skill training is a crucial part of a comprehensive program, considering the evidence that most students say they would turn to a friend when in difficulty (31, 35).

Comprehensive school suicide prevention programs make suicide awareness and education a mandatory part of the curriculum. For example, in Los Angeles suicide awareness units are mandatory in both the 7th- and 10th-grade health curriculums (39). The Calgary Board of Education (36) has made suicide prevention units mandatory in the 9th- and 11th-grade curriculums. Both of these school systems also support programs at the elementary school level that provide instruction in dealing with problems and feelings, but these programs do not deal directly with suicide unless special needs in a particular school become evident. The other programs have suicide awareness curriculums, although it is uncertain which grades are involved.

Teacher Preparation

A concomitant responsibility of making suicide prevention mandatory is the provision of inservice training for those who teach such curriculums. This involves familiarization with the subject and training in delivery of the lessons and learning experiences regarding suicide. Many of the teachers who receive this training in suicide curriculums also wish to have training in intervention in order to handle the case-finding situations that often occur in the delivery of affective education modules. As Kalafat and Underwood (42) have noted, this training is important because those who teach suicide awareness programs are often viewed as resources by their students. The Calgary Board of Education policy mandates that intervention training is provided on request to teachers presenting the suicide modules.

Suicide Awareness and Education for Staff and Parents

Comprehensive programs also include mandatory suicide awareness sessions on a repeated time schedule for all school personnel who have direct contact with students. These programs are aimed at everyone who comes in contact with students, including teachers, administrators, cafeteria staff, custodial staff, secretaries, school bus drivers, teacher aides, and community volunteers. In addition, suicide awareness sessions are frequently made available to parent groups to expand the resources available to young people and to enlist parents' support for and cooperation with school-based programs (37, 38, 42).

Intervention (Secondary Prevention)

Secondary prevention refers to prevention efforts in which the problem is identified early enough to allow for immediate intervention. Intervention aims at reducing the level and duration of the problem at an early phase so that it does not develop into more serious manifestations. As applied to suicide, it refers to the recognition of presuicide cues, engagement with the person, assessment of the level of risk, and immediate crisis intervention (27). In the school context, intervention involves (a) providing immediate intervention to students at risk of suicide, (b) establishing policy and procedures that mandate and guide such interventions, (c) establishing effective appropriate referral links with community resources, and (d) ensuring follow-up with the student, parents, and outside helping resources.

Providing Immediate Intervention to Students at Risk of Suicide

School staff are often in an excellent position to recognize the signs of potential suicidal behavior and to intervene early in a suicidal episode.

A number of school systems have school crisis–resource teams in place to deal with multiple types of crises and student problems (8, 38, 45). All members of these teams receive suicide intervention training in addition to other forms of preparation.

Comprehensive school programs provide suicide intervention training to a wide variety of staff members. All counselors, psychologists, and school nurses should be trained. It should not be assumed that these groups already possess such training. Suicide intervention training is seldom provided in professional training programs (46, 47). In terms of understanding resources and school procedures, there is also a benefit to training people within the system. Teachers, school resource officers, and administrators are also likely candidates for intervention training. Although training all staff would be beneficial, it is frequently impractical. The Dallas program is providing training for one counselor in each school. These Dallas counselors receive 18 hr of training spread over a number of weeks. In the Calgary Board of Education program all counselors and psychologists, as well as two resource people from each school, are being trained in a 2-day suicide intervention program. These resource people generally are teachers who have requested permission to attend the 2-day intensive training, or who have been selected by the administration. Many other teachers are requesting to attend as information about the training spreads through formal and informal networks.

Intervention training by school-system trainers has a number of advantages. They know their own system and its policies and can prepare those receiving the training for their own work environments. They also take on a certain ownership of the programs and may become intrinsically involved in program development and implementation. This has certainly been the case in the Calgary Board of Education program, where 12 staff members have been prepared to provide this training. This training mandate is incorporated into their current work roles as consultants, school counselors, or administrators. Members of the Suicide Prevention Unit of the Los Angeles Unified School District provide intervention training for their system staff (A. Dunn, personal communication, June 26, 1989). In turn, people trained in intervention can be prepared to provide the awareness–education inservices that all staff are required to attend. This brings the training to the school level, which is where it is most likely to be useful.

Additional training needs may arise out of the implementation of awareness and intervention training. The Calgary Board of Education (36) anticipates an interest in refresher training as well as a desire for additional training from those staff with longer-term case management responsibilities. We are presently developing such training for the Calgary Board.

Establishing Policy and Procedures That Mandate and Guide Suicide Interventions

Awareness and intervention training is insufficient on its own. Staff must have an understanding of what is expected of them and what is appropriate. Nelson and Slaikeu (48) noted that effective crisis intervention in schools requires three major components: a written policy on what to do when a crisis occurs, the physical resources to carry out the policy, and trained personnel to implement the service. This would certainly apply to suicidal crisis as well.

There has been a lack of written protocols for dealing with suicidal students, as noted by the Oakland County Child and Adolescent Suicide Prevention Task Force (49), the Connecticut Committee for Youth Suicide Prevention (50), Harris and Crawford (12), Ruof et al. (45), and others. Each of these groups has designed a series of suggested protocols for use in schools. Protocols typically cover expectations to intervene, intervention guidelines, procedures for reporting, informing parents, involving other resources, and follow-up. The Calgary, Los Angeles,

Denver, Fairfax, and Worcester school systems have all developed and implemented such procedures.

Different approaches to mandating intervention have been used. The Los Angeles and Denver programs require staff to report possible suicidal students to the school crisis–resource team. The Calgary policy (36) states that

> when a staff member notices signs that a student may be suicidal, he or she may meet with the student and inquire sensitively, yet directly, regarding the student's feelings and intentions. If a staff member is not in a position to carry out the above (an intervention), he or she shall share their concerns with the suicide resource people immediately so that this person, or another appropriate person may engage the student as quickly as possible. (p. 6)

All concerns and interventions must be reported to other system personnel (resource people, counselors, or administration). Thus, under the Calgary policy, staff are encouraged to intervene but are given an alternative if they feel unable to do so for any reason.

The question of legal liability is a problematic issue in the mandating of intervention. Although the issue is cloudy, it would appear at present that school staff have the responsibility to act as any prudent person would (45, 51). Milton Wilson of the California Department of Education, in an unpublished paper (52), stated that it would appear that schools could be held liable if they failed to provide services. It is our opinion that staff in positions of responsibility to young people are in more jeopardy if they do nothing than if they do something that was intended to be helpful. This issue would be far less problematic if all states and provinces adopted Wisconsin's legislation, which specifically excludes people from liability for intervening in suicidal situations (44).

Establishing Effective Appropriate Referral Links with Community Resources

Dealing effectively with highly suicidal and troubled young people will, on occasion, require more assistance than schools can reasonably provide. Educators require the assistance of the broader mental health community in dealing with this issue. Because of the emergency nature of crisis, rapid access to resources is required. It is important that resource links be developed with local hospital mental health emergency units and mental health centers for assessment and treatment assistance, and with child protection services for occasions when there are significant difficulties with parents. These agencies must be made aware of the school's policies and programs, and protocols for referral and follow-up assistance should be discussed. The Calgary Board is presently establishing these links through a series of meetings. Written protocols are ideal. These are most effectively developed through face-to-face meetings with the major service providers. Cooperation in this sphere benefits all parties. Wisconsin has done much to further the involvement of the community in school suicide prevention efforts, seeing their program as a community-based, but school-focused, program (W. Berkan, personal communication, November 29, 1989). Information regarding this area is not provided in the literature on the other model programs. Simmons, Comstock, and Franklin's (34) survey of services for suicidal adolescents reported a continuing lack of formal networking and coordination among agencies providing such services.

Follow-Up with the Student, Parents, and Outside Helping Resources

Effective suicide intervention involves appropriate plans and procedures for reintegrating a suicidal student into school and home life. In cases where treatment beyond crisis and supportive counseling is appropriate, involvement of other mental health professionals is necessary. Although schools typically do not provide therapy, they have the potential to be therapeutic in the way that a student is treated following major suicidal events. Cooperation and communication is necessary between the student, school staff, family, and helping resources to determine the most effective ways of proceeding.

Follow-up requires the formation of policies and procedures such as those delineated by Kalafat and Underwood (42). The Calgary Board of Education does not have follow-up procedures as a part of their policy. Rather, it is left to the individual school. The Dallas program does not spell out this component. The Los Angeles, Virginia, and Worcester programs have a clear procedure for following up individual students identified as being suicidal.

Tertiary Prevention (Postvention)

Tertiary prevention refers to treatment or rehabilitative efforts applied after something has happened. In suicide prevention it involves efforts to help those affected after a suicide has occurred.

One of the most difficult events for a school to cope with is the death of a student through suicide. Unfortunately, this tragic event is often the motivator for the establishment of suicide prevention programs (23, 45, 53). Schools are generally unprepared for student suicide (54). Comprehensive school programs have policies and procedures in place for dealing with the kinds of questions outlined by Dunne, McIntosh, and Dunne-Maxim (55).

How and when should staff be informed of a suicide?
How and when should students be informed of a suicide?
How should the school prepare for the reactions of students and faculty?
How, when, and where should students be allowed to express their reactions?
Which resources (system and community) should be alerted and asked for assistance?
Who is in charge?
What should be done about the victim's family?
What should be done about the victim's close friends?
What should be done about high-risk students?
Should the school hold a memorial service?
Will students be allowed to go to the funeral?
Who will discuss arrangements with the family?
What kinds of commemorative activities are appropriate?
What should be done about the concerns of other parents?
Who should deal with the media?
Are longer-term postvention activities necessary?

Fortunately, the past few years have seen the development of some excellent resources regarding the handling of postvention issues. Dunne et al. (55) have provided in-depth background material for understanding the issues and needs in postvention situations. The American Association of Suicidology is presently developing a set of postvention guidelines (56) that provide background and suggestions regarding managing the crisis, disseminating information, providing individual and group counseling, dealing with issues surrounding memorials and funerals, dealing with the bereaved family and other parents, responding to the media, linking with the community, and handling long-term effects and follow-up. Other task forces and school groups have designed specific recommendations for handling such crises in the schools (38, 49, 50, 57). The Dallas (37) and Los Angeles (39) school programs have a protocol in their board-mandated suicide prevention programs. The Calgary Board policy (36) does not have a protocol, but does require schools to have a set of procedures in place. The idea behind the Calgary Board policy is to let each school develop a plan suited to its own needs. Sample programs and a training inservice are provided to assist these schools in determining their plans.

Although it is tempting to design and develop postvention plans as the initial thrust, it is preferable to develop and implement intervention and awareness components first to help staff gain confidence in the belief that something can be done to prevent suicidal behavior in young people. Staff are then better prepared to handle completed suicide situations. Unfortunately, crises may not wait. Schools may use a "flying squad" of specially trained staff to assist schools in postvention until school-based policies and procedures are in place.

EVALUATION

Evaluation in the field of suicidology in general is a problematic area. Most of the research effort in the area has been to find out more about suicidal behavior and to attempt to assist those who are suicidal. In terms of schools, efforts have been directed toward designing and implementing programs, not evaluation (58). Little has been done to conduct comprehensive evaluations (29).

The need for evaluation in the area of suicide prevention has been commented on by many workers in the field (58–64). Comstock (65), in a review of developments over the 1970s, noted that there had been no progress in the application of program evaluation efforts to suicide prevention. No comprehensive, standardized models of evaluation have been developed whereby training and the effects of various forms of training in suicide prevention can be measured and compared (66). In part, this relates to the type and amount of effort expended, the narrow direction of that effort, the diversity of the programs involved, and the inherent difficulties encountered in carrying out such research. The National Task Force on Suicide in Canada (30) found that evaluation studies were few, and those that have been conducted proved to be either methodologically inadequate or based on systems of data collection that could not be compared across services owing to differences in behavioral definitions, selection and measurement of variables, and the outcome measures chosen.

Although comprehensive evaluation has not been conducted, limited evaluations have been carried out on components of suicide programs. Eddy, Wolpert, and Rosenberg (67) conducted a study to estimate the effectiveness of various interventions to prevent youth suicide. They pointed out that as little empirical research has been done, policy makers have to rely on the opinions of experts. Therefore, their study asked experts in the field to make judgments about the effectiveness of different interventions. One of the interventions on which opinion was sought was affective education, that is, suicide awareness–education applied to students to assist in coping skills, recognition of warning signs, and steps that they can take to assist themselves and others. The Eddy et al. results indicated that experts were uncertain regarding the effects of any of the various interventions. All interventions were rated relatively low in terms of the number of completed suicides that they were expected to prevent. There is some question regarding the outcome measure used here, that is, reduction in suicide. Suicide completions are not the only appropriate outcome measure. Attempted suicide, threatened suicide, and ideation must also be considered (14), as well as other program variables.

Ross (18) reported satisfaction among students with suicide prevention awareness programs. In program research on Project Lifesaver in Dayton, Ohio, Boggs (15) found that students showed significantly increased levels of knowledge regarding suicide after awareness–education programs were implemented in their schools. An interesting finding of the latter study was that secondary students already possessed sound knowledge about suicide. Johnson's (68) controlled study of the same project found no increase in suicidal thoughts or behavior as a result of participation. Shaffer et al. (14) evaluated three programs in New Jersey and found a similar result when they compared students who had been exposed to suicide prevention programs and those who had not. Shaffer et al. (69) reported in a later publication that students in general held attitudes and had knowledge that was sound. This was not changed through participation in a program. However, it was discovered that some students in both experimental and control groups held attitudes that were inappropriate. These were not changed through participation in the program.

There is a general concern with outcome measures. Shaffer et al. (14) looked at attitudes and knowledge. Although knowledge has been shown to change (15, 68), attitude change has shown less success (58). Research is required to determine if attitude and knowledge change translates to behavior and more effective abilities to recognize and act on warning signs of suicide in a friend. Long-term effects need to be determined as well. Empirical studies at this time will not fit or accommodate all the dynamics that would have to be measured to determine effect. Suicide is a multifaceted behavior that occurs in relation to a complex set of factors. Trying to measure the effect of primary prevention programs on such a rare, non-cause–effect behavior is most difficult.

The Dallas (37) schools have conducted some preliminary studies regarding the caregiver training components of their program, and found significant changes in knowledge and intervention skills. Tierney (70) found significant changes in attitudes, knowledge, and skills of participants in intervention training. This included educators and others. However, again it is unknown empirically how this increased intervention will translate into effects on outcome measures. No studies have been conducted regarding postvention programs in schools.

It is clear that the evaluation of comprehensive school programs lies in the future. At present, there is no conclusive empirical answer to questions regarding their effect. As an assist to this inquiry, we need to conduct what Kalafat and Ryerson (58) termed *action research*. In addition to outcome measures, evaluation must also focus on the materials and processes used in the programs (formative evaluation). There is extensive educational knowledge that can be applied in this enterprise. The attainment of specific objectives within the various components of comprehensive programs can be tested. Quantitative and qualitative methods of inquiry need to be applied to gain the most comprehensive results.

CONCLUSION

It is clear that conclusive evaluation of comprehensive school programs lies in the future. In the meantime, the need to respond to the problem of youth suicidal behaviors continues. Comprehensive school programs represent the culmination of a number of developments in suicidology and in the schools. Principles for the development of these programs are emerging, and model programs are being implemented. The major elements of comprehensive programs are summarized as follows for others to consider and evaluate their own programs.

I.   System-wide policy
     A. Written statements
     B. Policy approved by highest-level policy makers
     C. Policy formulated by multidisciplinary groups and all constituents
     D. Group planning committee for determining needs, policy, procedures, and implementation

II. Scope and content
     A. System-wide
     B. All elements of prevention, intervention, and postvention are included.
        1. Prevention includes education and awareness elements for students, staff, and parents.
        2. Intervention includes immediate and longer-term and follow-up elements.
        3. Postvention includes written protocols and the resources and mandate to implement them.

III. Resources
     A. System staff to provide assistance
     B. Established connections with external resources

IV. Training personnel
     A. Suicide curriculum delivery
     B. Intervention
     C. Awareness presentations
     D. Postvention protocols
     E. Inservice trainers

V.   Evaluation
     A. Formative
     B. Summative
     C. Comprehensive

VI. Follow-up
     A. Families
     B. Refresher courses
     C. Students

D. Staff survivors
E. Referral resources
F. Community coordination networks

A review of model programs indicates that although no one program has all components functioning as of yet, the Los Angeles, Fairfax County, and Worcester County programs come closest to being complete programs. The Calgary, Dallas, and Wisconsin programs are in earlier stages of implementation, but are following courses of development that will lead to comprehensive suicide prevention programs. Other systems can benefit from the experience of these programs.

REFERENCES

1. Shneidman, E. S. (1970). Recent developments in suicide prevention. In E. S. Shneidman, N. L. Farberow, & R. E. Litman (Eds.), *The psychology of suicide* (pp. 145–155). New York: Aronson.
2. Shneidman, E. S. (1979). An overview: Personality, motivation, and behavior theories. In L. D. Hankoff & B. Eisidler (Eds.), *Suicide: theory and clinical aspects* (pp. 143–163). Littleton, MA: PSG Publishing.
3. Caplan, G. R. (1964). *Principles in preventive psychiatry.* New York: Basic Books.
4. Shneidman, E. S., Farberow, N. L., & Litman, R. E. *The psychology of suicide* (pp. 145–155). New York: Aronson.
5. Shneidman, E. S. (1988). Some reflections of a founder. *Suicide and Life-Threatening Behavior, 18*(1), 1–12.
6. Berkovitz, I. H. (1985). The role of schools in child, adolescent, and youth suicide prevention. In M. L. Peck, N. L. Farberow, & R. E. Litman (Eds.), *Youth suicide* (pp. 170–190). New York: Springer.
7. Cooper, S., Munger, R., & Ravlin, M. M. (1980). Mental health prevention through affective education in schools. *Journal of Prevention, 1*(1), 24–34.
8. Glover, J. (1989). Establishing a suicide prevention program for secondary schools. *Student Assistance Journal, 2*(2), 15–20.
9. Herman, A. (1981). *Guidance in Canadian schools.* Calgary, Alberta, Canada: Detselig.
10. Shneidman, E. S., & Farberow, N. L. (1957). *Clues to suicide.* New York: McGraw-Hill.
11. Farberow, N. L., & Shneidman, E. S. (1961). *The cry for help.* New York: McGraw-Hill.
12. Harris, M. B. C., & Crawford, R. W. (1987). *Youth suicide: The identification of effective concepts and practices in policies and procedures for Texas schools.* Commerce, TX: East Texas State University.
13. Lieutenant Governor's Task Force. (1988). *Youth suicide prevention in Vermont.* Montpelier, VT: Author.
14. Shaffer, P., Garland, M. A., & Bacon, K. (1987), *Prevention issues for youth suicide.* Paper prepared for Project Prevention, American Academy of Child and Adolescent Psychiatry. (Available from Connecticut Committee for Youth Suicide Prevention)
15. Boggs, C. (Coordinator). (1986). *Project Lifesaver: Child and adolescent suicide prevention in two school systems.* Dayton, OH: Suicide Prevention Center.
16. Cantor, P. C. (1985). The role of crisis intervention centers. In N. L. Farberow, (Ed.), *Report of the National Conference on Youth Suicide* (pp. 213–218). Washington, DC: Youth Suicide National Center.
17. Joan, P. (1983). *The living alternative handbook.* Ithaca, NY: Suicide Prevention and Crisis Service of Tompkins County.
18. Ross, C. P. (1981). Teaching suicide prevention in schools. *Depression et Suicide.* New York: Pergamon Press.
19. Seiden, R. H. (1984). The youthful suicide epidemic. In *Public Affairs Report* (Vol. 25). Berkeley, CA: Institute of Governmental Studies, University of California.
20. Smith, J. (1984). *Suicide prevention: An introduction to crisis intervention; a curriculum for adolescents.* Dallas, TX: The Suicide and Crisis Center.
21. Colich, J. (1978). *Suicide prevention in the classroom: A teacher's guide to curriculum.* Denver, CO: American Association of Suicidology.

22. Cole, E., & Brotman, M. (1984). Suicide prevention: *A resource for student services.* Toronto, Ontario, Canada: Psychological Services, Toronto Board of Education.
23. Committee on Sudden Adolescent Death. (1984). *Teenage suicide: prevention, intervention, response: A handbook for schools.* New York: COSAD/Four Winds Hospital.
24. New York State Education Department, Office of General Education. (1984). *Suicide among school age youth.* Albany: State University of New York.
25. Ross, C. P. (1985). Teaching children the facts of life and death: Suicide prevention in the schools. In M. L. Peck, N. L. Farberow, & R. E. Litman (Eds.), *Youth suicide* (pp. 147–169). New York: Springer.
26. Heiman, M., Jones, F., Lamb, F., Dunne-Maxim, K., & Sutton, C. (1985). A training model for school personnel. In N. L. Farberow (Ed.), *Report of the National Conference on Youth Suicide* (pp. 213–218). Washington, DC: Youth Suicide National Center.
27. Ramsay, R. F., Tanney, B. L., Tierney, R. J., & Lang, W. A. (1987). *A suicide prevention training program: Trainers handbook* (3rd ed.). Calgary, Alberta, Canada: Canadian Mental Health Association/Authors.
28. Ryerson, D. M., & King, B. (1986). *Adolescent suicide awareness program (ASAP): A comprehensive education and prevention program for school communities.* Lyndhurst, NJ: South Bergen Mental Health Center.
29. Alcohol, Drug Abuse, and Mental Health Administration. (1989). *Report of the secretary's task force on youth suicide* (DHHS Publication No. [Adm.] 89-1621). Washington, DC: U.S. Government Printing Office.
30. Syer-Solursh, D. (Chairman). (1987). *Suicide in Canada: Report of the National Task Force On Suicide.* Ottawa, Ontario, Canada: Health and Welfare Canada.
31. Litman, R. E., & Farberow, N. L. (1986). *Youth suicide in California: Summary of assessment research as reported by the Institute for Studies of Destructive Behavior and the Suicide Prevention Center.* Sacramento, CA: California Department of Mental Health, CMU 85-2528.
32. State Council of Higher Education. (1989). *Incidence of clinical depression and suicide among college students and the availability of suicide prevention services at institutions of higher education in Virginia.* Richmond, VA: Author.
33. Cellota, B., Jacobs, G., Keys, S. G., & Cannon, G. (1988). A model prevention program. In D. Capuzzi & L. Golden (Eds.), *Preventing adolescent suicide* (pp. 269–297). Muncie, IN: Accelerated Development.
34. Simmons, J. T., Comstock, B. S., & Franklin, J. L. (1989). Prevention/intervention programs for suicidal adolescents. In *Report of the secretary's task force on youth suicide,* Vol. 3 (DHHS Publication No. (Adm.) 89-1621; (pp. 80–92). Washington, DC: U.S. Government Printing Office.
35. Nelson, R. E. (1988). Overview of prevention. In D. Capuzzi & L. Golden (Eds.), *Preventing adolescent suicide* (pp. 249–268). Muncie, IN: Accelerated Development.
36. Calgary Board of Education. (1988). *A policy for suicide prevention, intervention, and postvention in the schools.* Calgary, Alberta, Canada: Author.
37. Dallas Independent School District. (1988). *Project SOAR: Suicide options, awareness, relief.* Dallas, TX: Author.
38. Fairfax County Public Schools. (1987). *The adolescent suicide prevention program.* Fairfax, VA: The County School Board of Fairfax County.
39. Los Angeles Unified School District. (1988). *Youth suicide prevention program.* Los Angeles: Student Guidance Services Division.
40. Worcester County Board of Education. (1986). *Lifelines: Helping students find positive alternatives.* Worcester County, MD: Author.
41. Wisconsin Department of Public Instruction. (1986). *Suicide prevention: A resource and planning guide.* Madison, WI: Wisconsin Department of Public Instruction.
42. Kalafat, J., & Underwood, M. (1989). *Lifelines: A school-based adolescent suicide response program.* Dubuque, IA: Kendal/Hunt.
43. School Climate Unit. (1985). *Youth suicide prevention school program.* Sacramento, CA: Department of Education.
44. State of Wisconsin. (1985). Assembly Bill 180, LRB-0626/6 PG:It., Wisconsin Statutes 118.295, Suicide Intervention Civil Liability Exemption.
45. Ruof, S. R., Harris, J. M., & Robbie, M. B. (1987). *Handbook: Suicide prevention in the schools.* La Salle, CO: Weld BOCES.
46. Bongar, B., & Harmatz, M. (1989). Graduate training in clinical psychology and the study of suicide. *Professional Psychology: Research and Practice, 20,* 209–213.

47. Tanney, B. L. (1989). Preventing suicide by improving the competency of caregivers. In *Report of the secretary's task force on youth suicide Vol. 3* (DHHS Publication No. (Adm.) 89-1621; pp. 213–223). Washington, DC: U.S. Government Printing Office.

48. Nelson, E. R., & Slaikeu, K. A. (1984). Crisis intervention in the schools. In K. A. Slaikeu (Ed.), *Crisis intervention: A handbook for practice and research* (pp. 247–262). Newton, MA: Allyn & Bacon.

49. Oakland County Child and Adolescent Suicide Prevention Task Force. (1986). *School information packet dealing with attempted and completed suicides.* Detroit, MI: United Community Services of Metropolitan Detroit.

50. Connecticut Committee for Youth Suicide Prevention. (1989). *Connecticut state plan for youth suicide prevention: Recommendations.* Plainville, CT: Author.

51. Board of Education for the City of Hamilton. (1987). *A handbook for the caregiver on suicide prevention.* Hamilton, Ontario, Canada: Author.

52. Wilson, M. (1989). *Developing a school district suicide prevention policy.* Unpublished manuscript.

53. Hunt, C. (1987). Step by step: How your schools can live through the tragedy of teen suicides. *The American School Board Journal, 174,* 34–37.

54. Hill, W. H. (1984). Intervention and postvention in schools. In H. S. Sudak (Ed.), *Suicide in the young* (pp. 407–416). Littleton, MA: John Wright.

55. Dunne, E. J., McIntosh, J., & Dunne-Maxim, K. (Eds.). (1987). *Suicide and its aftermath.* New York: Norton.

56. American Association of Suicidology, School Suicide Prevention Programs Committee. (1989). *Postvention guidelines* (draft document). Denver, CO: American Association of Suicidology.

57. Sanchez, R. (1988). *Adolescent suicide: A prevention resource guide for the family and community.* Boise, ID: Bureau of Mental Health, Department of Health and Welfare.

58. Kalafat, J., & Ryerson, D. (Fall, 1989). A review of evaluation procedures and priorities. *Newslink, 15*(3), 1–6.

59. Allen, N. H. (1976). The health educator as a suicidologist. *Suicide and Life-Threatening Behavior, 6*(4), 195–201.

60. Bagley, C. (1971). An evaluation of suicide prevention agencies. *Suicide and Life-Threatening Behavior, 4,* 245–259.

61. Farberow, N. L. (1969). Training in suicide prevention for professional and community agents. *American Journal of Psychiatry, 125*(12), 116–119.

62. Heilig, S. M. (1970). Training in suicide prevention. *Bulletin of Suicidology, 6,* 41–44.

63. Smith, K., Eyman, J. R., Dyck, R., & Ryerson, D. (1988). *Report of the school program questionnaire.* Denver: American Association of Suicidology.

64. Resnik, H. C. P., & Hathorne, B. C. (Eds.). (1973). *Suicide prevention in the seventies* (DHEW Publication No. HSM 72-9054). Washington, DC: U.S. Government Printing Office.

65. Comstock, B. (1979). Suicide in the 1970's: A second look. *Suicide and Life-Threatening Behavior, 9*(1), 3–14.

66. Stein, D. M., & Lambert, M. J. (1984). Telephone counselling and crisis intervention: A review. *American Journal of Community Psychology, 12*(1), 101–126.

67. Eddy, D. M., Wolpert, R. L., & Rosenberg, M. L. (1987). Estimating the effectiveness of interventions to prevent youth suicides. *Medical Care, 25,*(12), 57–65.

68. Johnson, W. Y. (1985). Classroom discussion of suicide: An intervention tool for the teacher. *Contemporary Education, 56*(2), 219–326.

69. Shaffer, D., Garland, A., Gould, M., Fisher, P., & Trautman, P. (1988). Preventing teenage suicide: A critical review. *Journal of the American Academy of Child and Adolescent Psychiatry, 27*(6), 675–687.

70. Tierney, R. J. (1988). *Comprehensive evaluation for suicide prevention training.* Unpublished doctoral dissertation, University of Calgary, Calgary, Alberta, Canada.

8

Suicide Awareness Education in Schools: The Development of a Core Program and Subsequent Modifications for Special Populations or Institutions

Diane Ryerson
Peake/Ryerson Consulting Group, Inc., Englewood, New Jersey
South Bergen Mental Health Center, Inc., Lyndhurst, New Jersey

Suicide awareness education is a critical necessity in today's pressured school communities. The legacy of secrecy, taboo, and denial that prevented previous generations of educators and parents from speaking honestly about suicide is no longer relevant or even possible in today's media-educated society. Over the past 15 years, as professionals have been slowly and cautiously introducing suicide awareness programs into schools and human service agencies, the print and electronic media have focused a glaring spotlight on self-intentioned deaths. Newspapers, magazines, television news programs, docudramas, and movies have recognized, addressed, and occasionally sensationalized this tragic reality of today's society, while educators and mental health experts continue to agonize over how, when, and if one should talk to teens about suicide, and who should do it.

As a result of this media bombardment, a large proportion of preteens and adolescents are well, if inaccurately, informed about suicide. All too often their instructors are rock musicians, newspaper reporters, novelists, movie producers and directors, television nightly news editors, and even classmates or friends, while parents, educators, and mental health specialists remain silent and evasive. Sometimes the information preteens and adolescents receive is sensitively and accurately presented; sometimes warning signs and helping strategies are included—but not often enough.

DEVELOPMENT OF A SCHOOL-BASED SUICIDE AWARENESS PROGRAM

Not only youth, but also their parents and teachers—the adults most influential and prominent in children's lives—need to be systematically educated to understand the reality of suicide and other self-destructive behaviors within the continuum of adolescent development. All members of middle and high school communities need to be given the information and skills they need to identify, support, and obtain professional assistance for at-risk youth. To achieve this goal, sensitivity to the idiosyncratic qualities of each school or community and the special needs and vulnerabilities of different populations is needed. Teenagers, their parents, and their educators need clear, accurate, specific information to counter the sensationalism and superficiality of most media coverage.

Here I (a) briefly trace the evolution of a comprehensive, school-based suicide awareness program and (b) outline the various modifications of the program's structure and content that must be made to ensure its relevance for and realism in a variety of school settings and special populations (1–13).

In 1978, the communities in northeast New Jersey were shaken by what appeared to be a small cluster of adolescent suicides. A 13-year-old girl, the daughter of a local pediatrician, took a massive overdose of aspirin and died while her family was away for the day. Investigation into her history uncovered a long tale of alleged abuse and neglect by disturbed parents. Several weeks later, a popular, good-looking, 10th-grade athlete with a history of drinking and getting into fights hung himself after a party. A week later a depressed, withdrawn, shy classmate with a case pending in juvenile court left a group of friends, rushed home on his motor bike, and also hung himself.

While the survivor community was trapped in the national spotlight, surrounding towns reacted in varying ways. Several towns reached out to local mental health practitioners for assistance in training their educators about teenage suicide; others ignored the cluster or denied that it had any possible relevance to their schools and communities. Several years later, in 1981, the supervisor of physical and health education at a local regional high school that had not had a recent suicide, but had experienced several attempts, decided that suicide should be addressed in the school's family life curriculum. The educator believed that suicide was a sensitive topic that he wanted assistance in addressing, and called the local community mental health center for consultation.

The result was the gradual evolution of the Adolescent Suicide Awareness Program (ASAP), a comprehensive mental health education program for school communities. The ASAP is designed to be implemented as a cooperative project between community mental health providers and local school systems—a partnership that ensures cooperation between educators and therapists in identifying and assisting teenagers who are at risk. It has been expanded to more than 350 communities and has served as a model for programs in other counties and states, as well as in Canada and western Europe.

About ASAP

The rationale for ASAP is that each individual in a school community needs to become knowledgeable about depression and self-destructive behavior in teenagers.

Educators need to know because they are in a unique position to identify and refer students at risk. Individual classroom teachers have extensive experience with "average" adolescents, and have studied adolescent development during training. They also have daily contact with the same students, enabling them to compare behavior, are less defensive than a student's parents, and are not constrained by the strictures of peer loyalty to keep a suicidal confidence.

Parents desperately need this information because their children's lives are at stake. Parents are often inexperienced with, or ignorant about, the emotional difficulties of adolescents. Reluctant to acknowledge emotional difficulties in their own child, they frequently deny the seriousness of a teenager's despair until it is too late. Parents also need to know how to counsel and support their child when he or she has a friend who is depressed and potentially suicidal.

For students, having this information could be a matter of life and death. Teenagers have little experience with life and few well-developed coping skills. They do not realize that the feelings of depression they experience are usually time-limited and are not a sign of inadequacy or mental illness. Because a classmate or friend is the most frequent confidant of a suicidal adolescent, teens need to know how to recognize warning signs and know when, how, and where to get professional assistance for a troubled peer. Students need to learn that it is essential— sometimes even life saving—to take warning signs seriously and to break a confidence.

Goals of ASAP

The goals of ASAP are based on the tenets of public health education. The first goal is to disseminate critically important information about the recognition and prevention of adolescent suicidal behavior to all members of a school community.

Although it is essential that educators, parents, and students have this basic information, a school system also needs to have a close working relationship with the professional mental health system in the community to be able to manage suicidal crises, treat depressed students, and collaborate when a suicidal teen returns to school. The second goal is, therefore, to develop and maintain close, effective communication and referral procedures between the local educational and mental health systems in a community.

The secondary goals of ASAP evolved as the pilot program was developed and field tested. They focused on major attitudinal changes that were considered necessary if the program was to be effective in achieving the primary goals. They are as follows:

1. To detoxify participants' attitudes toward emotional difficulties.
2. To demonstrate that school personnel and therapists are caring, knowledgeable, and approachable professionals to whom a teen can turn for help with emotional problems; ensuring that teenagers will translate the information learned in a school-based awareness program into swift and effective action during a crisis is, of course, the ultimate objective.
3. To promote help-seeking behaviors and identify local crisis intervention facilities.

One of the most important and most challenging objectives is to encourage teenagers, as well as parents and educators, to overcome their natural reluctance to acknowledge that a fellow teen is in trouble and then to take action on the teen's behalf.

Content of ASAP

The initial task in the development of ASAP was to reduce the tremendous amount of clinical and research data about adolescent suicide into a succinct, meaningful, and action-oriented curriculum. After extensive sifting of information and fine tuning of design, the following six points were identified as the key information everyone in a school community must know for the school to become a prevention-oriented system.

The key areas of information selected include

1. The warning signs that an adolescent is potentially suicidal
2. The "facts" about adolescent suicide (i.e., local, state, and national rate; the demographic groups at high risk; the ratio of suicide attempts to completed suicide; relation of attempts to completed suicides; relation of numbers of suicides to other causes of adolescent deaths)
3. What depression looks like in adolescents and how it is different from depression in adults
4. The "causes" (societal, psychological, biological, environmental, and situational) of adolescent self-destructive behavior
5. What the educator, parent, or teenager can do to help in a suicidal crisis
6. Where in the community professional help can be obtained

Structure of ASAP

Once a school community decides to implement a suicide awareness program, the next major problem is designing a method for disseminating this sensitive material to parents, teachers, and students. In the past, and occasionally still today, denial of the possibility of suicide and the omnipresent fear of putting the idea of suicide in a vulnerable adolescent's head prove to be insurmountable stumbling blocks. As a result, comprehensive programs were seldom implemented or maintained past the initial phase until 10 years ago.

An established, well-accepted program with a lengthy track record and an extensively piloted curriculum often provides reassurance to school administrators who are still hesitant about introducing suicide awareness training. With this resistance factor in mind, the structure of ASAP was initially designed as three flexible, interrelated components that could be implemented sequentially, or could, because of special training requirements of a school system, be given individually. The process encourages school staff to take an active role in the installation of the program and ensures that parents and educators are trained before introducing the curriculum to the students. It is critical for the significant adults in a teenager's life—that is, parents and teachers—to be prepared to hear and deal with the student's potential reaction to the student workshop. It is a risky mistake to educate teens without first preparing their adult caretakers.

The components of ASAP include

1. *Educators' seminar.* This 3-hr intensive seminar for teachers, administrators, and support staff (guidance, child study team, nurses, cafeteria and maintenance workers, coaches, secretaries) uses lecture, audiovisuals, self-evaluation exercises, and small group discussion to develop a common understanding of the causes and warning signs of adolescent suicide, and to clarify school procedures for handling troubled teens. The seminar teaches crisis intervention strategies and informs educators about local mental health facilities.
2. *Parents' program.* This is a flexible program tailored to the needs and interests of each participant group. Programs vary from a 30-min overview to an intensive 2-hr workshop similar to the educators' seminar.
3. *Students' workshop.* This is a unique 4- to 6-hr workshop designed to inform

high school students about the realities of adolescent self-destructive behavior; it enables them to evaluate their own emotional well-being and prepares them to identify and deal with depression and suicidal behavior in friends, family members, and themselves. A variety of teaching methodologies are used.

Evaluation of ASAP

Each workshop is evaluated with a simple rating scale immediately after the program. Although the participants' scores have been routinely excellent, the long-term impact of the program on knowledge retention, attitudes, and behavior needs in-depth evaluation. The reported anecdotal impact of ASAP on a school system includes the following:

1. *An increase in the number of referrals to the local mental health provider.* Local mental health centers report between three and five referrals from a school system after the introduction of each program element; approximately one quarter to one third of these referrals become active cases. Many children who are referred are not actively suicidal, but are troubled young people in need of counseling. Suicide awareness programs have a "trickle-down" effect that alerts participants to a wide spectrum of adolescent problems. Students also appear more comfortable in referring themselves or a friend for counseling after they have participated in the student's workshop. They also make frequent and more appropriate use of local emergency phone services.

2. *Less resistance to asking for help.* Parents and teenagers alike appear less reluctant to accept a referral to a center and more willing to follow through on treatment recommendations after participating in ASAP.

3. *Improved communications.* Contact and communications are strengthened among the school administration, the child study teams, and the local mental health professionals.

4. *Enhanced trust between students and ASAP personnel.* As previously noted, most people are reluctant to discuss suicide with teenagers. Adolescents want and need this life-and-death information. They respect the agency personnel, and later the school staff, for talking directly about a taboo subject. Their level of trust and positive attitude toward the program presenters increases after participation. Guidance counselors and child study team personnel who conduct the program report better rapport with students.

5. *A decrease in the number of suicides in participating school systems.* Although it cannot be definitively stated that the decrease is a direct result of participation in ASAP, there have been numerous cases where a youngster at risk was identified *without* a suicide attempt's having taken place. The rescuers in these cases stated that they learned how to handle the situation in the ASAP program. Clinical experience indicates that ASAP has helped many critical interventions with previously undiagnosed teenagers. Long-term, in-depth research is needed to confirm these anecdotal reports and to investigate what parts of ASAP, as well as other suicide awareness programs, contribute to this positive outcome, what is unnecessary or potentially harmful, and what needs to be added or reinforced. This research is the next critical step in suicide awareness education.

Implementation of ASAP

Programs are tailored to meet each system's needs, and local school personnel may play an active role in the design and implementation of each component. The program uses existing school personnel and is designed to be cost effective and readily replicated. The entire program takes from 3 months to 2 years to implement, depending on the needs and wishes of each system.

The first step in introducing ASAP into a community is to train a team of mental health professionals from the local community mental health center, family service agency, or other mental health agency to deliver the program. This training format is similar to other school-based suicide awareness programs. The sponsoring mental health organization then provides the educators' seminar and parents' program in the school community.

Following the completion of the first two programs, a school is then ready, if it elects to introduce the students' workshop on an annual basis. In the first year of the program, trainers from the mental health agency conduct the students' workshop while simultaneously training the school's in-house ASAP team to deliver the program themselves. This team usually consists of a combination of guidance counselors, school social workers and psychologists, nurses, substance abuse or student assistance counselors, and health educators. The students' workshop may be given in special in-school field trips, during regularly scheduled class periods, or as part of the health or physical education program. The training schedule can be modified to meet the scheduling limitations of each school; otherwise the program may encounter unnecessary resistance.

In subsequent years, the school's ASAP team conducts the students' workshops with 9th or 10th graders, and the mental health agency continues to provide emergency and therapeutic services to troubled teens, as well as consultation regarding the program itself.

STRATEGIES FOR DISSEMINATING THE CORE CURRICULUM

The procedure for implementing ASAP described here remains the standard and most desirable method. The South Bergen Mental Health Center (SBMHC) was fortunate to obtain a grant from the Turrell Fund of East Orange, NJ, that enabled it to train the 22 private, parochial, and special needs schools in its service area to use this ideal procedure. Slight modifications were made to accommodate the needs of individual schools (e.g., one school had just had an in-depth seminar on adolescent suicide for the faculty by the school psychiatrist, so a modification was made to give the educators' seminar last instead of first). Also, several schools were "recuperating" from the completed suicide of a student or faculty member, which required special modification and timing of workshops.

By and large, the initial programs were conducted by the book, which enabled SBMHC to gain a great deal of experience under almost optimal conditions. When training for catchment-area school systems was completed, the positive reception and perceived successes of the program prompted many requests for ASAP from other schools outside SBMHC's service area, and from other cities, counties, and states.

In an effort to share the ASAP model with other communities, a number of different training methods have been tried. Various program modifications have also been piloted in order to meet the particular needs of a school community without diluting the impact of the program or altering its intent.

The major training methods used include the following:

1. *Mental health center training.* When numerous towns in Bergen County (but outside SBMHC's service area) requested ASAP training, the center experimented by replicating the training with its own service-area schools on a fee-for-services basis, using its own staff to conduct workshops. Although ASAP was successfully delivered in a turnkey basis to these schools, there were several drawbacks to this approach: (a) ASAP's second goal—to develop and maintain close, effective communication and referral procedures between the local educational and mental health systems in a community—was reduced. When these schools experienced a suicidal crisis, they first turned to SBMHC for emergency intervention and consultation instead of to their own community mental health provider. As SBMHC could not officially provide these services, a delivery gap emerged. Precious time was wasted while the school was reconnected with their designated provider. (b) The SBMHC staff had enough to do to keep up with their schools, as well as their regular caseload; the additional training load proved an unnecessary drain on the agency's resources.

To meet the needs of these towns while ensuring that they developed working relationships with their own mental health providers, a mental health center training program was developed and funding secured. Teams of therapists from five community mental health centers in Bergen County were trained in much the same manner as were service-area schools. They, in turn, offered ASAP to their catchment-area towns on a fee basis. Approximately three quarters of the 70-plus schools in Bergen County have voluntarily participated in ASAP in the past 8 years. Several towns had preexisting programs; several others elected not to participate. Three quarters of those who participated report they are still teaching the student's workshop curriculum annually and are periodically retraining teachers.

2. *ASAP professional seminar.* The second major method used to disseminate ASAP was the development of the 2½-day ASAP professional seminar designed for educators and mental health professionals who wanted to start a suicide awareness program in their school or community. The professional seminar is an intensive, hands-on, how-to workshop that focuses on introducing participants to the basic ASAP structure and curriculum.

A significant proportion of its time is spent helping participants tailor the basic program to their community's and school's particular needs and demographics. The seminar is offered semiannually in Lyndhurst, NJ, near SBMHC's main office. It is also available as a traveling seminar on a limited basis. This training method has enabled SBMHC to share the ASAP program with a wide range of professionals from across the United States and Canada and from western Europe as well. It also enables SBMHC to maintain a degree of quality control in the program's replication. Trainees who complete the full seminar are awarded a certificate that entitles them to order ASAP materials for use in their own programs.

3. *Pilot training programs.* These were developed to modify the basic ASAP program for special populations. Several in-depth training programs were conducted in a number of inner-city, multiethnic districts in 1986–1987. The purpose was to field test ASAP in large, urban, low-income schools with large Black and

Hispanic populations, and to make the appropriate modifications. ASAP has also been modified for use in private day and boarding schools and regional vocational technical schools. The urban modification process is described in more depth later.

ASAP Modifications for Specific Human Service Delivery Systems

In addition to modifying ASAP for a variety of school settings, SBMHC has received requests to develop training programs on adolescent suicide prevention for a variety of other systems dealing with troubled adolescents. In its effort to reach alienated youths who have dropped out, been expelled or suspended, placed on long-term home instruction, or incarcerated, it is now experimenting with a variety of training models for law enforcement personnel, including municipal police officers, juvenile officers, probation and parole officers, and detention and detention alternative facility personnel.

FACTORS IN MODIFYING ADOLESCENT SUICIDE AWARENESS PROGRAMS FOR SPECIAL POPULATIONS

As the result of SBMHC's extensive training inside its catchment area under near-optimal conditions, as well as SBMHC's experience in training others to deliver the ASAP model and "modified ASAP" for specific populations, it has developed a number of different program models. SBMHC's experience has demonstrated that two separate but interrelated issues must always be addressed for a suicide awareness program to be successfully integrated into a new school environment.

1. *Organizational issues.* Each school or school system is a unique social, political, and educational environment, even though its organizational structure may be identical on paper to that of the school next door. It is essential to recognize and deal with both the implicit and explicit organizational and political issues in a school to determine how best to introduce suicide awareness programs.

Several critical organizational issues include (a) the personal orientation and experiences of top school administration (superintendent, building principal, etc.); (b) the school's recent experience with suicide and life-threatening behavior or other sudden violent deaths in its own or an adjacent community; (c) the attitudes and experiences of key faculty, the board of education, and parents; (d) the size of the student body and the system's organizational complexity; (e) whether the school is located in an urban, suburban, or rural environment; (f) the availability, quality, and accessibility of community mental health providers and their present relationship with the school; (g) whether the school is a middle school, junior high school, or high school; (h) whether the school is public, parochial, private (day or boarding), or special needs (i.e., vocational–technical classified—learning and physical disabilities); and (i) the availability of recreation and support programs for teens in the community.

2. *Demographic issues.* The socioeconomic, racial, ethnic, and religious profile of school systems will have an impact on the program's emphasis and teaching style. A program director should obtain the following information before determining necessary program modifications: (a) the racial and ethnic composition of both the faculty and the student body; (b) the academic achievement level of

students in the proposed target grade(s); (c) the socioeconomic background of the community as a whole, and of the families of children attending the particular school; (d) percentage of non-English-speaking students or those for whom English is a second language; (e) percentage of children from single-parent homes; (f) percentage of students from families below poverty level (eligibility for school lunch programs); (g) the major social problems of the community as perceived by the administration, faculty, students, and parents; (h) the major religious groups represented in the student population; the estimate of the impact of religious values and doctrines on the lives of students and their families; (i) the rate of adolescent pregnancies and number of teen parents attending school; (j) the profile of alcohol and drug abuse in the school and community; and (k) the major employers and job categories of students' parents and of students themselves.

The gathering of information on a school's organizational structure and relationships and the demographics of the faculty and student body play two major roles in the introduction of a suicide awareness program like ASAP into any school community.

First, there are real differences between school communities and the students they serve. These must be addressed before a program commences. Second, the process of studying the structure, demographics, and current climate of the individual school assures educators and parents that the project director recognizes the unique characteristics of the school, and allays fears that a "packaged program" is going to be force fit into their system. The fact-finding interviews conducted by the project director will enable him or her to

1. Assess the attitude of key people toward both suicide and the program
2. Initiate working relationships
3. Determine the school's "hot spots"
4. Bring resistances and objections to the surface before formal training sessions begin
5. Enable key people to make appropriate programmatic suggestions for incorporation into the program
6. Permit the project manager to assess the training skills and comfort level of a potential in-house ASAP training team

The need to modify a basic suicide awareness–prevention program effectively, making it appropriate and acceptable to a school community, cannot be overemphasized. This is especially true when the program is being introduced by an outside mental health consultant or agency. SBMHC has repeatedly found worthwhile an extended "introduction" period during which the program manager has numerous meetings with key representatives from

1. *Administration* (superintendent, building principal, and disciplinarian and curriculum specialist)
2. *Faculty* (nurses, child study team or special services, department chairs or key faculty, guidance counselors, substance abuse or student assistance counselors, and peer listening program coordinator)
3. *Support staff* (coaches, cafeteria and maintenance workers, bus drivers and crossing guards, juvenile officers assigned to the school, and secretaries)

4. Board of Education
5. Parent association
6. Representatives of local human service and mental health providers

Many of these meetings can be quick, informal chats; group brainstorming meetings; or discussions following a formal presentation of the project. The project manager should repeatedly ask him- or herself and others, "with whom haven't we touched base with that we should?"

A professional collegial attitude, use of straightforward language, and a willingness to listen are all skills necessary to overcome a school staff's legitimate need to have their school's uniqueness, as well as their own competence and expertise, recognized and valued.

The preceding comments are intended to give a general outline of the areas a project manager should explore before beginning the formal portion of a suicide awareness program. Next, I demonstrate how these issues were addressed in modifying a basic school-based curriculum for a special population: large, inner-city schools with low-income, multiethnic and multiracial student populations.

In 1986, SBMHC began the modification of ASAP for low-income, multiethnic, urban school systems. The five pilot schools were in Jersey City, Orange, and East Orange, NJ, and included general high schools, a Roman Catholic girl's academy, and a public school for the academically talented.

The initial action plan for introducing ASAP into inner-city schools called for preliminary modifications to the educator, parent, and student curriculums that worked well in suburban schools. In-depth interviews with key school personnel (principals, social workers, guidance counselors, nurses, classroom teachers, and parents), together with suggestions from each project's staff and a brief review of the little literature that exists provided guidelines for initial alterations. Additional changes were made as the project progressed, and were based primarily on feedback from the trainers and participants.

At preliminary meetings local school personnel, community representatives, and project personnel agreed that suicide, especially adolescent suicide, was not perceived as a major problem in the inner city. National and state statistics, as well as local experience, indicated a substantially lower incidence of *reported* suicides among Black and Hispanic youth. Teachers and students pointed to the much more visible issues of urban adolescence: pregnancy and promiscuity, dropping out of school, risk-taking behavior, sexual assault, violence, and drug or alcohol abuse, as well as severe family dysfunction. Despite a large number of local suicide attempts (primarily among adolescent Hispanic girls) and a high mortality rate for urban youths, little connection was made between these self-destructive behaviors and suicide.

The content of ASAP was, therefore, broadened from a focus on adolescent suicide to include the pressures and problems of urban youth. Related changes were made in the large group presentations, as well as in the discussion guides used in the small group meetings. Emphasis was placed on making participants aware of the range of self-destructive behaviors of urban youth and their short- and long-term impact on their lives. Emphasis was shifted from recognizing depression and reacting to a suicidal crisis to identifying stressors, validating feelings, and discussing stress-management, problem-solving, and relationship skills.

In addition, considerable time was spent at the beginning of the inner-city project anticipating potential problems caused by organizational issues. The following were identified:

1. The lack of minority (Black and Hispanic) project trainers would result in resistance on the part of students and school staff.
2. The faculty and students in the urban schools would not relate to the available adolescent suicide prevention training films, most of which are set in suburban or rural areas and focus on the problems of White, middle-class teens.
3. The administrators and faculty would reject the project because suicide is not perceived as a major problem in inner-city schools.
4. The targeted 10th-grade students would be disruptive, uninterested, and even hostile.
5. It would be difficult, if not impossible, to bring urban parents out for the parent program portion of the project.

Surprisingly, only one of these issues (although they were all minor problems) caused the anticipated difficulties. This may have been because these issues were acknowledged in early meetings with school staff and their help in resolving them was engaged from the start. Once school staff were convinced that (a) although suicide is not perceived as a major inner-city school issue, their students are involved in a continuum of self-destructive behavior often resulting in diminished lives and damaged health, if not death; and (b) the ASAP project staff had something to offer the school, were willing to learn, and were reliable and caring, resistance to the program dissolved and a rewarding collaboration began.

The parents were, as predicted, difficult to reach. The same problems and resistances that keep suburban parents away from meetings (both parents working, lack of school involvement, denial of problems; i.e., pregnancy, drugs, alcohol, suicide), were compounded by cultural differences and language barriers (many parents spoke only Spanish), lack of transportation and baby sitting, fear of going out in the city at night, and a lack of understanding of the school structure and the problems of American teenagers. A major cause of family disagreement and depression in these schools came from the conflict between "Old Country" parents and their American teenagers.

Aggressive outreach programs were necessary to encourage parent participation. Numerous strategies such as phone chains, using community leaders as keynote speakers, combining the presentation with report card dissemination and even with raffles, were used with varying degrees of success. School personnel recommended that the parent program be renamed the "family program" because so many students lived with adults other than their biological parents.

Most encouraging was the students' reaction to the program. Initially they were quieter than their suburban counterparts, but they opened up once it became clear that the small groups were safe places in which to discuss feelings and fears. The small group discussions lasted from $1\frac{1}{2}$–2 hr, significantly longer than the suburban discussion periods, and were filled with identifying problems and searching for solutions. Suicide took a back seat to alcohol and drugs, teen pregnancy, peer pressure, and family stress—the students' major concerns.

The students' positive response to the opportunity to discuss feelings and problems generated enthusiasm in school staff, who not only accepted ASAP, but also undertook the creation of innovative programs to meet students' requests for more small group discussions. Rap groups and peer counseling programs were begun. One school started a crisis counseling service—the Time Out Program—where teachers volunteer to take turns staffing a room where troubled students can come for help at any time during the school day.

The major stumbling block in the inner-city project was the lack of organization and the resultant poor staff communication, which resulted in difficulties coordinating the implementation of workshops and meetings. Key staff did not receive meeting notices, necessary equipment was not delivered on time, other activities were scheduled during workshop times, and so forth.

A related difficulty was the urban schools' lack of resources that are taken for granted in suburban schools. Frequently projectors were broken, screens torn or missing, or "break out rooms" unavailable. Tight budgets often prevented sending meeting notices home by mail or providing simple refreshments. Several schools also had very limited access to school social workers and psychologists, which interfered with their participation in the project. Unlike suburban schools, meetings often started late, with several key faculty members not present and substitutes unavailable. Patience and persistence were essential.

Finding a key faculty leader sponsor was essential. It is also desirable but not mandatory that the lead trainer from the mental health agency be of the same socioeconomic or racial background as the majority of the school population. If not, the trainer should be prepared to study the local demographics in depth, as well as to spend extensive time meeting with school and community people and observing in the school.

A second problem was the degree of faculty frustration that often resulted when the overwhelming personal and family problems of many students were uncovered in the small discussion groups. The teachers were predominately White, middle-class professionals who lived outside the school district. These faculty members displayed an extraordinary degree of concern and compassion for their students. It was of vital importance to them and the program's success to have community-based mental health services immediately available when a troubled student was identified.

The personal and professional relationships that developed between the school staff and the mental health workers collaborating on the pilot program greatly facilitated these interventions and ensured ongoing cooperation between schools and therapists. The mental health centers' ASAP project managers and training teams continue to provide consultation to the schools on classroom management techniques, program implementation, and therapeutic intervention.

Training in the recognition and prevention of adolescent self-destructive behavior is a necessary and achievable goal for inner-city school communities. Although the introduction of the program requires more staff time than in resource-rich and psychologically sophisticated suburban schools, the payoffs appear to be even greater.

1. Students welcome the opportunity to identify feelings, discuss problems, and explore positive-coping and help-seeking skills.

2. Educators learn identification and referral skills and mental health professionals learn more about the school and family environments of their clients.

3. Some parents begin to identify and deal with their children's problems and behaviors and learn more about school structure and community resources.

4. Procedures are established for the identification and referral of troubled youth, and for ongoing school and mental health center collaboration. In many schools, procedures for managing a completed suicide or other sudden violent death was included in the training process.

CONCLUSION

School-based suicide awareness programs are rapidly becoming an accepted phenomenon in this country's junior and senior high schools. A majority of administrators and boards now recognize the need to have sympathetic, trained personnel address this critical mental health issue directly with teenagers as well as with their adult caretakers. The magnitude of the problem together with media-heightened awareness about suicide create a powerful incentive to address the issue head on. In addition to adding to school communities' knowledge about adolescent self-destructive behavior and teaching basic crisis management skills, suicide awareness education often provides the added benefit of alerting teens and adults alike to a wide continuum of adolescent problems. Because suicide is a topic of intense interest and concern for most teens, and a topic that most adults are reluctant to discuss with young people, suicide awareness programs are usually well received. The skills and knowledge learned are, of course, relevant to the broad scope of teen problems: substance abuse, promiscuity and sexually transmitted diseases, teen pregnancy, violence and risk-taking behavior, and so forth.

As was illustrated here, a basic suicide prevention curriculum can be successfully modified to meet a wide variety of organizational and demographic settings. It is essential that extensive research on the target school's structure and student population be done *before* implementation, and that as many key players as possible be involved in the tailoring process. When the core structure and content of the program is sound and the project director is experienced in implementing the program, the modifications are frequently minor, but nevertheless very important to the program's acceptance and success.

REFERENCES

1. Diekstra, R. F. W. (1989). Suicidal behavior in adolescents and young adults: The international picture. *Crisis, 10*(1), 16–35.
2. Frederick, C. J. (1984). Suicide in young minority group persons. In H. Sudak, A. Ford, & N. Rushfourth (Eds.), *Suicide in the young.* Boston: John Wright & Sons.
3. Gibbs, J. T. (1984). Black adolescents and youth: An endangered species. *American Journal of Orthopsychiatry, 54,* 6–21.
4. Gibbs, J. T. (1988). Conceptual, methodological and sociocultural issues in Black youth suicide: Implication for assessment and early intervention. *Suicide and Life Threatening Behavior, 18*(1), 74–89.
5. Hendin, J. (1969). Black suicide. *Archives of General Psychiatry, 21,* 407–422.
6. Mulder, A. M., Methorst, G. J., & Diekstra, R. F. W. (1989). Prevention of suicidal behavior in adolescents: The role and training of teachers. *Crisis, 10*(1), 36–51.
7. Ryerson, D. M., & King, B. (1985). *The adolescent suicide awareness program manual.* Lyndhurst, NJ: South Bergen Mental Health Center.
8. Ryerson, D. M. (1987). ASAP: An adolescent suicide awareness programme. In R. F. W. Diekstra & Hawton (Eds.), *Suicide in adolescence* (pp. 173–190). Dordrecht, The Netherlands: Martinus Nijhoff.
9. Seiden, R. H. (1972). Why are suicides of young Blacks increasing? *HSMHS Health Reports, 87,* 3–8.
10. Shaffer, D., Garland, A., & Whittle, B. (1988). An evaluation of three youth suicide prevention

programs in New Jersey. In *New Jersey Department of Human Services, Final Project Report* (unpublished).

11. Spano, N. A. (1988, June). *To be or not to be: Adolescent suicide, statewide action plan.* New York State Senate, Committee on Mental Hygiene.

12. Smith, J. A., & Carter, J. H. (1986). Suicide and Black adolescents: A medical dilemma. *Journal of the National Medical Association, 78,* 1061–1064.

13. *Youth suicide prevention: Meeting the challenge in New Jersey schools.* (1989). NJ: New Jersey State Department of Human Services, Governor's Advisory Council on Youth Suicide Prevention and the New Jersey Adolescent Suicide Prevention Project.

9

Sex Differences and Their Relevance to Primary Prevention of Adolescent Suicide

James Overholser
Case Western Reserve University, Cleveland, Ohio

Steven Evans
Western Psychiatric Institute and Clinic, Pittsburgh, Pennsylvania

Anthony Spirito
Brown University and Rhode Island Hospital, Providence

Adolescent suicide has become an increasing concern over the past few years. Epidemiological studies have shown an upsurge of suicidal behavior among adolescents. Although attempts have been made to address the incidence of suicide through preventive efforts (1), little is known about the sex differences relevant to such work. We begin by briefly describing some of the sex differences related to depression and suicidal behavior. We then focus on the findings of a series of studies exploring sex differences in the primary prevention of adolescent suicide.

SEX DIFFERENCES IN SUICIDAL BEHAVIOR

Suicide rates have been increasing over recent years, with most of this increase occurring with White males, whether adolescent or adult (2). Research in the area of child and adolescent suicide has revealed numerous differences between males and females. Sex differences have been found in rates of attempt and completion (3), techniques used to commit suicide (4), utilization and efficacy of suicide intervention centers (5), and imitative responses to media reports of suicide (6). Therefore, it is not at all surprising to observe sex differences in the success of primary prevention programs. To implement a successful primary prevention program targeting children or adolescents, it is essential that one is aware of and understands the relation between aspects of suicide and gender.

Differences between males and females in rate of suicide attempts change as a function of age. Suicide in children under 10 years of age is extremely rare (7). Within this young age group, boys attempt suicide more often than girls (4). However, in children more than 10 years of age, girls attempt suicide more often than boys (3), and this pattern continues into adulthood (8).

Although adolescent females attempt suicide at a greater rate than males, adolescent males complete suicide more often than females. Adolescent males between the ages of 10–14 successfully complete suicide at a ratio of greater than

5 : 1 over females (7). This ratio decreases as the age of adolescents increases. However, even after the gradual decrease, men between the ages of 25-29 complete suicide at a rate of almost 3.5 : 1 over same-aged women (7).

Part of the gender difference in rate of completed suicide is thought to be due to sex differences in the methods used (9). When males attempt suicide, highly lethal and violent methods are often used (10). Firearms and hanging are much more common methods for males than for females. Females tend to prefer less violent and less lethal methods, such as drug overdoses. The chances for discovery and recovery from the more passive methods used by females is greater than from the more violent methods used by males. These differences in method may help explain why more males complete suicide than females, even though fewer males attempt it.

Another phenomenon related to teenage suicide is clustering. Following incidents of suicide covered by the media, suicide in the local area significantly increases in proportion to the extent of the media coverage. Phillips and Carstensen (6) found the suicide rate for females increased 13.46% following the report of a suicide by the media. However, the suicide rate for males only rose by 5.18%. They contend that this is consistent with the popular belief that teenage girls are more easily influenced by social and imitative factors than are teenage boys.

Sex differences in symptoms associated with suicidal crises have been identified. In a study of more than 7,000 Black adolescents, females were three times more likely than males to report suicidal ideation or behavior (11). Also, in contrast to the males in the study, females who attempted suicide were more likely to express their self-destructive intent. Most important, adolescent males who attempted suicide without previously having expressed their suicidal intent were found to appear very similar to those males who showed no signs of suicidal tendencies. This suggests that adolescent males may hide their true feelings of depression and hopelessness, hindering preventive efforts. Conversely, externalizing, acting-out behaviors may be more indicative of suicidal tendencies in adolescent males than are more conventional warning signs such as depression and hopelessness (11).

Finally, there have been reports of sex differences in the use and effectiveness of crisis intervention centers. Miller, Coombs, Leeper, and Barton (5) have reported that counties that use crisis intervention centers experienced no change in the suicide rate when compared with the change found in counties that do not use these centers. However, when they looked at the data across sexes, they found significant differences. The suicide rate for females under 24 years of age in counties that offered crisis intervention centers dropped by 55%, whereas the suicide rate for females under 24 years of age in counties without these centers increased by 85%. There was no significant difference between the counties for male suicide rates. This finding is consistent with the observation that females are by far the most frequent users of crisis intervention centers. Therefore, females may be more amenable than males to the intervention and prevention strategies that are currently available.

ROLE OF SCHOOLS IN PRIMARY PREVENTION

Preventive efforts can take three semi-independent focal points: primary, secondary, and tertiary prevention (12). Primary prevention attempts to change the behavior of an unselected population in such a way as to prevent the occurrence of an undesirable behavior. Schools play an important role in the primary prevention of many disorders. By educating youth, schools can warn them of the potential dangers involved in many maladaptive coping styles, whether they be alcohol abuse, sexual promiscuity, or poor nutritional habits. In relation to suicide, primary prevention can serve two important functions: providing life skills training and improving social support networks (13). Prevention programs can focus on skills training, educating students about self-destructive urges, and informing them of treatment options that are available. Prevention programs can also attempt to improve the social supports available to teens, making students more sensitive to their classmates and facilitating their ability to identify and properly manage self-destructive tendencies in their peers.

Unfortunately, not everyone favors suicide prevention programs. Shaffer (14) believed that the discussion of suicide may serve to increase the rates of suicidal behavior, similar to the clustering that occurs following media presentations. There are no data to support this, as our own research has not found an increase in suicidality following our programs. Furthermore, most experts (e.g., 15) feel that open discussion about suicide offers the suicidal person a feeling of relief, of finally being able to discuss the problem openly, view it more objectively, and gather the information needed to deal with the situation.

Shaffer also questioned the cost effectiveness of a primary prevention program. According to Shaffer, Garland, Gould, Fisher, and Trautman (16), the primary prevention of suicide is not feasible because of the infrequent occurrence of death by suicide in the general population of adolescents. The cost of the prevention would be overwhelming. This line of reasoning focuses heavily on the false positives: those individuals who may appear suicidal although they have no intention of dying. However, any cost–benefit analysis must examine the tremendous "costs" involved in false negatives: those suicidal individuals who escape detection and are never offered treatment. Also, it is important to acknowledge that what is to be prevented is not only completed suicides but also suicide attempts.

SUICIDE AWARENESS PROGRAMS

In our first study, which examined the impact of suicide awareness curriculums in high schools (17), we used a sensitive research design in order to control for any indirect exposure to suicide information. A Solomon Four-Groups Design (18) was used to control for the effects of pretest sensitization. Specifically, we were concerned that completing the questionnaires would serve to sensitize the students to the issues being assessed and make it more likely they would learn about these issues through either the curriculum or other sources (e.g., television, news reports, etc.). Of the four groups in the study, one was tested by using a battery of measures both before and after participation in the curriculum. A second group served as the traditional control group and was tested during the same time periods as the first group, but did not participate in the curriculum. The third group completed the measures after, but not before, participating in the curriculum. Finally, the fourth group completed the measures only once and did not participate in the curriculum. With the assistance of the Rhode Island chapter of the Samaritans, we tested 473 high school students, using measures designed to quantify knowledge, attitudes, and coping strategies relevant to suicide. Then 291 of these students participated in a structured suicide awareness curriculum.

A prevention program must be described in adequate detail so that its effectiveness can be replicated with other groups of participants (19). The suicide awareness program used in our research had a well-defined structure and content. The structure of the curriculum was based on a 2-day teacher training session conducted by the local Samaritans chapter. A variety of background readings were provided to further explain issues such as self-esteem, developmental crises during adolescence, and the enigma of suicide. Following this training, the teachers conducted a 6-week curriculum with the students, which was typically presented as part of their health class.

A teacher's manual provided the framework for the content of the course. Classroom lectures and discussions were used to increase students' awareness of suicidal urges in themselves and in their peers. The curriculum content focused on knowledge, attitudes, and behaviors relevant to suicidality. The knowledge area placed emphasis on risk factors and warning signs indicative of a possible suicidal crisis. These warning signs were used as cues that a person needed help in managing a crisis situation. Also, an attempt was made to correct many of the myths surrounding suicide (e.g., someone who talks about suicide would never attempt it). The attitude section dealt with issues pertaining to attitudes, experiences, and emotions regarding death and suicide. Teachers attempted to cultivate a compassionate attitude toward suicide and its victims. The behavior section of the curriculum focused on coping styles and referral patterns that are useful when one is confronted with suicidal urges in oneself or others. The focus was primarily on the identification and management of suicidal urges. Management techniques emphasized social skills and active listening strategies to provide social support to isolated and withdrawn peers. When relevant, handouts from the teacher's guide were distributed to the students (more detailed information regarding the curriculum can be obtained from A. Spirito).

Approximately 10 weeks after the initial testing, all students were retested, using the same questionnaires. Results showed that, for the most part, students who had participated in the curriculum had benefited from it. They had increased their knowledge about suicide facts and myths, largely pertaining to the identification of factors associated with increased risk of suicide. Students also reported more adaptive attitudes toward suicidal peers, no longer feeling that suicidal teens are weak or disturbed. Finally, students showed a slight improvement in their coping behaviors. After the curriculum, students were less likely to rely on wishful thinking or social withdrawal when confronted with stressful situations.

However, pretest sensitization effects were also observed. Students who were in the assessment-only control group showed slight but significant increases on several of the dependent measures. The very act of completing the suicide questionnaires seemed to have a beneficial impact on some students. This is understandable, considering the applied nature of the questionnaires. Many of the measures assess interesting and thought-provoking issues. Any self-perceived knowledge deficits may stimulate an interest in finding the correct answer. For example, when asked "True or False; Someone who talks about suicide is unlikely to ever attempt it," many students may rightfully respond "I don't know." Subsequent to the assessment procedures, these students may be more sensitive to casual talk or professional descriptions of suicidal behavior in an attempt to contemplate and answer some of these very important questions. Thus, our early research showed that the assessment of suicide knowledge, attitudes, and behaviors can have indirect beneficial effects on subjects.

A more powerful finding of this first research project emerged in the strong sex effects that were observed. At the time of the initial testing, the female students consistently displayed higher levels of knowledge about suicide and less endorsement of common myths surrounding suicide. Females also reported more adaptive attitudes toward suicide, being cautious but not avoidant when confronted with suicidal urges in a peer. Finally, female students displayed better coping behaviors than the male students. Female students showed less passive and avoidant strategies, such as blaming others, wishful thinking, or social withdrawal when attempting to cope with a stressful situation. Also, despite their higher levels of knowledge, attitudes, and coping behaviors at baseline, female students were more likely than male students to benefit from the suicide curriculum.

Our second research project (20) attempted to expand on the first. Because of the strong sex effects already noted, this remained a focus of the study. However, we decided to examine a potentially more powerful sensitizing factor. Because the previous exposure to suicide-related material (pretest sensitization) was found to improve students' performance on subsequent retesting, we considered it useful to explore the impact of personal knowledge of a peer who had attempted suicide. We attempted to determine how such a life event may affect students and their knowledge, attitudes, and behaviors relevant to suicide.

In this study, we tested 471 high school students recruited from schools different than those used in the previous study. Approximately half of these students participated in the suicide curriculum, and the other half served as controls. Students who participated in the suicide curriculum were retested approximately 1 month after the completion of the program. When we analyzed the results, we again found the strong sex effects noted in the earlier study. Both before and after the curriculum, female students were more likely than male students to display higher levels of knowledge and more appropriate attitudes. Also, when specifically asked how they would cope with a suicidal peer, female students displayed a wider range of coping behaviors.

The effects of knowing a peer who had attempted suicide were less prominent than the sex differences. Personal exposure to suicidal behavior in a peer was found to increase the student's ability to benefit from the curriculum. In other words, these students were more likely to learn the factual material presented during the suicide discussions. Also, after the curriculum, these students were found to have reduced any negative attitudes they may have held toward suicidal peers.

In general, results from these two studies point to the importance of sex differences in educating high school students about suicide. The female students consistently displayed higher levels of knowledge, attitudes, and behavior before the curriculum, and they were more likely to benefit from the curriculum when it was provided. These findings suggest two conclusions: (a) in comparison to male students, female students appeared more sensitive to suicide and its management, and (b) male students may require suicide awareness curriculums that differ from the kind we have been providing.

IMPLICATIONS AND APPLICATIONS

An important finding culled from the research we have described is the fact that males were significantly different from females on most of the suicide-related assessment measures. Sex differences were observed both before and after participation in the suicide curriculum. More important, males were less likely to benefit from the curriculum despite the fact that they started off at lower levels. This would suggest that two factors come into play when attempting primary prevention programs in schools: (a) gender differences may set certain limits on the response styles of the different sexes, and (b) females may be capable of benefiting from a program such as the one used in our studies, but males may need a program with a different focus or technique.

Whenever attempting to change someone's behavior, it is important to teach to their strengths, attempting to build on already-established abilities. As stated earlier, suicide curriculums for females may follow procedures similar to our program as it has been found reasonably effective. However, different programs may have to be developed for males. At this point, we can speculate on what changes may be necessary for males to benefit from a suicide prevention program. On the basis of our research, it might be suspected that sex differences in learning styles could play an important role in the inability of males to benefit from our suicide awareness curriculum. However, research examining sex differences in learning styles has failed to identify any consistent patterns that could explain our findings (21).

Sex differences in coping styles may play a role in suicide prevention. Previous research examining coping-style differences across adolescent males and females found consistent differences in both the type of problems experienced and the coping strategies used. Females report more problems with parents and fewer academic problems than boys (22). Gender seems to mediate the way in which life events are perceived, and therefore determines what is considered stressful (23). Furthermore, strategies for coping with problems differed by sex. As compared with males, females were more likely to use emotional regulation and social support and less likely to use wishful thinking (22). Again, the increased social tendencies in females are seen, perhaps reflecting higher levels of emotional expressiveness. Previous research has found adolescent females to be less inhibited and more sociable than same-aged males (24). This may be because males have traditionally been socialized into suppressing their emotional and tender side, rarely revealing their true emotions (25). Facilitating basic communication skills may be important for many adolescent males, and should help reduce the risk of death by suicide in adolescents (26).

The societal norms that influence helping behavior are different for males and females (27). Heroic helping of strangers is more characteristic of males, and the nurturant caring of someone in a long-term relationship is more characteristic of females. Thus, socialization and emotional regulation issues may again be playing a role in the assistance provided by males and females. These basic affiliation patterns could regulate adolescents' ability to both provide and receive assistance during a suicidal crisis.

Another area of concern relevant to gender differences pertains to empathy. Across the lifespan, females have been found to be more empathetic than males (28). It has been suggested that males may need special training to improve their sensitivity to nonverbal cues, learning how to decode nonverbal messages (29). Because of this, males may learn to focus more on action than emotion, even when affective reactions would be more appropriate (28). Suicide prevention programs may need to address these issues when working with male students.

Effective prevention programs attempt to strengthen the natural social support that is available for helping the distressed person cope with the problematic situation (30). Although such support can come from family members, friends, coworkers, or the broader community, our research suggests suicidal adolescents are most likely to benefit from social support that is available from their own peers.

In conclusion, empirical studies have identified a variety of sex differences that have implications for the primary prevention of suicidal behavior in adolescents. Teachers and counselors working with adolescents must be aware of these differences and address them as needed. Researchers must explore the possibility of developing more extensive training programs to confront these issues. In this way, we may be able to refine our attempts at primary prevention and enhance the effectiveness of suicide prevention programs.

REFERENCES

1. Kean, T. (1989). The life you save may be your own: New Jersey addresses prevention of adolescent problems. *American Psychologist, 44,* 828–830.
2. Klerman, G. (1987). Clinical epidemiology of suicide. *Journal of Clinical Psychiatry, 48*(Suppl.), 33–38.
3. Hawton, K. (1986). *Suicide and attempted suicide among children and adolescents.* Beverly Hills, CA: Sage.
4. Sudak, H., Ford, A., & Rushforth, N. (1984). Adolescent suicide: An overview. *American Journal of Psychotherapy, 38,* 350–363.
5. Miller, H., Coombs, D., Leeper, J., & Barton, S. (1984). An analysis of the effects of suicide prevention facilities on suicide rates in the United States. *American Journal of Public Health, 74,* 340–343.
6. Phillips, D., & Carstensen, L. (1986). Clustering of teenage suicides after television news stories about suicide. *New England Journal of Medicine, 315,* 685–689.
7. Shaffer, D., & Fisher, P. (1981). The epidemiology of suicide in children and young adolescents. *Journal of the American Academy of Child Psychiatry, 20,* 545–565.
8. Wetzel, R., Reich, T., Murphy, G., Province, M., & Miller, J. (1987). The changing relationship between age and suicide rates: Cohort effect, period effect or both? *Psychiatric Developments, 3,* 179–218.
9. Robbins, D., & Alessi, N. (1985). Depressive symptoms and suicidal behavior in adolescents. *American Journal of Psychiatry, 142,* 588–592.
10. Otto, U. (1972). Suicidal acts by children and adolescents. *Acta Psychiatrica Scandinavia* (Suppl.), *233,* 5–123.
11. Bettes, B., & Walker, E. (1986). Symptoms associated with suicidal behavior in childhood and adolescence. *Journal of Abnormal Child Psychology, 14,* 591–604.
12. Caplan, C., & Grunebaum, H. (1967). Perspectives on primary prevention: A review. *Archives of General Psychiatry, 17,* 331–346.
13. Hamburg, D., & Takanishi, R. (1989). Preparing for life: The critical transition of adolescence. *American Psychologist, 44,* 825–827.
14. Shaffer, D. (1989, April). *Research findings and some common beliefs about adolescent suicide and its prevention.* Paper presented at the Society for Research in Child Development biennial meeting, Kansas City, MO.
15. Beck, A. T., Rush, A., Shaw, B., & Emery, G. (1979). *Cognitive therapy of depression.* New York: Guilford Press.
16. Shaffer, D., Garland, A., Gould, M., Fisher, P., & Trautman, P. (1988). Preventing teenage suicide: A critical review. *Journal of the American Academy of Child and Adolescent Psychiatry, 27,* 675–687.
17. Spirito, A., Overholser, J., Ashworth, S., Morgan, J., & Benedict-Drew, C. (1988). Evaluation of

a suicide awareness curriculum for high school students. *Journal of the American Academy of Child and Adolescent Psychiatry, 27,* 705–711.

18. Solomon, R. (1949). An extension of control group design. *Psychological Bulletin, 46,* 137–150.
19. Offord, D. (1982). Primary prevention: Aspects of program design and evaluation. *Journal of the American Academy of Child Psychiatry, 1,* 225–230.
20. Overholser, J., Hemstreet, A., Spirito, A., & Vyse, S. (1989). Suicide awareness programs in the schools: Effects of gender and personal experience. *Journal of the American Academy of Child and Adolescent Psychiatry, 28,* 925–930.
21. Hyde, J. (1981). How large are cognitive gender differences? *American Psychologist, 36,* 892–901.
22. Stark, L., Spirito, A., Williams, D., & Guevremont, D. (1989). Common problems and coping strategies, I: Findings with normal adolescents. *Journal of Abnormal Child Psychology, 17,* 205–213.
23. Newcomb, M., Huba, G., & Bentler, P. (1986). Desirability of various life change events among adolescents: Effects of exposure, sex, age, and ethnicity. *Journal of Research in Personality, 20,* 207–227.
24. Kashani, J., Hoeper, E., Beck, N., Corcoran, C., Fallahi, C., McAllister, J., Rosenberg, T., & Reid, J. (1987). Personality, psychiatric disorders, and parental attitude among a community sample of adolescents. *Journal of the American Academy of Child and Adolescent Psychiatry, 26,* 879–885.
25. Richmond-Abbott, M. (1983). *Masculine and feminine: Sex roles over the life cycle.* Reading, MA: Addison-Wesley.
26. Motto, J. (1984). Suicide in male adolescents. In H. Sudak, A. Ford, & N. Rushforth (Eds.), *Suicide in the young* (pp. 227–244). Boston: John Wright.
27. Eagly, A., & Crowley, M. (1986). Gender and helping behavior: A meta-analytic review of the social psychological literature. *Psychological Bulletin, 100,* 283–308.
28. Hoffman, M. (1977). Sex differences in empathy and related behaviors. *Psychological Bulletin, 84,* 712–722.
29. Hall, J. (1978). Gender effects in decoding nonverbal cues. *Psychological Bulletin, 85,* 845–857.
30. Price, R., Cowen, E., Lorion, R., & Ramos-McKay, J. (1989). The search for effective prevention programs: What we learned along the way. *American Journal of Orthopsychiatry, 59,* 49–58.

III

SUICIDE INTERVENTION IN SCHOOLS

Intervention relates to the treatment and care of a suicidal crisis or a suicidal problem. It is doing something during the event. Many people, including those in schools, can serve as lifesaving agents. Nonetheless, professionally trained people continue to play the primary roles in intervention. Part III outlines what has been learned about intervening with young suicidal people. It consists of four chapters: an outline for crisis intervention in schools, the therapeutic care of the suicidal student, countertransference when counseling school-aged youth, and family therapy with suicidal children.

10

Crisis Intervention in Schools

Lee Ann Hoff
Northeastern University, Boston, Massachusetts

This chapter discusses crisis management for suicidal adolescents that balances psychological with sociocultural aspects of crisis and follow-up treatment. It underscores both the opportunity and the danger that crisis entails. The dangerous side of crisis is more prominent in several instances: when the crisis originates from sociocultural factors, when it interfaces with psychopathology, and when significant others fail to mitigate these dangers through immediate, appropriate response.

Using case examples, Chapter 10 reviews the signs of a developing crisis state (including suicide risk assessment) and suggests techniques that an empathetic informed person might use at different stages to prevent a crisis whenever possible, help a person work through a crisis successfully, or make a referral for additional assistance depending on individual responses to traumatic events and the resources available. One case focuses on crisis originating from unanticipated events like parental divorce and the normal stress of adolescence. The second case highlights the additional trauma of events such as incest and violence springing from sociocultural sources like gender and racial bias. Case analysis includes examination of what went wrong and suggests what natural crisis managers (parents, teachers, and friends) and formal crisis managers (counselors, school nurses, and therapists) might have done to prevent suicidal behavior. The context of analysis is North American society and the cultural values and social problems that must be addressed if the epidemic of adolescent suicide in contemporary society is to be curtailed.

RECOGNIZING ADOLESCENTS AT RISK FOR CRISIS

A crisis does not develop instantaneously. There are identifiable interacting stages of development leading to active crisis (1, 2). These stages are psychosocial in character and vary somewhat depending on the kind of traumatic event being experienced. Catastrophic, shocking events such as rape or receiving a diagnosis such as AIDS include (a) a period of shock or impact, (b) a period of recoil, and (c) a posttraumatic period (3). The response to less catastrophic stressors, such as the turmoil and upsets of adolescence, is more gradual. Recognizing these phases and intervening in a timely fashion can prevent a stressful life event from becoming a full-blown crisis.

Example 1: Jay—Crisis of situational–developmental origins. *Jay, age 17, is from an upper-middle-class family and excels in school, especially in literature and writing. Jay's father* *is a physician, and his mother is a management consultant. His sister Karen, age 24, is completing her MBA degree at a prestigious university and has already signed on for a high-paying job in an advertising agency. Jay's parents frequently express their "approval" of his plans to major in literature, but Jay nevertheless feels their apprehension that he might not make enough money in such a field. Jay would like to talk with his parents about this issue but feels they never have enough time. Jay learned recently that his parents plan to divorce as soon as he graduates from high school, so he feels he is in the way of their plans. When Jay took an overdose of pills after an argument with his father, everyone wondered why Jay was so unhappy when he seems to have everything going for him.*

Example 2: Leah—Crisis of sociocultural origins. *During a workshop on suicide, a woman presented the case of her 16-year-old foster daughter Leah. After suffering years of incest from her father and the painful secrecy that surrounds this crime, Leah finally went to her pastor for help. The pastor apparently did not believe her. He said, "Your father is a respected member of this community; go home and do as you're told." Some weeks later the father turned himself in to the police. The police said, "You know, some members of the community might be upset by what you've done, so why don't you leave town for awhile until things cool down." When a workshop participant suggested that Leah needed psychotherapy for her depression, Leah's foster mother impatiently responded, "She's had that and it hasn't stopped her from wanting to kill herself. How can my daughter ever be healed as long as people ignore what her father has done?"*

Who cares? In Jay's case, his family seemed to care, although the parent's goals *for* Jay outweighed their support of his own goals. In Leah's case, certainly the pastor and police officer did not seem to care. In what follows I consider the development of crisis, the dynamic relation between personal despair and social support, and how the suicidal behavior of these two young people might have been prevented.

Phase 1

Events like Jay's argument with his father and his parents' impending divorce cause an *initial rise in anxiety.* This initial shock sets in order a series of reactions culminating in a crisis, but in itself does not constitute crisis. This depends on what happens next. People usually respond to traumatic events with familiar problem-solving mechanisms to reduce the stress and discomfort arising from excessive anxiety. In Jay's case, he initially kept the news to himself, as he has a tendency to be a loner and finds it difficult to ask for help. He wanted to talk with his parents but did not have the courage to demand time of their apparently busy schedules. Jay thought that if he just kept to himself for awhile he would feel better. Also, he secretly wished his parents' divorce were over so he would not have to observe their tension and could decide where he wants to live. Jay enjoys taking with his sister, but when he got more depressed he convinced her to just leave him alone until he felt better.

Early responses in incest cases may include guilt, fear, depression, isolation, anxiety about normal social relationships, and vague physical symptoms (4). Leah felt guilty and isolated and frequently had abdominal pain. Once at age 10 when Leah saw the school nurse for a "stomach ache" she wanted to tell her about the incest, but the nurse seemed too busy and Leah felt ashamed.

Phase 2

In this phase, the person's *usual problem-solving ability fails,* while the stimulus causing the initial rise in anxiety continues. In Jay's case, he grew more despondent, and the longer he stayed by himself the more anxious he became. The thought of suicide was scary and he reconsidered talking with his parents about his career choice. Jay wanted to assert his ideas about a career but at the same time wanted his parents' approval. The possibility of acute crisis for Jay increased but was not inevitable. It depended on what happened next.

As for Leah, she felt increasingly depressed and guilty about the continued incest as she approached puberty and had considered telling her mother. She did not do so, however, for fear of breaking up the family because her parents did not get along well.

Phase 3

In this phase, the individual's *anxiety level rises further*. The increased tension moves the person to use every resource available—including unusual or new means—to solve the problem and reduce the increasingly painful state of anxiety. In Jay's case, when his best friend Erin (a male) noticed his increasing quietness and asked how Jay was feeling, they had the following conversation one day in the school locker room:

Jay: It's pretty bad, Erin . . . but I'll be OK. Hey, Erin, do you think I could stay at your place
        tonight?
Erin: Sure, Jay . . . no problem. But what's the trouble, Jay? You seem really down?
Jay: It's OK, Erin, I really don't want to talk about it . . . But on second thought, I think I better go
        home.
Erin: What's goin' on, Jay? Did you have another fight with your dad?
Jay: You got it, Erin. I 'spose he means well, but he won't get off my back . . . just wants me to make
        big money like he thinks my sister's gonna do. Can't see that their big money's made them very
        happy . . . I've had it.
Erin: What do you mean, Jay?
Jay: Never mind . . . Thanks anyway, Erin . . . maybe another time.

Asking to stay over with his best friend when he was depressed was a courageous act for Jay, but he was unable to take the extra step of accepting the opportunity to get away from the source of his anxiety and be with someone willing to talk about his distress (he felt too obliged to his parents). Jay's new problem-solving attempt did not work and he was in full-blown crisis. Erin was worried, did not know what else to say to Jay, but went to the track coach and expressed his concern. The coach suggested that Erin urge Jay to see the guidance counselor the next day.

Leah's creative problem solving consisted of going to her pastor, with the unfortunate result cited earlier, a full-blown suicidal crisis.

Phase 4

This phase is *state of active crisis* that results when (a) internal strength and social support are lacking or the person is unable to use existing support, (b) the person's problem remains unresolved, and (c) tension and anxiety rise to an unbearable degree.

Jay responded to his predicament by taking a bottle of 50 aspirin after a tense dinner with his parents.[1] He did not really want to die, but also did not know what else to do. When Erin dropped by later to see Jay, Jay said that his ears were ringing and that he felt sick to his stomach. In response to Erin's concern, Jay told him that he took the aspirin. Erin told Jay's parents and Jay was rushed to a local hospital.

These cases illustrate several points about the crisis experience. Although Jay is a normal adolescent, he was at risk for crisis on several counts. He faces the developmental challenge of achieving adult independence. It is therefore important for Jay to assert himself regarding his career interests. However, he has the simultaneous challenge of relating to his apparently unhappy parents and deciding which home he wants to live in when they divorce. Meeting these challenges would have been easier if Jay were not so reluctant to ask for help.

Besides these factors, Jay was still grieving over the loss of his best friend, Lance, by suicide, as he never really talked with anyone about how deeply Lance's death affected him. Thus, although Erin was there for Jay, he could not persuade him to accept at least the temporary relief of getting away from his parents. But Erin's suspicions were proved correct when he stopped by to check on Jay. These actions appear to have saved Jay's life.

In Leah's case, full-blown crisis and response by a suicide attempt might have been avoided if school and health personnel had picked up on the earlier behavior signs common to incest victims, and if the pastor had not blatantly colluded in victim-blaming when Leah asked for help. System failures like these most likely contribute to the large number of abused youth feeling forced into runaway status, with further abuse and suicide attempts often the tragic result (5, 6, 7). Also, the crisis aspect of incest usually occurs at the time of disclosure, not around incest episodes (4). Because disclosure usually catapults the entire family into crisis, it becomes imperative for crisis intervenors in schools to have ready access to family and sexual abuse experts when such a crisis erupts.

In short, with knowledge of early signs and the confidence that this conveys, the initial traumatic events—news of Jay's parents' divorce and abuse by incest—need not have led to full-blown crises that these teens were unable to resolve except through a potentially fatal suicide attempt. These cases also reveal that suicidal responses to traumatic life events most often do not occur in places where mental health specialists are immediately available. This fact highlights the importance of front-line persons like a best friend, a school nurse, a pastor, or a track coach, not only in preventing a full-blown crisis from developing in the first place, but also in saving lives when the situation becomes life-threatening.

IDENTIFYING SIGNALS OF DISTRESS

Let us return, then, to the beginning phases of these crisis situations and see how the natural crisis managers surrounding Jay and Leah approached an impending life crisis that culminated in a suicide attempt.

Without playing therapist, it is important for teachers, classmates, and athletic and health personnel to know enough about their students that a loner like Jay and

---

[1]In general, a lethal dose of medicine is 10 times the normal dose. All first-aid kits should contain Ipecac, a substance to induce vomiting, in the event that emergency medical facilities are not immediately available.

a child with chronic physical complaints like Leah would signal the need to note any unusual behaviors and raise further questions. In general, crisis intervention demands alertness to what has been called "crisis plumage," the signals of distress that tell one a person is having trouble coping with a stressful or traumatic life event (8). These signals of distress encompass the emotional, biophysical, cognitive, and behavioral aspects of human functioning (2, pp. 80–89).

The most central emotional and biophysical manifestation of crisis is high anxiety. Commonly experienced signs of anxiety include a sense of dread, fear of losing control, inability to focus on one thing, and physical symptoms such as sweating, frequent urination, diarrhea, loss of appetite, nausea and vomiting, tachycardia (rapid heart beat), headache, chest or abdominal pain, rash, menstrual irregularity, and social or sexual disinterest.

Feelings, especially high anxiety, have a great impact on perceptions and thinking processes, the cognitive signals of crisis. In crisis, one's attention is focused on the acute anxiety experienced and a few items concerning the crisis event. Jay, for example, could not get his mind off his father's response to his acceptance in a small liberal arts college instead of a more prestigious school. Leah was always preoccupied about keeping her secret. As a consequence, the person's usual memory and perception may be altered. He or she may have difficulty sorting things out and concentrating on school work. For example, Jay kept asking himself, should I accept money from my parents for a college they do not really approve of? Should I bury my plans and do what my father wants me to do? Should I toss in the towel and just leave home? Leah wanted to tell her mother about the incest but thought things could get worse if her mother did not believe her.

People in crisis often have trouble defining who they are and what their skills are. Their anguish and resulting confusion can alter their ability to make decisions and solve problems, the very skills needed during a crisis—hence, the need to temporarily "borrow" some ego functions from a caring, significant other. These extra stressors are doubly burdensome when added to the necessary developmental tasks of adolescence.

A disturbance in perceptual processes and problem-solving ability increases the person's already heightened anxiety state and may lead to the fear of going crazy or of losing control. This distorted perceptual process should not be confused with mental illness, in which a person's usual pattern of thinking is disturbed.

In a crisis state, this disturbance is considered a normal part of the crisis experience, with a rapid return to normal perception once the crisis is resolved. The best guide to making this important distinction is the person's history. If there is no record of mental disturbance or abnormal functioning, the temporary perceptual changes should be regarded as part of the crisis experience. The last thing that a young person in crisis needs is the additional burden of a psychiatric label or unnecessary psychiatric hospitalization at a time when problem-solving assistance and increased social support are most critical.

High anxiety and distorted perception can lead to unusual ways of behaving. Assessment of another's behavior as unusual, however, begins with ascertaining what *that person's* definition of what is usual is, not what one's own is. Thus, in Jay's case his quiet behavior may be "normal" for him, but when facing a stressful life event the tendency is to exaggerate such normal behavior to the point of dangerous isolation and refusal of the additional help needed for avoiding catastrophe during crisis.

In sexual abuse cases, although behavioral cues and other symptoms are generally more blatant, they are likewise ignored more often, partly because of the legacy of "Freudian seduction theory" and its dismissing sexual abuse claims as mere products of children's vivid fantasy life (4, pp. 9–11). Similarly, in other crises stemming from sociocultural sources such as racially motivated or antigay violence, behavioral cues can more easily be reconstructed into psychopathological terms as a means of bypassing the deeper social change such personal crises signal (7; 2, pp. 42–43).

In general, the most significant behavioral signs to look for in assessing distressed adolescents are (a) their ability to perform normal school functions and (b) changes in interpersonal relationships and normal behavior patterns. For students in another language community, an additional sign is the temporary loss of foreign language ability, which would increase anxiety still further.

UNCOVERING SUICIDAL CLUES
DURING CRISIS ASSESSMENT

In addition to identifying emotional, cognitive, and behavioral signals in a distressed person, it is incumbent on *all* people—natural and formal crisis managers—to learn the clues to suicide and how to respond to and refer a person at risk. These clues include

- Giving away prized possessions
- Despondency and distress following a critical life event
- A verbal message like Jay's "I've had it" or "I just can't take it anymore . . . something's got to give"
- Any behavior that is unusual for the individual, for example, eating more or less than usual[2]

Also, suicidal people typically have a history of failed communication; that is, young people in particular express their needs behaviorally rather than by directly asking for the help they need, or, as is often true of men, they more rigidly interpret the traditional social expectation that "real men don't ask for help." Suicidal people are also more inflexible in their thought patterns, for example, *"either* this thing works out, *or* life isn't worth living."

Successful intervention in schools during early phases of crisis development implies that faculty become thoroughly familiar with these signals and suicidal clues and comfortable in integrating this knowledge and preventive responses into their ordinary work as teachers and academic advisors, for example, observing death themes in essays.

STRATEGIES OF CRISIS PREVENTION
AND INTERVENTION

Broadly, prevention (of dangerous outcomes) and intervention (to aid in coping and to promote growth) are based on the level and adequacy of the person's

---

[2]Among young women with eating disorders, a significant number have been sexually abused. These figures suggest that the sociocultural context or origin of teenage self-destructiveness must be central in assessment and successful treatment of depression and prevention of suicide.

emotional, cognitive, and *behavioral* functioning, including suicidal clues and other signs of unhealthy coping. Specific strategies appeal to these distinctive areas, which are, of course, interrelated (2).

Listen Actively and with Concern

This is perhaps the most basic thing one can do to help, because a key complaint of adolescents is that adults do not listen to them and because without listening, rapport and trust cannot be built. Without trust, all other strategies might be useless. Listening intersects with the next technique.

Encourage the Open Expression of Feelings

Listening counteracts the tendency of people like Jay and Leah to bottle up feelings such as anger, loss, fear, and hopelessness. By encouraging people to express their feelings and by accepting those feelings without judgment, one can help a person in crisis to feel better immediately and learn a healthier coping style. In instances of acute loss—a common theme in crisis—open expression aids in the all-important process of "grief work." Leah, for example, was internally mourning the loss of her normal adolescence. Also, she feared losing her family altogether if she disclosed her secret, which in fact is what happened.

A useful technique to elicit emotional expression is role modeling, such as "If that happened to me I think I'd be very angry" (or upset, etc.) or (in the case of rape or incest) "Do you really think it's appropriate to blame yourself for someone else's wrongdoing?" For extreme anxiety and accompanying changes in biophysical functioning, relaxation techniques and physical outlets can be encouraged to direct the high energy of the crisis experience into constructive channels. This point underscores the pivotal role of athletic directors, who can not only pick up subtle changes in physical performance resulting from depression, but can also initiate communication with a depressed student who "drops out."

As important as listening and emotional or physical expression are, however, alone they are usually not enough. Therefore, strategies directed toward the cognitive and behavioral elements of the crisis are also important.

Help the Person Gain an Understanding of the Crisis

The student in crisis may ask, "Why did this have to happen to me?" This question is sometimes accompanied by self-blame. A person may curtail self-blame if helped to see the complex factors that contribute to emotional crisis. For example, if Leah (or a rape victim) blames herself for her victimization, she can be told that no matter what she did, the abuse was not justified. Similarly, a rape victim needs explicit assurance that her decision to hitchhike or drink too much does not make her responsible for someone else's violence (9). In another example, the survivor of a no-fault car accident in which a friend is killed may feel "survivor's guilt" which must be worked through. This introduces the following technique.

130 L. A. HOFF

Help the Individual Gradually Accept Reality

In catastrophic crisis situations, this is particularly difficult but nevertheless central. It means allowing the person some time initially to deny the reality that may be too shocking or painful to accept at once. Just being there, listening, and making empathetic statements helps people to eventually let go of the denial and accept the reality in small doses. In cases of particularly cruel or unfair treatment, one also must control the temptation to join the victim in blaming others. Instead of blaming, empathy and acceptance of the person's feelings can help the person to escape from the position of a victim and move on.

Engaging the person in decision-making around the crisis situation is central to the growth-promoting facet of the crisis experience. It allows the upset person to put distorted thoughts, chaotic feelings, and possible disturbed behavior into some kind of order and appeals to a person's need for self-mastery and control. This point is particularly important in dealing with *all* adolescents and with anyone who is suicidal, as power and control issues are often central to the crisis. In decision counseling, a person is helped to decide

- What problem is to be solved? "Jay, what's happening? You've been hanging out alone for days now. I'm worried and want to help."
- How is it to be solved? "What do you think would be most helpful?"
- When should it be solved? Erin: "Jay, how about the two of us going to the health service or to see the counselor?" Counselor or school nurse: "Leah, why don't you and your mother and I talk about this together so we can do what's best for you and your family?"[3]
- Who should be involved in solving it? "Jay, is there anyone else besides your English teacher whom you feel comfortable talking to?"

These kinds of questions lead to active *exploration of new ways to cope with problems,* such as asking for an appointment with the counselor and feeling like this is an okay thing to do and not a blow to one's pride. This strategy implies *linking the person to social support sources.* Not only does this relieve the suicidal person's sense of isolation, but innovative, contemporary rites of passage provide youth the formal group support that is often lacking in today's society, especially around such issues as changing sex roles, substance abuse, and violence.[4]

CENTRALITY OF COMMUNICATION
IN SUCCESSFUL CRISIS INTERVENTION

With awareness of specific crisis signals and the special needs of adolescents, let us consider intervention approaches in further detail. One of the tactics that distinguishes crisis intervention from traditional psychotherapy is the directive action of a would-be intervenor. A sensitive coach, teacher, or school nurse might pay special attention to behavior changes and notice the "absence" of a loner like Jay and Leah's periodic vague physical complaints. In Jay's case, it would be important on the one hand to respect his request to be left alone for awhile. One's

[3]It is understood that school personnel are fully informed of mandated reporting laws and procedures regarding child abuse.
[4]For a fuller discussion of this crisis prevention strategy, see Hoff (2, pp. 379–389).

interpretation of "awhile" in a case like this, however, should be quite a short time. This is because a prominent characteristic of loners and despondent people is their reluctance or inability (depending on the degree of depression) to ask for help. Ideally, then, someone (friend, teacher, parent) needs to reach out to distressed teens in a proactive way, that is, seeking them out, expressing concern, listening, and in general creating an atmosphere that will counteract any reluctance to ask for and use available help and to share possible thoughts of suicide. All of this is much easier and more fruitful, of course, if good rapport already exists and school personnel attempt to anticipate students' needs and take leadership in initiating communication with those less likely to make their needs known.

Such communication is unlikely, however, for those who still harbor the myth that talking with people suspected of being suicidal will put the idea into their heads. Clinical experience and extensive research with suicidal people reveal that nothing could be further from the truth. The process of deciding to commit suicide is much more complicated than that. A person who is not already suicidal will not become so by a direct question from someone intending to help. In fact, experience suggests that suicidal people are *relieved* when someone is sensitive enough to respond to their despair and thus to help protect them from themselves. Sharing the scary feelings of suicidal impulses becomes possible when empathy is conveyed and thus lessens the possibility of acting out the feelings.

Persistence in this common myth about suicide serves a purpose, as all myths do. In general, it prevents one from having to deal with the fearful prospect that the person may indeed admit to feeling suicidal and that one then has to do something to prevent it or else be responsible for another's death. So at least subliminally, many people reason that it is better to be silent and hope for the best.

Yet nothing is more important in crisis intervention for a potentially suicidal person than direct communication. First, communication is the only way to find out exactly what is going on and to *assess* the degree of suicidal risk. People convinced of its importance for an upset or despondent adolescent and who have conveyed concern and empathy might say, "Jay [Leah], you really seem down . . . What's going on? Is there anything I can do?" Most often this will elicit relief and a willingness to communicate further. If it does not, however, one nevertheless needs to follow up with something like, "I'm here if you need me; I'll check back with you later," or "How about going for a walk and getting out of your room for awhile?" Statements like these illustrate the second and third functions of direct communication: *prevention* and *intervention*.

When considering that suicidal people often have difficulty communicating and that a person who commits suicide ultimately feels cut off from the human community, caring communication is the single most important thing anyone can do for a person contemplating suicide. Conviction regarding this fact should dislodge the myth about putting the idea of suicide into someone's head by talking directly about it and free one's energy to develop with distressed teens other solutions to their problems. This might have included the school counselor's suggestion to Jay that they make a conference call to his parents, as Jay seemed unable to reach out to them on his own. At the very least, someone could have recommended that Jay contact a 24-hr teen hotline for support and emergency response.

Let us assume, however, that thee preventive tactics were not used and Jay had moved on to Phase 3 when his friend Erin arrived. Similar tactics are indicated here. In fact, Erin made a very appropriate beginning when he asked, "What do you mean, Jay [by 'I've had it']?"

If Erin had come from a school where suicide prevention programs have been developed as part of national youth suicide prevention efforts, he would have known not to let Jay off the hook with his "never mind." Instead, Erin might have continued with something like, "Jay, I'm worried about you. When you say you've had it, does that maybe mean that you're thinking of killing yourself over this?" A direct question like this, in the context of a caring attitude, will almost invariably be welcomed as an invitation to go on living, because someone cares enough to ask.

Also, instead of going to the coach on his own, it would have been preferable for Erin to persuade Jay to go with him. Such participatory (vs. dominant-subordinate) action builds on the principle of doing things *with* rather than *to* people, thus bolstering their sense of self-mastery. Failing that, however, Erin should nevertheless have told Jay that, out of his concern for Jay, he intended to get help from the coach or counselor. These directive actions, including as much participation as possible by the person in crisis, become necessary during acute crisis states because high anxiety usually interferes with one's ordinary decision-making ability. In cases like Jay's his reluctance to ask for help underscored the need for direct action.

SPECIAL INTERVENTIONS FOR VICTIMS IN CRISIS

For abuse victims like Leah, some additional strategies are indicated. When crisis originates from sociocultural sources, the emotional healing process takes on a different tone than for those originating in developmental transitions or expected life events. This is because the crisis resolution process includes whatever people do to *explain* to themselves why traumatic events happen to them; that is, the event must fit into one's meaning system (10). Thus, among those whose emotional trauma originates from the social act of violence rooted in gender, racial, or other bias or social neglect, healing requires some kind of *social* response (11, 12). In practice, this means that a victim like Leah needs to hear from a community representative that her abuser—*not she*—is accountable for the abuse. Failure to incorporate this kind of *public* response into crisis intervention in such cases constitutes collusion in victim-blaming, which usually evolves into self-blame, depression, and danger of suicide (13, 14). Victim compensation policies are based on recognition of this dynamic. It is reasonable to conclude, therefore, that if, on her courageous decision to disclose, Leah's pastor had advocated for her rather than defending her abuser, she might never have become suicidal. Significantly, Leah's foster mother understood the link between Leah's continued suicidality and the failed mediation on her behalf—even with on-going psychotherapy.[5]

FOLLOW-UP AFTER ACUTE CRISIS EPISODES

These actions usually suffice in the immediate crisis situation. However, adolescents like Jay and Leah are vulnerable to other crisis episodes, and possibly suicide, depending on what kind of crisis specialty and follow-up services are avail-

---

[5]The common practice of removing *victims* from their homes rather than their abusers affirms in the victims' minds that they are the ones responsible for the abuse (4).

able. In general, even though Jay is known as a loner and has a less-than-harmonious family background, he is academically successful, is well liked by classmates, and has no history of psychological or behavioral problems. This suggests that Jay does not need psychiatric treatment. However, Jay's loner behavior and reluctance to communicate his needs seem to have increased his vulnerability to acute crisis when confronted with unusual challenges during the normal turmoil of adolescence. He therefore might benefit from counseling or psychotherapy in order to gain insight into this behavior and become comfortable with more healthy coping styles. Longer-term follow-up therapy after resolution of the acute crisis extends the learning potential of a crisis experience. A general rule of thumb is that follow-up psychotherapy is indicated for anyone who responds to a life crisis with a suicide attempt. This highlights the *opportunity* aspect of crisis: One's less-than-healthy response to a stressful life event can be the occasion for learning more about oneself and why one approaches life's ups and downs in certain ways. For adolescents, family therapy is the follow-up treatment of choice whenever possible. If a family approach (in addition to individual psychotherapy) had been used in Leah's case, she might not have continued to feel suicidal, as the focus would have been away from her purported psychopathology.

Similar principles apply if one discovers an acutely upset person who has a psychiatric history or a record of generally troublesome behavior and inadequate coping with everyday issues and demands.

GROUP APPROACHES TO INDIVIDUAL CRISIS

This brings us to the issue of response to and by the group as a whole when an individual student is in crisis for whatever reason or responds to a stressful life event with suicide, violence, or other negative behaviors. Life-threatening events, no matter where they occur, almost invariably elicit anxiety reactions and fear in the surrounding group. These responses are heightened in proportion to the closeness of the individual's relationship to the group.

In cases of suicide attempts or completed suicide, this phenomenon has been well documented in "cluster" suicides among young people (5). Such reactions are explained in terms of bonding among peer group members, learned behavior, and the misguided belief by some that suicidal tendencies are "contagious," which can result in a self-fulfilling prophecy.

When a person in one's group is victimized by violence, fear for one's own safety is one of the most common responses, along with the desire for revenge because of the false belief that the best way to handle violence is with more violence. In both kinds of crisis situation, one must also contend with the fact that taboos have been broken, the violation of which threatens the stability of the social fabric.

The powerful emotions of fear, anger, and anxiety that life-threatening behaviors can arouse are in themselves very frightening. Hence, the approach that many take is to try to keep the incident quiet, saying as little to the group as possible in the misguided belief that the fear and anger will thus be controlled and the group's anxiety level reduced. Nothing could be further from the truth.

The principle of open, direct communication with a suicidal person that is so central to successfully helping the individual student applies equally to the group. It is critical, therefore, to quell the impulse to keep things quiet and hope things will calm down. Basically the principal, guidance director, faculty member, or even one of the students, perhaps with some peer counseling experience, should call the group together as soon as possible.

Confidentiality should not be an issue here. First, the grapevine about a crisis event is highly effective, so almost everyone knows about it anyway; this knowledge and the anxiety it engenders should be channeled so that the group's energy and resources can be mobilized on behalf of the suicidal individual or survivors in crisis.

Second, to protect the individual's privacy rights and yet activate the group's resources on his or her behalf, the principal or whoever talks with the individual lays the foundation for group response with a statement such as,

> *Jay, since you took the aspirin everyone is worried and scared. I think we should have a meeting so you can explain your situation yourself and stop the rumors that won't do you or any one else any good. I know people are concerned, so it's better that you be there so we can all pull together on this.*

Bolstered with facts and confidence in the importance of open communication about anxiety-laden topics like suicide and violence, a principal or faculty member can more easily remain calm and bring some order and direction into the inherently chaotic nature of a crisis situation. If the principal's calm attitude does not beget calm, at least the group will not have to deal with the additional stressor of a principal's hysteria.

Many people underestimate the power of group members to pull together and take advantage of the high tension of a crisis situation to use existing strengths of members and develop innovative ways of solving a problem. It is not unlike the pilot or airline attendant enhancing personal resources for a sick passenger by asking the group if a physician or nurse is on board to help. Individuals like Jay and Leah are helped during crisis, but the group has also taken a forward step in the human community of natural and formal crisis managers.

REFERENCES

1. Caplan, G. (1964). *Principles of preventive psychiatry.* New York: Basic Books.
2. Hoff, L. A. (1989). *People in crisis: Understanding and helping* (3rd ed.). Redwood City, CA: Addison-Wesley.
3. Tyhurst, J. A. (1951). Individual reactions to community disaster. *American Journal of Psychiatry, 107,* 764–769.
4. Herman, J. L. (1981). *Father-daughter incest.* Cambridge, MA: Harvard University Press.
5. Coleman, L. (1987). *Suicide clusters.* Winchester, MA: Faber & Faber.
6. Russell, D. (1986). *The secret trauma: Incest in the lives of girls and women.* New York: Basic Books.
7. Gil, D. G. (1987). Sociocultural aspects of domestic violence. In M. Lystad (Ed.), *Violence in the home: Interdisciplinary perspectives.* New York: Brunner/Mazel.
8. Hansell, N. (1976). *The person in distress.* New York: Human Sciences Press.
9. Washaw, R. (1988). *I never called it rape.* New York: Harper & Row.
10. Antonovsky, R. (1980). *Health, stress and coping.* San Francisco: Jossey-Bass.
11. Lifton, R. J., & Olson, E. (1976). The human meaning of total disaster: The Buffalo Creek experience. *Psychiatry, 39,* 1–18.
12. Sales, E., Baum, M., & Shore, B. (1984). Victim readjustment following assault. *Journal of Social Issues, 40*(1), 117–136.
13. Cloward, R. A., & Piven, F. F. (1979). Hidden protest: The channeling of female innovation and resistance. *Sign: Journal of Woman in Culture and Society, 4,* 651–669.
14. Newberger, C. M., Melnicoe, J. H., & Newberger, E. H. (1986). The American family in crisis: Implications for children. *Current Problems in Pediatrics, 16*(12), 674–721.

11

Therapeutic Care of the Suicidal Student

Kim Smith
The Menninger Clinic, Albuquerque, New Mexico

Once a student has been identified as being potentially suicidal, various interventions should occur. The student's parents should be notified and involved, and the student should receive individual attention in the form of crisis intervention and therapy. But what should parents and school personnel reasonably expect of a sound treatment process for the identified student? What are the standards of care that follow the identification of a seriously depressed or suicidal student? There has been no formal dialogue about such standards, so this chapter begins that discussion. It focuses on therapy for the suicidal high school or college student, because teenagers aged 15–19 accounted for 88% of the completed suicides by people under age 20 in 1986 (1). Finally, where appropriate, distinctions are made between the processes of crisis intervention and therapy.

INITIAL ASSESSMENT ISSUES

Regardless of how the suicidal student is identified, it is crucial to make an initial assessment of the individual's imminent risk for suicidal action. A person's actual willingness to act on serious suicidal inclinations is generally brief, lasting from a few hours to a day or two, but that willingness can quickly return full force with little provocation. Thus, the assessment should be performed expeditiously, face to face with the student. It should be done by a school staff member who has been trained to perform such evaluations and who has demonstrated competence in the area. One way to ensure that the person possesses the minimum skills to perform such evaluations involves checking credentials; for example, "Individual Certification" from the American Association of Suicidology illustrates such competencies. If the student is judged to be in imminent suicidal danger, then the parents should be contacted so that protective, crisis intervention steps can be taken. Although the time immediately after crisis stabilization is usually inappropriate for beginning a reflective therapeutic process, decisions are required about whether and with whom to enter therapy. Up through their mid-teens, students usually benefit most from family therapy. Sometimes the family is so resistant and destructive, however, that the student needs the support and corrective investment of an individual therapist. For the older high school student, individual therapy may be preferable to a family process for several reasons. The individual structure of the therapy supports individuation, because the student's private thoughts and feelings are not diffused into the family process. Also, in this age group the issues concern relationships outside the family more than those with family members per se. Nevertheless, the family's propensity for symbiotic processes should be assessed; if these processes are strong, then family work is necessary. In addition, when the reasons for the suicidal ideation or action seem vague, muddy, and not compelling, then the therapist should become more suspicious that the student is acting out for the family. Thus, a thoughtful decision—after appraisal of the circumstances—should be made about whether individual or family therapy is most appropriate. The structure or type of therapy shapes the types of goals that can be attained.

CONCEPTUALIZING THE SUICIDE SYMPTOM

Suicidal behaviors that are motivated by a variety of feelings and wishes have various aims or purposes. Suicide is the acting out of a symptom; that is, it is motivated by the resultant compromise between destructive and adaptive forces. To attempt to find *the* cause of the suicide would be a serious oversimplification. Searching for a single cause is apt to highlight only the triggering agent (e.g., a breakup with a boyfriend or a fight with a parent).

Because suicide is not a succinct disease entity, such as pneumonia, it is difficult to predict its occurrence or even to recognize its antecedents in a person's character structure. To treat the suicidal student, a therapist must therefore keep in mind that people arrive at suicidal thoughts by different paths and by wishes to achieve different, often conflicting goals. Therapists should also appreciate that the impetus and meaning of suicide for a given individual can be understood and then examined in a therapeutic process.

Certain generalizations about suicide can help conceptualize the therapeutic tasks. The first is that suicidal behaviors, regardless of their seriousness, are indications that the student is feeling impotent and potentially out of control about a current, seemingly vital life transaction. Second, suicidal behavior appeals to the person as a tool to help him or her regain a personal sense of power and control. Although a student may have no intention of dying, suicide-like behaviors usually serve to make significant others feel more responsive or affectively punished for perceived neglect or rejection.

To those students who are willing to actually take their life, suicide can be seen as causing or preventing the occurrence of certain consequences that they are otherwise powerless to influence. For example, when a 17-year-old girl named Alexis was restricted from going on an important date because she had stubbornly and repeatedly violated her curfew, she hung herself at the time the date was to have occurred. Alexis had told her best friend that she would prevent her mother from controlling her and humiliating her. Her suicide was a powerful action that was partially motivated by her determination to prevent or negate a sense of herself as being powerless. Her suicide may also have been compelled by her angry wish to cause her mother to hurt forever because she had so deeply frustrated and hurt Alexis.

These motivations would have been conscious or close to Alexis's awareness, but they were, of course, only derivatives of an even deeper and more empowering set of unconscious constructs. In certain types of therapy, uncovering these constructs is desirable. Whether a therapist focuses primarily on conscious or unconscious motivations depends on the therapist's style of working and on the patient's psychological or emotional resources.

ALWAYS DIAGNOSE

With all suicidal and depressed students, diagnosis is essential. A formal *Diagnostic and Statistical Manual of Mental Disorders* (third edition, revised; 2) diagnosis is a beginning point that helps the therapist conceptualize such things as the student's level of ego organization, the duration of symptoms, the presence of associated substance abuse, the impact of environmental stresses, and the presence of affective disorder. As many as 70% of the youth who commit suicide may have an affective disorder (3, 4) for which medication is often helpful. Treating an affective illness without appropriate antidepressive medication is substandard work that is bound to lessen the impact of otherwise sound psychological interventions.

Some seemingly withdrawn, depressed youth are actually attempting to fend off psychological disorganization. Cues of such disorganization are strained obsessional defenses, peculiar word usage, paranoia-tinged concerns, overly inferential logic, sudden intense rages, and social withdrawal. When such behaviors are noted, a more detailed workup, often including a battery of psychological tests, is warranted. As with affective disorders, medications to help tighten defenses against psychotic processes may be an indispensable part of the treatment. Of course, when drug or alcohol use (not just abuse) is involved, those substances must be discontinued during the diagnostic and treatment processes. If this is not possible for the student, a direct focus on the substance dependence or addiction, often with an inpatient component, must be made before further therapy can be successful. If the patient is admitted to an inpatient substance abuse unit, the therapist must clearly inform the admitting staff that the patient is seriously depressed and is a potential suicide.

SPECIAL ISSUES IN THE THERAPY

Although these formal diagnostic issues are important, the therapist must also develop more subtle and dynamic diagnostic formulations about the timing of the student's suicidal impulse and about the conscious and unconscious aims of the suicidal impetus. This aspect of diagnosis is actually an integral part of therapy that is accomplished with therapeutic skills such as empathic resonance, clarifications, mild confrontations, and nongenetic, non-transference-based interpretations. Clinicians must therefore listen to *how* the student responds to such interventions even more than to *what* the student relates.

Among adolescents, for example, there is a common area of divergence between the patient's response to the therapist and the content of what the patient reports. This divergence occurs around the person's ability to make use of helping figures. Some youth will complain that no one understands or listens to them, which causes them to feel alone and alienated. The therapist may observe, however, that such patients easily become contemptuous or angry whenever anyone attempts to be empathic. The therapist may also observe a countertransference reaction that involves an emotional retreat, a loss of interest in the patient's point of view, and a tendency to overcontrol and tell the patient what is "wrong" with him or her. Dynamic conflicts associated with suicide despondency are evident in the patient's spoiling negation of others' efforts to empathetically connect and in the therapist's knowledge of the reactive tendencies that this stimulates.

A gentle confrontation of the patient will help establish that the patient's dependency conflicts are part of the suicide problem. The way that patients respond to this confrontation is indicative of their defensive tendencies and of their ability to have their observing ego stimulated into recognizing such self-defeating behavior. Such therapeutic interventions can help establish whether, at least for the moment, a patient can become introspectively curious about unconscious motivations rather than automatically act on them.

The clinician must achieve a clear understanding of the student's logic of why suicide makes sense or is the "only" thing that can be done in the given circumstance. Gaining this appreciation requires that the therapist obtain the student's perspective on his or her family, special relationships, peer and classroom pressures, and so forth. The therapist begins this process of understanding by communicating an acceptance of why the patient is suicidal, as well as an uncontentious puzzlement about the patient's "logical" conclusion to commit suicide.

Sometimes the patient's logic can be fairly compelling, as with 15-year-old Meg, who was pregnant. She was aware of her mother's strong pro-life stand on abortion and believed that her parents would "kill" her if they found out she was pregnant. She did not like the father well enough to marry him, nor did she believe she could support herself and a baby. Her physician father and psychologist mother had long held ambitions for her to obtain advanced degrees. Every possible non-suicidal solution to her problem seemed blocked, resulting in Meg's perception that killing herself was the only way out of her dilemma.

Another "reasonable" explanation was offered by 16-year-old Mark, who had been diagnosed as a diabetic at age 9. He lived with his mother and young brother, supported only by his mother's work and occasional, unpredictable financial assistance from his maternal grandfather. Mark's diabetes had been troublesome and costly to his mother, who often discussed the problem with anyone who would listen. Mark's healthy, younger brother was more attractive, popular, and athletically talented, which caused Mark to feel even more flawed and devalued. Mark's eyesight and one kidney were seriously threatened by his poorly controlled blood sugar level, which often ranged between 450–600 mg/dl (80–130 mg/dl is the normal range). Mark hated his restrictive diet, which precluded consumption of many of the foods popular with teenagers and made him feel all the more outcast. He believed that his diabetes would only worsen and that he would be progressively isolated from the acceptance and admiration he so wanted. His present life seemed excruciatingly painful, but his future seemed unbearable. Suicide was the only way Mark could imagine having an impact on his own fate.

The problems faced by both Meg and Mark had significant family components to them. Meg's busy parents relied excessively on rules and rigid adherence to structure to keep the family functioning and to ensure predictable, albeit meager, nurturance. Neither parent had received much love or attention as a child, so they therefore had little to give Meg. In spite of this handicap, both parents cared deeply for Meg, and after their initial shock at her pregnancy and suicidal state of mind, they were able to help her explore alternatives. The hardest task faced by the therapist was to convince Meg of the wisdom of a joint session with her parents. Meg's desperation ultimately served as a stimulus for the family to reflect on how poorly their individual needs were being met, including the parents' needs for intimacy. Meg decided not to have an abortion but instead carried the baby to term and then gave it up for adoption.

Unlike Meg's parents, Mark's mother refused to participate in his therapy, choosing to see Mark's desperation as yet another burden he inflicted on the family. Mark was seen in individual psychotherapy of a mildly supportive, mainly expressive nature (insight oriented and interpretive of unconscious processes). The initial work centered on the function of his suicide wishes. If he placed himself into the diabetic coma he imagined, he would be saying to his illness "Fuck you! I will eat what I want and kill you." Also, he thought that killing himself would relieve his mother of her pain and would allow her to be happy. He was willing to commit suicide, then, partly because he loved her. His anger at her grew, however, as it dawned on him that his mother seemed to have long wished for him to die. The cathartic release of these intense affective discoveries began to supplant Mark's suicide wish. At one point, he raged that he would not "buy her peace of mind" with his death. In spite of his overt anger, his blood sugar level dropped below 200, which he viewed as a sign that he did not have to swallow his anger and die for his mother. Several months after entering therapy, Mark required a kidney transplant. Because of Mark's lingering resentment toward his family, the hospital staff refused to accept a kidney from any of Mark's relatives out of concern that his body would reject it.

These brief vignettes necessarily oversimplify the complex, long-term therapy processes of these cases. They do illustrate, however, that the logic of "reasonable" rationalizations that conclude that suicide is the only option can be made to give way to more complex perspectives in which suicide becomes less compelling.

In other cases, the logic makes absolute sense to the student but is only vaguely plausible to the clinician, for example, the boy who becomes suicidal in response to the rejection of a lover; the girl who feels worthless and "ruined" because of date rape; the girl who is angry and humiliated by her mother's restrictions on her social activities; and the boy who always feels misunderstood and wrongly accused by parents, teachers, and even his friends. These are the types of patients that clinicians are most likely to see.

In most instances, therapists will discover that the youth's angry despondence about a painful precipitating event has its roots in active family dynamics. A crisis intervention approach alone will usually not venture into the murky waters of family issues unless the patient persistently directs attention to them. Instead, a crisis intervention approach tries to identify areas of support in the family rather than to elucidate conflicts. Therapists who use a crisis approach focus on relieving the tension that arises from the problems presented by the patient and also strive to infuse hope, simplify the problems, and identify reasonable alternatives. Individual and family therapy, however, with their common goal of resolving conflict (as opposed to stopping a suicide) encourage such exploration.

Clinicians will occasionally see a student whose suicide logic is difficult to appreciate. Often these students seem to have abundant personal resources; however, on "stubbing their toes," they are plunged into suicidal rage or despondency.

One such student was 18-year-old Julie Ann, who ultimately destroyed herself with a shotgun blast. She had won state beauty contests, graduated second in her high school class, and made "all state" in golf. Her parents were admired by the community for their business acumen, their social generosity, and their civic investment. At the end of Julie Ann's first semester at college, however, she was admitted to an inpatient unit because she had become acutely suicidal as a result of a skin condition. In treating a facial pimple, she had developed swollen, purplish welts in reaction to a prescribed medication. The inpatient staff members were astonished when Julie Ann asserted that the welts were the cause of her suicide wishes.

A family history revealed that Julie Ann's seemingly perfectly happy parents had separated and become engaged in bitter divorce proceedings when she had first left for college. Julie Ann had then begun to have trouble with her grades and in her peer relationships. Her grumpy, moody, withdrawn demeanor was unappealing and caused others to avoid her. By late in the semester, before her complexion problem occurred, she had already become quite depressed.

The treatment team began to understand that Julie Ann's suicide ideation had erupted as an escape from the sudden and rapid deterioration of her "perfect" family and her "perfect" self. The team interpreted to Julie Ann that although she was focused on her blemished face, it was her blemished life that was producing her despair. She acknowledged that she was upset about her parents' impending divorce and her school difficulties but reiterated that she was *suicidal* because of the welts.

The staff members continued their interpretive work by pointing out that Julie Ann had seemed to be doing fine until she had received news of her parents' separation. Only then had she seemed depressed, as indicated by her difficulty concentrating on her studies, her irritability, her withdrawal from social interactions, her need to sleep 12–15 hr a day, her loss of appetite, and her apathy about school. She responded to this interpretation by becoming more adamant that those were not the reasons for her feeling worthless and wanting to die.

This antagonistic struggle lasted several days until one evening Julie Ann said that she suddenly realized that what the staff had been saying was true. She indicated that their confrontations suddenly made a lot of sense to her and that just acknowledging that made her feel better and less depressed. Julie Ann telephoned her father to come pick her up.

The treatment team realized that this sudden reversal was either a conscious avoidance of treatment or an unconsciously motivated flight into health. They advised against her leaving, because severely depressed people rarely experience such an obvious and major adjustment to their views of themselves and others without intensive, long-term therapy. Julie Ann skillfully convinced her father, however, that she was better and that the "excellent staff" were just being "overly protective." She left the hospital against medical advice and killed herself 3 days later.

This vignette illustrates the point that the therapist must first accept the student's explanation of why suicide is desirable. Then, with compassion and curiosity, the therapist must ask the patient for help in understanding how it is that feeling devastated about a seemingly minor problem, such as one's appearance, can lead to a conclusion to commit suicide. Usually the patient will respond by reviewing these self-perceptions, but with more elaboration.

In Julie Ann's case, on the basis of other comments she made to staff members, she may have also been anxious that her classmates would always regard her with pity as "that poor girl with all those ugly welts." The therapist could have thoughtfully responded that this might indeed make Julie Ann feel angry and hurt and asked her, "help me to understand how that can make you feel that life is no longer worth living." This type of interchange is generally experienced by patients as an attempt to understand them, which often results in an acceptance of the therapist's encouragement to delve more deeply into the reasons for the suicidal impulse.

Had this unhurried, listening, and accepting but clarifying paradigm continued, Julie Ann might well have revealed that the thought of being pitied made her hate herself and those who pitied her. She had always been able to achieve whatever she wanted and had always been able to fix or have her parents fix any problem in her life. Now she was one of those people to whom she had formerly felt superior and on whom she had bestowed "kindness." This acknowledgement could have opened the door to Julie Ann's fractured, narcissistic sense of perfection, which the treatment team had correctly diagnosed as the core of her despondency. The hospital staff members, who were certainly invested in working with the patient, were correct in many of their understandings of Julie Ann. However, they were so eager to help her that they did not take the time to explore what was on the other side of the door she had opened.

As bizarre as it seemed, Julie Ann was indeed suicidal because of her welts, to which she had bound her worries and anger about her unconscious conflicts, her shattered expectations of herself and family, and her defenses against fully experiencing her devastation. Suicide is often the final defense against accepting crushed views of oneself and one's future. Karl Menninger has often said that the patient is always right; that is just up to the therapist to be diligent enough to find out how.

Another characteristic of the therapy of suicidal patients is its constant focus. The therapy should remain focused on understanding the dynamics of the suicide while maintaining a vigilance for changes, usually environmental, that might increase the risk of imminent suicidal action.

An unfocused therapy that allows the student to wander over the entire landscape of his or her mind, or, as is even more common, to seize on and obsessively overwork the superficial aspects of the current problem, is often indicative of the therapist's paralyzing anxiety in response to the patient's intense suicide ideation. The lack of focused, judicious activity (e.g., sharpening comments, requesting clarification, and presenting interpretations about the functions of the death wish) can convey to the patient that the therapist feels similarly outwitted and helplessly trapped by events. On the other hand, only in crisis management should therapists suggest that they have *the* answer or solution.

COMMUNICATING HOPE

Therapists should allow their confidence in the therapeutic process and their hope for resolution to be *implicitly* evident to their patients. It is best to indirectly communicate hope that a patient can, with the therapist's consultation, view his or her life differently. By carefully listening and responding with empathy, the therapist conveys a sense of the patient's worth, which fuels hope.

Empathy, however, is rarely sufficient in itself. Just as important is the therapist's attention to the patient's action-oriented defenses against therapeutic work, such as late arrivals, attempts to finish early, long silences, or even verbosity. These defensive maneuvers reflect the patient's discouragement and subtle self-deprecation, as if he or she were not worth the therapist's time. Guarding against even the suggestion of an anxious need to rescue, the therapist's activity conveys caring and hopefulness.

In all cases, the therapist must resist the urge to promise the impossible or minimize the seriousness of the patient's problems. Narcissistic and action-prone patients will occasionally minimize their suicide ideation and even their past attempts at suicide. These young, high-risk students usually approach therapy in a detached and uninvolved manner. They may have a history of many prior therapies, none of which was particularly successful. Their often haughty demeanor is a defense against the rejection they associate with attachment, but it often elicits distancing, rejecting responses from their therapists.

For such patients, the therapy itself threatens further failure and disillusionment. As a result, when the therapy becomes confrontational and difficult, they often flee without notice. Therapists must learn to anticipate these issues from the beginning and convey to the patient the serious, life-threatening nature of the depressive disorder.

By conveying this sober evaluation, the therapist reassures the patient that the seriousness of the patient's pain is understood. Feeling understood usually stimulates hopefulness. Such preparatory work also enables the patient to anticipate, understand, and allay the impulse to flee as it emerges.

THERAPEUTIC USE OF HOPELESSNESS

It is often surprising to read in the literature and to hear from other clinicians that the best response to a suicidal person's hopelessness is a vigorous attempt to remove or negate the hopelessness and then to infuse the suicidal person with hope. In such cases, the therapist treats hopelessness as a toxic affective state that must be removed before the patient is destroyed.

The surprising aspect of this view is that it ignores the specific understanding of what the patient is feeling hopeless about. If one asks the patient what he or she is hopeless about, the response will usually be "everything." However, if asked, "but what do you feel *most* hopeless about," the patient can usually be much more specific (e.g., "I'm hopeless . . . that I'll ever have a decent relationship with a woman"; "that I can ever make my husband happy"; "that I'll ever be good enough for my father"; "that I'll ever stop screwing things up"). When the therapist and the patient can reduce the suicidal malaise from a vague feeling about everything in life to a state of hopelessness involving something specific, then the problem is in a form that allows further therapeutic work.

How the therapist next approaches the patient's hopelessness depends on the nature of the therapeutic process. In crisis work, it is not useful to define hopelessness as a therapeutic problem. The parallel task in crisis intervention is to break the patient's stated problems down into solvable components. The overall goal is to stabilize the situation by simplifying and reframing the "unsolvable" problem to make it solvable.

In psychotherapy, however, avoiding a direct focus on the hopelessness dilutes the effectiveness and significance of the therapy. Many therapists, especially those more oriented to short-term and cognitive psychotherapies, find that patients' conscious beliefs about their suicidal motivations are a suitable basis from which to work. Other therapists will want to examine the underpinning of these conscious constructs in order to evaluate the realism in the patient's expectations of self and others.

The case of Jason, a smallish 16-year-old, illustrates how faulty such expectations can be. Jason often attempted to feel "big" and equal to other boys by "not taking anything off of them." He entered therapy after attempting to electrocute himself when a girl with whom he was infatuated suddenly became interested in an older, taller, and more athletic boy.

Although Jason survived the attempt, he remained sullen, angrily depressed, and rejecting of help. His resistance began to dissolve, however, as he responded to the therapist's inquiry about his hopelessness. "I'll never be able to get the girl I want," Jason stormed. When the therapist asked why that might be, he replied that girls never took him seriously. "They think I'm 'cute' or a 'good friend.' "

The therapist asked again why that might be. After a long silence, Jason said that he was "too short . . . girls want tall guys with a great build . . . I always believed I'd grow out of this but I'm 16 and I'm not tall, so there's no sense in going on!" Later, he added that his mother always "smothered" him and told others how "cute" he was. As a result, he felt he needed to become tall and strong in order to break away from her. She humiliated him and made him feel like a little boy. He imagined that all girls saw him as a "cute little boy."

Several aspects of Jason's self–other expectations stimulated his hopelessness and were important to the therapy, including his self-hatred for his perceived defectiveness and his cocky, boorish efforts to prove his manliness. He faultily assumed that such a swaggering demeanor impressed others rather than put them off.

His hopelessness about growing taller, however, was probably realistic and reflected his good judgment. To constantly hold out hope for significant growth would only continue his angry depression. This time-consuming work was exceedingly difficult, because Jason's hope for additional growth tended to resurface with media coverage of hormone-induced growth experiments. In fact, Jason was at the lower limit of the normal range of height for his age, so he was not a suitable candidate for endocrine treatment.

Finally, Jason's struggle to separate from his mother was of major importance. He learned the power of using words to express his exasperation to his mother and, during a family process, persistently addressed her tendency to hang on to him as her "baby." Because she had been unable to bear more children, she felt like a failure. Pretending that Jason was still her baby was part of her denial. When she finally saw how destructive her tendencies were, she backed off but became depressed and required her own individual treatment.

EXPECTATIONS OF THE THERAPIST

Therapists who treat suicidal patients should have some specific preparation for their work. They should give careful, systematic thought to their concept of suicide and to what modifications of their therapeutic technique it might require. Special seminars or workshops on the psychotherapeutic issues generated by suicidal patients are warranted, because most graduate programs, including residency training programs, do not study suicide sufficiently.

Beyond their formal training, therapists of the suicidal patient should have certain personal characteristics, including the capacity to recognize their own aggression. Because suicidal patients feel miserable, they often consciously make others angry or unconsciously attempt to provoke their hostile impulses.

Therapists who have difficulty recognizing their own anger, or who too readily and intensely feel and act angrily, are not going to work well with a suicidal patient. The patient will evoke the therapist's hostility and then feel more wounded and rejected by the therapist's response to that provocation. When the therapist acts out or displays anger, it may further damage the patient's vulnerable, quixotic internal sense of goodness and worth. This reaction increases the risk that suicidal action will be seen as a tool to stop the painful deterioration of the "good" self and as a weapon to hatefully destroy the "bad" self (and "bad" other, including the therapist).

Several authors have described the suicidal patient's impact on the therapist's unconscious processes and treatment of the patient (e.g., 5–7). In a particularly clear articulation of the therapist's contributions to suicide, Zee (7) pointed out that some therapists may be unable to recognize or therapeutically express the hostile feelings that the patient stimulates. Instead, the hostility comes out in a "kill them with kindness" approach. Suicidally prone patients are often painfully aware of their envy, rage, and wishes for others to also feel miserable. Because of their positive regard for the therapist, these patients also guiltily worry about harming the "good" therapist who is so allied with their own wish to emerge from pain. Therapists who have difficulty acknowledging their patients' hostility toward them can cause their patients to feel diminished, unworthy, and guilty, as if the patients were very bad children standing before an all-seeing, desperately needed parent who must reject their greedily complaining, disgusting demeanor.

So how can therapists deal appropriately with the hostile urges they observe in their ideation or behavior? First, therapists should cease acting on these urges and should instead vigorously attempt to determine how much of their behavior is being stimulated by their patients and how much is related to their own unresolved and familiar neurosis. Furthermore, whatever is stimulated by the character and transference tendencies of the patient must be understood in terms of its function (e.g., how does it serve the patient to make me mad in these circumstances? Does the patient want me to act like a demeaning parent who chastises a child for appearing weak? Does the patient feel so hopeless about being capable that he or she wishes me to attack to confirm his or her perceived worthlessness?)

As the patient's hostility is understood, it should be interpreted calmly and matter-of-factly (e.g., "You are attempting to make me angry enough to attack you because you are so angry with your plight. If you can get me to act like your father, then you can feel hopeless about changing. You can also then be angry with me. In such a state, your wishes to kill the hated parts of yourself and to attempt to punish me for hurting you might be compelling"). Complete interpretations of this nature will usually facilitate movement from provocative acting out into more self-observing, thoughtful work. (A complete interpretation involves stating an observation of the patient's behavior as well as providing a suggestion about its motive or cause.) Incomplete interpretations, however, tend to escalate the patient's anger while unconsciously expressing the therapist's hostility toward the patient.

For instance, it is inadequate to tell the patient that he or she is acting angrily or with hostility without interpreting the likely intention or function of the hostility. To merely say "You are finding fault with everything I say today. It seems that you are angry with me" can make the patient feel shamed, argumentative, or parentally corrected, but it probably will not provide insight to the patient's unconscious motivations and goals. Despite uncertainty about the transferential aspect of an interpretation, therapists can still make a structurally complete interpretation by wondering aloud with their patients about the hostility's intended effect (e.g., "You seem to ignore my comments as if you were trying to provoke me. Is that how you would deal with your mother when she would say things that you didn't want to hear?'' or "Can you think about why you might want me to struggle with you for control of this session?'')

Sometimes, especially with patients who function in the borderline ego range, such interpretive efforts will not affect the patient's angry acting out. The therapist can then attempt more directly to elicit the patient's observing ego and the ego state that is aligned with the therapeutic effort. The therapist might say, for example, "You seem so angry with me that you would rather attack than allow us to think about the meaning of your anger. It's as if you wish to destroy our relationship or test me to see if I can be provoked into hurting you.''

When the therapist believes that actually revealing anger to the patient is essential to setting limits and restoring therapeutic order, an opportunity for important insights is lost. Those connections made in the context of intense feelings are often very powerful and psychologically mutative. On the other hand, the therapist should not submit to being the target of a sadistic patient who will not think about and modulate hostility.

It is often reassuring to the patient (and to the therapist) when the therapist simply restates the therapeutic frame of thinking and understanding. Some patients will repeatedly test whether the therapist can survive, control, and protect them from greedy, hateful internal self-aspects. In this author's experience, however, most therapists too readily act out their anger at such patients. Although a patient may be acting provocatively, the therapist's own neurotic issues often become quickly activated and displaced onto the patient. This acting out aborts the understanding of the patient's need to be hostile and may permanently arrest the therapy.

The therapist who is disinclined to analyze the patient's idealization of him or her is also a poor therapist for the suicidal student. Suicidal patients often view their therapist as a perfectly sensitive, kind, protective, and nurturing person who exists for them. The therapist who needs or enjoys the patient's idealization too much may arrest the patient's ability to identify and relinquish unrealistic expectations, not only of others but also of themselves.

This type of therapist can also unconsciously encourage and enjoy a symbiotically tight, mirroring transference that can be disastrous. In these cases, the patient's self-esteem is regulated by his or her attachment to the idealized therapist. This connection can be ruptured, however, by an insensitive or incorrect interpretation or by the therapist's illness or vacation, plunging the patient into rage and despair. (For further discussion and clinical examples of this type of therapist–patient relationship, see 8.)

Such therapists often idealize themselves as well, which leads to their narcissistic view of themselves as being above common constraints such as not cultivating the patient for personal satisfaction, including sexual relations. Identifying with the patient's projections, these therapists often view themselves as the *only* person who can really meet the patient's needs.

SUMMARY

I have briefly outlined the major aspects of therapy with suicidal students. In the past several years, certain modifications to traditional therapeutic processes have been found to enhance a therapist's ability to treat the underlying psychological abscess that pressures a person to commit suicide. I believe that all students who are depressed or angry enough to have persistent suicide ideation, or to have made a suicide attempt, should participate in a therapy process similar to that described in this chapter. Crisis intervention may be lifesaving, but it is not therapy and it does not resolve the suicide impetus.

REFERENCES

1. National Center for Health Statistics. (1988). (Unpublished final data, Trend Table C, p. 292). Washington, DC: Public Health Service.
2. American Psychiatric Association. (1987). *Diagnostic and statistical manual of mental disorders* (3rd ed., rev.). Washington, DC: Author.
3. Brent, D. A., Perper, J. A., Goldstein, C. E., Kolko, D. J., Allan, M. J., Allman, C. J., & Zelenak, J. P. (1988). Risk factors for adolescent suicide: A comparison of adolescent suicide victims with suicidal inpatients. *Archives of General Psychiatry, 45*(6), 581–588.
4. Shafii, M., Steltz-Lenarsky, J., Derrick, A. M., Beckner, C., & Whittinghill, J. R. (1988). Comorbidity of mental disorders in the post-mortem diagnosis of completed suicide in children and adolescents. *Journal of Affective Disorders, 15,* 227–233.
5. Maltsberger, J. T., & Buie, D. H. (1974). Countertransference hate in the treatment of suicidal patients. *Archives of General Psychiatry, 30,* 625–633.
6. Searles, H. F. (1967). The "dedicated physician" in psychotherapy and psychoanalysis. In R. W. Gibson (Ed.), *Crosscurrents in psychiatry and psychoanalysis* (pp. 128–143). Philadelphia: Lippincott.
7. Zee, H. (1972). Blindspots in recognizing serious suicidal intentions. *Bulletin of the Menninger Clinic, 36*(5), 551–555.
8. Stone, A. A. (1971). Suicide precipitated by psychotherapy: A clinical contribution. *American Journal of Psychotherapy, 25*(1), 18–26.

12

Countertransference when Counseling Suicidal School-Aged Youth

James R. Eyman
Menninger Clinic, Topeka, Kansas

Counseling suicidal adolescents can be rewarding yet problematic and emotionally taxing. Difficulties that impinge on the counseling process may involve students, families, and school personnel. For example, students who do not view the counselor as a resource might be reluctant to report concerns about themselves or their friends. In some educational systems, antagonism between counselors and other school personnel compounds the reporting problem. Sometimes family members interfere with the treatment or referral of a suicidal adolescent.

Diagnosis of suicidal risk constitutes another area of difficulty. Missed diagnoses of lethality could be due to a lack of clinical experience or training, unreliable suicidal assessment instruments (1), or the adolescent's unwillingness to articulate intent and lethality. To establish and reach agreed-on goals, the counselor should try to form a collaborative relationship with the suicidal adolescent. Counselors can do much to foster an adolescent's sense of trust, openness, and receptivity to a treatment process. However, this rapport is not always easily achieved with suicidal adolescents, who can be quite mistrustful, angry, provocative, and rejecting of help.

Another problematic area involves the counselor's relationship to himself or herself. Counseling suicidal adolescents can provoke intense and often unconscious feelings in oneself. Anxiety, anger, and wishes to rescue or abandon the adolescent are all typically evoked when counseling suicidal adolescents. These intense feelings can not only profoundly affect how counselors view themselves and the ways in which they relate to suicidal adolescents but can also affect their ability to effectively counsel these youth. It is crucial in any counseling situation to be aware of and to understand one's thoughts, feelings, and reactions to the person being counseled. Harnessing these feelings will aid the counselor in understanding the individual, rather than allowing them to impede the treatment by affecting judgment and causing the counselor to act nontherapeutically.

In the psychoanalytic literature, the feelings a counselor has toward the person being counseled are called *countertransference*. The countertransference that can be generated when working with suicidal youth is the focus of this chapter.

DEFINITION OF COUNTERTRANSFERENCE

The concept of countertransference has undergone a metamorphosis since Freud first used the term in 1910. Freud (2) wrote,

> We have become aware of the "counter-transference," which arises in him [the treater] as a result of the patient's influence on his unconscious feelings, and we are almost inclined to insist that he shall recognize this counter-transference in himself and overcome it. (pp. 144–145)

Although Freud did not write extensively on countertransference, he insisted that the treater's feelings toward a patient were the result of the treater's own unconscious conflicts and therefore constituted a hindrance to treatment and to a thorough understanding of the patient.

> A male psychotherapist was seeing a young male homosexual in treatment. The patient had sought psychotherapy because he had been feeling increasingly depressed, was having difficulty sleeping, and was losing interest in previously enjoyable activities. Much to the psychotherapist's surprise, he found himself becoming increasingly uncomfortable and anxious whenever the patient discussed his homosexual encounters. When the therapist tried without success to divert discussion away from this topic, he experienced anger at the patient for his homosexual liaisons. Aware that this reaction was interfering with an empathetic understanding of the patient's experience, the psychotherapist discussed his confusing array of feelings toward his patient in his own psychotherapy. In so doing, he eventually became aware of the guilt he still felt about his own adolescent homosexual activities. This patient had stirred within the psychotherapist conflicts about his own homosexual yearnings. The anxiety, anger, and discomfort resulting from the psychotherapist's unresolved conflict were interfering with his ability to effectively treat the patient.

The first article specifically on countertransference, entitled "On the Countertransference and Psychoanalysis," was published by Stern in 1924 (3). Stern suggested, as did Freud, that countertransference originated in the treater's own unconscious conflicts and in the resulting impulse to act out those conflicts with patients. However, Stern deviated from Freud by proposing a second source of countertransference that resulted from the patient's real, objective interaction with the therapist.

> A female school psychologist was counseling a bright young man who had been having considerable difficulty in school. He had missed many classes and was spending most of his time at home in his room listening to music or watching television. Although he often failed at schoolwork, he could do well when he made the effort. The school psychologist found herself assuming more and more responsibility for the boy. For example, she convinced his teachers to extend the time that several papers were due in classes, and then when the boy failed to turn in the papers, she tried to excuse his behavior and negotiate another extension. She accompanied the boy to the school library and even selected the topics and books for his papers. She eventually realized that this out-of-the-ordinary behavior was being elicited by the youth's seeming helplessness and inability to cope with the demands of school. Although she realized that the boy was in fact quite intelligent and capable, she was responding to his intense dependency by being overly involved and by doing things for him that he was actually quite capable of doing himself.

Despite Stern's assertion that countertransference can be generated by the real interaction with the patient, until Winnicott's 1949 article "Hate in the Countertransference" (4), most people continued to believe that countertransference derived solely from the treater's unconscious conflicts and was therefore only a hindrance to effective treatment (5). Although Winnicott acknowledged that countertransference can come from the treater's unconscious and unresolved conflicts, he placed greater emphasis on Stern's view that countertransference can also be based on the real relationship between the treater and the patient. Winnicott discussed his work with psychotic and antisocial patients and suggested that very intense feelings toward these patients can often arise and that these intense feelings are to be expected and should be explored and understood by the treater. In an elaboration of Winnicott's position, Heimann (6) stated that because countertransference can be largely created and elicited by the patient, it is therefore part of the patient's personality; thus, understanding countertransference reactions becomes a way to understand the patient.

Later authors discussed countertransference as in inevitable and normal response to a patient that can form the foundation for the treater's empathy toward, and understanding of, the patient. This view is a radical departure from Freud's early conceptualization of countertransference. No longer was countertransference seen solely as a hindrance to treatment; rather, it was now being discussed as another source of information for understanding and treating the patient (5, 7). In the previous example, the school psychologist was able to use her countertransference to develop her understanding that the boy was so intensely afraid of failing that he tried to get others to do things for him, or that he preferred to give up rather than try and fail. She was then able to discuss with him his fear of failure and to help him develop strategies to alleviate his anxiety.

COUNTERTRANSFERENCE WITH SUICIDAL INDIVIDUALS

With a few notable exceptions (8–12), little attention has been given to countertransference elicited by treating suicidal individuals. The paucity of literature on the subject is surprising, given the knowledge that suicidal individuals can evoke strong reactions in treaters. However, the very intensity of these feelings and the resultant wish to rid oneself of intense affect may, in part, be responsible for the lack of articles in this area.

Many writers (8, 10, 12) believe that strong negative feelings by treaters toward suicidal individuals are inevitable. In the following section I describe the most common sources of countertransference, typical countertransference reactions, and how the countertransference might unfortunately be acted out by a treater. The focus is on suicidal individuals' conflicted dependency yearnings, their ineffective management of aggressive urges, and the treater's anxiety about death. Although the emphasis here is on counseling, similar countertransference difficulties may also arise in many other circumstances, such as psychotherapy and hospital treatment. Likewise, although the countertransference reactions common to the treatment of suicidal clients are discussed in this context, they can also occur when treating individuals with other complaints.

Conflicted Dependency Wishes

Many seriously suicidal adolescents are profoundly concerned about abandonment and are ambivalent about closeness. They secretly search for an all-powerful, perfectly attuned mother figure who will supply them with endless comfort and gratification, and who will meet their every desire or need and help them recapture the pleasures of infancy. Of course, this is an unrealistic wish that can never be satisfied. These individuals are also seriously conflicted about their strong dependency wishes, so they often act in counterdependent ways. On the one hand, they desperately want nurturance, on the other hand, because of problematic early depriving or traumatic childhood experiences, they often fear that expressing their desire for dependency will leave them vulnerable to a depriving and critical bad mother (8, 13–16).

Suicidal adolescents often rapidly develop an ambivalent dependent relationship with their treater. They often secretly and unrealistically hope that all possible gratification will now come from the counselor, because they wish to see the treater as perfectly good, caring, and understanding and with an unlimited ability to soothe and gratify (8, 9, 13, 17). They often try to entice the counselor into gratifying their dependency needs and then become upset and angry when this strategy inevitably fails to satisfy them. Within the counseling situation, the adolescent can demonstrate this behavior in a variety of ways. Suicidal adolescents often expect their counselor to magically know what they are thinking and feeling without having to clearly convey their experience in words.

> A young male adolescent was told to build models when feeling suicidal because such activity had in the past made the boy less despondent and suicidal. One day he told his counselor in detail about building an aircraft carrier the previous evening and described the sense of accomplishment he had felt on completing the model. The next day, however, the boy told his counselor that he was furious at her because she should have known that his building a model was a sign that he was feeling suicidal.

The counselor's failure to intuit the boy's suicidal feelings lead to his no longer feeling that she was omnipotent and could magically understand and soothe him. A suicidal adolescent's demands for many unnecessary appointments or attempts to entice the counselor into doing things that the adolescent is capable of are other behaviors that illustrate such dependency yearnings.

Because suicidal adolescents are conflicted about their dependency wishes, they also simultaneously use a variety of maneuvers to distance the counselor and to avoid true intimacy because they fear the counselor will somehow harm them or abandon them. They may convey to the counselor that he or she is not important or helpful to them (e.g., appointments may be missed). Suicidal adolescents may fail to bring their experiences to their counselor, thus thwarting their counselor's efforts to know and understand them. As a result, their counterdependency does not allow them to take advantage of whatever realistic nurturance and support is available.

Treaters often have countertransference reactions to the suicidal individual's intense, ambivalent dependency yearnings. The countertransference often involves a fear of being engulfed, used up, and overwhelmed. The suicidal adolescent can be experienced as so excessively needy and demanding that all the treater's resources will be depleted without ever satisfying the adolescent. Counselors are vulnerable to acting out this countertransference by distancing themselves from the suicidal adolescent. For example, to mitigate the anxiety generated by such a situation, counselors may mistakenly deny their importance to suicidal adolescents by missing appointments or scheduling them too infrequently. They may also attempt to prevent future contact with the adolescent and may even unconsciously try not to be helpful. Suicidal adolescents will usually interpret these distancing maneuvers as signs of abandonment. Consequently, they will feel more desperate and alone, with a resultant increase in their suicidality.

Another typical way that treaters may act out their countertransference fear of being engulfed is to expect and insist on mature, independent behavior that is beyond the adolescent's capability. Such insistence comes from the treater's wish to deintensify the dependency rather than from an understanding and appreciation of the adolescent's ability. The adolescent may react to such demands by feeling hopeless or like a failure, with an increase in suicidal urges.

A 15-year-old boy's father had just recently been incapacitated by a severe stroke when the boy began to see the school's social worker. The teenager's grades had quickly deteriorated, he was chronically tired and would sometimes fall asleep in classes, and he appeared depressed and lethargic. The boy told the social worker that his father had been partially paralyzed by the stroke and "just didn't seem the same." His father would not be able to resume work for at least a year, if at all. The family was worried about their financial resources, as they had limited saving and the father was self-employed and did not have insurance to effectively cover an extended illness. There were three younger children in the family, and the mother was chronically depressed and frequently unable to take care of the children and perform other daily tasks. Before his stroke, the father took care of the family.

Even before this tragedy, the boy had often contacted the social worker to discuss such things as whether to try out for the football team. They boy usually had difficulty ending the sessions, and the social worker frequently had to lead the boy out of his office in order to end their meetings. These contacts with the boy puzzled the social worker because they concerned relatively minor problems that he thought should be discussed with the boy's parents, rather than with someone with his experience and expertise. The boy's mother had recently told her son that now that his father was ill, it was his job to take care of the family, including her. He was told to get another job, help with the family's finances, and pay the bills. He was expected to coordinate the household chores and prepare meals. Not only was he responsible for how the family functioned, but he also became the primary source of support and nurturance for his depressed mother and his incapacitated father.

In discussing these affairs with the social worker, the boy was understandably feeling overwhelmed, frightened, depressed, and grief stricken. He was not doing well with any of these additional responsibilities. The social worker's approach with the boy was to help him schedule his activities so that he could accomplish everything his mother had asked him to do. The family's circumstances continued to deteriorate, and the boy felt increasingly like a failure, with no hope of resolving the situation. He became more depressed and suicidal.

Rather than trying to realistically assess what the boy was capable of doing in this situation and then intervening to help the boy and his family cope with this trauma, the social worker had colluded with the family in expecting the boy to function at an unrealistically mature and independent level. The social worker was reacting not only to the chaotic family situation but also to his correct understanding of the boy as a very characterologically dependent and needy young man. His resultant countertransference (that to become too involved with the boy would be like "trying to fill up an empty well") caused him to avoid a therapeutic process that he unconsciously feared would never end and would deplete his resources.

Another typical countertransference paradigm that results from the adolescent's conflicted dependency yearnings occurs when the treater believes that he or she is in fact the omnipotent "all-good mother" that the adolescent is so desperately seeking. The treater feels compelled to try to compensate for past and current deprivations. As a result, the treater may become overindulgent and may inadvertently fuel these adolescents' unrealistic beliefs that someone can totally take care of them and solve all their problems. The counselor may also promote the suicidal adolescent's view of being helpless and in need of a powerful, protective, soothing parent. The second example in this chapter, about the school psychologist who helped the boy with his schoolwork, characterizes how a treater might act on the wish to be an "all-good mother." Once the counselor unconsciously colludes with these impossible ideals, disappointment is inevitable. Inability to live up to this e expectation is often perceived as failure by the adolescent, who may ngrily and provocatively against the treater.

Aggression

Suicidal adolescents are often quite devaluing and hostile. They act out their anger provocatively through substance abuse, physical altercations, promiscuity, and various other acts of misconduct. In counseling, they may either covertly or directly reject help, engaging instead in hostile verbal or physical activities. Such aggressive onslaughts can undermine a treater's self-esteem. Freud (18) noted that the desire to help people is related to the natural conflicts that people as treaters have about their own hostile tendencies. By becoming someone who helps other individuals, treaters reassure themselves that this hostility is under control. Instead of being destructive, they become constructive (12). They want to be seen as good and omnipotent helpers, and they wish to receive gratitude and love in return (10). Suicidal adolescents, through their devaluing, help-rejecting, and aggressive assaults on their treater's feelings of competency and hopes to help others, challenge this self-concept and concomitantly call into question the treater's management of his or her own hostility (12), thus adversely affecting the treater's self-esteem and sense of competency. Countertransference that may arise from such aggressive attacks on the treater's self-esteem involves a wish to hurt and punish.

> *A young female school psychologist had been counseling a seriously suicidal 17-year-old boy. The adolescent first came to the school psychologist's attention when a teacher asked for her advice on how to deal with the boy's classroom preoccupation with death. He would often talk about death to his friends before and after class, and he had recently written a paper on suicide and signed his name as "Mr. Death." The school psychologist, obviously concerned, offered to meet with the boy. The boy laughed at the psychologist's concern, saying it was "all a funny joke" and "a big game." Even though the psychologist knew that the boy was having severe family problems and had appeared quite depressed, the student insisted that everything was all right.*
>
> *The next day the boy was found outside the psychologist's office holding a bottle of aspirin and telling a friend that he would probably die if he ingested the entire bottle. The psychologist again met with the boy, who said that if he really wanted to kill himself then she could not stop him. Furthermore, he insisted that her talking with him was not helpful. The psychologist, correctly believing that the boy was at risk for a suicide attempt, tried to get him seen at a community mental health center, but neither the boy nor his family would cooperate. She felt that all her efforts to help were being thwarted by the boy and his family. That night, the psychologist dreamed that she was a concentration camp guard leading a group of prisoners to be executed, one of whom was the suicidal adolescent. She was quite upset by this dream until she recognized that it conveyed her understandable anger toward the boy who was hostilely rejecting all her well-intentioned efforts to help.*

One common way in which anger toward a suicidal adolescent is often acted out is by the counselor's reacting to such growing hostility by becoming an overly solicitous and kind model of omnipotence and goodness. Searles (19) has stated that presenting oneself as totally compassionate and understanding in reaction to one's growing hostility toward the patient can cause the treater to fail to adequately address the patient's aggression. It can also make the suicidal individual feel small and worthless in comparison to such a model of godly goodness (12).

> *A young female adolescent had been sexually abused as a child and had a history of promiscuous relationships with males in which she was emotionally abused and sexually exploited. After an abusive relationship with a boyfriend ended, she became suicidal and entered counsel-*

ing with a male school psychologist. She was chronically hostile and provocative toward the school psychologist. She would frequently miss counseling sessions and was often contemptuous when she did appear. The young girl alternated between complaining that the psychologist did not have enough time for her and saying that the psychologist was a cold, incompetent person who did not understand her. She would often go into rages and scream at the psychologist about how she felt misunderstood and uncared for. At times, her anger became so intense that she threw books and knocked objects off a table. A few times after such outbursts of anger toward the psychologist, she became inebriated and had sexual liaisons with boys she barely knew.

The psychologist reacted to this hostile and provocative behavior by being overly kind and understanding. He often apologized for making her so angry, and he spent considerable time trying to convince her of his good intentions. He also did special favors for her, such as buying her soft drinks.

During a consultation process, the psychologist realized that he was avoiding having to address the patient's aggressive behavior. He was neither attempting to explore with the adolescent what the aggressive onslaughts meant nor limiting the provocative behavior in his office. He was gradually able to discuss his understandable anger toward this young girl. He realized that the intense hostility this provocative adolescent generated in him made him so uncomfortable that he attempted to avoid any awareness of his anger by being overly kind and understanding toward her. Understanding his countertransference reaction to the girl then allowed him to modify the counseling situation.

Another typical way that such sadistic countertransference can be acted out is by being overly hostile. There is a distinction between being openly and appropriately angry at a suicidal adolescent, which can at times be therapeutic (as in the previous example), and being overtly hostile in ways that undermine the patient's self-esteem and ability to grow.

Anxiety about Death

In the treatment of suicidal adolescents, death is a salient issue that always looms as a possibility; it is present in the counseling situation in various forms. Suicidal adolescents will often flaunt suicide threats in an effort to manipulate the counselor or their environment. Others can become so absorbed by thoughts of death that they read stories about it, fantasize about it, and dream about it. Because the threat of losing a patient by suicide can be very frightening to a counselor, it affects the counseling experience. Empathy often fuels the treater's painful and intense reactions to a suicide, but so too does a fear of being blamed for the suicide. Feelings of guilt and doubt about professional competency are often intensified by a concern about how colleagues will view the treatment and the treater. Because the possibility of death is ever present, counseling suicidal individuals often stirs the counselor's own thoughts and feelings about death and can even trigger latent suicidal urges. Thus, the anxiety not only involves the possibility of the adolescent's death but also touches whatever suicidal thoughts the counselor might possess and whatever feelings and concerns about death he or she might have.

A common countertransference reaction to anxiety about death is to feel totally responsible for whether the suicidal adolescent lives or dies. This countertransference is particularly problematic because counselors and other treaters have so little control over any person's decision to die. However, many suicidal adolescents can sense their counselor's anxiety about death and will use suicide threats or attempts to manipulate the counseling process. Countertransference elicited by such anxiety can be acted out either by overestimating or underestimating the adolescent's suicide potential. Out of a wish to suppress the adolescent's suicidal urges and control the suicidal behavior, a treater might interpret the adolescent's intent as more serious than it is and overreact by instituting too many safeguards and controls. For example, a counselor might insist that family members immediately hospitalize the student when such measures are not really needed. On the other hand, a counselor might react to this anxiety about death by underestimating the seriousness of the adolescent's intent and thus fail to take appropriate action. A false sense of security can be generated by the wish to avoid dealing with anxiety generated by the possibility of death.

> A 17-year-old boy was referred to the school counselor because his friend had told a teacher that the boy had been talking about shooting himself with his father's gun. The counselor met with the boy, who shared with him his suicide plan. He had recently had many conflicts with his teachers, and his grades were deteriorating. His parents had filed for divorce, and he was feeling despondent and hopeless. After talking to the boy, the counselor said that he would talk to the boy's parents within the next week or so to suggest referral to a mental health professional. Four days later, the boy shot and killed himself.
>
> Traumatized by this event, the counselor sought psychotherapy. As the psychotherapy progressed, the counselor was able to realize that although he had believed that the boy was seriously suicidal and should have immediately referred him, he had convinced himself that there was little suicide risk because of his own conflicts and concerns about death. Three years earlier, the counselor had supported his own mother during a long and painful illness in which she suffered intense physical pain and gradually deteriorated. He had been close to his mother and had not adequately mourned her loss. The adolescent boy's wish to die had angered the counselor, because his own mother had so valiantly tried to live. The boy had reawakened the painful feelings the counselor had experienced during his mother's long illness, as well as his grief over her death. By attempting to minimize the seriousness of the boy's suicidal urges, the counselor was trying to avoid addressing his own anxiety about death and lack of mourning for his mother's death.

Although helping the suicidal adolescent find a zest for life is an important therapeutic goal, treaters must also realize that each adolescent must decide whether to commit suicide or to work collaboratively with the counselor to understand the wish to die. Counselors are often erroneously drawn into the role of "saving" these adolescents from suicidal despair. They assume that if they can only provide the love and concern that others have not, they will somehow transform the wish to die into a desire to live (20).

A WISH TO ABANDON

The intense feelings of anxiety and anger that can be generated in treaters by suicidal adolescents can lead to a wish to abandon these persons. Maltsberger and Buie (10) have said that the wish to leave the suicidal person is not primarily a wish to get away from the patient's ambivalent dependency yearnings, hostility, and devaluing or from the possibility of the person's death. Instead, this wish primarily involves the difficulty that counselors have in tolerating their own unpleasant feelings in response to these suicidal individuals. The wish to abandon the suicidal patient is connected with the wish to suppress the unpleasant feelings that are surfacing within the treater. Attempting to deal with these feelings by abandoning and rejecting the individual will, of course, only heighten the suicidal crisis.

> A young adolescent girl came to the school nurse's office complaining of nausea. While examining the girl, the nurse noticed a cut on her wrist that was healing. The nurse asked about the wound, and the girl told her that she had made a suicide attempt by cutting her wrist with a razor blade but that her psychologist knew about the suicide attempt.

During the next few months, the girl often came into the nurse's office to talk, and a relationship began to develop between them. Because the girl often talked about her personal problems, the nurse was concerned about how this might affect her treatment, so she obtained the girl's permission to contact her psychologist. The psychologist felt that the relationship was important to the young girl and should be continued. A month later, the girl made a nearly lethal suicide attempt by overdose. She had not conveyed her suicidal urges to either the nurse or the psychologist. The nurse then told the psychologist that she believed her relationship with the student was no longer helpful and should be terminated.

After the nurse explored with the psychologist her own reaction to the girl's suicide attempt, she realized that her wish to stop seeing the student resulted from her anger at the girl for "betraying my trust." The girl's suicide attempt had made the nurse feel that her friendly overtures were being rebuked and that she was impotent to help. She no longer felt helpful and caring, and as a result she had begun to question her skill and professional competency. The nurse was eventually able to discuss her anger toward the girl with the psychologist. Although understandable, her anger had made her doubt her competency even more because she believed that a caring and professional person should not feel angry at someone so desperately in need of help. Thus, the nurse's wish to abandon her relationship with the young girl was based on her anger toward the girl for injuring the nurse's self-esteem and sense of competence and on her inability to tolerate her own angry feelings. Once she understood her countertransference, the nurse decided to continue to meet with the girl.

DEFENSIVE MANEUVERS

Counselors may use a variety of defensive maneuvers to fend off the unpleasant feelings that are generated when working with suicidal individuals. Defense mechanisms can thus prevent counselors from becoming aware of countertransference. Maltsberger and Buie (10) described four typical defense mechanisms that treaters use to dim their awareness of their animosity toward suicidal patients: (a) repression, (b) turning anger inward, (c) reaction formation, and (d) projection. Treaters can better recognize and guard against these defense mechanisms when they can identify the feeling and fantasy generated by the specific defense and the behavioral manifestation of each defense mechanism.

Repression is a defense mechanism in which undesirable thoughts and feelings are kept from conscious thought. A counselor who represses feelings toward a suicidal adolescent may not be empathically attuned with the adolescent and thus may experience minimal feeling toward the person. This repression of feelings might be manifested in the counseling situation by apparent boredom and disinterest, with the counselor yawning, acting restless, and watching the clock.

The animosity a counselor feels toward a suicidal adolescent can also be turned against the self. Attempts to deal with the hostility may result in a masochistic succumbing to the adolescent's anger and devaluation of the treater. Thus, a counselor might have conscious self-devaluing fantasies, ideas of self-punishment, and doubts about his or her capacity to be helpful to the adolescent. Feelings of worthlessness, hopelessness, and inadequacy can predominate.

The defense of reaction formation involves preventing a thought or feeling from reaching consciousness by reversing its meaning. Treaters, through reaction formation, can attempt to avoid their hostility toward their patients by becoming overly solicitous and by wishing to rescue them from their painful despair. Rather than feeling angry and wishing the patient to suffer, the counselor feels an urgency to cure and help.

In projection, the treater defends against unacceptable thoughts and feelings by attributing them to an external source. These thoughts and feelings are then seen as a part of the environment rather than as a part of the person. Maltsberger and Buie

(10) explained that projection serves to defuse the treater's unconscious wish to kill the patient, a wish that is elicited by the patient's aggressive and provocative behavior. Thus, the treater may believe that the patient wishes to kill him- or herself. This defense is often accompanied by a pervasive sense of fear within the treater, who consequently becomes preoccupied with concerns that the patient will act out suicidal urges even when there is no objective data for such a belief.

THERAPEUTIC USE AND MANAGEMENT OF COUNTERTRANSFERENCE

Countertransference can arise from a treater's unresolved conflicts and from the objective relationship between the treater and the patient. A treater must be willing to explore himself or herself in order to understand whether the countertransference originates from the treater's internal conflicts and, if so, to take appropriate steps to manage or resolve those conflicts. However, countertransference that is not based on the treater's internal conflicts does not need to be taken away through psychotherapy and self-understanding but is instead an inevitable and intrinsic aspect of the treatment process. The goal is to be aware of any countertransference feelings and to understand what they might be communicating about the counseling experience with the patient. When countertransference is understood, it can aid in diagnostic formulation, help to clarify how others may respond to the individual, and facilitate therapeutic intervention.

Not being attuned to, and not understanding, countertransference can cause a treater to act on these feelings with potentially deleterious consequences. In particular, counselors who work with difficult patients such as suicidal adolescents should be aware that these patients can evoke strong feelings. Counselors must also be willing to accept and tolerate these feelings without unnecessarily defending against them or acting them out. Unfortunately, countertransference can be difficult to discern. For example, projecting hostility onto the patient (and thereby believing that the patient is more lethal than is actually the case) is often difficult to distinguish from an accurate assessment of the patient's lethality.

Because of the intense countertransference that is generated by suicidal patients and the potential for acting out these feelings, treaters should schedule regular consultations with knowledgeable professionals. A successful consultation process requires the treater's willingness to openly share his or her thoughts and feelings toward the suicidal patient with the consultant. Effective treatment of suicidal adolescents requires an exploration of the treater's internal state, as well as an understanding of the suicidal patient's motivation.

REFERENCES

1. Eyman, J. R., Mikawa, J. K., & Eyman, S. K. (1990). The problem of adolescent suicide: Issues and assessment. In P. McReynolds, J. C. Rosen, & G. Chelune (Eds.), *Advances in psychological assessment: Vol. VII* (pp. 165–202). New York: Plenum Press.
2. Freud, S. (1957). The future prospects of psycho-analytic therapy. In J. Strachey (Ed. & Trans.), *The standard edition of the complete psychological works of Sigmund Freud* (Vol. 11, pp. 139–151). London: Hogath Press. (Original work published 1910)
3. Stern, A. (1924). On the countertransference in psychoanalysis. *Psychoanalytic Review, 2,* 166–174.
4. Winnicott, D. (1949). Hate in the countertransference. *International Journal of Psycho-Analysis, 30,* 69–74.

5. Slakter, E. (1987). The history of the concept. In E. Slakter (Ed.), *Countertransference* (pp. 7–42). Northvale, NJ: Jason Aronson.
6. Heimann, P. (1950). On countertransference. *International Journal of Psycho-Analysis, 14,* 81–84.
7. Chessick, R. (1986). Transference and countertransference revisted. *Dynamic Psychotherapy, 4,* 14–30.
8. Eyman, J. R. (1987, May). *Unsuccessful psychotherapy with seriously suicidal borderline patients.* Paper presented at the Joint Meeting of the American Association of Suicidology and the International Association of Suicide Prevention, San Francisco, CA.
9. Hendin, H. (1981). Psychotherapy and suicide. *American Journal of Psychotherapy, 35,* 469–480.
10. Maltsberger, J., & Buie, D. (1974). Countertransference hate in the treatment of suicidal patients. *Archives of General Psychiatry, 30,* 625–633.
11. Modestin, J. (1987). Counter-transference reactions contributing to completed suicide. *British Journal of Medical Psychology, 60,* 379–385.
12. Zee, H. J. (1972). Blindspots in recognizing serious suicidal intentions. *Bulletin of the Menninger Clinic, 36,* 551–555.
13. Eyman, J. R., & Conroy, R. (1988, April). *Suicide: The loss of a fantasy.* Paper presented at the meeting of the American Association of Suicidology, Washington, DC.
14. Richman, J. (1986). *Family therapy for suicidal people.* New York: Springer.
15. Richman, J., & Eyman, J. R. (in press). Psychotherapy of suicide: Individual, group, and family approaches. In D. Lester (Ed.), *Understanding suicide: The state of the art.* Philadelphia, PA: Charles Press.
16. Smith, K., & Eyman, J. (1988). Ego structure and object differentiation in suicide patients. In H. D. Lerner & P. M. Lerner (Eds.), *Primitive mental states and the Rorschach* (pp. 175–202). Madison, CT: International Universities Press.
17. Stone, A., & Shein, H. (1968). Psychotherapy of the hospitalized suicidal patient. *American Journal of Psychotherapy, 22,* 15–25.
18. Freud, S. (1959). The question of lay analysis. In J. Strachey (Ed. & Trans.), *The standard edition of the complete psychological works of Sigmund Freud* (Vol. 11, pp. 177–258). London: Hogarth Press. (Original work published in 1926)
19. Searles, H. (1967). The "dedicated physician" in psychotherapy and psychoanalysis. In R. W. Gibson (Ed.), *Crosscurrents in psychiatry and psychoanalysis* (pp. 128–143). Philadelphia, PA: Lippincott.
20. Gabbard, G. O. (1990). Affective disorders. In G. O. Gabbard (Ed.), *Psychodynamic psychiatry in clinical practice* (pp. 177–198). Washington, DC: American Psychiatric Press.

13

Family Therapy with Suicidal Children

Joseph Richman
Albert Einstein College of Medicine, Bronx, New York

This chapter is about family therapy, because the family is instrumental in the suicidal behavior of young people and central to the success of the healing process.

Family relationships are inseparable from the emotional well-being or ill-being of all children, either within or outside the family. This is because the family is a social system at the interface between the individual and society, that is, where the child first learns the roles and rules of living with others. That is why difficulties often first become apparent at the point where the child must leave home to attend school or engage in other outside activities.

This is not to discount the importance of other relationships or of biological, constitutional, and genetic factors, but their fate, too, is inseparable from the family. For example, mentally retarded or disabled children may be rejected and become the object of anger, may be loved and accepted, or may receive a combination of these attitudes. Targum (1) has described how family relationships in people with biologically based bipolar disorders help shape the course of the illness.

A comparison might also be made between Madam van de Put, a Dutch woman who killed her infant girl because she was a thalidomide baby, born without limbs (2), and May, of "May's Miracle" (a 1989 public television program), who raised an infant who had been abandoned by its mother. This little boy was blind and severely damaged. With the patient help and care of the woman who adopted him, he grew up to be a musician, a mimic of popular singers, and an object of admiration by others.

Parental influences were studied almost half a century ago by Adelaide Johnson and her coworkers (3–5). They demonstrated how antisocial acting out was related to covert messages by the parents encouraging these actions. They reported similar findings in studies of homosexuality and other behaviors.

Other research studies have described the parent–child context of separation anxiety disorders (6) and of depression and other psychiatric disturbances (7). Earlier, Bowlby (8) had described a strong relation between school phobias in children and suicidal threats by the mothers. Bowlby also found that it was only in family meetings that the relation between fears of going to school in children and suicidal communications by the mother was revealed.

Suicidal behavior in children and adolescents has continued to receive a great deal of attention, with many of these works recognizing the importance of family factors (e.g., 9) not only in terms of early upbringing and experiences but in the present, where the current situation helps determine either well-being or emotional distress.

On the basis of such studies and my clinical experience, I believe that family therapy, usually combined with individual counseling, group psychotherapy, or both, can help the young person deal constructively with suicidal impulses.

Family therapy is the most effective means of reducing the tensions that contribute to suicidal behavior, permitting growth and individuation, and at the same time maintaining family cohesion. Family therapy also offers the best opportunity for utilizing and strengthening the positive forces that may be present. Families have been given bad press. Fortunately, there has been a growing recognition of the positive resources of the family, even in those with a disturbed member (10).

This is good reason to redouble efforts to prevent and treat youthful self-destructive behavior. These deaths form a record of unnecessary and, in a sense, man-made tragedies that have permanently shattered the lives of the living.

This is not to discount the great importance of peer relationships and pressures. However, their effects cannot be understood apart from the family's reactions to the child's developmental struggles. Family therapy, therefore, can help the young person deal constructively with conflict and stress, without a self-destructive or suicidal resolution.

Family therapy is the most effective means of reducing the tensions contributing to suicidal behavior, of permitting growth and individuation, and at the same time maintaining family cohesion. It is the treatment of choice for suicidal people of all ages (11).

In the past 15 years, the suicide rate among young people has tripled and in Canada has caught up with or outstripped the suicide rate among the elderly. To compound the tragedy, the child at risk for suicide is often the one who is most sensitive, perceptive, bright, and creative.

Vivienne (12) is an example. She was a 14-year-old girl whose personal qualities and gifts were apparent in her beautiful poetry; but she committed suicide. Thomas Chatterton is a more noted representative. He was a gifted poet whose poetry, 200 years later, is still read, but he ended his life at age 17. How many more Viviennes and Chattertons have there been who ended their lives, unknown and unmourned except for their families and those who knew and loved them?

It is primarily in family therapy that I am constantly impressed by the perceptiveness of these potentially suicidal prepubertal and adolescent children. Carl, age 11, is a typical example. When he becomes upset, I know the family is in trouble and needs help. For example, Carl's aunt had been hospitalized because of a psychotic breakdown. Carl asked if she was going to die and was reassured. To me, this concern was valid, because his aunt had attended a family session, and I thought she exhibited covert suicidal signs.

PUBERTY AND PREPUBERTY

Although my original intent was to present on adolescent suicide, beginning with the teens, it became evident that suicidal behavior from an earlier age contained similar dynamics and treatment implications. A chance finding in a perusal of the literature and my clinical notes suggested that particularly sensitive events in those who then or subsequently became suicidal occurred at age 10. Examples include the following:

1. Ernest G.'s parents separated when he was 10, and in the process his mother attempted suicide. Ernie, who had been a lively and successful child, became quietly incompetent, a failure in his school, love, social, and vocational life. In his mid-20s, when he entered therapy, he was living alone and working at menial tasks.

2. James R. was another patient whose parents separated when he was 10, following an extremely frightening quarrel that he witnessed. In therapy at age 30, James described an enduring sense of apprehension, with a conviction that his world was no longer secure and could disintegrate at any moment.

3. David K. was brought into the clinic when he was 12. His mother was worried because he was depressed and suicidal, ostensibly because of school and peer problems. He told his mother that he was a complete failure and that death was the only answer. His father had committed suicide when David was 10, although he was told, and apparently believed, hat his father had died of a heart attack.

The parents of such vulnerable children also report traumatic experiences when they were 10. Dora P., for example, now in her 30s, is chronically depressed, and her son, now also 10, has become a school and behavior problem and is suicidal. When Dora was 10, her father grabbed a knife in the course of a quarrel with his wife and stabbed himself, then an ambulance took him away. He survived, but the memory of that event has haunted his then 10-year-old daughter for a quarter of a century, and the depressive and self-destructive trends have continued into the next generation.

Another example is Joel M. At 11 years of age, he hung himself during his sister's 10th birthday party. Ironically, in the family therapy that followed, his sister was his most vociferous and understanding ally.

Most of these events, in fact all of them in my experience, involved the family, especially the parents, and often included the actual or threatened dissolution of the family or the marriage.

Why should these deaths, suicidal attempts, and suicides occur while a vulnerable child is 10? There is no particular reason that I can see. However, there are also anecdotal records of other experiences at age 10 that are more positive and that also seem to have had an enduring influence.

One woman recalled that her dream or fondest wish at age 10 was to spend all her time reading. She grew up to become a historian of literature, and her wishes of age 10 came true. Another 10-year-old boy had a record of failure in school, where he spent most of his time daydreaming. At age 10, a teacher made special demands on him, and for the first time he was successful. His dream, then, was to become a scholar and to intellectually and symbolically win the praises of his demanding teacher over and over again. And so he did.

My heuristic conclusion is that it is not that traumatic events occur more frequently at age 10; they occur at all ages. The decades, however, have a particularly important symbolic significance in marking the beginning and ending of a developmental phase. Age 10, therefore, may be a symbolic marker, with events transferred in memory to that new decade. In addition, 10-year-olds who are bright and precocious are then feeling the early stirrings of physiological and social changes, which are the harbingers of adolescence.

Table 1 Characteristics of families with a suicidal child

An inability to accept necessary change
    An intolerance for separation
    An association of change with separation
    An association of development with separation
    An association of separation with death
    A symbiosis without empathy
    A clinging to early attachments at the expense of later ones
    An inability to mourn
Role and interpersonal conflicts, failures, and fixations
    An intolerance of failure
    A fear of success
    A fusion of self and social role
A disturbed family structure
    A closed family system
    An association of the open family with loss
    A prohibition against intimacy outside the family
    An isolation of the potentially suicidal person within the family
    Fragility of a key family member
Unbalanced or one-sided intrafamilial relationships
    A specific kind of scapegoating
    Double-binding relationships
    Sadomasochistic relationships
    Ambivalent relationships
    An association of relationships outside the home with loss
Affective difficulties
    A one-sided pattern of aggression
    An association of aggression with death
    A family depression
    An association of autonomous emotions with separation
Transactional difficulties
    Communication disturbances
    An excessive secretiveness
    Open communication associated with danger
An intolerance for crises
    An association of crisis with separation
    An association of crisis with preventing separation

Note. Adapted from *Family Therapy for Suicidal People* by J. Richman, 1986, New York: Springer-Verlag. Adapted by permission.

ADOLESCENCE

The turmoil of the adolescent years, the social, family, and other demands, become more urgent and disruptive. These years are when psychosexual changes, and an overall increase in drive pressure, become pressing and cannot be denied. That is why aggressive and sexual behavior become an issue. The increased role demands include succeeding in school, with friends, and in sexual relations: establishing the beginnings of a career; and, in later adolescence, leaving home for college or marriage. All of these are activities that move the person out of the home and away from the family. Table 1 presents the salient characteristics of the family during a suicidal crisis. In a family that cannot tolerate separation, the result can be an enormous amount of family disruption and crises.

A direct line can be traced from the stress aroused in the family by the threat of change and separation to the closed family system and other disturbances in family structure and relationships and to disturbed roles and relationships outside the family. Both unforeseen life events and the nature of these family interactions lead to frequent but never resolved crises, which accumulate until stress and tension become overwhelming and the suicidal act takes place.

The affective disturbances in the family and the maladaptive rules regarding the expression and discharge of drive and the increase in social demands combine with the physiologically based increased arousal of sexual and aggressive tensions in the adolescent, thus escalating the risk of destructive and self-destructive reactions.

The key variables in the family include the association of separation with death combined with unresolved mourning and unfinished business with past relationships and significant others. Change has also become associated with separation. Any change in the behavior of one key family member, therefore, such as an adolescent who is trying to meet the demands of everyday life, may have an impact on the functioning of other family members. Conversely, changes in the behavior and functioning of other family members, such as job losses and changes, increased drinking, escalation of parental conflicts, and divorce, affect the adolescent. Physical and sexual abuse by parents or other adult figures, drug or alcohol abuse and other maladaptive behaviors by the adolescent, school strain or failure, and peer or sexual conflicts often escalate in response to these pressures.

The adolescent, in sum, is assaulted from both without (by family, peer, and school pressures) and within by the surge of instinctual pressures. How the adolescent crisis is resolved has much to do with how the parents have navigated their own passages through childhood and adolescence.

In addition, if other family members have also resorted to self-destructive or suicidal messages and acts, then suicidal behavior in the adolescent is more likely to occur. The major thesis of this chapter, is therefore, that a suicidal state in a young person is part of a struggle for personal individuation and social integration in the entire family. In other words, the suicidal state in a child or adolescent is based on a developmental crisis in the family system. There is a danger, as well as a positive and hopeful aspect, to a suicidal episode.

Theresa Benedek (13), an eminent analyst of the 1930s and 1940s, reached similar conclusions regarding emotional disturbances from her psychoanalytic work with children and with parents. She postulated that a child runs into a developmental roadblock and emotional distress at the stage of development the parents have failed to master. That situation with the suicidal child may include a crisis of middle age or aging in the parents, old age in grandparents, and the crises of youth and childhood in older and younger siblings. All are involved, for what happens to one person in a family cannot be separated from what is happening to others. The suicidal child is also burdened with the developmental crises of parents and others in the family. Orbach (14) described similar dynamics, where the child is given the task of solving a problem in the family that is at the time beyond the child's or anyone else's ability to resolve. That is why the suicidal act communicates the presence of a family system in trouble and in need of help. If the child can be treated and helped out of an impasse, the result becomes a growth experience for everyone.

Because the family is implicated in these tensions, it makes sense to see the family in order to reduce the family-based pressures and anxieties related to suicidal behavior in the young person (Table 2). In addition, with the reduction of

Table 2   The psychotherapeutic process: From hello to goodbye

The initial phase
  Dealing with referrals, first meeting, clarification of ground rules
Crisis intervention
  Assessment of risk
  Assessment and involvement of the suicidal person and the family members
  Pinpointing the crisis, evaluation of suicidal risk, determination of disposition (e.g., hospitalization
    or outpatient), determination of target symptoms and a tentative treatment plan
  Intervention: Crisis intervention may be sufficient; if not, the contact continues into the next stage.
Early phase of family therapy
  Continuation of crisis intervention and assessment, including "monitoring" and further
    clarification of target goals and symptoms
  Establishing rapport and commitment
First crisis in therapy
  Arousal of separation anxiety
  Negative therapeutic reaction
Repeated crises in therapy
  Continued monitoring of symptoms or danger signs
  Dealing with discouragement, scapegoating, and sabotage
Dealing with special and typical problems
  Contacts with outside agencies, hospitals, caregivers, therapists, and other professionals
  Constructive use of transference and (especially) of countertransference
  Resolution
Ending phase
  Importance of timing and possible arousal of separation anxiety
  Termination
  Arrangement for periodic follow-up.

anxiety and an airing of the conflicts between the child and adolescent at risk for suicide, the family has an opportunity to become a healing, caring, and maturing force for all its members.

Separation anxiety is the major source of tension in the suicidal child and family. The first task, therefore, aside from immediate lifesaving measures, is to reduce this anxiety. The major procedure is to gather the family members, including the suicidal person, in a task-oriented meeting with a positive and problem-solving emphasis.

The basic procedure for the first contact consists of a series of brief individual meetings, followed by a more extended family session. I first meet with the participants in the hall or waiting room, where I introduce myself and explain that we are meeting for the purpose of making things better and that first I want to see them individually and then all together.

I then see each participant, establish the beginnings of a rapport, obtain their perception of the situation, ask for a figure drawing (which I use as a screening device), and invite their participation in the therapeutic endeavor. These individual meetings are followed by the family session, where the bulk of the action, assessment, and therapy takes place.

I try to bring in as many family members as possible; however, I work with whomever I can get and will not turn down a suicidal person for family therapy even when key members will not appear. Such rules are flexible. In general, I follow the procedures recommended by Langsley et al. (15) and Pittman (16) on the crisis treatment of families in general and my earlier work (11) on suicidal families in particular.

THE SUICIDAL STATE IN AN ADOLESCENT

Nancy G. was 16 when she attempted suicide by slashing her arms so violently that she cut through an artery and almost bled to death. Behind her act were tensions aroused by school pressures, feelings of social failure, a preoccupation with death, and a number of family crises. The family components included the death of her maternal grandmother, who lived in another state. Nancy was sent to represent the family at the grandmother's funeral. When she returned home she found that her parents had separated. She was then placed in the double-bind dilemma of deciding which parent to live with. She moved back and forth, becoming increasingly conflicted and undecided. She was also assigned the tasks of simultaneously mourning for grandmother, whose death was seemingly ignored by the rest of the family, and becoming a replacement for the grandmother. The unfortunate effect was to enable the family, especially the mother, to avoid the painful mourning process.

Nancy also worried about her father, who had an illness that made careful dieting essential, but who flamboyantly defied the medical regimen. He had not worked for years and remained at home, spending his time eating, drinking, and sleeping. Nancy's preoccupation with death was centered around fears that her father would die. Her mother disliked her job, but had to remain in order to support the family. Her father was overinvolved in Nancy's schoolwork, as well as her menstrual cycle, and he attributed her suicidal act primarily to premenstrual syndrome.

Nancy's mother relied on her for emotional support and mothering, whereas her two older siblings were free to pursue their careers, friendships, and social attachments. (In actual fact, they were by no means as free as it appeared.)

Nancy was seen in a combination of family and individual therapy, and the parents were also seen separately. Nancy became less of a parent figure and more of an individual. In their marital sessions, the great conflicts and antagonisms dividing the parents were aired.

Therapy was discontinued after 6 months, when Nancy left for college. Follow-up contact after 3 years indicates that she is living away from home and doing well in school. Her father returned to work, having decided to swallow his pride and accept a beginner's job and salary. He has since received several raises and promotions. Her mother changed her job for one less conflictual and more congenial to her interests. The parents also reconciled and are again living together.

Nancy's case illustrates several of the principles and processes of suicidal behavior and family in young persons. Her adolescent turmoil and crises were intertwined with suicidal urges, and these in turn were intertwined with the unresolved problems of the parents. The parents had tried to deal with, or avoid dealing with, their marital and other tasks of maturity by placing these conflicts into their daughter. The crises of the parents involved separation, death anxiety, and failure or strain in meeting social role obligations both in the home and outside. These all became intertwined with Nancy's adolescent turmoil and efforts to cope with her own developmental and role demands.

Nancy's story centered on the two major components of adolescent growth that are implicated in suicide—individuation and cohesion (by Freud and Durkheim, respectively). Part of individuation consists of leaving home for college. The parents acknowledged that their older daughter could not tolerate the separation and had to return home to attend a local school. The older son, too, did not complete college—although both parents are professionals with college degrees—and for a time he became an alcoholic.

THE SUICIDAL STATE IN A PREADOLESCENT

In the pubertal or prepubertal child, the suicidal state combines inner pressures around school, friendships, and other demands of childhood with the family situation.

Carl P., for example, was 10 when he and his family entered therapy. The major precipitant was the death of his paternal grandfather by suicide 2 years earlier. Carl was the recipient of much anxiety, owing to fear that he carried a hereditary trait inherited from the grandfather. He became a severe behavior problem in school and with peers, which was seen as evidence that the parents' fears were justified. In therapy sessions he reacted to complaints about him by placing an imaginary gun to his head and making shooting sounds and by scratching his wrists with his fingernails.

The parents were overinvolved with his activities, especially in school. His father coached or tutored him unmercifully, and both parents went over his homework with a fine-tooth comb, searching for any errors. They refused to desist until Carl threatened to run away from home or to refuse to do any homework. They finally agreed to place responsibility for school and homework on Carl himself, and both school and peer relationships became less of an issue. Carl is now considerably less symptomatic. He was also emerged as being very bright and artistically gifted.

Carl's father had been very distant from the family but became more involved. The result was a temporary escalation of marital conflicts, as the parents were unused to working together, and Carl's mother saw his father as more of a hindrance than a help until they both changed their patterns and started becoming partners. The father also needed to work on his own depression, the mourning for his father, and the fears for his own biological and genetic predispositions, which had been projected onto Carl.

As in the case of Nancy's family, Carl's father also changed his job. Carl's mother, too, left her work to return to school full time, not because of any difficulties with her job, but because the further education was needed for her advancement.

In virtually 100% of my patients in family therapy, both parents work. That is also true of most of the families I know who are not in therapy. The relation between suicidal behavior in children and this changing family pattern, where it is more the exception than the rule for the mother to remain home while father works and is the sole or main breadwinner, deserves a much fuller investigation.

With suicidal children, the parents are at the extreme of either overinvolvement with a flavor of incorporation or underinvolvement verging on neglect. It is well recognized that the merging of boundaries is the major aspect of symbiosis. Less known is the relation between symbiosis and isolation of or withdrawal from a symbiotic other. Both extremes are part of the symbiosis in the suicidal situation, for the symbiotic parents of suicidal children think in polarities and extremes.

To summarize, the developmental tasks of prepubertal and adolescent children interact with the developmental tasks and life vicissitudes of other family members, especially the parents. The clash and interplay between these determine the fate of the young person's suicidal impulse.

In both the cases presented in this chapter, the death of a grandparent was a major precipitant. In both cases, the parents were not able to mourn the deaths appropriately. The legacy of failed mourning was the parents' increased difficulties in meeting their parental roles, with a special impact on the child who became suicidal.

Nancy's mother tried to make her a replacement for her lost parents, as someone to mother and care for her. Carl's parents tried to make him a replacement in another way, as the tainted person into whom all the fears of mental illness and suicide were placed. The danger in this case was that of isolation and exclusion.

Early in the therapy, Carl's parents wanted to send him away to a boarding school. They also wondered about sending him for individual therapy to another therapist. I thought that separate treatment for Carl might leave unresolved the family's projections, introjections, and unfinished problems with their families of origin, especially incomplete mourning. My response was to say cheerfully, "You're going to have to deal with him," which they did.

Communication

This is a broad area that for some scholars encompasses the entire human condition (17). Communication is one of the basic needs of humans. It is the basis of all the arts, and some, such as Susanne Langer (18), saw communication as the foundation of all culture and civilization.

Our concern, however, is with the area I have called "the suicidal communication system" (11), which refers to all messages that contribute to the development of a suicidal episode. Some communications can kill and some can heal. Communication is relationship: Open, honest, positive, and caring communications heal; negative communications may kill. Covert messages are insidious, and silence may be the most insidious of all.

Secretiveness, which combines the silent with the covert, may draw one individual into a conspiracy to help another commit suicide. The deadly power of secrecy appears when a young person confides a suicidal intent to a friend with the admonition "but don't tell anyone; it's a secret." What is the friend to do? The only resource is to be on the side of life, to refuse to enter into such a secret alliance, and even to violate a confidence. Such moves have prevented suicides and saved lives.

The words *it's a secret* are not to be accepted literally. Secretiveness is characteristic of the families of suicidal people, and the suicidal child may be repeating what is learned in the home. A misplaced sense of family loyalty is another reason why the suicidal person demands secrecy. The very act of confiding in someone outside the family violates a family rule. There is a "myth of exclusiveness" in the families of suicidal people, based on the false and sometimes deadly belief that to establish a close new relationship outside the family means the end of a primary close relationship inside the family, most often between a parent and the child at risk.

A second characteristic is the multilevel nature of all communication, combined with the ambivalent and double-binding nature of suicidal communications. A statement can mean one thing and its opposite at the same time. The words *don't tell anyone* ask for secrecy, but to tell someone asks for rescue. There is a tendency among suicidal people to select one person, who is then made responsible for the life or death of the suicidal one (19). This becomes the terrible responsibility of the friend.

An example was presented in the book *Vivienne* (12), about the gifted 14-year-old. She chose two such conspirators, whom she confided in separately: both were sworn to secrecy, and both obeyed. One was a friend and the other was her sister. They felt obligated to keep the secret, even though they perhaps realized that, as the old saying goes, "wherever there is a secret there must be something wrong." They did not realize that sometimes there is something wrong in keeping a secret.

Another aspect of such secrecy is the ambivalent and double-binding nature of relationships in suicide. Great secretiveness often alternates with great openness, as though the world had become one huge confessional. In addition, a statement such as "don't tell anyone" may mean one thing and its opposite simultaneously. At a conscious level, "don't tell anyone" is a request for secrecy. At a more covert level, it reflects a wish for the confidante to tell others and thus be the rescuer.

One of the great values of survivor groups for those who have experienced the suicide of a family member or of someone close is that the group offers a place where one can share one's feelings and experiences. The value of such open, direct, and honest communication can only be appreciated by those who have experienced it with receptive and understanding others. Open communication combined with caring is lifesaving and makes the right kind of therapy—whether it be group, family, or individual—uniquely valuable, both for the suicidal person and for others.

In family therapy, the airing of strife, anger, and conflicts can have a positive outcome when these take place in a therapeutic atmosphere where they are part of the treatment process. Although such exchanges or communications can be deadly at home, in therapy they can become the beginning of the healing process in the entire family.

Communication, of course, is a transaction. It is not only the identified suicidal person who communicates. There is also the communication of messages from others that may be conducive to suicide. And there are messages of pain, emotional distress, suicidal states, and suicidal ideation by other family members. The family members often think these are concealed because they are not verbalized. As Pittman (16) said, "In a misguided effort to avoid embarrassment or pain or blame or change, many people keep secrets and thereby compound the confusion." However, children respond to the emotional, behavioral, and existential state of their parents, not necessarily to what they say.

It is a myth to think that children do not know things because they have not been told about them. Carl's father became depressed, with suicidal ideation; he grew increasingly withdrawn, irritable, and subject to sudden outbursts of rage. Carl left for camp during this period and immediately began to fight with other boys and to display provocative behavior, such as throwing rocks.

The parents attributed these problems to his general interpersonal difficulties. They were astounded when I suggested that Carl's behavior was a response to anxiety over his father. I also praised Carl's understanding and how much he had realized his father was not himself and did not hold his father up to scorn. I emphasized how such awareness by Carl pointed up the importance of being open and upfront with the family. I ended by saying, "Thank God for the telephone."

Carl's father, depression and withdrawal notwithstanding, said he would phone Carl the next day and reassure him that all was fine at home. He did so and reported at our next session that Carl had settled down in camp and was now doing well. The father himself appeared less depressed.

The family can become *the* major helping and support system of the suicidal young person. In the process, the other family members can also become major recipients of help and support, based on the optimal integration of personal individuation and social or family cohesion.

Conclusion

Suicidal behavior in adolescence and puberty is associated with school pressures and failure. Many schools have accepted responsibility for such tragic acts and have worked valiantly to organize suicide prevention and educational programs. These activities are to be highly commended. However, suicidal behavior in response to school tensions and conflicts may be only one part of the total situation. School difficulties can be understood fruitfully as a displacement from more fundamental family problems in the child at risk. Working only with children may be leaving out those who are most concerned and who possess the greatest potential for preventing suicide. All therapeutic efforts with young suicidal people, therefore, should be integrated with the family.

Some families with a suicidal child are unapproachable and rejecting of help. Then, fortunately, there are the others. Those who accept and become engaged in family therapy after an attempted or completed suicide are very special people, in my experience. They are willing to go through the pain of mourning for the past and for lost loved ones and to tolerate the struggles required for growth and the establishment of more loving and healing relationships. The greatest promise for preventing suicide lies not so much in families who have never known a suicide, but in those in which completed or attempted suicides have occurred. How the family deals with such events makes all the difference. The courageous ones can set the standard for the rest of society and truly become the families that prevent suicide.

I would like to conclude with a word to the helpers and therapists, distilled from my 25 years of intensive work with suicidal people and their families. Working with suicidal young people is an anxiety-laden task. If this chapter can reduce some of the stress and anxiety associated with treating suicidal youth, arouse the interest of more family therapists in working with the youthful suicide patient, and help them see the therapy as a rewarding challenge, then it will have achieved its goal.

REFERENCES

1. Targum, S. D. (1988). Genetic issues in treatment. In J. F. Clarkin, G. L. Haas, & J. D. Glick (Eds.), *Affective disorders and the family* (pp. 196–212). New York: Guilford.
2. Maguire, D. (1975). *Death by choice.* New York: Schocken.
3. Johnson, A. (1949). Sanctions for superego lacunae of adolescents. In K. Eissler (Ed.), *Searchlight on delinquency: New psychoanalytic studies* (pp. 225–245). New York: International Press.
4. Johnson, A., & Szurek, S. A. (1951). The genesis of antisocial acting out in children and adults. *Psychoanalytic Quarterly, 21,* 323–343.
5. Kolb, L. C., & Johnson, A. M. (1955). Etiology and therapy of overt homosexuality. *Psychiatric Quarterly, 24,* 506–515.

6. Last, C. G., Hersen, M. Kazdin, A. E., Francis, G., et al. (1987). Psychiatric illness in the mothers of anxious children. *American Journal of Psychiatry, 144*(12), 1580–1583.
7. Weissman, M. M., Gammon, G. D., John, K., Merikangas, K. R., et al. (1987). Children of depressed parents: Increased psychopathology and early onset of major depression. *Archives of General Psychiatry, 44,* 847–853.
8. Bowlby, J. (1973). *Attachment and loss. Vol. II: Separation.* New York: Basic Books.
9. Pfeffer, C. R. (1986). *The suicidal child.* New York: Guilford Press.
10. Karpel, M. A. (Ed.). (1986). *Family resources: The hidden partner in family therapy.* New York: Guilford Press.
11. Richman, J. (1986). *Family therapy for suicidal people.* New York: Springer.
12. Mack, J., & Hickler, J. (1981). *Vivienne.* Boston: Little, Brown.
13. Benedek, T. (1973). Parenthood as a developmental phase. In *Psychoanalytic investigations: Selected papers.* New York: Quadrangle.
14. Orbach, I. (1986). The "insolvable problem" as a determinant in the dynamics of suicidal behavior in children. *American Journal of Psychotherapy, 40*(4), 511–520.
15. Langsley, D. G., & Kaplan, D. M. (and collaborators). (1968). *The treatment of families in crisis.* New York: Grune & Stratton.
16. Pittman, F. S. (1987). *Turning points. Treating families in transition and crisis.* New York: Norton.
17. Watzlawick, P., Beavin, J. H., & Jackson, D. (1967). *Pragmatics of human communication.* New York: Norton.
18. Langer, S. (1948). *Philosophy in a new key.* New York: Harvard University Press.
19. Jensen, V. W., & Petty, T. A. (1958). The fantasy of being rescued in suicide. *Psychoanalytic Quarterly, 27,* 327–339.

IV

SUICIDE POSTVENTION
IN SCHOOLS

Postvention refers to those things done after the dire event has occurred. Post-vention deals with the traumatic aftereffects in the survivors and involves offering psychological services to them. School systems are an especially critical force in such endeavors with youth. Part IV outlines postvention strategies for schools. It consists of four chapters: a conceptual model for postvention, a suicide postvention program with a case illustration, a discussion about counseling such survivors, and consultants' viewpoints regarding postvention.

14

Posttraumatic Stress Disorder: A Conceptual Model for Postvention

Antoon A. Leenaars
Windsor, Ontario

Susanne Wenckstern
Board of Education for the City of Windsor, Ontario

Suicide is a trauma for the survivors. Our own experience with such survivors—in schools and other systems—suggests that this type of bereavement is associated with a prolonged stress response in many individuals. Research supports this view (1, 2). Wilson, Smith, and Johnson (3) have reported that the loss of a significant other, including that by suicide, results in significant distress; indeed, the greater the degree of loss or its symbolic implication (such as might be experienced in relation to a previous death), the more severe the stress syndrome. Freud in 1917 (4) had already noted that loss of an object (related primarily to attachment) results in trauma with symptoms of depression. It would appear from our view that this is especially true for suicide because more than any other death in our society, there is a social (and often personal dynamic) stigma for the survivors. We personally believe that it is heuristic to view this event from the *posttraumatic stress disorder* framework.[1]

DEFINITION AND DIAGNOSTIC CRITERIA

The literature on victims of traumatic events is composed of more or less distinct areas (5). This is certainly true for suicide. Often suicide is not even discussed in texts on trauma. Yet there are common psychological

We thank the Board of Education for the City of Windsor for its support of our effort. The views in this chapter are ours, not necessarily those of the Board of Education for the City of Windsor.

This chapter is a version of a section of a paper entitled "Suicide Postvention in School Systems: A Model" presented at the conference *Helping Children Cope with Death,* King's College, London, June 1988.

Diagnostic criteria for posttraumatic stress disorder were reprinted with permission from the *Diagnostic and Statistical Manual of Mental Disorders, Third Edition, Revised.* Copyright 1987 by the American Psychiatric Association.

[1]By no means do we wish to suggest that posttraumatic stress disorder (PTSD) occurs after all suicides or in all survivors. For example, if the suicide is anticipated in a chronic repeater or in a terminally ill individual, PTSD may not occur. We wish to stress only that, from our view, it is a common response. There are no universals in people's response to suicide, only commonalities.

experiences.[2] Recognition of the commonalities has recently been furthered by the American Psychiatric Association's (APA's) *Diagnostic and Statistical Manual of Mental Disorders,* third edition (*DSM-III;* 6). In this diagnostic manual, there is a new classification—the posttraumatic stress disorder (PTSD)—that spells out characteristic symptoms that may follow "a psychologically traumatic event that is generally outside the range of usual human experience" (p. 16). PTSD is most often associated with military combat, particularly in veterans of the Vietnam War (7). Yet, as Janoff-Bulman (5) pointed out, PTSD can be associated with other traumatic events (e.g., serious crimes, accidents, or disasters). Suicide is clearly outside the usual human experience. It indeed evokes "significant symptoms of distress in most people" (8, 9).

Traumatic stress disorder refers to those natural behaviors and emotions that occur during a catastrophe. Figley (10) defined *post*traumatic stress disorder "as a set of conscious and unconscious behaviors and emotions associated with dealing with the memories of the stressors of the catastrophe and immediately afterwards" (p. xix). In addition to the existence of a recognized stressor, PTSD, as defined by APA's revised *DSM-III* (*DSM-III-R;* 11), includes the following: reexperiencing the trauma (e.g., recurrent recollection, recurrent dreams, associations that the event is recurring), numbing of responsiveness or a reduced involvement with the external world (e.g., diminished interest, detachment, constricted affect), and persistent symptoms of increased arousal (e.g., hyperalertness, sleep disturbance, survivor guilt, problem in memory or concentration, avoidance of events that evoke recall). Table 1 presents the diagnostic criteria for PTSD as outlined in the *DSM-III-R* (11).

Our own experience with survivors of suicide would suggest that many would fir such a description. Although few people (with the exception of police, hospital staff, firemen, and guards), will, for example, ever experience finding a body, one only has to imagine what it would be like for a father to find his son dead from a gunshot wound to the head, the boy's brains and blood all over the wall—a survivor's real experience. Or to imagine a student killing himself in front of his classmates—also real experience. Or to imagine a principal cutting down a body, trying to provide resuscitation—another real experience. For them, the likelihood of experiencing PTSD is high; however, even hearing about a suicide can evoke a response, as is evident from the contagion effect. In Japan a few years ago, an 18-year-old pop idol, Yukiko Okada, after a fight with her lover, leaped to her death from the building that housed her recording company In Tokyo. In the 17 days following her suicide, the suicide toll reached 33 young people. Phillips (12, 13) has recently documented that teenage (and adult) clusters do exist. We vividly recall a number of cases in our local school system. One young man, who clearly exhibited PTSD, only fortuitously survived his own attempt 4 days[3] after his girlfriend tried to kill herself. There is a ripple effect.

All this is not meant to suggest that the realization of a posttraumatic reaction is new. Freud in 1917 (14) described what he called a psychical trauma; he saw this as a process started by a threatening situation that is acute and overwhelming. He

---

[2]By no means do we wish to suggest that the reactions after all traumas are the same. For example, we know that there are, despite commonalities, differences for survivors of a suicide, homicide, or sudden accidents.

[3]In our model, we do not strictly adhere to the criterion that the disturbance have a duration of at least 1 month. That is a criterion for diagnosis; ours is a response model (of postvention).

Table 1 Diagnostic criteria for posttraumatic stress disorder

A. The person has experienced an event that is outside the range of usual human experience and that would be markedly distressing to almost anyone, for example, a serious threat to one's life or physical integrity; serious threat or harm to one's children, spouse, or other close relatives and friends; sudden destruction of one's home or community; or seeing another person who is being, or has recently been, seriously injured or killed as the result of an accident or physical violence.

B. The traumatic event is persistently reexperienced in at least one of the following ways:
   1. Recurrent and intrusive distressing recollections of the event (in young children, repetitive play in which themes or aspects of the trauma are expressed)
   2. Recurrent distressing dreams of the event
   3. Sudden acting or feeling as if the traumatic event were recurring (includes a sense of reliving the experience, illusions, hallucinations, and dissociative [flashback] episodes, even those that occur on awakening or when intoxicated)
   4. Intense psychological distress at exposure to events that symbolize or resemble an aspect of the traumatic event, including anniversaries of the trauma

C. Persistent avoidance of stimuli associated with the trauma or numbing of general responsiveness (not present before the trauma), as indicated by at least three of the following:
   1. Efforts to avoid thoughts or feelings associated with the trauma
   2. Efforts to avoid activities or situations that arouse recollections of the trauma
   3. Inability to recall an important aspect of the trauma (psychogenic amnesia)
   4. Markedly diminished interest in significant activities (in young children, loss of recently acquired developmental skills such as toilet training or language skills)
   5. Feeling of detachment or estrangement from others
   6. Restricted range of affect, for example, inability to have loving feelings
   7. Sense of a foreshortened future, for example, does not expect to have a career, marriage, children, or a long life

D. Persistent symptoms of increased arousal (not present before the trauma), as indicated by at least two of the following:
   1. Difficulty in falling or staying asleep
   2. Irritability or outbursts of anger
   3. Difficulty concentrating
   4. Hypervigilance
   5. Exaggerated startle response
   6. Physiologic reactivity on exposure to events that symbolize or resemble an aspect of the traumatic event (for example, a woman who was raped in a elevator breaks out in a sweat when entering any elevator)

E. Duration of the disturbance (symptoms in B, C, and D) of at least 1 month.

Specify delayed onset if the onset of symptoms was at least 6 months after the trauma.

Reprinted with permission from the *Diagnostic and Statistical Manual of Mental Disorders* (3rd ed., revised). Copyright 1987 by the American Psychiatric Association.

described the reaction as a developmental sequence to a traumatic event (15). More recently in 1985, Janoff-Bulman noted that "much of the psychological trauma produced by victimizing events derives from the shattering of very basic assumptions that victims have held about the operation of the world" (5, p. 17). Most people hold that "Johnny, the 10-year-old, doesn't kill himself." Everyone has constructs, a theory of the world. With a suicide, say Johnny's, one's view of the world may be shattered, resulting in possible PTSD.[4] One has to cope with "Johnny killed himself."

---

[4]We wish to point out that the response in survivors is not always—or even usually—a disorder. We even planned to develop a neologism: posttraumatic stress response, or PTSR. It is more accurate. Yet, the tradition, noted by Figley, is to use *PTSD*.

ADJUSTMENT TO SUICIDE

Adjusting to a suicide is remarkably difficult. Freud (16) distinguished between the positive and negative effects of trauma. He saw remembering, repeating, and reexperiencing as positive, which is opposite of the more typical denial approach. Forgetting, avoidance, phobia, and inhibition were described by Freud as negative. These are common responses in many victims after a suicide, even in adults who are to guide youngsters, such as principals, psychologists, and so forth. A common response is to deny it: "Don't talk about it; after all, talking about suicide causes suicide." We firmly believe, as has been so well documented with Vietnam veterans, that this approach only exacerbates the trauma. However, as Wilson, Smith, and Johnson (3) have pointed out, it is important for people to see that the victims of a suicide may be caught in a no-win cycle of events. They noted the following:

> To talk about the powerful and overwhelming trauma means risking further stigmatization; the failure to discuss the traumatic episode increases the need for defensive avoidance and thus increases the probability of depression alternating with cycles of intensive imagery and other symptoms of PTSD. (p. 169)

Survivors must be helped to work through it. Positive adjustive strategies must be fostered.

PTSD: CHILDREN AND ADOLESCENTS

It should be noted that PTSD was intended for adults; however, *DSM-III-R* (11) makes direct application to children (see Table 1). Eth and Pynoos (17) had earlier presented convincing arguments that it can be applied to children and adolescents. They noted that children of trauma have exhibited such symptoms as "deleterious effects on cognition (including memory, school performance, and learning), affect, interpersonal relations, impulse control and behavior, vegetative function and the formation of symptoms" (p. 41). Terr (18) and Lifton and Olson (19) have both observed in studies of abducted children and in children who survived a disaster (e.g., Hiroshima) that there is a posttraumatic reaction, and that, indeed, there are amazing commonalities in how children respond to various unusual trauma. Bowlby (20) has made a number of observations about traumatic reactions to loss, most notably anxious attachment behavior. Often children do not appear to exhibit a reaction—for example, there are few recognizable overt verbalizations—but there may well be a negative reaction, which could be fostered by an adult who also wants to deny the loss. Anna Freud (21) noted that children often rely on various forms of denial, evident in fantasy, action, and affect, all in order to ease (numb) the pain.

One of the authors recalls working with a school-aged child who had found his teenage brother hanging; he simply would not believe it had happened—it did *not* happen. A child may sit for hours in front of a dead parent without responding. Denial may not be the only reaction. Aggressiveness, obsessive fantasies (recurrence), anxious arousal, behavioral problems, poor peer relations, school failure, and even imitation have been documented in children and adolescents after a suicide. For example, regarding the latter concerning characteristic, one 8-year-old was found scratching himself with a knife in his classroom, reacting to his teenage brother's serious attempt 6 months earlier. The reaction may not be immediate.

One of the authors saw a teenage girl for therapy 4 years after one of the children for whom she frequently babysat had killed himself. She recurrently imagined that if only she had been babysitting that night, she could have saved the boy.

Despite commonalities in young people's response to a trauma, Erickson (22) has pointed out that there are differences, depending on one's developmental age, in how one responds to a crisis. Eth and Pynoos (17), in their studies of children who had seen a parent killed, noted that differences exist related to developmental age. In response to a suicide, one too must consider developmental lines. Newman (23) has noted that adolescents' posttraumatic symptoms more and more resemble adult symptoms, especially posttraumatic acting out, truancy, precocious sexual actions, substance abuse, and delinquency. A. Freud (21) has suggested that such behaviors are defensive mechanisms, and Nagara (24) has postulated that much has to do with identifying with the victim (e.g., the suicide). These symptoms are ways of adjusting to the trauma; however, they are not adaptive.

INDIVIDUAL DIFFERENCES AND PTSD

All individuals do not respond to a trauma in a similar fashion. There are individual differences; not all develop PTSD. Wilson, Smith, and Johnson (3) have found in various survivor groups that one needs "to specify how the nature and complexity of the stressor event impacts on the unique personality of the survivor" (pp. 167–168). In the same vein, it is important to realize that not all survivors of suicide are alike; they bring with them their own way of adjusting to a trauma (9). It is unreasonable to believe that the psychological distress produced by a suicide will produce the same effect in everyone. We have found that the closest "objects"—family, boy- or girlfriend, close friend—are most at risk. We have, however, found people with PTSD who were distant (although maybe not psychologically) from the suicide. One recurrent marker appears to be if they had very seriously contemplated or attempted suicide themselves or if they knew someone who had killed him- or herself. In one case, for example, the person at immediate risk was the principal at a school—his parents had died in a homicide–suicide themselves. In another case, a teacher had been suicidal for years.[5] In general, however, Wilson and colleagues (3) have suggested that the more severe and complex the stressful life event, the greater the likelihood that an individual might develop symptoms of PTSD. All this also suggests, for intervention, that anyone might be the client.

THE ENVIRONMENT AND PTSD

Research on PTSD suggests that an individual's adjustment to a trauma is largely affected by the type of response provided (10). There have been a number of special programs introduced soon after trauma (e.g., prisoners of war, Iranian hostages, rape victims). Scurfield (25) has noted that such intervention (postvention) appears to have a positive effect in preventing and lessening the severity of

---

[5]Recent research by Brent and his colleagues (44) supports these clinical observations. They found that young—and we would add older—people who developed suicidal ideation and/or plans in response to early suicide were more likely to have made suicide attempts before and/or qualify for a diagnosis of major depression. Close friends of suicide victims become suicidal at lower levels of psychopathology than other people.

PTSD. Figley (26) has suggested that the critical question is this: Is the environment supportive or not?

The school is one such important environment. We have outlined elsewhere our postvention model for schools, designed to address PTSD (27–29). Other models include Carter and Brooks (30); Comstock (31); Lamartine (32); Lamartine-Anderson and Sattem (33); Lamb and Dunne-Maxim (34); Lane-Malbon (35); Pelej and Scholzen (36); Shulman (37); Valente, Saunders, and Street (38); and Zinner (39). Shneidman (40, 41) has outlined a series of more general meta-guidelines for any postvention. There are a number of important commonalities evident in these models.

Postvention in school is seen as

1. Addressing possible psychological damage (PTSD) and facilitating the grief process.

2. Addressing the contagion effect.

3. Needing preplanning. There is a need for schools to have a sound policy or plan in place before a suicide occurs.

4. Needing a coordinator—not administrative staff, but a mental health expert—to take charge and to provide structure in such highly traumatic situations.

5. Needing a school consultation, planning meeting, or both as soon as possible. Consultation with school staff, including but not limited to the teaching staff, is seen as essential. Students cannot be helped until faculty is helped. Someone in the faculty may well be most at risk.

6. Conducting staff, student, and parent workshops or services shortly after a suicide. *Postvention becomes prevention.*

7. Assessing and identifying high-risk individuals as soon as possible.

8. Providing individuals at risk with or directing them to therapeutic intervention.

9. Establishing support groups as needed.

10. Networking and linking with community agencies.

11. Conducting an academic autopsy and consultation with colleagues.

12. Handling the media effectively. A media policy should be formulated.

More agreement than disagreement exists in the literature on postvention in schools. There appears to be some controversy about concrete, content issues (29). The most critical aspect, aside from a clear formulation about PTSD, of suicide postvention in the future is evaluation. Is what one is doing effective? What else needs to be done? Why does it work?

CONCLUDING REMARKS

To conclude, although there are individual differences, Green, Wilson, and Lindy (43) have noted that the social environment may contribute to a person's recovery.

There is most likely an interaction between person and event. Social supports, especially schools, are critical. As Green and colleagues (43) have noted the "more supportive environments tend to be associated with better adjustment to stress" (p. 61). Regrettably, as already noted, adults, even in schools, foster denial. We frequently promote negative adjustment. It would appear from our view that much of this has to do with people in authority in school systems. We believe that response needs to begin with administration, followed by school staff and the other individuals involved. People's attitudes toward suicide (44) also need to be addressed. People can learn from the best-known victims of PTSD, Vietnam veterans. Their PTSD was so severe because the attitude toward the Vietnam war was so negative—the war was a loss!

REFERENCES

1. Gleser, G., Green, B., & Wignet, C. (1981). *Buffalo Creek revisited: Prolonged psychosocial effects of disaster.* New York: Simon & Schuster.
2. Horowitz, M. (1979). Psychological response to serious life events. In V. Hamilton & D. Warburton (Eds.), *Human stress and cognition.* New York: Wiley.
3. Wilson, J., Smith, W., & Johnson, S. (1985). A comparative analysis of PTSD among various survivor groups. In C. Figley (Ed.), *Trauma and its wake* (pp. 142–172). New York: Brunner/Mazel.
4. Freud, S. (1917). Mourning and melancholia. In J. Strachey (Ed. and Trans.), *The standard edition of the complete psychological works of S. Freud* (Vol. 14, pp. 239–258). London: Hogarth Press.
5. Janoff-Bulman, R. (1985). The aftermath of victimization: Rebuilding shattered assumptions. In C. Figley (Ed.), *Trauma and its wake* (pp. 15–35). New York: Brunner/Mazel.
6. American Psychiatric Association. (1980). *Diagnostic and statistical manual of mental disorders* (3rd Ed.). Washington, DC: Author.
7. Figley, C. (Ed.). (1978). *Stress disorders among Vietnam veterans.* New York: Brunner/Mazel.
8. Leenaars, A. (1988). *Suicide notes.* New York: Human Sciences Press.
9. Shneidman, E. (1985). *Definition of suicide.* New York: Wiley.
10. Figley, C. (1985). Introduction. In C. Figley (Ed.), *Trauma and its wake* (pp. xvii–xxvi). New York: Brunner/Mazel.
11. American Psychiatric Association. (1987). *Diagnostic and statistical manual of mental disorders* (3rd Ed., rev.). Washington, DC: American Psychiatric Association.
12. Phillips, D., & Carstensen, M. (1986). Clustering of teenage suicides after television news stories about suicide. *New England Journal of Medicine, 315,* 685–689.
13. Phillips, D. (1986, April). *Effect of the media.* Paper presented at the conference of the American Association of Suicidology, Atlanta, GA.
14. Freud, S. (1917). Introductory lectures in psychoanalysis. In J. Strachey (Ed. and Trans.), *The standard edition of the complete psychological works of Sigmund Freud* (Vol. 16, pp. 243–463). London: Hogarth Press.
15. Freud, S. (1926). Inhibitions, symptoms and anxiety. In J. Strachey (Ed. and Trans.), *The standard edition of the complete psychological works of Sigmund Freud* (Vol. 20, pp. 77–174). London: Hogarth Press.
16. Freud, S. (1939). Moses and monotheism. In J. Strachey (Ed. & Trans.), *The standard edition of the complete psychological works of Sigmund Freud* (Vol. 23, pp. 3–137). London: Hogarth Press.
17. Eth, G., & Pynoos, R. (1985). Developmental perspective on psychic trauma in childhood. In C. Figley (Ed.), *Trauma and its wake* (pp. 36–52). New York: Brunner/Mazel.
18. Terr, L. (1979). Children of Chonchilla: Study of psychic trauma. *Psychoanalytic Study of the Child, 34,* 547–623.
19. Lifton, R., & Olson, E. (1976). The human meaning of total disaster: The Buffalo Creek experience. *Psychiatry, 39,* 1–18.
20. Bowlby, J. (1977). The making and breaking of affectionate bonds. *British Journal of Psychiatry, 130,* 201–208, 421–431.
21. Freud, A. (1966). *Ego and mechanism of defense.* New York: International Universe Press.
22. Erickson, E. (1932). *The life cycle completed:* New York: Norton.
23. Newman, C. (1976). Children of disaster: Clinical observations at Buffalo Creek. *American Journal of Psychiatry, 133,* 306–312.
24. Nagara, H. (1970). Children's reactions to the death of important objects: A developmental approach. *Psychoanalytic Study of the Child, 25,* 360–500.
25. Scurfield, R. (1985). Post-trauma stress assessment and treatment. Overview and formulation. In C. Figley (Ed.), *Trauma and its wake* (pp. 219–256). New York: Brunner/Mazel.

26. Figley, C. (1983). Catastrophes: An overview of family reactions: In C. Figley & H. Cubbin (Eds.), *Stress and the family, Volume II: Coping with catastrophes*. New York: Brunner/Mazel.
27. Leenaars, A. (1985). Suicide postvention in a school system. *Canada's Mental Health, 33*(4).
28. Leenaars, A., & Wenckstern, S. (1986, April). *Suicide postvention in a school system*. Paper presented at the conference of the American Association of Suicidology, Atlanta, GA.
29. Leenaars, A., & Wenckstern, S. (1988). Suicide postvention in school systems: A model. In J. Morgan (Ed.), *Helping children cope with death*. London: King's College.
30. Carter, B., & Brooks, A. (1986, April). *An exploration of group postvention techniques*. Paper presented at the conference of the American Association of Suicidology, Atlanta, GA.
31. Comstock, B. (1985,). Youth suicide cluster: A community response. *Newslink*.
32. Lamartine, C. (1985). *Suicide prevention in educational settings: After a suicide death*. Dayton, OH: Suicide Prevention Center.
33. Lamartine-Anderson, C., & Sattem, L. (1986, April). *After a suicide in an educational setting*. Paper presented at the conference of the American Association of Suicidology, Atlanta, GA.
34. Lamb, F., & Dunne-Maxim, K. (1987). Postvention in schools: Policy and process. In E. Dunne, J. McIntosh, & K. Dunne-Maxim (Eds.), *Suicide and its aftermath: Understanding and counseling the survivors*. New York: Norton.
35. Lane-Malbon, L. (1986, April). *After suicide: Crisis intervention in the school*. Paper presented at the conference of the American Association of Suicidology, Atlanta, GA.
36. Pelej, J., & Scholzen, K. (1987, May). *Postvention: A school's response to a suicide*. Paper presented at the conference of the American Association of Suicidology, San Francisco.
37. Shulman, N. (1986). Tragedy in Concord: Crisis intervention in a school following a student fatality. *Newslink*.
38. Valente, S., Saunders, J., & Street, R. (1986). *Adolescent bereavement programs in the schools*. Paper presented at the conference of the American Association of Suicidology, Atlanta, GA.
39. Zinner, E. (1986). *Survivor intervention strategy in the suicide of a sixth-grader*. Paper presented at the conference of the American Association of Suicidology, Atlanta, GA.
40. Shneidman, E. (1981). Postvention: The care of the bereaved. In E. Shneidman, *Suicide thoughts and reflections, 1960–1980* (pp. 157–167). New York: Human Sciences Press.
41. Shneidman, E. (1983). Postvention and the survivor-victim. In *Deaths of man*. Jason Aronson.
42. Brent, D., Kerr, M., Goldstein, C., Bozigar, J., Wartella, M., & Allan, M. (1989). An outbreak of suicide and suicidal behavior in a high school. *Journal of the American Academy of Child and Adolescent Psychiatry, 28*, 918–924.
43. Green, B., Wilson, J., & Lindy, J. (1985). Conceptualizing post-traumatic stress disorders. A psychosocial framework. In C. Figley (Ed.), *Trauma and is wake* (pp. 53–72). New York: Brunner/Mazel.
44. Domino, G., & Leenaars, A. (1989). Attitudes toward suicide: A comparison of Canadian and United States college students. *Suicide and Life-Threatening Behavior, 19*, 160–172.

15

Suicide Postvention: A Case Illustration in a Secondary School

Susanne Wenckstern
Board of Education for the City of Windsor, Ontario

Antoon A. Leenaars
Windsor, Ontario

Postvention, a term introduced by Shneidman (1–3), refers to the following:

> *Those things done after the dire event has occurred that serve to mollify the after effects of the event in a person who has attempted suicide, or to deal with the adverse effects as the survivor-victims of a person who has committed suicide. (1, p. 385)*

Postvention includes service(s) to all survivors of such a dire event who are in need—children, parents, teachers, friends, and so forth. Suicide (and death) postvention are seen as important future developments. We believe that school systems will be an especially critical force in these endeavors (1–5).

The literature on suicide postvention in schools is very scant (e.g., 4, 5). Increased attention, however, is being paid to this topic as was evident at recent conferences of the American Association of Suicidology (6–12).

School postvention programs represent an "organized response of a caring, humanistic institution in addressing the traumatic loss of a student in such a way that the emotional needs of those remaining are dealt with effectively" (10, p. 387). They are designed specifically to address the traumatic loss of a student by forestalling possible psychological damage within our posttraumatic stress disorder (PTSD) framework (as outlined elsewhere in this book; 13) and to facilitate the grief process (4). A major concern and thrust of such programs is addressing the contagion or "copycat" effect (14) by preventing suicide role modeling (7).

We wish to stress that postvention work is not merely grief counseling. We view the grieving process as part of or embedded within a posttraumatic framework. Some postvention programs have gone awry in regarding it as a bereavement process alone. Postvention in schools requires a different understanding and training. In our view, it is more like responding to a disaster, such as, for example, addressing the space shuttle disaster in Christa McAuliffe's school.

Preplanned postvention efforts are viewed by Leenaars and Wenckstern (9) as

We thank the Board of Education for the City of Windsor for its support of our effort. Discussions with Dr. E. Shneidman are greatly appreciated. The views in this chapter are the author's, not necessarily those of the Board of Education for the City of Windsor.

being embedded within prevention efforts that strive to address the suicidal problem among youth.

STRATEGIES FOR POSTVENTION

Our postvention efforts essentially represent a synthesis of *educational strategies* largely selected from the American Association of Suicidology and the Canadian Association for Suicide Prevention; *consultative intervention* acquired in part from Goodstein (15) and Watzlawick, Beavin, and Jackson (16); *crisis intervention strategies* from Farberow (17), Hoff (18), Parad (19), and Shneidman (20, 21), and a few specifically related to trauma response, for example, Lifton (22) and Lindemann (23); *and especially postvention strategies* from Shneidman (2).

Our postvention program includes the following generic aspects, although modifications will be necessary depending on such factors as time, situation, and nature of the suicide. Postvention requires a constructivist approach within a general, heuristic framework.

1. *Consultation.* Discussion, coordination, and planning are undertaken at every phase, beginning with school administration and then followed by school staff and by other involved individuals, such as students and parents, under the direction of the postvention coordinator, that is, a mental health expert who takes charge and provides structure. Concurrent peer consultation and review among professional staff who are involved in the postvention program (postvention team) are undertaken to review the plans that were implemented and to plan or coordinate further action. For example, a flexible contingency plan must be preplanned to allow for alternative actions, if needed.

There is some controversy in the field of suicidology at this time regarding whether the consultants to the program should be inside or outside consultants vis-à-vis the school. It has been our experience that at least one consultant should be an insider. A difficulty may arise when an outside consultant needs to quickly penetrate a school's barriers or resistances in times of trauma. We believe that regardless of whether a consultant is inside or outside, territorial problems need to be addressed.

2. *Crisis intervention.* Emergency or crisis response is provided, using basic problem-solving strategies. We believe that students and staff of the local school are likely to need support in response to a suicide trauma. It is crucial not to underestimate the closeness of relationships or the intensity of reactions of individuals who might be experiencing a posttraumatic stress reaction. (See Hoff in this book.)

3. *Community linkage.* As we believe that it is imperative that survivors of suicide be provided with the appropriate support, we assist these individuals to obtain such services. Educational systems need to develop a linkage system or network to aid in making referrals to the appropriate community services and to exchange information and coordinate services with appropriate community services as needed. Such a network should be predefined. As an example, following the space shuttle disaster, people found it helpful that they had already established relationships in the school to call (24). Setting up a suicide prevention–awareness committee has assisted people in our community, for another example, to know what is available and has allowed us to liaise with other providers in our area. No

one agency can provide all the services necessary after a trauma. Equally as important, a school is not likely to be able to address all the needs.

4. *Assessment and counseling.* Evaluation and therapy are provided as needed or when requested by the school administrator, for example, the principal or his or her designate. (See Part III of this book.)

5. *Education.* Information about suicide and its prevention (e.g., clues, myths, causes, what to do, where to go for help, etc.) is provided through discussion, seminars, workshops, and small assemblies (35–50 people) at the school and within the community. (See Part II of this book.)

6. *Liaison with the media.* Information about the suicide in the form of publicity, especially that which tends to sensationalize or glamorize the suicide, should be avoided. It is not and should not be the school's responsibility to provide information about the actuarial details of the suicide to the media. This falls within the jurisdiction of the police department, coroner's office, or other authorities. However, our experience has shown us that (a) a media spokesperson for the school must be appointed at the outset of the crisis, and (b) this role should be filled by the postvention coordinator and not by a school administrator (e.g., the principal). Not only does this ensure the accuracy and consistency of information being given out, but most important, it ensures that this information is being provided by someone who understands the postvention procedures and positive impact of the program. It is the procedures and their impact that should be emphasized to the media.

7. *Follow-up.* Periodic follow-ups are undertaken with the school administrators, school staff, and mental health professionals (e.g., as in our case, school board psychological and social work services staff). A formal final consultation is provided several months after the suicide to facilitate a formal closure to the program. However, every attempt is made to let all concerned know that we are available on request for follow-up if the need arises.

PRINCIPLES OF POSTVENTION

Shneidman (2) provided us with some principles of postvention that are common to understanding the event. They are largely based on his extensive work with survivors in a psychotherapeutic context.

The following principles of postvention are derived from Shneidman but have been liberally modified for application within a school setting:

1. In working with the survivor-victims of suicide, it is best to begin as soon as possible after the tragedy, within the first 24 hr if that can be managed with the students at the school. Consultation and networking between all concerned personnel (i.e., school administrators, teachers, mental health professionals [e.g., psychological and social work services staff]), under the direction of a postvention coordinator, are critical at this time. Equally important as the program initiated through these efforts is the compilation and sharing of accurate, reliable information about the event as it becomes known, in order to combat often mounting hysteria as misinformation, often of a sensational nature, quickly proliferates. Further, the mechanism for establishing clear lines of communication, as quickly and as effectively as possible, occurs at this time. Schools require the *early* actions of professionals to help promote the appearance of strength and reassurance in a

situation that is not only unanticipated but also overwhelming to many survivors. Intervention with survivors before funeral arrangements are made is especially helpful to youth. For many of them this traumatic event represents their first encounter with death and funerals. Early intervention can facilitate the planning of specific individual and group leave-taking rituals within a supportive milieu. These can be combined with formal funeral ceremonies that allow young people not only to acknowledge their relationship to the decedent but also to be a part of larger, culturally embedded leave-taking ceremonies.

2. Resistance may be met from the survivors; some—but not all—are either willing or eager to have the opportunity to talk to professionally oriented persons. Others only wish to deny the event—a negative posttraumatic stress reaction. Our experience has shown us that this resistance may come from a source that is essential to the cooperative effort of postvention: the school administration.

In our own attempts, we have, however, fortunately received cooperation from all parents; they play a critical, indirect role in our efforts at the school.

A book recommended to us as being helpful by a number of survivors of suicide is *After Suicide* by John H. Hewett (25). Hewett reminds one of the root origin of the word *survive:* It comes from two Latin words—*super,* which means *over,* and *vivere,* which means *to live.* The survivor has a chance to start over or continue to live a life that he or she might have felt to be over. The survivors at the school (the school family) need to learn to go on living—to work and to play.

Before this step, within a school setting, it is important to identify the survivors. Within a fairly large, heterogeneous school setting, one can usually anticipate that some subgroups within the larger school context may be more affected by the suicide than other groups or individuals, for example, the deceased student's class or grade or teacher in comparison with other more distant classes or grades at that school. At the same time, it is often difficult to identify potential PTSD victims; for example, in one case a student who was several years junior to the suicide victim but who was "psychologically close," that is, who identified closely with the deceased student, was most at risk. We know of one case in which the principal, whose own parents had died as a result of homicide–suicide, was most at risk. It has been our experience that, although it is difficult, many of those survivors who have been identified as potential PTSD victims are not only willing to talk about the tragedy and their feelings, cognitions, and so forth but are relieved to be provided with the opportunity to do so. Identifying and intervening with survivors reassures more peripheral members of the group that appropriate and beneficial actions are imminent.

3. Negative emotions about the decedent (the deceased person) or about death itself—such as irritation, anger, envy, shame, guilt, and so on—need to be explored, but not necessarily at the very beginning. Timing is very important.

It has been our experience that this is true whether one is in a dyadic therapeutic relationship or is a professional assisting individuals or groups in a school setting. The individual or group should not be prematurely pushed into confronting or dealing with negative emotions, cognitions, and so forth at a time when defenses may be strong and necessary.

4. The postvener should play the important role of reality tester. He or she is not so much the echo of conscience as the quiet voice of reason.

It is very important to provide survivors, especially young people, with sound adult role models to guide and assist them through the posttraumatic stress process. Assisting adult survivors first not only provides reassurance but also allows them to facilitate the process as adult role models for their young charges.

5. Referral to community services may be crucial in some cases. One should be constantly alert for possible decline in physical health and overall mental well-being and for other symptoms of PTSD.

As stated earlier, we believe networking among service providers is important, as it is imperative that survivors of suicide be made aware of and be provided with appropriate short- and long-term support if it is needed. It is simply not the school alone that needs to respond but other services in the community as well—bereavement services, community crisis services, clergy, family physicians, and so on.

Posttraumatic stress is itself a dire process, almost akin to a disease in that there are subtle factors at work that can take a heavy toll unless they are treated and controlled. In the case of suicide, the death of a significant other is fraught with the emotional and psychological aspects of a death that was self-inflicted, which when coupled with the human need to understand and make meaning of what often is a nonunderstandable event, makes the adjustment process very difficult. For children, the latter may be hindered by their developmental level, most notably their understanding of death (26).

6. Needless to say, pollyannaish optimism or banal platitudes should be avoided. Statements such as "Don't worry, Sally, this too shall pass," "You'll get over it," and "Everything will be okay, Billy, now run out and play" are in no way helpful. Not only do survivors find these kind of verbal statements not helpful, they may be PTSD enhancing. They exemplify a lack of empathic understanding that may in fact alienate the survivor at a time when support is critical. Providing an atmosphere of compassionate, empathic understanding without being judgmental in any way is more helpful. One must be a good active listener to be helpful.

7. Trauma work takes awhile: anywhere from several months to the end of the person's life, but certainly more than 3 weeks or six sessions.

Although our efforts in the school typically last about 3–4 months, a greater length of time may be required in addressing posttraumatic stress reactions in some individuals. The door is always left open. That is, within our framework the length of time or number of sessions cannot be prescribed in either an arbitrary or a priori fashion. There are no predictable, sequential stages to PTSD. Similarly, from the survivor's framework, it is not a definitive 6 months, 10 months, and so on. To illustrate, one girl required therapy 2 years after her brother committed suicide, when she was at the same age her brother was when he killed himself. This is not an uncommon phenomenon among siblings of suicide victims. Research shows that our society sanctions a fairly consensual mourning period of approximately 1 year's duration with a well-known individual and group rituals that demarcate the beginning and end of mourning. However, we know of a widow in her 50s who had lost her husband 8 years earlier. This woman was castigated by her 80-year-old mother for attending a dance with a widowed woman friend. There is no simple or single rule of thumb to the posttraumatic stress process; it is very individual. In some cases it may take several months or years, and it may take considerably longer or even to the end of life, as Shneidman has indicated. The latter may occur if the posttraumatic stress response is partially or not worked through. For children and adolescent survivors, the suicide of a close "object" may leave

Table 1 Principles of postvention

1. In working with survivor victims of suicide, it is best to begin as soon as possible after the tragedy, within the first 24 hours if that can be managed with children at the school.
2. Resistance may be met from the survivors; some—but not all—are either willing or eager to have the opportunity to talk to professionally oriented persons.
3. Negative emotions about the decedent (the deceased person) or about the death itself—irritation, anger, envy, shame, guilt, and so on—need to be explored, but not at the very beginning. Timing is so important.
4. The postvener should play the important role of reality tester. He or she is not so much the echo of conscience as *the quiet voice of reason.*
5. Referral to community services may be crucial in some cases. One should be constantly alert for possible decline in physical health and in overall mental well-being.
6. Needless to say, pollannaish optimism, or banal platitudes, should be avoided.
7. Trauma work takes awhile—from several months to the end of life, but certainly more than 3 weeks or 6 sessions.
8. A comprehensive program of health care on the part of a benign and enlightened community should include preventive, interventive, and *postventive* elements.

irrevocable and perennial scars, depending on such factors as that youth's level of cognitive, emotional, and psychological development.

8. A comprehensive program of health care on the part of a benign and enlightened community should include preventive, interventive, and postventive elements.

As many school settings become increasingly diversified in terms of the students, families, and communities they serve, flexibility within the program (e.g., contingency plans) and its time lines will become necessary to take into account and appropriately address demographic and sociocultural factors. One must be sensitive and empathic to the needs of survivor-victims who may not share one's culturally prescribed leave-taking and funeral rituals.

Table 1 presents the basic principles.

SEQUENCE OF POSTVENTION

Figure 1 is a flowchart diagram in time-sequence format of our program for school postvention of a student suicide. Preplanned postvention efforts are crucial. A plan must be in place before a suicide, not after. Appropriate modifications can be made to address PTSD associated with other traumatic deaths or for the suicide of significant others (e.g., parent, sibling, or school staff).

The program calls for the postvention team to engage in a number of preplanned consultations. This team consists of critically identified school personnel and mental health professionals under the direction of a postvention coordinator, ideally a mental health professional with prior experience in this area. The size of the team will vary in each case depending on a number of factors, such as the availability of resources, size of school, and so forth. In-servicing of key personnel (e.g., school psychologists, social workers, teachers, and principals) provides them with basic postventive skills for future efforts. We believe it is paramount to the program's effectiveness that a professional remain in charge to provide structure and direction at important junctures. The program calls, however, for joint coordination of efforts, as one individual cannot effectively deal with such a large-scale trauma and also to prevent stress overload. The principal, for example, will

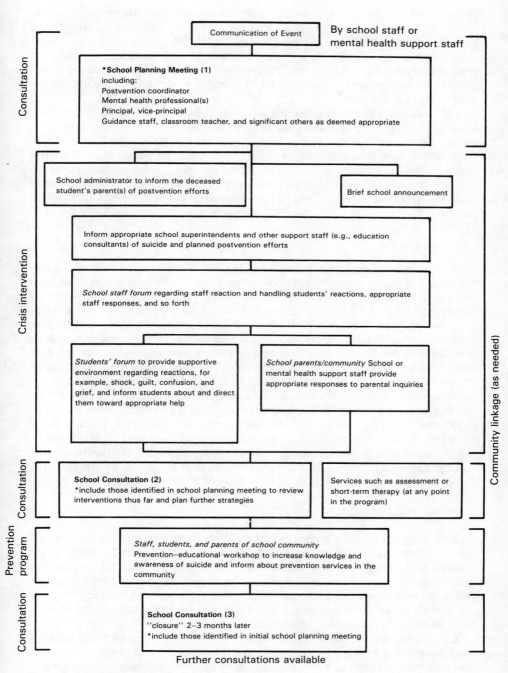

Figure 1 School Postvention of a Suicide

be another key person on the team in regard to the administrative issues that will occur. Joint postvention team efforts also ensure the provision of ongoing coverage, a number of contacts and supports for posttraumatic stress victims, and alternative sources of information and perspectives. At each and every level of the program, individual or group consultations are available with any mental health professional on request. This is clearly reiterated to the school throughout the postvention efforts.

Our experience has shown that the emphasis in such consultations and reviews should be supportive, positive, and constructive (e.g., "What did you do?" "What other factors might be important?" "What can we do next?") This contrasts with a more assaultive, overly critical approach or emphasis (e.g., "Did you do ?" "Why didn't you consider ?" etc.) that can easily become the tenor of the consultative process under such professionally stressful, anxiety-provoking conditions. A supportive approach is helpful to the postvention team and to the program as well.

Consultation

As shown in the flowchart presented in Figure 1, following a report of suicide, the school planning meeting (1) is conducted to ensure that the postvention team meets to (a) acquaint everyone with the basic concepts and steps in the postvention program and (b) formulate problem-solving strategies and plan how best to implement the program with immediate focus on crisis intervention response for that school's particular time, place, and situation. It is important to engage in a prior meeting with postvention team members who are unfamiliar with the program in order to acquaint them with it. Clarification of roles and response to the media by the postvention coordinator are addressed here.

Before formulating a plan and specific strategies, clarification of the event must occur. Facts surrounding the death must be verified, for example, from the police department (such as a victim's referral unit) or medical examiner. When it is not clear that the death was a suicide, this uncertainty can be acknowledged. However, the suicide of a teacher or student cannot be kept secret, even if the family requests it. One must address the needs of the students and staff in trauma. The trauma goes beyond the family: One needs to address possible PTSD in all survivors.

Crisis Intervention

Following consultation arising out of the school planning meeting (1) a school administrator, usually the principal, informs the deceased student's family of the planned postvention efforts. Concurrently, school administration are requested to give a brief message of condolence that serves to publicly acknowledge a student's death. We have found that the vehicle for imparting this information varies according to such factors as school size, time of day, and so forth. Appropriate superintendents and others are also informed at this time.

Crisis intervention with students and school staff (including all staff, not only teaching staff) is engaged in as soon as possible after the tragedy (both formally and informally). Goals include providing basic support, accurate information discussed openly and frankly, and the message that assistance is forthcoming. Targeting the deceased student's classmates, teachers, and close friends for immediate support and identifying potential posttraumatic stress victims are critical at this stage. School staff, and especially the school secretaries, are sought out for consultation to aid them in appropriately addressing parental and community inquiries, calls from the media, and so forth. School secretaries are often the initial contact person and need to know how to respond appropriately and consistently to parental and community inquiries. Secretaries should not be media spokespersons or give out detailed information. The role of providing basic facts and knowing who to refer inquiries to should be the limit of their responsibility. In a similar vein, all team members and the coordinator need to be aware of their limits of responsibility regarding the provision of information to parents, media, and so forth.

At this point, school staff is worked with in a fairly informal workshop format (see Figure 1, School Staff Forum) *before* engaging the students, as we believe it is crucial to address the staff's needs and reactions and to prepare them to assist the students. We have found that staff need to be assisted before they can be expected to help their students. Information regarding planned efforts is also provided.

Subsequently, a forum is provided for individual students, groups, or classes (see Figure 1, Students' Forum) identified in the school planning meeting in order to provide an immediate, supportive environment to handle initial posttraumatic stress reactions. Information about where to go for help if needed is provided. Information regarding the planned sequence of postvention efforts and what students can expect related to these efforts is also provided. An opportunity to answer questions, concerns, and so forth is an important aspect during this session or sessions with the students.

Consultation

Following immediate crisis intervention efforts, the significant people identified in the school planning meeting (1), and others deemed appropriate, are called together (see Figure 1, School Consultation; 2) to process postvention efforts to that point and to plan further strategies, including those that begin to address suicide prevention. We have found that the consultative process is the key to an appropriate response, even when needed, for the coordinator him- or herself. However, such supervisory consultation should only be provided by someone with some expertise in suicidology.

Services such as assessment or short therapy are provided at any point in the program. Networking in the form of community linkage also occurs at any point (e.g., medical, crisis, or mental health services and others), especially for follow-up and long-term treatment, if needed.

Prevention Program

Educational or informational workshops focusing on suicide prevention are implemented. Prevention should not be seen as a substitute for postvention. They are not the same thing. Prevention, however, is an essential part of postvention. School staff, students, parents, and any other interested individuals or groups within the community are targeted for prevention or education workshops in order to increase awareness and knowledge about suicide prevention and inform people about local services available.

For student workshops, we have found it good practice to have parents informed in writing by school administration of the purpose and content of the workshop. Parents should be encouraged to contact designated school administrators or the postvention team regarding questions, concerns, and so forth.

Consultation

The third formal consultation (see Figure 1, School Consultation; 3) is essentially a time to wrap up. It is a forum for providing some closure, although the doors remain open. It is also a time to process what has occurred in the form of an academic autopsy, which is invaluable in attempting to assess the effectiveness of the postvention efforts and will aid in future preplanned efforts in terms of revising and refining the program.

SUICIDE CASE ILLUSTRATION
AT THE SECONDARY LEVEL

We illustrate our program with a suicide case, using a time-sequence format: The postvention coordinator (Susanne Wenckstern) was notified of the suicide of a 17-year-old boy by the boy's secondary school principal (in consultation with the school psychologist) as soon as school began the morning following his suicide.

1. At the principal's request, the coordinator provided immediate basic support to the suicide's sibling and friend (who were found sitting in the school counseling office) and gave them assurances that immediate follow-up by mental health school professionals (in this case, the school psychologist and school social worker) would occur.

2. The postvention team then met for the school planning meeting (1). The team included the postvention coordinator, mental health professionals, principal, vice-principal, guidance department head, and other key school personnel (e.g., guidance staff, head secretary, community personnel, etc.). The meeting was chaired by the postvention coordinator. The meeting agenda was to process what had happened, that is, to clarify known "facts" related to the suicide and to coordinate the team's efforts in a systematic way (using the outline presented in Figure 1). Discussions about appropriate response to students, parents, and others were undertaken at this time. It is very important to include not only teachers but also other school staff, such as the school crossing guard, secretary, and maintenance staff, who also have contact with students and their families.

3. At this particular secondary (or high) school, the *usual* response to a student's or staff member's death is to briefly express a message of condolence. It is important that a suicide be acknowledged as would any other death. The principal therefore issued a brief announcement, as was his norm, over the public address system, although we personally believe that no death should be announced by this means. It would be more desirable to have classroom teachers inform their students within the classroom; however, this often is not feasible in a practical sense, especially in large schools, given the many "pulls" for coordination of efforts in the immediate aftermath of a suicide. In this case, the deceased boy's classmates were informed of the specific nature of the death within their classrooms at regular class time by their teachers. The principal accepted the responsibility of informing the deceased student's parents and Board of Education administrative personnel of planned postvention efforts.

4. Individual support and encouragement were provided throughout the day by the postvention team to several of the deceased boy's teachers at their request. Again, anyone can be identified as a survivor or as being in need of help through the posttraumatic stress process (e.g., principal, parent, sibling, teacher). These teachers sought some direction in how to handle the situation with their students and expressed some guilt feelings about whether they had missed a suicidal clue. One teacher had just experienced a personal suicide tragedy and required additional support and counseling, which, as we have learned, is not an uncommon event. Throughout the day the door of the counseling office was left open to any student or school staff member. A mental health member of the postvention team and counselors were on call throughout the day to provide support, answer questions, make appropriate community referrals, and so forth. Counseling staff were thus involved directly in our postvention efforts in order to facilitate their visibility and accessibility as contact–support people.

5. All members of school staff were informed about and requested to attend a staff meeting–workshop (see Figure 1, School Staff Forum) that first day. The deceased student's eight classroom teachers in particular were targeted for this session. A number of staff, including classroom teachers, counselors, the school librarian, and the secretary, were present and shared their reactions and concerns, asked questions, and so forth and were prepared for the following day's and subsequent postvention efforts at the school.

6. At the start of the second day a school consultation was undertaken to review and update information (that had not come to light in the previous day's immediate aftermath) and to plan that day's postvention efforts. In providing guidelines for intervention the program simultaneously serves to reduce the team's and school's perceived stress in what are often emotionally charged and chaotic PTSD situations. However, the program needs to be flexible to allow modifications to occur, depending on case-by-case specificity. In this case, it became necessary to accommodate to that day's funeral services as arranged by the immediate family with little advance notice to the school community (i.e., 40 hr after the death).

7. The plans devised the previous day to address student needs (see Figure 1, Students' Forum) were reviewed. Specifically, designated members of the postvention team (postvention coordinator, school social worker, school psychologist, and counselor) went into all eight classes in which the deceased boy had been a member (with the teacher present) during regular class time to provide basic support; deal with the students' reactions to suicide generally, their guilt feelings, and other reactions; answer questions; inform participants where help was available both within the school and community as well as inform them of current postvention and future planned prevention efforts. Just as counseling staff need to be actively involved in the process (each of the school's three counselors were in at least two classrooms), similarly teachers need to be involved so that they are aware of student reactions and are prepared for follow-up if needed. Teachers, as we have found in the past, were very helpful in identifying at-risk students.

Basically, this aspect of our postvention program provides a forum or opportunity for students and their teachers to discuss the suicide openly and frankly in a supportive fashion. An invitation was extended to peers (i.e., other than classmates) of the deceased student to attend any of the classroom discussions. All students were provided with the option of participating or leaving the classroom at any point. Some of the deceased boy's classmates attended more than one classroom session. To accommodate approximately 12 close friends and classmates who missed all classroom discussions throughout the day (primarily because of their attendance at the funeral services), the postvention team met with these students in small groups at the end of the day. These were very cohesive, close-knit groups resulting in intensive group interaction, with members of the group more openly sharing emotions, questions, and so forth within a supportive setting.

8. The second formal consultation (see Figure 1, School Consultation; 2) was undertaken after school with persons identified in the school planning meeting (1) in order to review and process the second day's efforts and plan further efforts such as the provision of suicide prevention–educational workshops to students, school staff, and parents. We believe it is important in posttraumatic stress situations for the postvention team to meet frequently in the days following the event with key people within the school in order to process ongoing efforts, to continue to clarify facts as they emerge, and to share up-to-date information and suggestions or ideas and, very important, to provide support to one another. Working very closely with top school administrators and obtaining their support and commitment to the postvention program are essential.

9. Throughout the initial days following the suicide and subsequently, individual assessment and short-term counseling were provided on a request by a student, his or her parents(s), or school staff. Linkage with appropriate community services (e.g., a survivor group) was made as needed. Involving other professional caregivers within the community is essential to aid in follow-up and in providing services such as short- and long-term treatment when needed.

10. On the third day, following peer consultation, the postvention team again reviewed the efforts undertaken to date and coordinated further specific action for the week (e.g., providing ongoing coverage at the school for the remainder of the week). Throughout the first week, the postvention team in general and mental health members of the team in particular were available for consultation, discussion, or counseling. The school reported that the availability of mental health support, especially during the first days after the suicide, was deeply appreciated; we were there if needed. Being highly visible served to reduce some of the stress and anxiety experienced by adults, who may normally view themselves as totally in control or in charge. The postvention team serves as role models not only to students but also to staff in such posttraumatic stress situations.

The postvention team continued to be available through the first week as needed, with ongoing consultation of the coordinator.

11. Approximately 3 weeks after the suicide, a mandatory staff educational workshop was conducted by the school psychologist and school social worker. We have found that it is critical to emphasize the mandatory nature of attendance, as our experience has shown that those people who would clearly benefit most from attending such a workshop often engage in denial and avoidance by not attending, both negative, maladjustive reactions. In fact, despite having had several other fairly recent suicides at this secondary school, and having had no previous inservicing on this topic, the principal reported that many teachers felt that they did not need to learn more about suicide prevention.

12. Approximately 1 week following the staff prevention workshop, an educational workshop was presented to one third of the student body who had signed up to attend. Small group workshops (i.e., 20 students) were conducted by the mental

health members of the postvention team, accompanied by a counselor. The participation of counseling staff again served to make local, in-school personnel highly visible to students as accessible contact or resource persons.

A similar workshop was planned and offered at the school for the school parents and community (prevention program).

13. In the following weeks, periodic follow-ups with the principal, school staff, school psychologist, and school social worker, as well as community contacts, were undertaken. A more formal wrap up (i.e., School Consultation; 3) was undertaken several months later to provide a sense of closure to these postvention efforts and included an *academic autopsy* to aid in future refinements of the program. The doors were left open to the school, as we believe that potential for contact with indefinite extended periods should be included in any crisis intervention program designed to address possible PTSD.

Throughout these postvention efforts, *informal* discussion and consultation with school staff and, in particular, peers has been important not only in terms of obtaining collegial support and enhancing our own educational and professional development, but also in assisting us in reviewing the program's effectiveness.

A NEGATIVE CASE ILLUSTRATION

We have come to learn that the system—or more accurately, an individual's (e.g., principal's) denial of the event or trauma—may hinder a response. Here is an example:

1. The postvention coordinator was notified of the student's suicide by the school.

2. That same day (Day 1), the postvention team (the coordinator and school mental health professionals) met with the vice-principal to assess the situation and to plan implementation of the appropriate intervention plan. By this time, despite previous available in-service training, the school staff had already arranged, without consultation, a meeting with those students who had been classmates of the deceased student—an unfortunate first deviation of the program. The structure and direction follows from the program under the direction of the postvention coordinator. One does not implement one's own program.

3. Despite reluctance (given the milieu of that particular school), the postvention team had no choice but to meet with the students. During the meeting with students (see Figure 1, Crisis Intervention—Students' Forum), attempts were made to begin discussions with students with an understanding that follow-up, as our program calls for, would be provided. Students were in fact informed of the planned sequence of follow-up efforts, with details to follow (e.g., dates, times, etc.).

4. The next day (Day 2), the principal stopped all response, saying that it would only aggravate the situation ("After all, we don't want to put ideas in their heads"). Even the follow-up was not allowed.

This case highlights the critical need to have a program for suicide postvention in schools. A number of serious attempts followed at that school—the contagion effect that postvention is designed to address occurred. Even years later, there has been fallout at the school. The need to respond must be stressed in schools; *a principal or other school administrator simply should not be allowed to make the decision.* There is not only a need to respond positively to the possible posttraumatic stress reaction but also to respond to obvious liability issues. To address this often encountered "system" concern, we suggest that one begin by establishing a postvention project with upper administration, followed by lower administration and school staff, and other involved individuals.

CONCLUDING REMARKS

Suicide does occur, and although most people will never experience such an event, it is important that everyone increase their knowledge about it. Schools need to learn to respond positively to such a trauma, to provide assistance to the survivors, and to address possible contagion phenomena—not to deny the event. Development of suicide postvention in school systems within the framework of a comprehensive trauma response program is a critical force in these efforts. School staff, with support from mental health professionals, need to develop postvention skills to address PTSD. Our most important future endeavor lies in the area of evaluation of our efforts, especially as it provides a sound, empirical basis for further development and refinement of postvention programs.

We know of many school staff who have saved a life. Everyone, not just the school has a role in addressing trauma when it occurs. The belief that suicide postvention is only temporary is a myth. With timely, appropriate assistance, individuals can be helped through trauma (e.g., a suicide, a disaster). Perhaps the words of Dr. James O. Wells (24)—one of the psychologists who addressed the Challenger disaster in Christa McAuliffe's home school—may provide hope: "The crisis of disaster can be an opportunity to learn from experience and to form the relationships which may be tapped in future crises."

REFERENCES

1. Shneidman, E. (1973). Suicide. *Encyclopedia Britannica.* Chicago: Benton.
2. Shneidman, E. (1981). Postvention: The care of the bereaved. In E. Shneidman (Ed.), *Suicide thoughts and reflections, 1960-1980.* (pp. 157-167). New York: Human Sciences Press.
3. Shneidman, E. (1983). Postvention and the survivor-victim. In *Deaths of man* (pp. 33-41). New York: Aronson.
4. Lamb, F., & Dunne-Maxim, K. (1987). Postvention in schools: Policy and process. In E. Dunne, J. McIntosh, & K. Dunne-Maxim (Eds.), *Suicide and its aftermath: Understanding and counseling the survivors* (pp. 245-260). New York: Norton.
5. Leenaars, A. A. (1985). Suicide postvention in a school system. *Canada's Mental Health, 33*(4).
6. Carter, B. C., & Brooks, A. (1986, April). *An exploration of group postvention techniques.* Paper presented at the conference of the American Association of Suicidology, Atlanta, GA.
7. Lamartine-Anderson, C., & Sattem, L. (1986, April). *After a suicide in an educational setting.* Paper presented at the conference of the American Association of Suicidology, Atlanta, GA.
8. Lane-Malbon, L. (1986, April). *After suicide: Crisis intervention in the school.* Paper presented at the conference of the American Association of Suicidology, Atlanta, GA.
9. Leenaars, A. A., & Wenckstern, S. (1986, April). *Suicide postvention in a school system.* Paper presented at the conference of the American Association of Suicidology, Atlanta, GA.
10. Pelej, J. P., & Scholzen, K. C. (1987, May). *Postvention: A school's response to a suicide.* Paper presented at the conference of the American Association of Suicidology, San Francisco.
11. Valente, S. M., Saunders, J. M., & Street, R. (1986, April). *Adolescent bereavement programs in the schools.* Paper presented at the conference of the American Association of Suicidology, Atlanta, GA.
12. Zinner, E. S. (1986, April). *Survivor intervention strategy in the suicide of a sixth-grader.* Paper presented at the conference of the American Association of Suicidology, Atlanta, GA.
13. Leenaars, A., & Wenckstern, S. (1990). Posttraumatic stress disorder: A conceptual model for

postvention. In A. Leenaars & S. Wenckstern (Eds.), *Suicide prevention in schools* (pp. 173–180). Washington, DC: Hemisphere.

14. Phillips, D., & Carstensen, M. (1986). Clustering of teenage suicides after television news stories about suicide. *New England Journal of Medicine, 315,* 685–689.
15. Goodstein, L. (1978). *Consulting with human service systems.* Menlo Park, CA: Addison-Wesley.
16. Watzlawick, P., Beavin, J., & Jackson, D. (1967). *Pragmatics of human communication.* New York: Norton.
17. Farberow, N. (1967). Crisis, disaster and suicide: Theory and therapy. In E. Shneidman (Ed.), *Essays in self-destruction* (pp. 373–398). New York: Science House.
18. Hoff, L. (1984). *People in crisis* (2nd Ed.). Menlo, CA: Addison-Wesley.
19. Parad, H. (Ed.). (1965). *Crisis intervention: Selected readings.* New York: Family Service Association of America.
20. Shneidman, E. (1980). Psychotherapy with suicidal patients. In E. Shneidman (Ed.), *Suicide thoughts and reflections, 1960–1980* (pp. 149–156). New York: Human Sciences Press.
21. Shneidman, E. (1985). *Definition of suicide.* New York: Wiley.
22. Lifton, R. (1969). *Death in life: Survivors of Hiroshima.* New York: Vintage.
23. Lindemann, E. (1944). Symptomatology and management of acute grief. *American Journal of Psychiatry, 101,* 141–148.
24. Wells, J. (1982, June). *The community in crisis.* Paper presented at the conference of the National Council of Community Mental Health Centers. Miami, FL.
25. Hewett, J. (1980). *After suicide.* Philadelphia: Westminster Press.
26. Pfeffer, C. (1986). *The suicidal child.* New York: Guilford Press.

16

Clinical Opportunities in Suicide Postvention

Bonnie Frank Carter and Allan Brooks
Albert Einstein Medical Center, Philadelphia, Pennsylvania

In our clinical experience with the aftermath of suicide and suicide attempts in school settings, convergent postvention has resulted in optimal intermediate outcomes. Working with small groups of survivors in a time-limited format of several weeks to a few months, we have provided thorough processing of grief; accommodation of the inevitable shifts in family and peer relationships; complete absence of permanent self-harm; increased acceptance of peer, family, and professional resources; and significant development of insight through convergent postvention (1–4).

Our entry into postvention therapy included reviewing the limited but growing literature on suicide postvention plus the broader and earlier resources on crisis intervention following other catastrophically traumatic events. These combined literatures fully document the risks created for youngsters through suicide survivorship that are the indications for postvention (e.g., for suicide postvention, 5–14, and for crisis intervention, 15–21).

The concerns presented by these sources may be summarized as follows. After the loss of a significant other by suicide, a young person experiences severe grief, significant bereavement, and extreme anxiety; such a youngster is also susceptible to posttraumatic stress disorder (22). Serious developmental interference is increasingly likely at younger ages. Regression to behaviors of earlier stages of development and serious suicidal activity are likely. Physical symptoms of emotional shock are also common. The emotional disturbance may be severe enough to constitute acute depression or psychosis. Many manifestations occur immediately following the suicide, but serious problems may arise at unpredictable times later in life.

The literature clearly demonstrates the crushing impact suicide has on family and other support systems. Although familiar sources of help remain dependable in other crises, these are frequently paralyzed in the aftermath of suicide. Affected support systems include friends, peers, school staff, and even medical professionals and clergy. Suicide inevitably catches everyone by surprise, and support people experience symptoms similar to those of the more proximate survivors. Everyone touched by a suicide experiences anger, blame, helplessness, and denial, emotional reactions that can limit the availability of assistance. Each subsystem's capacity to respond honestly and effectively is further impaired by the fear of being ostracized as a result of the stigma our society imposes on suicide. The resulting wall of secrecy further insulates survivors from the human contacts so essential for recovery, and the impact of this distancing is especially damaging to children and adolescents because they are so dependent on the structures generated in their environment by significant adults.

A survivor of any disaster is in crisis immediately following the traumatic event and is likely to experience impairment in functioning. Sometimes these immediate effects worsen; other times they seem to disappear, only to be reexperienced later as some more dysfunctional symptom. It is our view that survivors always require intervention in order to avoid becoming completely overwhelmed, although further clinical and research efforts are needed to more fully understand the various parameters of psychological invulnerability (e.g., 23, 24). Assistance is needed for dealing with the external tragic events and with the internal psychological responses. Frequently, the offering of such assistance must be proactive because physical shock and psychological denial cause survivors to refuse the help they most clearly need. The provision of such help for suicide survivors has been termed *postvention* (12–14). By strengthening previously existing coping skills and introducing additional supports, both from within individual survivors and from the outside, postvention enables survivors to manage their powerful and frightening emotions, including even their own suicidal feelings, and thereby diminishes the negative effects that constitute posttraumatic stress disorder (PTSD) and clinical depression. While the supportive actions are occurring, the postvener also identifies specific areas of distress and risk that might warrant more comprehensive and intensive forms of therapy and for which referrals are needed. Suicide postvention in the schools creates unique opportunities to work with young people, as it occurs in the setting where they spend the most time and where there is the widest range of supportive resources. Three responses to crisis intervention have been described (25), differentiated by the degree of therapeutic comprehensiveness and intensity provided. In addition to brief (or short-term) interventions and long-term treatment of indefinite duration, a third intermediate form exists. This approach is "convergent" between the other two, in terms of methods, goals, and accomplishments (Yalom, as cited in Farberow, 26; see tabulation in Carter and Brooks, 3). We have adapted a 12- to 16-session format for postvention therapy following acts of suicide, parasuicide, homocide, and interpersonal violence. Although the specified number of sessions should be recognized as arbitrary, and in fact has been unattainable in some of our clinical endeavors, this format accommodates many pragmatic considerations. Concentrated therapeutic intervention for an intermediate period of time affords reasonable closure and insight development in a manner feasible with limited staff availability and funding. Principles from self psychology, in particular (see Carter, 27, 28, for further elaboration), and dynamic psychiatry, in general, are significant for clinical postvention. Use of a two-person cotherapy team is advisable to minimize overload on the postvention therapists and provide adequate assimilation of the many simultaneous processes. An additional auxiliary therapist or consulting review group is further recommended for recognizing and diffusing potentially toxic countertransference reactions, for example, identification with the survivors or anger at seemingly responsible authorities.

We describe here several of our student postvention groups in order to illustrate the clinical opportunities that arise within postvention, therapeutic themes typical to this therapy, and frequent concerns of the postvention therapist (or *postvener*). This examination of clinical material has two purposes: (a) review of positive and negative outcomes in order to further refine clinical procedures and (b) empirical documentation of the efficacy of suicide postvention. Along with some of our colleagues (e.g., 24, 29, 30), we continue to view case studies as legitimate sources of data regarding therapeutic outcome.

The work presented here has been reported previously (1–4, 31). In all cases, pseudonyms are used and confidentiality is otherwise protected by altering details not essential to the clinical validity of the cases.

CASE 1

The first postvention group involved four 10th-grade girls, aged 14–15, and two 12th-grade boys, aged 17–18, who attended a prestigious and academically competitive high school. The friend who died, Karl, was 16 and had been attending the same school until that autumn. The seven youngsters formed the core of a larger group of friends, the full extent of which was never clearly identified. Although several other youngsters were in lesser or greater contact at various times, the core group of seven, and after the suicide the six survivors, constituted a strong and supportive peer group. The boys lived with both parents, whereas all four girls lived with a single parent. Of greatest clinical significance are the data showing a relative absence of previous psychiatric or psychological services (only one girl had been in any individual treatment, and the three other girls had experienced some minimal family counseling), despite extensive previous suicidal activity (most of the youngsters had previously survived attempted or completed suicides in close family members or friends and/or was a previous parasuicide himself or herself). For example, in Ellen's family, suicide attempts had been made by both parents and all four grandparents, with the maternal grandfather completing suicide several years before the time of the present event. In a sense, then, with Anton the only exception, all of these youngsters were suicide survivors long before the death of their friend.

Following the reported suicide over the weekend, school officials found themselves required to address more emotion among the boy's friends and peers than could be handled adequately by the available counseling staff and contacted our group (Bonnie Frank Carter). The first arrangement was for a small group discussion, consisting of the close friends of the suicide victim and other students who were highly distressed. These students numbered about 20 and were identified by school personnel, with specific plans coordinated by the counseling staff. The purpose of that session was to assess the emotional needs of the suicide survivors, provide immediate support of short-term needs, establish viable options for accessing further therapeutic support where needed, and, overall, to prevent additional deaths among these suicide survivors. Accordingly, the following actions and themes dominated the session. A specific request was made for a box of tissues to be placed at the center of the long table around which we met. This emphasized the acceptability of tears, a proclamation that stood in contrast to other messages the students were hearing to "stop crying already." It was noted that the long-range purpose of crying was to help the students feel better, but it was also noted that they might feel worse before feeling better.

In addition to needing acceptance of their sadness, the students were in great need of tolerance for their anger. Some were able to express anger at their friend's action ("Why didn't Karl think our caring was enough reason for him to continue living?"), but most directed anger at authority figures. Specifically, anger was addressed at school officials and school policies, as certain administrative actions were interpreted as precipitating factors to the suicide. Defense of school policies was not the central issue, however, and accepting this anger was valuable as one means of facilitating further expression of the strong emotions involved. In addition, feelings toward the school were used later as a medium for decreasing risk of suicide, through an increase in future orientation and feeling of worth, which was accomplished by engaging the students in a sharing of suggestions for changes in school policy. This would have been less productive if it had been the first response to their anger.

As an additional means of demonstrating the acceptability of anger, the initial "promise" that the students would feel "somewhat better" after talking was focused on near the end of the scheduled time of that first meeting. Although most participants stated that they felt better, two said that they did not. One girl repeated the family dictum that sorrows are not to be spoken about. She seemed resigned to this and actually seemed capable of accommodating this purportedly necessary consequence of her parents' Holocaust experiences. Diane was the other girl who stated she felt no better, and she was openly angry. Simple acceptance of this, and interpretation of other students' defense of the postvener, was enormously effective in establishing open talking (i.e., "therapy") as a reliable and effective resource.

The first session ended with the postvenor's going around the table to check on each student's plans for who to speak to and rely on both over the weekend (this was a Friday) and when they returned to school (Monday). It also became clear that further group support would be appropriate, and plans were made to return the following week and meet again, this time with only those students who were close friends of the suicide victim.

At the second session (also held at the school) the six students agreed that further talking would be helpful. It was decided to move to the Psychiatry Outpatient Clinic in order to avoid confusion about the school's role, and the concept of a "postvention group" emerged with a plan to meet once a week for 10 additional sessions. This second session also included detailed descriptions of available support. Despite this support, including 24-hr access to the primary therapist, further crises remained.

Teenagers who attempt or complete suicide have usually tried other ways to make their needs known but have found those paths blocked somehow. Such disappointments can cause people to have great difficulty trusting that others are reliable or dependable. Newly presented support systems are, therefore, often "tested." In this case, Bret did the "testing." He took a dangerous overdose of an over-the-counter medication, which required stomach pumping plus an overnight hospital stay to monitor his vital signs. Student members of the group were actively involved in available support, and telephone communication included the therapist and the boy's parents.

While the group was being developed, and before and after Bret's suicide attempt, telephone contact was established with the parent (or parents) of each group member. Reactions from these parents clustered into two categories: (a) overtly positive, in that parents stated appreciation of the additional support for the youngster or solicited further support for self or family; or (b) ambivalent, in that parents rejected the value of counseling. The ambivalent comments included the concern that attention to feelings in the aftermath of tragedies, such as the recent suicide, would destructively prolong emotional reactions and delay recovery, including delaying return to usual competence in school performance. In some cases this rejection was stated at the same time as comments were made cultivating further contact and support. Beyond the obvious fact that teenage behavior is embedded within a family system, these contacts with parents made it empirically clear that family issues were contributing to the distress felt by these youngsters. One option would have been a multifamily group, with the identified group being joined by parents and other family members. Although suggested and explored on several occasions, this option was never accepted by the group. To the contrary, they all seemed invested in maintaining the group as a forum separate from their family involvements. Although incorporating the families into the group could have afforded support to these youngsters' separation, it evolved that keeping the group process relatively isolated from the families provided similar support, albeit through different channels.

Following his suicide attempt, Bret was able to attend the next session (actually the first held at the outpatient clinic), and the group expressed feelings of anger, sadness, and despair at being inadequate to protect him from the suicide attempt. The same feelings were present regarding Karl's completed suicide, and the relation between the completed suicide and the risk of suicide by the survivors themselves was made explicit by including the following in an individual treatment plan: Problem—As a suicide survivor, "Jane" is at risk for suicide; goal—"Jane" will not attempt suicide.

The predominant theme of the group was the inevitability of losses and the means of accepting or surviving this. The conflict of protecting oneself adequately while remaining open to interpersonal commitment was explored via the changing terrain of the group's relationships. As this group had been friends before the start of the formal "group," much of their interactions occurred outside the treatment setting. Nevertheless, the shifting sands of their alliances were clearly evident in the group sessions. For example, Diane had the role of outcast when the group began. This was partially due to her previous romantic relationship with Anton, who was involved with Frances as the group began. This exacerbated the rift between Diane and Frances, which then evolved from total noncommunication to renewed (although less intense) friendship over the course of the group's therapy involvement. As this occurred, Diane regained her status as a fully accepted group member, even though certain other differences remained (e.g., she was the only group member whose school performance remained unimpaired by the emotional effects of the friend's suicide). In part, the focus on Diane, first as an outcast and then as a returning pilgrim, acted as a distraction from the focus on irretrievable losses, specifically the loss of the friend. Later it seemed that the group was working through that kind of loss by specifically setting up retrievable losses. Thus, concurrent with Diane's reentry to the group, Anton took on the outcast role. In fact, by the end of the formal group, he was separated enough from the original process to attend neither the last session nor the 3-month follow-up "reunion" session. The term *reunion* was suggested by Bret, a senior with little certainty in his future plans who needed reassurance that friendships could be maintained after graduation. It was Bret who bore the brunt of Anton's departure, as the two boys had been close friends, and the resulting mourning contributed to his need for treatment on an individual basis.

A wide range of content areas was used in service of the theme of remaining psychologically sound despite inevitable losses. These included

1. Recounting and anticipating other major losses, such as those through death, divorce, major geographical moves, or social transactions, including high school graduation;

2. Discussion of religious beliefs, including views of death and the omnipotence, or lack thereof, of God;

3. Occurrences that contributed to or hindered the development of a safe environment in the group, including addressing what people said, how others reacted to what was said, and then how the first people reacted themselves;

4. Psychological concepts introduced by group members, especially Anton, including use of a sociogram to identify group members' functional roles in the group and the position in the group of one or another individual as a "tragic figure" (in the literary sense);

5. Problem-solving tactics, including support from others, intellectualization, and escape, and the different appropriateness of various strategies at different times; and

6. Feelings regarding the holidays, in relation to families, in relation to each other, and in relation to their deceased friend.

The emergence of sensitive feelings was the central feature of this postvention group, and accordingly the feelings of the primary therapist played a significant role in the ongoing process. From the start, countertransference included a strong sense of identification with the suicide survivors. It was tempting to see the school officials as the "bad guys" in order to retain a feeling of order despite the senseless death of a 16-year-old boy. After all, if the school administrators or "somebody" had done something proximally to "cause" the boy's death, then it would be a simple thing to change such causes. Or, more accurately, such a view would make it simpler to adopt the comforting belief that teenage suicide could *always* be prevented—a comforting belief, perhaps, but unfortunately not a reality.

Thus, countertransference also included substantial anxiety, both in relation to the real responsibilities taken on when working with people at risk of suicide and also derived through identifying with the youngsters, that is, feeling their anxiety over the recent loss and other losses. Auxiliary support was provided by a psychiatrist (Allan Brooks) and was most critical at the beginning and near the completion of the postvention. At the beginning, support was vital as we addressed the inevitable administrative concerns surrounding the initiation of such intensive activity. Consultation continued to be essential once the group sessions started, as the security of the support systems was tested, as previously described, even to the point of that ultimate test, a suicide attempt. During the termination phase of the process, consultation again became critical, as the process was again tested during the transitions from formal group support to the support of friends, family, and individual therapy. On the surface, the several consultations merely conveyed information about recent occurrences, in the group sessions and in telephone contacts with the youngsters and their family members. Underlying this reporting structure was the more important opportunity for sharing countertransference affect in a way that could be nondamaging to both the group members and the primary therapist. Separated from the intensely engaging circumstances of direct contact with the suicide survivors, the auxiliary therapist could function as a more fully objective observer, relieving anxiety and increasing the effectiveness of the primary therapist in the group process.

In this first incarnation, the convergent approach to teenage suicide postvent (i.e., multiple sessions of network therapy in a time-limited format) was evaluated as reasonably successful. All six participating group members were alive 6 months after their friend's completed suicide. At that time, five of the six readily stated their feelings that the group process was helpful, as further indicated by their willingness to volunteer as group coleaders should a future opportunity arise.

The ability to further use psychotherapy is an additional area for evaluating the effectiveness of this group, and here, too, evidence is available regarding the apparent success of the process. Two of the group members entered individual treatment, and the same was being established for a third group member. Given the previous history of these youngsters and their families for nonuse of psychological or psychiatric services, this 50% utilization was viewed as clinically significant.

CASE 2

Lee was a 14-year-old Cambodian immigrant whose early life had been tragic. Lee's family had been in the United States for 6 years at the time of his death. His mother was a casualty of the Cambodian civil war and died before the family left Cambodia. As the family fled the country, Lee witnessed his older sister's death from poison gas. His older bother was attending a prestigious high school and a younger sister was at the same middle school as Lee. A rather serious, driven youngster, Lee had only a small circle of friends. On the day of his suicide, he was involved in an uncharacteristic prank: He scared some girls with a garter snake. One of the girls reported him. A school disciplinarian severely reprimanded him and gave him a note threatening suspension from school to take home to his father. Later that night, Lee hung himself from a tree in front of his house. (Months later, a community liaison representative identified a relevant primitive belief maintained in some Cambodian villages: When a person is ostracized from the community or otherwise dishonored, he or she is expected to stand by a tree, where some type of winged mythic creature takes the individual up into the branches and "takes him or her away" through something equivalent to hanging.)

The school was in a state of turmoil, with shock and blaming apparent. The primary postvener (Allan Brooks) met extensively with the administrative staff and the five teachers directly involved. These debriefing sessions provided responsible information about school psychodynamics, what to expect regarding student participation at memorial services, and other predictable aspects of the immediate suicide aftermath. Initial suggestions were provided about helping staff and students alike through the crisis of suicide survivorship. This key group identified communication regarding feelings and day-to-day issues as a general problem the staff experienced with the students and their families. They spoke of their own feelings of helplessness in the face of the current tragedy and wondered aloud how they might have anticipated (and thereby averted) the death. Many blamed school administration policies and particularly wanted to lay responsibility heavily on the individual who had reprimanded the child. They also discussed the economic and cultural plight of the neighborhood Asian communities and what they saw as rigid standards of discipline in certain subgroups (e.g., Korean, Pakistani, Cambodian, and Vietnamese people). This important issue was to become a prominent one and was further addressed in a later session involving the full faculty.

The postvention actions of deliberately taking charge, sorting through recent events, and prioritizing further actions calmed these key staff. Initially uncertain about endorsing a complete postvention program, pursuant presentations of the needs persuaded school officials to accept proferred services through the end of the ensuing school term.

Next there were two sessions held for the entire faculty. The first was a didactic in-service on recognizing suicidal danger and intervening effectively with depressed or suicidal children. The second was an open meeting for faculty to air their own issues. There were concerns about responding appropriately to the students' emotional needs while concurrently preserving the usual decorum of the school. A school support network of teacher volunteers was established to provide someone for the students to talk with at any time. These school personnel repeated the previously mentioned concern about cross-cultural differences. Many instances were reported in which Asian parents had responded to school disciplinary actions with levels of at-home punishment regarded as inappropriate by the faculty. Options for acquiring improved understanding of local Asian cultures were explored, and additional support from Asian community groups was arranged.

With the conclusion of the second meeting, the faculty appeared to have attained some closure. They were invited to continue seeking assistance as the year progressed. Several teachers took advantage of this, seeking curbside consultations or more thorough telephone contacts. The principal, guidance counselor, and school psychologist frequently conferred on multiple issues. To obtain additional assistance, the school district arranged for the school psychologist to spend more time at the school, and his activities included referring students for therapy where indicated.

With anger diffused and greater calm permeating the school, the faculty gained the understanding that not all suicides can be prevented even by the most vigilant professionals. Similarly, they gained the confidence of being better equipped to help future suicidal youngsters. As the emotional atmosphere of the school improved from the previous despair and blaming, postvention therapy could now be facilitated for the children without the possibility of opposition by school staff. With these preliminary preparations completed, postvention for the students proceeded. A psychiatrist (Allan Brooks) and a psychiatry resident (Charles McGlynn) were cotherapists, with a psychologist (Bonnie Frank Carter) consulted on a continuous basis. Involvement of two therapists ensured effective intervention for high-risk individuals.

The student postvention sessions were conducted in a school classroom. Seven boys and 5 girls were identified as being most at risk. All 12 were eighth-grade students, with the exception of 1 seventh grader who was friendly with Lee's peers. A mental health questionnaire completed by the students provided information relevant to suicidal risk, including personal and family history of suicidal behavior, emotional disturbance, medical stressors, and drug usage.

Flexibility was essential in order to provide an outlet for all to express their feelings, concerns, and confusions.

Ultimately, this postvention effort was limited to a total of seven sessions because of the approach of graduation. Sometimes the size of the group increased as teachers designated a few additional students as further at-risk survivors. One of these additional youngsters was Linda, Lee's sister, who was in the sixth grade. Linda attended only two sessions and continued to appear somewhat depressed.

Many unsuccessful efforts were made to involve her family in her therapy, but available support people were found outside her family.

The members of the group exhibited an array of at-risk characteristics: (a) Three youngsters had histories that included an important family member's natural death, such as death of a sibling; (b) one boy was anticipating his mother's imminent death from emphysema and cancer and had made a suicide attempt the year before; (c) late in the postvention, one boy revealed that his mother had committed suicide, a revelation that greatly shocked the group; (d) several children acknowledged use of drugs and alcohol; (e) three youngsters had a long history of severe suicidal preoccupation; (f) during the current intervention, another four developed a preoccupation with suicide that could not be easily shaken; (g) fully half of the group came from disrupted families; (h) many of the girls complained of male pressures to perform sexually; and (i) nearly all the youngsters felt their parents and other adults failed to understand them.

The group members readily spoke of their need to cry, and permission for this all-important expression was implied by the presence of a box of tissues in the center of the table and direct verbal encouragement of openness about grief. In another useful technique, one therapist (Allan Brooks) moved around the room, adopting different body postures to provide the varying closeness required by different students at different times. This studied encroachment on personal body space used physical proximity to convey accessibility and encourage emotional openness from the youngster's perspective. Through such strategies, this upset, dismayed, and sometimes disorderly group gradually became engaged in an active therapeutic process, with contributions from most of its members.

Occasionally the group coalesced into three subgroups. This sometimes appeared to consolidate internalized feelings of cohesion, but at other times the process of subgrouping was divisive. It is possible that meeting in smaller groups would have eliminated some of the divisiveness. Our experience suggests that disruptions in relationships are inevitable in the aftermath of trauma, and it is more therapeutic to contain such disruptions in the postvention process, where they can be addressed and mended or accepted.

Overall, the students expressed multiple emotions.

1. Students felt shock about the suicide, anger at Lee for his actions, and anger at the school and all authority figures.

2. Students also expressed feelings of loss and disillusionment with the world.

3. Blame was prevalent but alternately placed on various individuals.

4. The survivors particularly expressed a sense of futility in communicating with adults.

5. Nearly all suffered distortions about the future, wherein they perceived bleak dead ends rather than bright opportunities.

6. Some students openly admitted their own thoughts of suicide.

7. Other students were obsessed with thoughts that other Asian students at the school would commit suicide, although the therapists (and ultimately the students themselves) recognized these concerns as indications of anxiety about their own suicidal wishes.

Two of Lee's friends warranted particular attention owing to their closeness to Lee. Robert appeared to be functioning rather well, but Achmed, an immigrant from Pakistan, was the least cooperative and most angry member of the group. He often turned his body away from the others and usually wanted to leave the group before the end of the session. He was typically dissuaded from learning by the other youngsters, and the therapists explored and supported his feelings of grief, anger, and guilt. By the last session, Achmed seemed to have regained his previous sense of humor, sometimes even smiling quite brightly.

Three students reported recurring dreams of Lee's suicide, with two of these also experiencing nightmares of their own deaths and one still having vivid flashback dreams at the time of the last postvention session. Two of these children seemed to exhibit the "omen" phenomenon (20, 21). In this phenomenon, individuals review the events preceding a tragedy and conclude that they should have known what was coming, that they could have done something to prevent it, or even that they had specifically caused the tragedy. Feelings of guilt were clearly involved in both occurrences of the omen phenomenon in this case. Mary was one of the girls involved in the original prank, and she had responded to the announcement of Lee's suicide by running out of the school. In the postvention sessions, she spoke of her horror and guilt feelings. John was supposedly not close to Lee, but ultimately he revealed that Lee had told him how upset he was and that he felt like dying several weeks before his death. Of course, John was horror-stricken that he had done nothing to warn anyone. Both John and Mary were completely immersed in their role of guilt-bearer. They seemed to benefit from the group's reassuring support, especially from several discussions about causality. The omen phenomenon is said to include recurrent reminiscences of the precipitating event, but this intensity was not reported by these youngsters.

By the end of the seventh postvention session, the group had discharged enormously intense feelings of anger, guilt, blame, and sadness and had attained some measure of control over their behavior, including their suicidal thoughts. A relatively satisfactory closure was created for all as available resources were identified for all group members, including referrals by the school psychologist and guidance counselor to our clinic and others around the city.

CASE 3

Ann was a 15-year-old sophomore at an academically prestigious high school at the time she took a potentially lethal overdose of tranquilizers. Although she made this suicide attempt after carefully extricating herself from familiar surroundings where she might have been found and "rescued," she changed her mind after swallowing the medication and immediately sought emergency room help. From there, she was medically cleared and referred to a psychotherapist.

Ann's friends remained highly alarmed and enormously involved, and we were contacted to provide on-site assistance at school. Eleven youngsters (8 15-year-old sophomore girls and 3 17-year-old senior boys) accepted the school administrator's invitation to join a psychologist (Bonnie Frank Carter) to talk about what had happened. The first two sessions were held at the school with the benefit of strong faculty support and provided initial exploration about what had happened, who had known what at each point along the way, and who was feeling what now that Ann was back at school. After two sessions at the school, 10 youngsters (including Ann but excluding another girl) continued in a weekly postvention at the Psychiatry Outpatient Clinic for the ensuing 6 weeks until the semester ended.

This group generally exhibited a low level of suicidal risk: Most were from intact families with healthy and age-appropriate relationships with parents; most had not experienced any suicidality previously; and most reported little to no substance use. The exceptions were two of the boys and one girl who had become suicide survivors after friends' deaths during the 2 years before this postvention. In addition, Ann continued to struggle with issues of emotional and physical abuse, including the usual insistence that the abuser be protected through silence.

The third session provided the transition from school grounds to the outpatient clinic. At this time, a psychiatry resident was introduced in the role of cotherapist (Patricia Wright). Additional "business" at this session included review and signature of individual treatment plans, worded as follows:

1. Problem—As a close friend of someone who made a suicide attempt, "Jane" is at risk for self-destructive behavior; goal—to engage in no self-destructive behavior.

2. Problem—"Jane" is concerned about her friend who attempted suicide; goal—to provide support within the limits possible as a friend.

3. Problem—this recent suicide attempt raises many feelings regarding losses and separations; goal—to talk about feelings at each session in order to experience and accept the full range of affect.

As in Case 1, relationship changes constituted a major arena for expression of suicide-related issues. Ethan began dating Delores during this time period. Hank had been dating Delores, and significant conflict over his being "rejected" was brought into the sessions. Later Hank began dating Ann, a relationship through which he seemed to fulfill his need for nurturance and to attempt control over his fear of rejection by aligning himself with someone who had similar characteristics *and* who was receiving substantial attention around these parameters.

The issue of confidentiality took on major significance in this academically and psychologically sophisticated group. Initially, concern was aroused when the group learned that a schoolmate knew more than many of them preferred about this therapy group. The "leak" of information was ultimately attributed to Janet (although this accusation could never be verified), and this became the basis for the group's open hostility toward her. This focus provided a diversion for the group from a more basic and more frightening anger. Janet had been the recipient of Ann's "suicide" letter on the day of her suicide attempt. (It remains unclear whether the letter was overtly suicidal; it was never shared with the therapists.) The group maintained some belief that Ann should have been saved from her suicide attempt and was less uncomfortable addressing anger at Janet (whom they viewed as personally strong and well-protected by her relationships with adults) than at Ann (whom they saw as fragile and vulnerable). Unfortunately, expressions of hostility were not managed sufficiently to enable Janet to remain in the group, and she dropped out, both from the postvention and from the group's social interactions, midway through the postvention. Similarly, Ann was sometimes unable to tolerate attending the sessions. Here, as in Case 1, relationship losses seemed to be a vehicle for processing actual and potential losses to death. A similar concern was voiced with regard to anger, as the group struggled with maintaining friendships through periods of open anger. Some relationships remained constant; some survived but with alterations; some ended.

Confidentiality and trust persisted as central themes and later were directed at the therapists. Carmen became sufficiently concerned to organize a noncooperation pact with Irene and Karen before the fifth session; not only did they remain virtually silent throughout the session, they also disrupted any development of emotional intensity through minor distractions. Carmen's healthy skepticism continued as a challenge to the primary therapist throughout the postvention, but this barrier to necessary talking was also addressed directly and legitimate confidentiality concerns were accommodated. In addition to its own legitimacy, the confidentiality issue was symbolic of the broader issue of when to talk and when to remain silent. Specifically, the group explored parameters for differentiating those times when a friend should be encouraged to talk versus times when leaving things alone is more responsive to the friend's needs. Within this issue, the group identified and expressed feelings of guilt at not having been able to sufficiently recognize Ann's intentions to have prevented her parasuicide, as well as feelings of anger at Ann for placing them in an impossible position where only mental telepathy would have enabled them to "see" any more than they did.

Although Ann remained central to the group process, whether she was present or absent at any given moment, discussions of guilt, anger, and loss were significant for all the group members. Issues similar to those in Cases 1 and 2 emerged, including a feeling that no one, peer or adult, listens sufficiently to the predicaments of young people. The responsibility shown by these youngsters in continuing with a 2-month postvention and a 6-month follow-up session is evidence not only of their pain, but also of the strength of their coping abilities. In contrast to benefits derived by the group members, Ann's feeling at the close of the postvention was that "the meetings . . . were pointless [although] the first [session] helped a lot because everything was put in the open." It may be that our interventions were less accessible owing to the less extreme aftermath of parasuicide, but it seems equally likely that Ann's final summation is an expression of her ambivalence between open exploration of her dysfunctional family and the need for protective silence in the absence of trust in other sources of safety. Overall, pursuant postvention after parasuicide provided a unique opportunity to help survivors learn constructive ways to cope with painful issues.

CONCLUSION

Our postvention activities continue to confirm our conclusion that time-limited group therapy is an effective method for addressing the aftermath of teenage suicide. At the present time, we are continuing the development of a convergent approach to clinical postvention, using cotherapy teams to extend the application to the aftermath of other violent events (27, 28), as well as following completed suicide and serious suicide attempts (1–4).

An additional clinical finding in our postvention work is that suicide survivors are more likely to become involved in providing support for suicidal ideators than are people with no prior exposure to suicide (31). As suicidal ideators seek individuals capable of "seeing" the warning signs that they present, they are more likely to choose people with prior experience as suicide survivors or who are otherwise sensitized to the problem of suicidal behavior. In some cases, this sensitivity has a healthy basis in enhanced awareness and empathy; in others it derives from problematic or pathological pressures of unresolved guilt, whether conscious or unconscious. In either case, constructive results are possible, as in Case 2 where students and staff alike translated personal feelings of responsibility into constructive general concern for Asian youngsters. This indicates the potential ripple effect of postvention, as postvention can create a responsiveness that is positive for the responder as well as the potential suicide, rather than a sensitivity that is helpful to the potential suicide but creates problems of overwhelmed resources in the responder. As described in the clinical material presented here, the purpose of postvention (second only to protecting against imminent self-destructive behavior) is to enhance previous strengths and introduce new resources for developing additional coping skills. Not only are recipients of postvention assisted in resolving their feelings about the suicide or parasuicide that has occurred, they are also empowered to respond effectively in future interactions with self-destructive individuals.

Throughout the postventions described here, as with many other descriptions of the experience of suicide survivorship (e.g., 6, 32) as well as of others suffering posttraumatic stress disorder, "What could I have done differently?" and "Why didn't I see what was wrong?" are repeated refrains. Strong feelings of guilt often dominate the emotions of survivors, in combination with grief and anger. The belief that people can become more sensitive to the messages of despair that usually precede suicide or parasuicide is the basis of suicide prevention education efforts. But the conviction that more can be done in the future must be tempered with compassion about events that have already occurred in the past. Not only is there nothing to be gained by creating guilt among suicide survivors by blaming them for their actions or for their silences, but the guilt they already feel is probably the core element in their increased risk for suicide and other expressions of distress.

When feelings are adequately supported so that appropriate processing occurs, a survivor can emerge from the crisis capable of sharing wisdom from the tragedy with others similarly assaulted. Adequate tolerance of affect is particularly important for the volatile feelings of anger, guilt, and shame. We have seen numerous examples of this among our patients, where youngsters who previously attempted suicide themselves, or who were otherwise exposed to suicidality, become very effective and much sought-after amateur counselors to their friends and peers. The factors that characterize positive versus negative responders to a potentially suicidal person are the same issues that must be addressed in discussion following a suicide or suicide attempt. If the intervention is to constitute an effective postvention rather than a further assault on already distraught survivors, there must be sufficient time and attention for the accommodation and processing of negative affect. Each person will have his or her own individual time needs for grieving, and this internally determined time-line cannot be altered without creating additional distress. It is probable that similarly enhanced sensitivities can be derived through loss experiences other than suicide.

Postvention efforts can do more harm than good if they become disguised and misguided attempts to protect survivors from the painful emotions they must process if they are truly to survive. There is a very fine line between facilitating the psychological process and interfering with that process. The effects of a given intervention can even change from being one side of that line to the other, depending on the particular person being helped. Postvention, therefore, must be a "clinical" (i.e., an *individual*) intervention, even within the context of a didactic approach to suicide prevention. It is essential to maintain a focus on the survivor as an individual and to provide opportunities for emotions to evolve in a manner appropriate to that individual. For example, many survivors respond affirmatively to a reframing of their feelings of guilt as representing positive caring for others more than any real culpability. One should remember, however, that as useful as this reframing may be for some people, if improperly timed it could function as an impediment to the processing of the grief and anger that gave rise to the guilt feelings.

Time is probably the most important element for competent postvention. Although the prognosis for recovery from posttraumatic stress disorder remains uncertain and entails many insufficiently understood premorbid factors (see, e.g., 24) in addition to circumstances of the external trauma itself, it is clear that processing of the inevitable feelings of anger, guilt, and despair involves varying amounts of time for different people. Another essential component is tolerance for these emotions. Many people find it so difficult to accept anger, guilt, and despair that denial prevents adequate processing of the pain experienced after suicide or parasuicide. Obviously, denial is involved when an action is labeled *accidental* rather than *suicidal,* but denial is also involved when professionals or friends attempt to protect survivors by curtailing emotional reactions or, conversely, by trying to hasten emotional resolution. Postvention is a difficult activity to conduct; it is always time consuming, frequently unappreciated, and often feared. Postvention also offers incredible opportunities: to respond at times of greatest tragedy, to find the continuing strength beneath the crumbled facade of grief and stress, to restore the health that existed before the tragedy, and to build on that health for further growth. Postvention offers, in essence, a classic opportunity for healing and nurturance.

REFERENCES

1. Carter, B. F., & Brooks, A. (1986). An exploration of group postvention techniques. In R. Cohen-Sandler (Ed.), *Proceedings, Nineteenth Annual Meeting, American Association of Suicidology* (pp. 242–243). Denver, CO: American Association of Suicidology.
2. Brooks, A., & Carter, B. F. (1987). Suicide postvention using convergent intervention strategies. In R. I. Yufit (Ed.), *Combined proceedings, Twentieth Annual Meeting, American Association of Suicidology and Nineteenth International Congress, International Association for Suicide Prevention* (pp. 243–245). Denver, CO: American Association of Suicidology.
3. Carter, B. F., & Brooks, A. (1990a). Suicide postvention: Crisis or opportunity. *School Counselor, 37,* 378–390.
4. Carter, B. F., & Brooks, A. (1990b). *Child and adolescent survivors of suicide.* In A. Leenaars (Ed.), *Suicide across the lifespan.* New York: Plenum Press.
5. Caine, A. C., & Fast, I. (1972). The legacy of suicide: Observations on the pathogenic impact of suicide upon marital partners. In A. C. Caine (Ed.), *Survivors of suicide* (pp. 145–154). Springfield, IL: Charles C Thomas.
6. Dunne, E., McIntosh, J. L., & Dunne-Maxim, K. (Eds.). (1987). *Suicide and its aftermath: Understanding and counseling the survivors.* New York: Norton.
7. Lamb, F., & Dunne-Maxim, K. (1987). Postvention in schools: Policy and process. In E. J. Dunne, J. L. McIntosh, & K. Dunne-Maxim (Eds.), *Suicide and its aftermath: Understanding and counseling the survivors* (pp. 245–260). Norton: New York.
8. Lane-Malbon, L. (1986). After suicide: Crisis intervention in the school. In R. Cohen-Sandler (Ed.), *Proceedings, Nineteenth Annual Meeting, American Association of Suicidology* (pp. 234–236). Denver, CO: American Association of Suicidology.
9. Leenaars, A. (1985). Suicide postvention in a school system. *Canada's Mental Health, 33*(4).
10. Leenaars, A., & Wenckstern, S. (1986). Suicide postvention in a school system. In

R. Cohen-Sandler (Ed.), *Proceedings, Nineteenth Annual Meeting, American Association of Suicidology* (pp. 237–239). Denver, CO: American Association of Suicidology.
11. Seiden, R. H. (1968). Suicidal behavior contagion on a college campus. In N. L. Farberow (Ed.), *Proceedings: Fourth International Conference for Suicide Prevention* (pp. 360–367). Los Angeles: Suicide Prevention Center.
12. Shneidman, E. S. (1971). Prevention, intervention, and postvention of suicide. *Annals of Internal Medicine, 75*, 453–458. (Reprinted from *Suicide and Life-Threatening Behavior*, 1981, *11*, 349–359).
13. Shneidman, E. S. (1975). Postvention: The care of the bereaved. In R. O. Pasnau (Ed.), *Consultation-liaison psychiatry* (pp. 245–256). New York: Grune & Stratton.
14. Shneidman, E. S. (1985). *Definition of suicide*. New York: Wiley.
15. Bowlby, J. (1980). *Loss: Sadness and depression (Attachment and loss: Vol. 3)*. New York: Basic Books.
16. Caplan, G. (1964). *Principles of preventive psychiatry*. New York: Basic Books.
17. Lindemann, E. (1944). Symptomatology and management of acute grief. *American Journal of Psychiatry, 101*, 141–148.
18. Pynoos, R. (1988, April). *The traumatized child*. Paper presented at Abbott Northwestern Hospital, Minneapolis, MN.
19. Pynoos, R., & Eth, S. (1984). Developmental perspective on psychic trauma in childhood. In C. R. Figley (Ed.), *Trauma and its wake* (pp. 36–52). New York: Brunner/Mazel.
20. Terr, L. (1979). Children of Chowchilla. *Psychoanalytic Study of the Child, 34*, 547–623.
21. Terr, L. (1983). Chowchilla revisited: The effects of psychic trauma four years after a school-bus kidnapping. *American Journal of Psychiatry, 140*, 1543–1550.
22. Leenaars, A., & Wenckstern, S. (1989). The suicide and post-traumatic stress disorder. In D. Lester (Ed.), *Proceedings, Twenty-second Annual Conference American Association of Suicidology* (pp. 98–99). Denver, CO: American Association of Suicidology.
23. Anthony, E. J. (1987). Risk, vulnerability, and resilience: An overview. In E. J. Anthony & B. J. Cohler (Eds.), *The invulnerable child* (pp. 3–48). New York: Guilford Press.
24. Ulman, R. B., & Brothers, D. (1988). *The shattered self: A psychoanalytic study of trauma*. Hillsdale, NJ: Analytic.
25. Baldwin, B. A. (1980). Styles of crisis intervention: Toward a convergent model. *Professional Psychology, 11*(1), 113–120.
26. Farberow, N. L. (1976). Group psychotherapy for self destructive persons. In H. J. Parad, H. L. P. Resnik, L. G. Parad, & M. D. Bowie (Eds.), *Emergency and disaster management: A mental health source book* (pp. 169–185). Bowie, MD: Charles.
27. Carter, B. F. (1989). Applications of self psychology for postvention. In D. Lester (Ed.), *Proceedings, Twenty-second Annual Meeting, American Association of Suicidology* (pp. 210–212). Denver, CO: American Association of Suicidology.
28. Carter, B. F. (in press). The "self" in postvention: Empathy, self psychology, and personal commitment. In B. Danto (Ed.), *Postvention*. Philadelphia: Charles.
29. Chassan, J. B. (1961). Stochastic models of the single case as a basis of clinical research design. *Behavioral Science, 6*, 42–50.
30. Chassan, J. B. (1979). *Research design in clinical psychology and psychiatry, 2nd edition*. New York: Wiley.
31. Carter, B. F., Brooks, A., & Katz, S. H. (1988). Postvention: An answer to contagion. In D. Lester (Ed.), *Proceedings, 21st Annual Meeting, American Association of Suicidology* (pp. 115–116). Denver, CO: American Association of Suicidology.
32. Lukas, C., & Seiden, H. M. (1987). *Silent grief: Living in the wake of suicide*. New York: Scribners.

17

Postvention from the Viewpoint of Consultants

Frederick Lamb and Karen Dunne-Maxim
University of Medicine and Dentistry of New Jersey, Piscataway

Maureen Underwood
New Jersey Youth Suicide Prevention Project, Trenton

Charlesetta Sutton
University of Medicine and Dentistry of New Jersey, Piscataway

Schools often turn to outsiders for help after a suicide. The school's administration, no matter how competent, can never be fully prepared for the shocking impact of a death by suicide. Students, faculty, and the administration itself will, to varying degrees, be caught up in the wave of anxiety, denial, anger, and unwarranted guilt that naturally follows such events (1, 2). The administration can be among those most affected because of its burden of responsibility for the entire school. Given the intense emotionality of the situation combined with the fear that other students are also at risk, it is natural that expert advice is sought (3).

The term *postvention* was coined to describe the process of helping the survivors of suicide deal with their feelings (4). Originally, *survivors* meant the close family members of the victim. However, as it became recognized that a suicide can affect a much wider circle of people (i.e., friends, classmates, an entire school, and even whole communities), postvention principles began to be applied to larger groups (5). Today, there is a developing body of literature on postvention in schools and a growing number of professionals with experience in this area (1, 2, 5–8). However, little attention has been given to the actual process of postvention consultation itself or to the experiences of the consultants. Therefore, this chapter examines postvention from the point of view of the professionals who actually do it.

A MEETING OF CONSULTANTS

In the spring of 1989, the New Jersey Youth Suicide Prevention Project, supported by the state's Department of Education and Division of Mental Health and Hospitals, brought together a group of 16 mental health professionals: psychologists, social workers, psychiatric nurses, and pastoral counselors with postvention consultation experience. Also participating were 2 observers from the education system. The 16 consultants had carried out a total of 75 postsuicide consultations in schools or other organizations. They came together not as experts but as colleagues all doing the same work and were eager to learn from, and share with, each other. They were a very experienced group clinically, many of them holding senior positions in their organizations. The number of postventions they had done varied considerably. Some had been involved in as many as 15; others had done only 1. Many of them had been involved in training, presenting, and writing on suicide prevention, postvention, or both. However, for almost all, this work was only a part of their professional lives. Most were doing direct treatment, administration, or consultation and education in their primary capacity.

The format for this meeting was a structured roundtable discussion that allowed the participants to describe what they did, what problems they encountered, and what they thought would make them more effective. The participants had also filled out a questionnaire in advance. This helped them to focus on issues of common concern and to identify points of agreement and disagreement. What follows is based on that questionnaire and the discussion, with elaboration by us (who were also participants).[1]

GAINING ENTRY INTO THE SCHOOL

One of the first issues to be discussed, and a recurring topic, was the process of gaining entry into the school. For many, this seemed to be one of the most significant challenges they faced. In this context, *entry* meant both the process of being invited into the school to help and defining that help, that is, contracting for the consultation. Many participants addressed the ambiguity of their role vis-à-vis the school and the wide variety of ways in which their efforts were received or understood. Barriers to interorganizational cooperation were given much attention. Almost all the participants were employees of local public mental health agencies. This was partially because of the auspices of the conference. However, that there were so many people with so much postvention experience demonstrates how common it is for schools to turn to the mental health system for help after a suicide. Nonetheless, the relations between the two systems sometimes proved problematic. Some issues are to be expected whenever an outsider becomes closely involved with an organization. All systems need to protect their boundaries from those who may not accept or understand their internal norms. However, these normal system-entry issues are compounded by the fear that the consultant will in some way judge or blame the school for the suicide. Such fears are common in survivors (9). It may well be that schools, with their usual close ties and accountability to the community, are especially vulnerable to these concerns. It was recalled that after a suicide cluster in one community, intense blame was directed at the school even though most of the victims were not students.

Participants saw the problem of gaining entry to the school as being directly connected to defining what the school wants from consultation. Some schools seek advice and guidance on how to deal with the crisis, and others look for direct

[1]We wish to recognize the active and thoughtful participation of the following professionals in the Conference on Postvention sponsored by the New Jersey Department of Education and the Department of Human Services, Division of Mental Health and Hospitals in June 1989: Frank Acocella, MA; Dave Armor, MSW; Carol Billow, ACSW; Sally Campbell, ACSW; Doug Halverson, MSW, M.Div.; Nina Johnson, ACSW; John Kalafat, PhD; Sonia Klimoff, PhD; Sandra Wright McCaw, RN, Ed.S; Richard McKeon, PhD; Diane Ryerson, ACSW; Bonnie Siddons, BA; Carolyn Turner, RN, MA; and Roberto Weiss, MA. The content of this chapter represents an attempt to synthesize and expand on their and the authors' views and experiences, supported by the available literature. This chapter could not have been written without their contributions to the conference, but we take final responsibility for its contents.

clinical services, usually specific help in screening and evaluating potentially suicidal students. The fear of suicide contagion, or a copycat effect (10), is often one of the first openly stated concerns of schools (11). The consultants reported that frequently when schools initially contacted their agencies, the first request was for assistance in identifying and screening high-risk students. Nonetheless, it is significant that a majority of the consultants reported that they spent less than 50% of their time providing direct services to students. Instead, the greatest proportion of time was spent focusing on the needs of staff (teachers, special services, and administrators). They explained that this was often a more efficient and appropriate use of their skills. Many had adopted a "helping-the-helpers" model with the aim of empowering appropriate school staff to carry out the necessary student assessment functions. Besides maximizing their available time, this approach had the added advantage of minimizing the resentment of those who might feel displaced by outside "experts."

However, it was also recognized that providing direct clinical services to students, to the extent feasible, could facilitate the entry process. Providing such help was more common when consultants were working with schools within their agencies' service area. Entering the schools to provide a specific, concrete service seemed to smooth the acceptance process. This was enhanced as the consultants provided evidence of their skills and knowledge in working with students. Their willingness to engage in this demanding clinical work helped break down the barriers and legitimized their consultative role.

Overall, there was a general consensus that it is necessary to adopt a flexible approach to postvention. There are too many variables to adopt a rigid model of what postvention should be. Factors such as geography, size of the school, available resources, preexisting relations between school and agency, tensions or problems within the school or community, and perhaps most important, the details and impact of the suicide itself must guide the intervention choices open to the consultant.

MANAGING THE CRISIS

One of the most important outcomes of the conference was the degree of consensus that existed on how to manage the crisis in a school after a suicide. In the preconference questionnaire, they had been asked about the advice they would give in five areas of concern:

- Dealing with the media
- Involving the community
- Interventions with parents
- Meeting faculty needs
- Interventions with students

Their responses showed substantial agreement about crisis management recommendations in most of these areas. What follows reflects the advice and thinking of the consultants in these areas, with particular emphasis on those topics that generated the most discussion: community, media, and parents.

INVOLVING THE COMMUNITY

There was a consensus among consultants about the critical importance of involving the larger community in postvention planning and implementation (Question 4k). A variety of reasons were cited. First, involvement of key agencies and leaders within the community recognized that the burden of postvention should not fall solely on the school; the entire community bears responsibility for healing after the suicide of one of its members. Second, utilizing community resources increases the people-power available to deal with both the immediate crisis and its longer term ramifications. The clergy, who are often underutilized in their pivotal role as community advocates and supports, and funeral directors, who by the nature of their work can facilitate community mourning, should be recognized as valuable postvention resources. Third, and perhaps most important, community involvement addressed the reality that the impact of a student suicide frequently reaches beyond a single school. Consultants recounted examples of high school students whose siblings or friends attended other schools and whose reactions had an impact there as well. Others recalled how a suicide in a nonpublic school that brought together students from differing areas had an impact on a variety of communities. In a well-publicized cluster of suicides, consultants described the dramatic distress and even panic that involved the entire community. Without community support and advance planning, containing the sequelae of suicide is almost impossible as "opportunities are often missed in the crucial first hours" (12, p. 3).

Consultants offered several models for encouraging and maximizing community involvement. In several locales, preexisting organizations that brought together various youth-serving groups assumed responsibility for the development of postvention crisis management response plans. Administration of these plans was carried out by an advisory committee that included key leaders in education, religion, health, municipal government, law enforcement, and the human services fields.

In another area, mental health centers took the leadership role in encouraging municipalities to develop plans for dealing with mental health emergencies. Each municipality was invited to join a team that included representatives from key agencies, public services, and community resources. This team participated in the development of a crisis management plan.

THE COMMUNITY CRISIS TEAM

Regardless of how they were formed, all community crisis management teams or committees were similar in function. The responsibilities they assumed included the following:

1. Planning and developing awareness of community resources
2. Developing workable communication networks
3. Mobilizing and coordinating school, community, and mental health intervention resources
4. Reviewing municipal and school crisis management plans
5. Providing technical assistance in the development of school board-approved crisis management plans

The communitywide crisis management team serves as a resource to the school and community and delegates important responsibilities following a tragedy. Consultants reported increased effectiveness of such groups when they had been organized before the occurrence of a crisis. In communities that had the benefit of preplanning by this critical group of leaders, the delays and turf battles that often hamper crisis response efforts were minimized.

DEALING WITH THE MEDIA

The consultants were unanimous in recommending that schools limit their contact with the media after a student suicide (Question 4a). However, in discussion, they were also unanimous in defining media issues as among the most complex and difficult issues they faced. This is consistent with the findings of the Centers for Disease Control (CDC). In their report on suicide clusters (12), they stated that, although

> the roles of the media in causing or exacerbating a suicide cluster is [sic] controversial, . . . some investigators will no longer even discuss an evolving suicide cluster with media representatives for fear that the newspaper or television accounts will lead to further suicides. (p. 10)

However, the CDC also recommended that a timely flow of accurate and appropriate information should be provided to the media. It is achieving this balance that proves to be so difficult for the consultant and the school.

The kind and amount of coverage the event receives is usually a consequence of a number of factors, such as the status of the student, whether the death was carried out in public, and whether there had been other recent suicides in the community (13). The consultants noted that suicides often become news after a particular angle is emphasized. In one case, a youngster fatally shot himself on the school grounds. Among the things found in his pocket was a tape of a particular kind of rock music. Subsequent news articles contained condemnation of this kind of music by local officials. This story then begat other stories from those defending the music. Thus, the story of a single death was kept alive in the media for several weeks and probably contributed to the continuing highly charged atmosphere in the school. Another consultant reported on the heavy media coverage that followed the murder of a parent and suicide by a 15-year-old boy. This was certainly a major tragedy that generated understandable media attention. However, the story was given new life by speculation about the boy's possible involvement in satanic activities.

Clinicians reported that in cases where the suicide received heavy media coverage, there was a significant increase in the number of suicide attempts reported to their agencies. They recognized that it was an open question whether the actual increase was in suicide attempts or merely in referrals. They also reported on the distress caused by intense media attention. For example, a student arrived at his local school to find the front door almost blocked by TV camera crews. As he passed by, another student pointed to him, saying, "If you want to know about suicide, ask him." The youngster ran home in tears and later told his counselor that he was fearful that the story of his suicide attempt of the previous year would be on the evening network news.

However, despite their reservations, consultants felt it was necessary to work with the media. They recognized that reporting that informed the public of preven-

tion strategies and community resources and that did not glamorize or sensationalize the death could be helpful. Still, they found themselves anxious about making
statements that could inadvertently contribute to escalation of the story. For example, a consultant was asked her opinion on the situation in which rock music had
been blamed for a suicide. Her comment that suicide is not usually related to one
simple cause was accurately reported. But the next day there was another story
quoting a local official with a different view.

Positive experiences with the media were also reported. Mental health professionals in one county met with the editor of a large suburban newspaper to express
their concerns about contagion. The editor heard them out, then agreed to review
their policy. Since then, a more low-key approach to these stories has been noted.
The consultants generally recognized the complexity of this issue and were sensitive to first amendment issues and the controversy over the impact of media coverage on suicide (14). It was noted that the CDC plans to bring media and mental
health professionals together for a more thorough discussion on this topic. Nonetheless, until there is a better understanding of the factors that lead to suicide
contagion, the following recommendations were adopted by the consultants.

Guidelines for Consultation with the Media

1. Establish relationships with the media before a community crisis. Use this
opportunity to explain concerns about the possible impact of sensationalized coverage and the risks of copycat behavior when the precise method of suicide is spelled
out.

2. Designate persons from the school and from other involved community
agencies to act as media spokespersons. In events where there is widespread impact on the whole community, establish a central location, away from the school,
for media inquiries.

3. Coach media liaisons on meeting the goals of both reporters and the institution they represent. Emphasize prevention resources and avoid blaming others.

4. Educate survivors, such as family members and friends, that they have the
right not to speak to the press.

Interventions with Parents

There are really two different groups to be considered, the parents of the victim
and the families of the other children in the school. Contemplating approaching the
parents of the victim is understandably anxiety provoking. Nonetheless, it is something that everyone agreed school officials need to do (Question 4j). In this way,
the school can join with the family in their grief, and the family is able to give the
school guidelines for attendance at memorial services, and so forth. Also, working
together can prevent misunderstandings. Usually this happens as a matter of
course. However, in at least one case that was described, a family reported never
hearing from the school after their son's death. They felt alone, isolated, and in a
subtle way blamed.

The issue of dealing with the parents of the other children in the school generated much controversy among the consultants. In everyone's experience, a school
suicide raises concern and anxiety among all the parents. As has been previously
reported (8), parents showed great concern: "fear that this one suicide could

trigger others; identification with the bereaved parents; guilt over not being able to prevent or somehow 'know' that [another child] was in trouble." (p. 309). The consultants all agreed that it was necessary to make a special effort to address these concerns, but there was considerable disagreement on the best way to do this. To Question 4b, "Should schools hold a large meeting with parents within one week after the suicide?" 9 consultants answered no and 6 answered yes. A main issue in dispute was the timing of the meeting, although some questioned the wisdom of any large, open forum. Those who favored an early meeting were mainly guided by the principles of crisis intervention, which state that there is a critical period in the life of a crisis when intervention can be most effective. They reported on meetings that were calm and orderly, with few if any negative consequences, and that seemed to immediately reduce the level of anxiety within the community. And the fact is suicide clusters do happen. A suicide does put others at risk. It is crucial that parents be given necessary information and guidance as soon as possible. They need to know about warning signs, about where to turn for help, and what to do if their child confides in them about concerns about a friend. A large parent meeting is one way to disseminate information to the largest number of people in a clear, concise, timely manner. It is also a way to reassure parents that the school administration is on top of the situation and is doing everything possible to ensure the well-being of the students. That such meetings can be difficult is not denied by those who favor them, and for that reason they recommend that the consultant be very active in planning and running the meeting.

On the other side of this issue were those who had been involved in parent meetings that became forums for blaming and scapegoating others. It has been these consultants' experience that in the first few days after a suicide, people can be so anxious and reactive that a meeting, no matter who leads it, can turn into a mob. Such meetings can be extremely painful to school staff, occurring just when they are most vulnerable and concerned about being blamed. Any attempt to explain their position may be misunderstood as defensiveness.

Some indicated less concern about holding a meeting at a later date, when people can take a more objective view of the situation. However, others warned against giving the wrong message by holding such a meeting at any time. After all, they noted, such meetings are not usually held if a student dies of illness or an accident. There is a danger that such a meeting contributes to the mystique or specialness of this death, as if the youngster's power extends beyond the grave. Anything that takes place that has the potential for heightening the emotional involvement of the entire community must be approached with extreme caution. Research findings on youth suicide and factors involved in copycat suicide and contagion suggest that imitative behavior may play a role in subsequent attempts and deaths (10, 14). Therefore, anything that heightens awareness of a specific suicide, no matter how well intentioned the purpose, might increase the risk factor.

Despite the strongly held views on both sides of this issue, a compromise position did emerge. It was agreed that the crucial issue was meeting the immediate needs of the parents without escalating the crisis. Various suggestions were made that could be used with or without also having a large meeting. Among the suggestions were (a) providing small group discussion groups, staffed by postvention consultants, to all parents who wished to participate; (b) sending a letter home to parents outlining the school's postvention plans and offering telephone consultation; and (c) providing alternative counseling by community resource people (e.g., clergy, mental health professionals, etc.) and using the parent–teacher associations to disseminate information.

AGREEMENT ON POSTVENTION BASICS

In contrast to the strongly held views and differing opinions on such issues as the preceding, agreement was so universal on some issues that little discussion was generated. However, because they represent some of the most basic areas for postvention decision making, a brief summary of these commonly held views is in order. What follows is based in the main on the results of the questionnaire (Appendix) with brief elaboration. For more details on these issues, see *Youth Suicide Prevention: Meeting the Challenge in New Jersey Schools* (15) and Lamb and Dunne-Maxim (5).

Meeting Faculty Needs

A faculty meeting should be held as soon as possible after the news of a suicide is known (Question 4d). Faculty should be given the facts about the suicide as they are known. However, despite the need to disseminate information quickly, the school public address system should not be used as a means of informing people about the suicide (Question 4e) or for providing follow-up information. Instead, the faculty meeting, supplemented by a telephone network, can provide staff with information and guidance on how to announce the death and deal with students' questions and reactions.

This type of proactive intervention is important in order to help staff contain the crisis. It clearly signals the leadership role of the administration in managing the situation and addressing staff support and morale issues. As one teacher dealing with the class immediately after the news of a suicide said, "It was like working in the dark. I was frightened for my students and myself." However, immediately providing in-service training to staff on suicide prevention is not recommended (Question 4l). It would, to quote one consultant, "be like putting salt in the wounds." Instead, the focus needs to be on helping them with exaggerated and unwarranted feelings of guilt and responsibility for the death and on how to understand and deal with student reactions. Faculty will also need to be aware that the impact of a suicide on a school is long lasting and that reactions may be anticipated many months after the event (Question 4m). Follow-up training at a later date, therefore, is appropriate and can help put events in perspective.

Interventions with Students

The distinction between addressing staff needs and student needs is somewhat arbitrary. The consultant's guidance and support in addressing student distress will also go a long way in answering many of the staff's most pressing concerns. For example, teachers will be reassured to know that some classroom discussion of the event is appropriate (Question 4h), provided they have been given some guidance on what to expect. As has already been suggested, this guidance will be especially welcome in the context of the initial announcement of the suicide.

On the other hand, it is necessary to maintain a balance. Schools need to keep within their routine as much as possible, while also providing opportunities for students to express their feelings and concerns. Teachers need to know that there are other resources available beyond their classroom. Opportunity for small group discussion is recommended (Question 4f). Crisis stations manned by counselors from the school and community were recommended by some consultants. Another technique for addressing concerns without generating more disruption is to have students submit their concerns and questions in writing so they can be followed up individually or in groups by appropriate staff. Because of the special demands and skills required for this kind of work, the use of a crisis management team (which ideally was already in existence) is encouraged (Question 4d). This team, made up of school staff with the appropriate training, experience, and expertise, is given the major responsibility for student screening and in-school interventions. This team approach has the added advantage of providing a mutual support group for those engaged in this stressful work.

Other student issues that are frequently raised related to funeral and memorial activities. The consultants felt strongly that formal on-site memorial services should be discouraged (Question 4d). Not only will a large memorial service bring dramatized attention to the event, but it may also set a difficult precedent. In one case that was reported, a large memorial service was held for a student who had killed himself. He happened to be a popular football player. Later, when there was another student suicide, the school decided such memorial activities were not a good idea. Unfortunately, this was misinterpreted by some as meaning the school felt the second student was less important.

Schools should commemorate the life of the deceased and help students do the same. However, this needs to be done without glamorizing, dramatizing, or mystifying a suicide. Permanent memorials such as plaques, benches, or, at least in the opinion of some, scholarship funds named after the deceased should be avoided. Instead, a time-limited memorial activity dedicated to raising funds for a youth-related cause or a school improvement work project could be encouraged. Students should also be allowed to attend the funeral (Question 4i), provided they and their parents wish it. This decision should be made with family support and without peer pressure. Forcing or preventing student participation may only increase feelings of anxiety, fear, and guilt.

RESISTANCE TO POSTVENTION EFFORTS

Everyone involved in the helping professions has experienced the phenomenon of having advice and help rejected or undermined. It is related to the natural human tendency to avoid painful truths and feelings, even when to do so is counterproductive. In the roundtable discussion, it was recognized that in response to a suicide disturbed grief reactions are normal (16). People have a need to protect themselves from being overwhelmed by their feelings. The task of the professional is to create a supportive atmosphere for the expression of these feelings, freeing the person to then take the necessary corrective actions. This is what postvention is all about. As the questionnaire results showed, the consultants were in general agreement on what corrective actions a school should take after a suicide. The challenge is to help create an atmosphere in the school in which these measures can take place. This topic, specifically acknowledging and managing resistance to postvention efforts, was a major focus of discussion.

DIFFERENTIAL RESPONSES

There was significant consensus on which groups showed the most and the least difficulty in accepting postvention help. Most students, including friends of the victim and teachers who knew the dead students personally, seemed to welcome postvention efforts. In contrast, greater reluctance was shown by school administrations, school boards, the faculty in general, and students who, although they were not close to the victim, showed a high-risk profile because of their past history. These results lend themselves to a good deal of speculative analysis that is beyond the scope of this discussion. However, the experience of the consultants seemed to bear out certain findings reported in the literature, namely that,

• Adults have more trouble talking about their feelings after a suicide than do young people (1).
• The burden of professional responsibility for other survivors can make it difficult to acknowledge one's own survivor status. (Similar reactions have been noted in hospital staff; 17.)

GAINING SCHOOL COOPERATION

There were a number of suggestions on gaining the cooperation and participation of faculty and administration:

1. The connection between successfully resolving entry issues and gaining administrative support was emphasized by many. Often, the key to this depends on establishing a positive relationship before the crisis. Such a relationship could be based on the provision of clinical services to the school's students, suicide prevention work, or joint participation in a community crisis initiative. The consultants also recommended anticipating postvention needs with local schools as part of any in-service training.

2. The limits of the consultative role must be recognized. The consultant needs to guard against being overly responsible. The consultant's role is primarily to provide advice, feedback, and technical assistance. The ability to influence how that help is used is limited. Generally, an empowering strategy was recommended that involved validating and supporting the school's efforts. Alternatives may be suggested, but decision-making authority rests with the school. The consultant helps guide these choices by identifying the probable consequences of various courses of action.

3. Whenever direct intervention is planned, special attention needs to be paid to clarifying mutual expectations; that is, who is going to do what? Communication breakdowns are especially common in crisis situations. Confusion may be especially likely when the school is asked to make arrangements for the consultant (i.e., scheduling meetings, interpreting the consultant's plans, or recruiting staff for a task). Whenever possible, the consultants advise, "check and recheck the details."

THE STRESS OF CONSULTATION

Without exception, the consultants reported that postvention work, despite its infrequency, was one of the most stressful and demanding activities in their professional lives. The nature of this stress falls into two general areas: (a) feelings of powerlessness and vulnerability in the face of systemic resistance and (b) consultants' own reactivity to the distress of those around them. The experiences of two consultants were representative. One described how after a particularly shocking suicide took place in the school, the administration wanted the consultant to ensure that there would be no other attempts but at the same time had difficulty following suggestions. Another described how the school would tend to justify actions as having been recommended by the consultant, even when they were not, and when in some cases they were contrary to the advice given. Sometimes consultants found themselves unwittingly caught in the middle of longstanding conflicts or tensions within the school. Such problems are common to all complex organizations and are exacerbated during times of conflict. Often the outsider became the target for these accumulated tensions. Thus, in one school with a long history of conflict between faculty and administration, the consultant was seen as siding with the administration in making the faculty stay after school for a postvention meeting. The consultant had in fact not known that the time was an issue and would have rescheduled the meeting if asked.

The greatest stress of all is also the most predictable. In the words of one conference participant, it is the stress of "negotiating how much one can give out in caring for others' needs before becoming emotionally exhausted or caught up in the anxiety yourself" or, in the words of another, the challenge of "managing your own and others' rage, frustration, and despair." As these two statements illustrate, consultants are not immune from the intense emotionality that follows a suicide. However, as professionals and as consultants, they need to maintain their equilibrium during crisis situations in order to lend support and objectivity to those in distress. One of the most critical functions of the consultant is to role-model crisis management for the school leadership. One person described it as being like a spongy ping-pong paddle that absorbs the anxiety, pain, and anger, then attempts to redirect it in constructive and healing ways. A more common tactic used by many of these mental health professionals is to view the school as requiring the same kind of nonjudgmental and nonreactive acceptance as is provided to the individual client.

A TEAM APPROACH

Many of the consultants recommended a team approach to ease the burdens and isolation of this work. In a school system where there will be hundreds of people with survivor reactions, the more professionals available to tend to postvention tasks, the better. Even within a small group of staff or students there will be a wide range of needs, often too much for one person to attend to. Joint leadership in any kind of group process is almost mandatory.

Another advantage of team intervention is the availability of collegial support and feedback. Even the most experienced consultant can lose objectivity in such a charged emotional atmosphere. Administrators and faculty are often suspicious of outside helpers and also feel helpless themselves. Consultants find themselves alternately idealized and devalued. Staff feedback may not be reliable, especially when there is great fear that it could happen again and great pressure to do something. It is especially in these situations that consultants may fall into the trap of feeling overly responsible and try to do too much. The best antidote to this is having the opportunity to check out reactions and ideas with knowledgeable colleagues. Besides the informal process of frequent "huddles" between consultants, some reported making a daily debriefing session part of their postvention process. This involved ending each day with a meeting of the consultant team to talk over the day's events and to develop a strategy for the next day. Such a process provides an opportunity for better planning and helps the consultants share their stresses and validate their experiences.

THE NEED FOR RESEARCH

Although the process of institutional postvention has its origins in crisis intervention and systems theory, combined with knowledge of suicide prevention and bereavement counseling, it apparently has not been the subject of formal investigation. The consultants were unanimous in their regret that their efforts, although numerous, did not include a research component. This failure to carry out adequate study of postvention methods or outcomes is widespread (18, 19). The consultants pledged to work toward the development of a uniform method of reporting and data collection as a first step in encouraging and facilitating scientific research.

A SUMMARY OF POSTVENTION PRINCIPLES

Despite the lack of validating research, the remarkable degree of consensus among those who have actually engaged in postvention activities should offer valuable guidance to others faced with helping a school, or other institution, deal with the trauma of suicide. To summarize, some key principles of postvention consultation, as suggested by the responses of some 16 mental health professionals engaged in this work, are as follows:

1. Postvention efforts will be greatly enhanced if there is a well-defined, comprehensive, and mutually understood consultation contract with the school.

2. The process of achieving entry into the school is facilitated by a positive, preexisting relationship between the school and the mental health professional.

3. Although circumstances will dictate specific intervention choices, the consultant should be prepared, as indicated, to provide guidance and support, empower faculty and administrators, and intervene directly with students and staff.

4. Almost everyone in a school can be affected by a suicide. As survivors, both students and staff may react with feelings of anger, anxiety, denial, shame, and guilt. Such feelings are normal but must be addressed because they can interfere with individual and group resolution of the crisis.

5. The general framework of crisis management advice will be guided by the need to avoid glamorizing or dramatizing the suicide, the maintenance of a stable and supportive atmosphere for students, and recognition of the needs of the survivors.

6. Some degree of reluctance to participate in postvention efforts must be expected and accepted.

7. Consultants, no matter how experienced, can never be immune to the pain and anguish that follow a suicide. They need to take the necessary steps to preserve their capacity for empathy and objectivity.

8. Consultants need to recognize the limits of their role and avoid becoming overly responsible for how the school chooses to deal with the suicide.

9. Schools and communities need to be encouraged to work together in joint crisis resolution initiatives. For both, the best postvention efforts will come from anticipating crisis issues before they arise.

As with all crisis intervention work, the focus in postvention is in supporting the client's (in this case, the school's) own strengths. Schools, by their very nature, are exceptionally resilient and resourceful organizations. They successfully overcome crises every day. The job of the postvention consultant is to validate the school in a reassertion of its abilities to cope with even the terrible tragedy of a suicide.

REFERENCES

1. Hill, W. H. (1984). Intervention and postvention in schools. In H. S. Sudak, A. B. Ford, & N. B. Rushporth (Eds.), *Suicide in the young* (pp. 407–416). Boston: John Wright/PGS.
2. Peck, M. L., & Berkovitz, I. H. (1987). Youth suicide: The role of school consultation. *Adolescent Psychiatry, 14,* 511–521.
3. Kalafat, J., & Underwood, M. (1985). *Lifelines: A school based adolescent suicide response program.* Dubuque, IA: Kendall/Hunt.
4. Shneidman, E. S. (1973). *Deaths of man.* New York: Quadrangle Books.
5. Lamb, F., & Dunne-Maxim, K. (1987). Postvention in schools: Policy and process. In E. Dunne, J. McIntosh, & K. Dunne-Maxim (Eds.), *Suicide and its aftermath.* (pp. 245–260). New York: Norton.
6. Webb, N. B. (1986). Before and after suicide: A prevention outreach program for colleges. *Suicide and Life-Threatening Behavior, 16,* 469–480.
7. Gaffney, D. (1988). Death in the classroom: A lesson in life. *Holistic Nursing Practice, 2,* 20–27.
8. Lamb, F., Dunne-Maxim, K., & Gaffney, D. (1990). In M. J. Rotheram, J. Bradley, & N. Oblensky (Eds.), *Evaluating and treating suicidal teens in community settings* (pp. 309–328). Tulsa, OK: National Resource Center for Youth Services.
9. Cain, A. C. (1972). Introduction. In A. C. Cain (Ed.), *Survivors of suicide* (pp. 5–33). Springfield, IL: Charles C Thomas.
10. Davidson, L. E. (1989). Suicide clusters and youth. In C. R. Pfeffer (Ed.), *Suicide among youth* (pp. 83–99). Washington, DC: American Psychiatric Press.
11. Range, L. M., Goggin, W. C., & Steede, K. K. (1988). Perception of behavior contagion of adolescent suicide. *Suicide and Life-Threatening Behavior, 18,* 334–341.
12. Centers for Disease Control, (1988, August 19). CDC Recommendations for a Community Plan for the Prevention and Containment of Suicidal Clusters. *Morbidity and Mortality Weekly Report, 5–6,* 37.
13. Dunne-Maxim, K. (1987). Survivors and the media. In E. Dunne, J. McIntosh, & K. Dunne-Maxim (Eds.), *Suicide and its aftermath* (pp. 45–56). New York: Norton.
14. Phillips, D. P., Carstensen, L. L., & Paight, D. J. (1989). In C. R. Pfeffer (Ed.), *Suicide among youth* (pp. 101–116). Washington, DC: American Psychiatric Press.
15. Governor's Advisory Council on Youth Suicide Prevention and The New Jersey Adolescent Suicide Prevention Project. (1989). *Youth suicide prevention: Meeting the challenge in New Jersey schools.* Trenton: New Jersey State Department of Human Services.
16. Rynearson, E. K. (1986). Psychological effects of unnatural dying on bereavement. *Psychiatric Annals, 16,* 272–275.
17. Soreff, S. M. (1975). The impact of staff suicide on a psychiatric inpatient unit. *The Journal of Nervous and Mental Disease, 161,* 130–133.
18. Schaffer, D., Garland, A., Gould, M., Fisher, P., & Trautman, P. (1988). Preventing teenage suicide: A critical review. *Journal of the American Academy of Child and Adolescent Psychiatry, 27,* 675–687.
19. Henley, S. H. A. (1984). Bereavement following suicide: A review of the literature. *Current Psychological Research and Reviews, Summer,* 53–61.

APPENDIX: QUESTIONNAIRE
FOR POSTVENTION CONSULTANTS

Please answer the following questions based on your experience in doing postvention work in schools after a student suicide.

1. How many school postventions have you done? _____

2. On average, how many hours does your postvention require? _____

3. Approximately what percentage of your total time in a postvention is focused on the following:

High risk students _____ (%)
The general student population _____ (%)
School administrators _____ (%)
Guidance and special services staff _____ (%)
Teachers _____ (%)
Parents of the victim _____ (%)
The other parents _____ (%)
Community resources _____ (%)
Others (specify) _____ (%)

4. In general, after a suicide, do you advise schools to

Limit contacts with media?	Yes ____ No ____
Hold meeting with all parents within 1 week after the suicide?	Yes ____ No ____
Hold school memorial service?	Yes ____ No ____
Hold faculty meetings about the suicide?	Yes ____ No ____
Use public address system to provide information about the suicide?	Yes ____ No ____
Encourage student small-group discussion?	Yes ____ No ____
Establish a crisis management team?	Yes ____ No ____
Avoid classroom discussion of the suicide?	Yes ____ No ____
Allow students to attend the funeral?	Yes ____ No ____
Contact the victim's parents?	Yes ____ No ____
Establish contact with relevant community agencies?	Yes ____ No ____
Include suicide prevention training for staff in postvention activities?	Yes ____ No ____
Anticipate long-term reactions to the suicide?	Yes ____ No ____

5. In general, how would you rate resistance to postvention efforts among the following:

The general student population?	High ____	Moderate ____	Low ____
The school administration?	High ____	Moderate ____	Low ____
Parents of the victim?	High ____	Moderate ____	Low ____
Parents of the other students?	High ____	Moderate ____	Low ____

Close friends of the victim?   High ____ Moderate ____ Low ____
High-risk students?   High ____ Moderate ____ Low ____
School boards?   High ____ Moderate ____ Low ____
The faculty as a whole?   High ____ Moderate ____ Low ____
Teachers who knew the victim?   High ____ Moderate ____ Low ____
Guidance/special services staff?   High ____ Moderate ____ Low ____

6. What do you find to be the most stressful part of doing postvention work?

_____

_____

_____

Name _____

Organization _____

V

CONCLUDING REMARKS

Prevention, intervention, and postvention in our schools are important in addressing suicide in youth. In this volume we have attempted to outline the state of the art of prevention in schools. Yet, critical reflection and research are urgently needed. Part V presents some concluding remarks. It consists of three chapters: the important of evaluations for programs, some critical reflections, and a brief summary.

18

Evaluation of School-Based Interventions

John Kalafat
St. Clare's Riverside Medical Center, Denville, New Jersey

Maurice Elias
Rutgers University, New Brunswick, New Jersey

During the past decade large numbers of school-based suicide intervention programs have arisen in response to increases in youth suicidal behavior. Other chapters in this volume review the scope and nature of these programs, as well as the issues associated with their proliferation. In this chapter we review the findings of efforts to assess the impact of these programs on their participants.

Our review places these findings within the context of the effects of youth-oriented prevention programs in general, and we identify some important questions that remain to be addressed. We also suggest a strategy and a methodology for addressing these questions.

AN EVALUATION FRAMEWORK

Program evaluation in general, and the evaluation of prevention programs in particular, can be organized into a framework that specifies the purpose of the evaluation and the steps or components of the evaluation process (1, 2). We present our review and recommendations within such a framework.

First, one purpose of a program evaluation is to provide information to program developers that will assist in the development and improvement of their programs. This type of evaluation has been called "action research" or the "amelioration model" (3), and is in contrast to the experimental model, the purpose of which is to generate formal theories or uncover universal laws (4). This distinction is important because the amelioration model attenuates the likelihood of drawing premature or overgeneralized conclusions about school-based programs—a phenomenon that has plagued the early stages of other preventive educational efforts (5).

Next, program evaluation basically consists of the following components:

1. *Needs assessment* not only establishes a general need for the program, but also may help identify the appropriate target population, key program elements, and preferred delivery methods.

2. *Program specification* requires a detailed specification of the goals of the program, procedures that will be used to reach the goals, resources needed to support the adequate implementation of the procedures over time, the program's theory of the way in which the intervention procedures are to lead to proximal and

distal goals (i.e., is the program of sufficient scope, intensity, etc., to achieve the intended objectives, at least in theory), and the expected time required to attain the various goals.

3. *Process evaluation* basically assesses the extent to which the program was delivered as it was conceived and sheds light on a variety of other program variables, such as whether the program

- goals and objectives were clearly specified and conceptually grounded;
- goals are limited to specific, observable, or measurable objectives;
- design and components address the objectives;
- follows established (in this case) instructional, consultative, developmental, or crisis principles;
- is of sufficient scope to achieve the objectives;
- implementation is linked to benchmarks that can be observed or measures to provide monitoring and feedback of the progress of the program over time; and
- whether there is assessment of "consumer satisfaction" with the various components of the program (consumers are defined as recipients of training and of the program).

4. *Proximal outcome* assesses the immediate impact of the program on its participants (in this case, the knowledge and attitudes of students, educators, and other target groups).

5. *Distal outcome* assesses the effects associated with processes and proximal outcomes (for school-based programs in this area, these might include referral rates and suicidal behavior).

6. *Exportability and adaptability of the program* refer to the extent to which it is known how, or if, a program needs to be modified with regard to basic program structure and assessment/monitoring or instrumentation needed to maintain its effectiveness despite variation in types of settings, population mixes within settings, implementors, etc.

We now review the results of current evaluation studies in each of these areas.

EVALUATION STUDIES

The need for school-based programs and the specific elements and targets required in these programs have been established by epidemiological data on youth suicide and by a variety of surveys of students and educators. Surveys of adolescents reveal that between 10 and 15% have made a suicide attempt (6–8) and between 40 and 60% have thought about suicide (8, 9). These and other surveys (10–12) indicate that troubled youth are most likely to turn to peers for assistance, and that up to 25% say they would not make a referral to a professional or other adult.

Surveys of educators consistently reveal a core of needed program elements including identification of risk (warning signs), crisis procedures, stress reduction, and knowledge of resources (13–16). These needs correspond with topics rated most important in a survey of 114 school programs (17). Top-rated topics were (1) myths, signs, facts, and symptoms; (2) referral sources; (3) identification/ acceptance of feelings; and (4) how to respond to suicidal crisis. These programs, then, would appear to be addressing the areas indicated in the surveys of students and educators. The survey of school programs also revealed that 94 such programs included a classroom component for students, the mean length of which was 3.5 hr. Sixty-one percent of those respondents indicated that they had written evaluation procedures. This leads to a consideration of the current evaluation concerning the impact of these programs.

Taken together these surveys indicate a need for school-based interventions addressing troubled youths and, perhaps more importantly, their peers, who most often know about their suicidal feelings. These data also point to the need for programs that attempt to increase the likelihood that youths will obtain appropriate help for themselves or their peers. Such programs would include knowledge of warning signs and referral procedures and resources; attitudes toward suicide, help-seeking, and breaking a confidence; and attitudes toward school and community-based helpers.

The formal evaluation of programs is clearly in the early stages of development. As recently as 1987 a review of the literature (18) revealed no published reports of systematic controlled studies of school-based educational intervention. A follow up of the programs identified in the Smith, Eyman, Dick, and Ryerson (17) survey that indicated that they had carried out some type of evaluation yielded data from 20 respondents (19). In general, these data revealed that:

- Nearly all of the programs surveyed so far keep tract of the number of classes and students reached.
- About half regularly obtain written feedback from students, faculty, administrators, and parents.
- Most consultants conduct the classes themselves rather than train teachers to do so.
- About half have assessed changes in knowledge and attitudes of students.
- Very few have assessed changes in knowledge and attitudes of teachers, administrators, or parents.
- Over half track changes in referrals to school personnel; about half have tracked referrals to community agencies.
- The majority have not assessed changes in rates of suicide attempts or completions.

In addition, more detailed data were obtained from two programs. Project Lifesaver (6) was a one-session classroom presentation provided by the Suicide Prevention Center of Dayton, Ohio, in two school systems. Pre- and post-questionnaires addressing knowledge and attitudes about suicide were obtained from students in seventh, eighth, and ninth grades who attended the program. Comparisons with students who did not attend were reported for some, but not all, items.

An early version (1982) of the Project Lifesaver questionnaire yielded significant increases in the ability to recognize warning signs and the willingness to confide in a teacher on the part of students who attended the program. On the 1986 questionnaire significantly more program attenders, as compared to nonattenders, indicated that they would tell a friend's parents, another friend, or a teacher if a friend were in crisis; and a lower percentage of attenders would tell no one if a friend were in a crisis. Program attendance appeared to have no effect on students' actions if they, as opposed to a friend, were in crisis.

About 8% of seventh graders and 13% of eighth graders reported having made a suicide attempt, and a smaller percent of these students indicated that they would tell an adult about their own or a friend's crisis (13 vs. 33% would tell a parent; 20 vs. 30% would tell a counselor). A greater percentage of attempters (34 vs. 23%) would tell no one. Both attempters and nonattempters who attended the program showed increases in expressed willingness to call a crisis service.

Bowers and Gilbert (10) reported a study of the impact of the Richmond, Virginia, crisis center suicide education program for grades 8, 10, and 12 in a local school system. Pre- and post-program measures without comparison groups were obtained. Grades 8 and 12 showed significant increases in percentage of correct responses to a true-false questionnaire and in the knowledge of and comfort in using the crisis center. A mixed pattern of results was found among sexes and grades as to program effects on actions taken if oneself or a friend were in crisis. Between 7 and 11% reported having made a suicide attempt, with the exception of 12th-grade females, 23% of whom reported having made an attempt.

Late in 1987 Nelson (20) reported an evaluation of the California suicide prevention school program. An 18-item pretest measuring knowledge (facts about suicide, resources, and intervention techniques), attitudes toward suicidal peers, and confidence in one's ability to respond to those peers was administered to 189 students participating in a 4-hr curriculum. A different sample of 181 students completed the measure after the curriculum. The posttest group showed slightly higher, but statistically significant, scores in knowledge and helpful attitudes toward suicidal peers than the pretest group.

After 1987 the literature reveals four program evaluations that used pre-post self report measures on treatment and matched comparison groups. Schaffer, Garland, and Whittle (7) evaluated the impact of three suicide education programs (5, 4, and 2 hr) carried out in six New Jersey high schools. Pre- and post-program questionnaires assessing knowledge and attitudes about suicide and help seeking, and suicidality, were administered to 1,140 ninth and tenth grade students in the treatment schools, and 1,043 students in five control schools.

Results indicated that:

• Approximately 90% of the students felt that the programs should be delivered in other schools. Less than 10% were distressed by the program or knew someone who was. A main reason for any distress was regret over a missed opportunity to help a suicidal friend. A large number of students felt the program made it easier to deal with their own and their friend's problems.

• There was no evidence that the programs had induced suicidal behavior in any of the students.

• Seeking help for one's own problems was not generally done prior to the programs. Only 5% of students usually talk over their problems with a teacher or counselor, and only 13% would definitely take their troubles to a mental health professional. These proportions were unchanged by exposure to a program. There was, however, an increase in the number of program students who would make use of a hotline (24% to 34%) and who would recommend a hotline to a suicidal friend.

• Helping a friend was no more likely after receiving the programs. About 65% of the students would share another student's suicidal disclosure with an adult, about 10% would keep it a secret, and about one third would share it with another friend. These proportions were unchanged by exposure to a program. A pattern of responses, whereby a majority of students would behave responsibly and a minority unfavorably, with neither group being influenced by the program, recurred in several areas.

• Students' knowledge of suicide warning signs increased after exposure to a program, but the number who knew of community mental health resources (40%) remained unchanged.

• As with the Dayton study, those students who reported having made an attempt (11%) differed from the nonattempters in that they were two times less likely to give up a secret if a friend were suicidal, or to tell anyone if they felt suicidal. They also held a more negative view about help from professionals and, not surprisingly, were more likely to endorse suicide as a solution to problems. With the exception of calling a hotline, none of these attitudes was affected by the programs. Attempters were also more likely to rate the programs as boring (38 vs. 23%), providing little new information (39 vs. 21%), and distressing (12 vs. 6%), again largely because after the program they responded with regrets about missed opportunities to take constructive action for themselves or a troubled peer.

Educators responded in a generally favorable fashion to the programs. A majority indicated that, although they knew that school policies for the management of emotional disturbances in students existed, they were generally ignorant about how these were implemented. Their knowledge increased dramatically as a result of exposure to the programs. Knowledge about treatment resources and suicide warning signs also increased after exposure to the programs.

In one of the better designed studies to date, Spirito, Overholser, Ashworth, Morgan, and Benedict-Drew (11) employed a Solomon four-groups design to assess students' responses on self-report knowledge and attitude measures. Two experimental groups went through a 6-hr curriculum provided by trained teachers; one group received pre- and post-measures and one received only post-measures. Two matched control groups were drawn from schools in similar geographical locations. Again, one received pre- and post-measures and one only post-measures. Posttests occurred 10 weeks after the curriculum, thus measuring fairly long-term effects. Scores on their Suicide Knowledge test showed significant effects (gains) for curriculum, pretesting, and sex: knowledge score gains after the curriculum occurred only in the pretested groups and gains were greater for females. Attitudes toward suicide changed in a positive direction (more understanding, less prejudicial, increased tendency to assist peers), occurred mainly as a function of having completed the pretest and were unaffected by the curriculum. Also, females were more likely than males to endorse positive attitudes toward suicide regardless of whether they took part in the suicide awareness program. Females in the pretesting group also showed decreases on a standard (Beck) hopelessness inventory after the curriculum.

In another evaluation of this suicide awareness program (21), the same measures were employed to conduct pre- and post-assessment of students who took part in the curriculum in two schools and a comparison group of students from another school. This study was designed to assess the effects of gender and personal experience with suicidal peers.

Gender differences were again found in that, on baseline measures, females had higher knowledge scores and were less likely to evaluate suicide behavior in a negative manner. The curriculum was associated with a slight reduction in hopelessness for female students and small, but statistically significant, increases in hopelessness and negative evaluation attitudes in males. Females showed a significant decrease in negative evaluations of suicidal behavior after the curriculum.

On the pretest, students who had personal experience with a suicidal peer displayed more negative evaluation attitudes than did students without such experience; such personal experience was associated with greater learning of relevant information during the curriculum. This variable is important, because one question raised about the preventive strategy of exposing all students to a suicide awareness curriculum is the salience of the material to them. Learning research indicates that students best learn the material that is relevant to issues they are currently addressing in their lives (22). The personal knowledge form used in a pilot study for this program revealed that an average ninth-grader had contact with two or three peers who spoke of attempting suicide. The average student spoke to about four peers who expressed some suicidal intentions, but reported referring only one student for professional help. These findings confirm informal assessments by the first author and reports from other surveys (6, 7). It would appear the widespread knowledge of suicidal peers raises the salience of the programs for students in a manner that can affect their learning. Pretesting may also alert students to issues in this area in such a way as to enhance learning.

Before discussing the general implications of the pattern of findings from these studies in regard to high school awareness curricula, we review one other study that deals with college students.

Abbey, Madsen, and Polland (23) conducted a study to assess whether a short-term awareness curriculum would demonstrate effects on knowledge about suicide and responses to suicidal situations contained in (a) an established Suicide Intervention Response Scale that has been used to assess posttraining competence of paraprofessional hotline workers, and (b) responses to five suicidal vignettes rated by raters who had established appropriate levels of reliability.

There were three groups of participants in this study: a control group receiving pre-post measures only; one treatment group receiving self-study handouts only; and a treatment group receiving handouts plus three practically-oriented lecture/discussion sessions.

This study, then, is unique in that it not only assessed two learning conditions, but also attempted to assess performance, albeit in an analog situation, rather than simply relying on self reports of knowledge and attitudes.

The results indicated that both treatment groups significantly outperformed the control group on all measures. The lecture-plus-handouts group outperformed the handouts-only group on knowledge and responses to the suicide related vignettes. The researchers reviewed some evidence that all of the measures (except the vignettes) may be drawing their variance from similar constructs (i.e., measuring basically the same thing). While these results are encouraging, the authors state they were obtained with college students and may not generalize to high school or middle school students.

OVERVIEW OF EVALUATION STUDIES

The overall pattern of results for students and educators showed gains in knowledge and little or no impact on attitudes, except for reported confidence in talking to a suicidal peer. Other health curricula addressing substance abuse and sexual behavior have shown similar lack of success in affecting attitudes (24, 25). Also, research on other health education programs (26, 27) and on help-seeking in adolescents (28) has found little correlation between self-report measures and behavior. No studies measured distal outcomes, although two reported significant increases in calls to local hotlines after the program (11, 29). Thus, there is a need to measure behavior (distal outcomes) in order to assess whether these programs achieve their objectives. The stated objectives and outcome evaluation criteria (dependent variables) are, of course, one in the same (1). It is therefore interesting to note the ratings of importance of various evaluation criteria as obtained in the Smith et al. survey. Mean ratings on a seven-point scale with 1 being most important were:

Measurable increase in student knowledge about suicide: 2.29
Measurable increase in helping skills (e.g., listening, coping): 3.40
Measurable increase in knowledge of referral services: 3.50
Increase in the number of suicidal students using referral services before acting: 3.53
Measurable reduction in the number of suicide attempts/gestures reported to school staff and/or local emergency rooms: 4.87
Measurable reduction in the number of suicidal deaths: 5.34
Measurable reduction in the number of unplanned pregnancies, and/or alcohol or drug discipline cases reported to school staff: 6.28

These priorities make sense as objectives for educational programs. Students must acquire practical knowledge about suicide, such as warning signs; skills in responding to troubled peers; and knowledge of referral sources as a prerequisite to increased use of referral sources. Use of referral sources may result in reduction of suicide attempts and completions, but many other variables will affect this outcome, including the efficacy of these referral sources and changes in the troubled students' lives. In light of the well-documented negative attitude among youths toward seeking help from formal sources (28), it would also seem appropriate for programs to include strategies to address such attitudes as one of their objectives. Moreover, the results reviewed so far in regard to impact on student attitudes are not predictive of much success in affecting such entrenched attitudes. Again, the impact of these programs on student behaviors remains unclear, as this has yet to be assessed. This state of affairs—some initial proximal outcomes and little or no measured distal effects—is fairly common for first generation assessments of preventive/educational youth programs.

Useful information can be gleaned from briefly examining the history of research into the effectiveness of programs in the area of social competence promotion and the prevention of mental disorders, because these programs received their modern impetus in the 1960s. After almost 30 years the research record shows considerable variation across studies that assessed the effectiveness of these programs with regard to their proximal and distal outcomes. However, neither significant program effects nor failures to generate predicted changes allowed one to be certain what practical intervention recommendations logically followed. Kelly (30) was among the leaders in pointing out the inadequacy of the existing knowledge base because too little was known about the extent to which programs were carried out as planned. As implementation monitoring becomes recognized as a necessary aspect of program evaluation (31), researchers and program developers will be required to understand and explicate more fully the critical components, range, and exportability of their preventive and competence-enhancing interventions. If programs are to impact on public health, they must address questions as to what kinds of modification can be made/and in what kind of settings, which will allow them to approximate their claimed proximal and distal effects. This question can be answered for very few programs and even when the answer is known it has tended to be disappointing (32).

Within the field of suicide prevention it must also be said that efforts at program improvement or program amelioration will not accelerate until there is greater systematic attention to implementation process evaluation. It is not enough to say that one has a carefully developed, published curriculum as the basis of one's program. Assessment must be made of the various key steps that occur between a setting's agreement to use one's program and the collection of outcome data (33).

For example, the first author was a consultant on a project that evaluated three New Jersey awareness programs (7). This study was the only systematic evaluation that did not show knowledge gains. However, for a variety of reasons beyond the control of the evaluators, each of these programs may have been implemented under less than optimal conditions. The lack of process evaluation data prevents the formal assessment of this suspected scenario. One example of a potential link between a process variable and program outcome can be drawn from this project. One attitude change that was found in this study was an increase in the number of students who indicated a willingness to use a hotline. This was the referral source most emphasized in each program, particularly through the use of wallet-card handouts. This is an important possible effect, as hotlines possess certain qualities such as anonymity and temporal and financial accessibility that may make them more acceptable to adolescents.

It is informative to assess a variety of other process variables as noted in the examples that follow.

• Smith et al's (17) survey revealed that some programs were provided by school personnel, others by external consultants. Do different presenters have differential effects, for example, by increasing the salience of particular adult caregivers? Would, for example, peer presenters yield different effects, given the preference of many youth for peer helpers?

• There is considerable literature on the program elements that may enhance the transfer of knowledge and skills gained in training programs to enhanced performance in actual settings (34). Do school-based programs include such elements?

• It is now generally agreed that school-based programs must go beyond curricula for students and educators to assessment and interventions aimed at enhancing and mobilizing a wide scope of school and community resources (35). It is not effective, for example, to train students and educators to refer to a community human service system that is unprepared to respond. Such context or environmental variables are, in fact, considered important for the transfer of learning from the classroom to real life situations (36).

These variables, then, must also be included in process and outcome evaluations. The amelioration model would call for careful specification, systematic variation, assessment, and exploration of program characteristics that would yield clear feedback to enhance the desired impact of our school-based efforts.

CONCLUSIONS

From the program evaluation framework articulated at the beginning of this chapter and the research reviewed subsequently, several specific recommendations can be made to advance research in the field of school-based suicide intervention.

1. Comparability of research across sites and teams can be increased, particularly by providing more detailed descriptions of intervention activities and by greater standardization of measurement instruments.

2. Program developers and evaluators must be more specific about the program goals, their theory of the pathways through which change is expected to occur, their intended implementation procedures, and the plan for monitoring implementation. The full range of evaluation variables noted in the beginning of this chapter can serve as guidelines for a thorough conceptualization of one's planned study.

3. When designing interventions, the literature on program elements that may enhance transfer of knowledge and performance outside the training context should be consulted so that these elements are included in the intervention plan.

4. Research should note that program outcomes often reflect an interaction of the dosage (or amount) of an intervention and its salience (or meaningfulness and relevance) to the target population. Programs are most likely to be effective if and when they combine high dosage and high salience; when either is low, a program might yield disappointing results. Yet, if both factors are not assessed, researchers will be at a loss to attribute the findings to program design, inappropriate targeting, or both. This has data analytic implications as well, as it is possible that the group for which a program might have high salience and effectiveness is too small for its gains to produce an overall statistically significant effect in the treatment group. Clarity about one's theory of change can help one determine appropriate data analytic techniques and avoid such pitfalls.

5. To a much greater extent, comprehensive, ecological case studies should be used as a format for writing interventions and evaluations. In a number of other fields this method is gaining increased legitimacy as an effective way to capture the contextual variation that influences the success or failure of intervention efforts (37).

Initial school-based interventions have been grass roots collaborations between mental health consultants and educators attempting to address pressing, practical needs. These efforts may include significant public health contributions, and early evaluation returns are encouraging, if not sufficiently informative. As these collaborative efforts continue and begin to incorporate evaluations that include some of our recommendations, and are carried out over time by a number of different investigators, the field of suicide prevention will be able to establish a more secure, confident knowledge base. We contend that this could contain implications for public health practice that are likely, literally, to save lives and avert the tragedies that even unsuccessful suicide attempts represent.

REFERENCES

1. Price, R. H., & Smith, S. S. (1985). *A guide to evaluating prevention programs in mental health.* Rockville, MD: National Institute of Mental Health.
2. Kelly, J. G. (1988). *A guide to conducting prevention research in the community.* New York: Haworth Press.
3. Windle, C., & Neigher, W. D. (1978). Ethical problems in program evaluation: Advice for trapped evaluators. *Evaluation and Program Planning, 1*, 97–108.
4. Fishman, D. B., & Neigher, W. D. (1982). American psychology in the eighties: Who will buy? *American Psychologist, 37*, 553–546.
5. Elias, M. J. (1987). Establishing enduring prevention programs: Advancing the legacy of Swampscott. *American Journal of Community Psychology, 15*, 539–553.
6. Boggs, C. (1986). *Project Lifesaver: Child and adolescent suicide prevention in two school systems.* Dayton, OH: Suicide Prevention Center, Inc.
7. Schaffer, D., Garland, A., & Whittle, B. (1988, March). An evaluation of youth suicide prevention programs. *New Jersey adolescent suicide prevention project: Final project report.* Trenton, NJ: New Jersey Division of Mental Health and Hospitals.
8. Smith, K., & Crawford, S. (1986). Suicidal behavior among "normal" high school students. *Suicide and Life-Threatening Behavior, 3*, 313–325.
9. Curran, D. K. (1987). *Adolescent suicide behavior.* Washington, DC: Hemisphere.
10. Bowers, C., & Gilbert, J. (1987). *Survey of effectiveness of suicide education program in Richmond schools.* Richmond, VA: Crisis Center.
11. Spirito, A., Overholser, J., Ashworth, S., Morgan, J., & Benedict-Drew, C. Evaluation of a suicide awareness curriculum for high school students. *Journal of the American Academy of Child & Adolescent Psychiatry, 6*, 705–711.
12. North, J. E. (1978). Developmental changes in preferences for help. *Journal of Clinical Child Psychology,* Summer, *7*, 129–132.
13. Grob, M. C., Klein, A. A., & Eisen, S. V. (1982). The role of the high school professional in identifying and managing adolescent suicide behavior. *Journal of Youth and Adolescence, 12*, 162–173.
14. Davis, J. M. (1985). Suicidal cries in schools. *School Psychology Review, 3*, 313–324.
15. Mariano, F. (1989, April). *Educators' views of school-based suicide awareness programs.* Paper presented at the Annual Conference of the American Association of Suicidology, San Diego, CA.
16. Wise, P. S., Snead, V. S., & Huebner, E. S. (1987). Crisis intervention: Involvement and training needs of school psychology personnel. *The Journal of School Psychology, 25*, 185–187.
17. Smith, K., Eyman, J. J., Dick, R., & Ryerson, D. (1987, October). *Report of the school suicide programs questionnaire.* Albuquerque, NM: The Menninger Clinic.
18. Schaffer, D., Bacon, K., Fisher, P., & Garland, A. (1987, January). *Review of youth suicide prevention programs.* New York, NY: New York State Psychiatric Institute.
19. Kalafat, J., & Garland, A. (1988, April). *Evaluation of school-based suicide programs.* Paper presented at the Annual Conference of the American Association of Suicidology, Washington, DC.
20. Nelson, F. L. (1987). Evaluation of a youth suicide prevention school program. *Adolescence, 88*, 813–825.
21. Hemstreet, A. H., Overholser, J. C., Spirito, A., & Vyse, S. (1989, August). *Suicide awareness programs in the schools: Effects of gender and personal experience.* Paper presented at the Annual Convention of the American Psychological Association, New Orleans, LA.
22. Knowles, M. (1973). *The adult learner: A neglected species.* Houston, TX: Gulf Publishing.
23. Abbey, K. J., Madsen, C. H., & Polland, R. (1989). Short-term suicide awareness curriculum. *Suicide & Life-Threatening Behavior, 2*, 216–227.
24. Botvin, G. J. (1986). Substance abuse prevention research: Recent developments and future directions. *Journal of School Health, 77*, 89–92.
25. Barlett, E. E. (1981). The contribution of school health education to community health promotion: What can we reasonably expect? *American Journal of Public Health, 71*, 1384–1391.
26. Arborelius, E., & Bremberg, S. (1988). "It is *your* decision!"–Behavioral effects of a student-centered health education model at school for adolescents. *Journal of Adolescence, 11*, 287–297.
27. Tracey, T. J., Sherry, P., Bauer, G. P., Robins, T. H., Todaro, L., & Briggs, S. (1984). Help

seeking as a function of student characteristics and program description: a logit-loglinear analysis. *Journal of Counseling Psychology, 1,* 54–62.

28. Aaronson, S. L., Underwood, M., Gaffney, D., & Rotheram-Borus, M. J. (1989, April). *Reluctance to help-seeking by adolescents.* Paper presented at the Annual Conference of the American Association of Suicidology, San Diego, CA.

29. Ross, C. (1987). School and suicide: Education for life and death. In R. F. W. Diekstra & R. Hawton (Eds.) *Suicide in adolescence* (pp. 155–172). The Netherlands: Martinus Nijhoff Publishers.

30. Kelly, J. G. (1979). T'aint what you do its the way you do it. *American Journal of Community Psychology, 7,* 244–261.

31. Elias, M. J., & Brandon, L. R. (1988). Primary prevention of behaviors and emotional problems in school-aged populations. *School Psychology Review, 4,* 581–602.

32. Haskins, R. (1989). Beyond metaphor: The efficacy of early childhood education. *American Psychologist, 44,* 274–282.

33. Elias, M. J., & Clabby, J. F. (1984). Integrating social and affective education into public school curriculum and instruction. In C. A. Maher, R. J., Illbacks, & J. E. Zins (Eds.). *Organizational psychology in the schools: A handbook for professionals* (pp. 143–172). Springfield, IL: Charles C Thomas.

34. Camp, R. R., Blanchard, P. N., & Huszco, G. G. (1986). *Toward a more organizationally effective training strategy and practice.* Englewood Cliffs, NJ: Prentice-Hall.

35. Kalafat, J., & Underwood, M. (1989). *Lifelines: A school-based adolescent suicide response program.* Dubuque, IA: Kendall/Hunt.

36. Rummler, G. A., & Brache, A. P. (1988). The systems view of human performance. *Training,* September, *25,* 45–53.

37. Yin R. (1984). *Case study research: Design and methods.* Beverly Hills, CA: Sage.

19

Suicide Intervention in Schools: Critical Reflections

Alan L. Berman
American University, Washington, DC

NASALVILLE: A PARABLE

Imagine a small midwestern town for which you serve as a public health specialist. In the early spring months your attention is alerted to an outbreak of nasality among students in the local high school. In its most alarming and prevalent form, specific behaviors (e.g., nose picking) are leading to serious medical consequences (e.g., excessive nose bleeding: morbidity) requiring emergency treatment at Nasalville General Hospital and, in extremis, death (mortality). Reports of these events in the Nasalville *Gazette* have fueled community concern and, to your dismay, threaten the possibility of contagion or imitative behaviors (e.g., teachers at Nasalville High School have noted a rash of nasal behaviors, particularly among groups of students prone to being nosy).

The mayor of Nasalville has asked you to develop a prevention–intervention program to quell these disturbing behaviors and their consequences. However, even before you begin to focus an interventive strategy you are overwhelmed by the community's response. Editorials in the *Gazette* have urged quick action and proposed the adoption of public information campaigns ("Say No to Nose Picking," "Take a Bite Out of Nosiness"). The citizens of Nasalville have already formed group influence campaigns ("Students/Mothers Against Nose Picking") and more severe measures of environmental control have been proposed by members of your staff eager to demonstrate their crisis intervention skills (e.g., "All students will wear nose guards during school hours"; or "Students will be required to wear mittens . . .").

At Nasalville Senior High counselors and teachers, in consultation with the staff of the Nasalville Community Mental Health Center, have developed and instituted a school-based nasality prevention program. This multipoint intervention strategy primarily is educational in format, using lectures by experts on nasality, interviews with teens who had survived serious nasal episodes, and handouts of warning signs of risks associated with nasal behavior. Students are being taught not to keep secrets when told by friends of planned nose picking and where to refer someone in need of help. Similar programs have been developed for parents and teachers, as well as school gatekeepers (bus drivers, cafeteria workers, etc.) needed to observe students at risk. A peer counseling program proposed initially by several students has begun with the support of a faculty advisor.

By everyone's account these are significant and successful interventions. Students report that they benefitted from their training and have evaluated their educational program with much satisfaction and can, indeed, demonstrate that they are able to better identify nasal behavior risks on posttraining tests. Student peer counselors are meeting weekly with a number of students observed to be vulnerable and they themselves report considerable satisfaction with their training and growth in understanding and responding to peers in trouble. Parents, teachers, and gatekeepers are pleased at the speed and intensity of response by the school community and point, perhaps most profoundly, to the fact that no new incidents of nasal related mortality have been observed in the several months since these programs began.

In spite of these reports you feel cautious and uneasy. You remain uncertain about the effectiveness of these school-based approaches, instituted in urgency, and are hesitant to commit limited resources prematurely without more behaviorally focused outcome data. You wonder aloud about the efficacy, efficiency, and long-term impact of these programs.

In the meantime communities nationwide have sought information about the Nasalville School-Based Prevention Program in order to institute prevention programs of their own. Program manuals and correlative material are being disseminated, speakers from Nasalville High are delivering workshops at national educational and mental health conventions, and a network of nasal prevention program coordinators has been formed to share information. Stimulated by such national attention and reinforcement, Nasalville's efforts appear to have achieved considerable popular validation and acceptance as a significant community-based preventive program.

Parables are meant to teach through simple illustration. The snowball effect of Nasalville's programmatic interventions, spurred by public demand, support, and the reinforcement of those involved and those seeking models, mirrors efforts in recent years to intervene in the emerging problem of youth suicide. A zeitgeist has developed, similar to that fostered by the volunteerism of the 1960s–1970s that reinforced the development of telephone counseling and crisis intervention services; a zeitgeist that feeds on its own energy and good intent, on the felt urgency of the problem in need of resolution. The need for resolution, however, is not sufficient reason for simple solutions to complex problems. Suicide and self-destructive behaviors are outcomes of a very complex set of interactive factors and dynamics. Interventions born out of urgency rather than research, analysis, and rigorous planning may lead to false impressions about the problem and the truly impactive solutions (1).

PREVENTION OF PUBLIC HEALTH PROBLEMS

Any community-wide preventive intervention such as that instituted in our mythical Nasalville rests on the consensual response of the community to a number of significant questions. These questions apply irrespective of whether the problem focus is that of nasality or suicidality, or for that matter, AIDS, teenage pregnancy, drugs, or alcohol. For our purposes we will focus on the problem of youth suicide, referencing what we have learned from efforts in other problem areas as appropriate.

First, do we agree that there is a problem (i.e., a threat to the public well-being) sufficient to define a need to prevent? As is well illustrated throughout this volume, there is significant epidemiological data to alert us to an alarming rise in the incidence of youth suicide when current rates are compared to those of earlier decades. Recently reported rates in the United States for 1985 reflected an all-time high for youth aged 15–19 years (2). Similar increases have been noted on an international level (3). However, a nationwide or worldwide observed increase in suicide among youth does not make for sufficient agreement that a need for preventive response will be felt on a local level such as in Nasalville. Thus, a condition of problem–definition to be met before a response can be considered is raised by a second question: Is there sufficient local (community) concern to mobilize response efforts?

Human behavior is such that we generally deny problems until they are undeniable or are of such threat that our anticipatory anxiety overwhelms our defenses. The normative theme appears to be: If not in my town (or school), it is not my problem. There is no rule of thumb or measurable threshold for defining when a community might mobilize a response to a perceived threat. Those familiar with suicide prevention efforts in the schools readily will affirm the resistance of individual school principals to such efforts when their schools have not had a suicidal crisis. Such denial and resistance are reinforced by the mistaken and grandiose belief that the lack of a suicide to date is indicative of the lack of risk for such an untoward event. Thus, it is often the case that a crisis must first occur in the community or be sufficiently close to its front door before a response can be mobilized.

When a response is mobilized, the extent of such a response will be governed by parameters that are both material and measurable (e.g., available funds and resources) and subjective and emotional (e.g., the extent and duration of the threat, the demands placed on the community by the response effort, the empathic identification with the victims, etc.). Such parameters may be tied to a third question that frames our response: Are there conditional limitations to our response capabilities?

In illustration of these subjective parameters, let me offer the following: In October 1987 a dramatic rescue took place in a small Texas town. An 18-month-old toddler named Jessica McClure was trapped in a narrow well, 22 feet below ground, for 58 hours. An enormous rescue effort was mobilized, demanding significant resources of monies, equipment, and volunteer manpower at a total estimated value of well over $1 million. Media attention to the rescue effort was intense and riveting of the nation's focus, including that of a united sense of joy when she was successfully brought to the surface and given hope of continued life (4).

In October 1988 a similarly dramatic rescue effort was extended over several weeks to the Barrow 3, three whales trapped by an ice flow off Point Barrow, Alaska. Again, more than $1 million was spent, including an enormous corporate investment by an oil company, culminating in the successful release of two of the whales to the open seas (5).

These examples illustrate the strength of the humanitarian spirit that can drive efforts of good Samaritanism in a crisis, particularly when the victim of that crisis is perceived as trapped and helpless, even hopeless, absent interventive effort. But it must be understood that there is a conditional morality underlying such responses. The suicidal person, irrespective of age, arguably might be presented as equally trapped, helpless, hopeless, and in need of external intervention. But the stigma of pathology or of perceived responsibility for one's "decision" to act in a suicidal manner clouds the typical community's response, often inhibiting ready interventions and at times even provoking responses of "jump already" to the individual on the proverbial ledge. The national effort to support youth suicide prevention in the United States involves less federal dollars annually than were given to the rescue of the Barrow 3, and only minimal corporate interest to date.

The Jessica McClures and Barrow whales of our lifetime are individual crisis events demanding and receiving specific and expected time-limited interventions. The prevention of an aggregate of future suicides is much more difficult and raises additional questions for our consideration. Among the more significant of these are the following:

1. Do we know enough about prevention, in general, and about suicide prevention, in particular, to know what works and what doesn't work?
2. Do we agree on the definition of the problem, allowing us to target preventive efforts?
3. Can we agree on a strategy? Are there constraints to our efforts to effectively respond?
4. Are we sufficiently aware of iatrogenic effects?
5. Are we appropriately measuring impacts and outcomes and revising our approaches accordingly?

DO WE KNOW ENOUGH ABOUT PREVENTION OF PUBLIC HEALTH PROBLEMS?

The implicit assumption in most preventive efforts is that education equals prevention. This is particularly true when applied to problems of youth where our schools are the natural sites for preventive efforts (get them where they are) and wherein education is the obviously appropriate strategy for prevention (teaching is what we do).

The most extensive and long-term effort in this regard in the United States has been that of school-based sex education to combat unwanted teen pregnancy. Yet after years of experience at this effort, the United States continues to lead the world in teen pregnancy rates (6) and there is no evident change in either these rates or in the frequency of unsafe sexual intercourse (7). Thus this effort may hold important lessons for us to consider when we think about youth suicide prevention programming.

The responsibility for this apparent failure of preventive efforts may not be that of education, per se, but, rather, the approach. Mashaw (6), comparing the United States with Sweden, notes that in Sweden sex education begins in the lowest grades and continues throughout the school years. Swedish children learn early about contraception, which is available at no cost and with full confidentiality from county health centers and school-based clinics. In contrast, American sex education begins too late, is too cautious in scope, and varies even within the same school system in content and quality. Ninety-percent of American students are taught about contraception *after* they reach the average age of first intercourse; almost no school districts include sexual decision-making as a goal of their sex education program (8); and Mashaw (6) appropriately observes that teaching facts about human reproductive biology does little to alter human reproductive behavior!

Similar approaches are common to other preventive efforts. Evaluations of efforts in the schools to prevent drug abuse show "no dramatic or long-term reductions in drug use," (p. 77) and of one of the most popular and widely marketed curriculum to only significantly achieve an increase in knowledge about alcohol (9). Authors of one of these evaluations concluded that as now conceived, school alcohol abuse prevention fails because what students learn in the classroom is entirely unrelated to alcohol problems in the real world (10). If knowledge alone were sufficient to change behavior, then years of well-publicized warnings about the negative health consequences of smoking would have lowered the prevalence of smoking behavior. The number of women who smoke has actually increased since health warnings were first mandated by the Surgeon General over two decades ago (11).

DO WE AGREE ON THE DEFINITION OF THE PROBLEM?

Definition underlies goals, methods chosen to achieve those goals, and appropriate evaluation of those efforts. With regard to youth suicide prevention, the most obvious goal is that of preventing suicide among our youth. Yet, as a normative event in any community, no less individual schools, the lack of a suicidal death might readily fool a program administrator into believing that one's methods have been successful. Stated in contrast, as a rare event suicide might not occur in any given time period by chance; if one does *nothing* preventively, one might still reach a goal of no suicides.

Should we focus our efforts at preventing suicide, suicidal behaviors (e.g., attempts, gestures, threats, ideations), or predisposing conditions that make one vulnerable to and at risk for being suicidal? Or would we be more successful by adopting long-term goals of teaching more health-enhancing behaviors and coping skills beginning in the primary grades?

CAN WE AGREE ON A STRATEGY?

The answers we propose to the foregoing question are inextricably tied to our choice of approaches. If we agree that we should develop school-based suicide prevention programs, how should we proceed? We need a model and a theory of change that define when we should intervene, what our targets should be, and who should do the intervening.

The now classic approach to the prevention of mental and public health problems is that of Gerald Caplan (12), who distinguished the concepts of primary (antecedent to problem development), secondary (early intervention and treatment), and tertiary (postvention for survivors) prevention. As applied to school-based youth suicide prevention, the predominant level of response is that of early intervention (secondary prevention). As I will argue shortly, the more cost efficient and potentially constructive intervention is that of primary prevention, a strategy, however, which demands great patience and the long-term commitment of resources. As a contrasting approach, Jessor (13) has proposed a model to minimize, insulate, and/or delay the onset of health-endangering behaviors. This model, for example, might promote an approach directed at containing adolescent drug and alcohol use as a method of suicide prevention.

The targets of any proposed intervention might be the system as a whole (e.g., all youth in a school), the individual (e.g., youth identified as at risk), and/or the environment (those conditions that are known to be suicidogenic). Lastly, who should develop and implement the intervention: professionals from without (e.g., suicidologists) or within (e.g., school counselors) the school, and/or students (e.g., peer counselors)? This volume is replete with recommended answers and models for responding to these questions; each is appropriate for adaption depending on an individual school or school system's constraints (e.g., available monies, personnel, community support, etc.) and resources. Significant among those constraints is the relative competition posed by other health-endangering behaviors that also demand preventive programming. In a typical American high school at the threshold of the 1990s there are rightful demands for educational programs in areas such as sex, drug abuse, AIDS, and child abuse, etc. Can we afford to develop significant preventive education programs in all these areas, or should we be developing models to deal with antecedents common to these separate foci?

Perhaps because of these demands, schools that are, moreover, struggling at the most basic level to effectively teach the three Rs, are hesitant to commit the necessary time and resources to educate about a multitude of demanding social problems, including youth suicide. Perhaps for that reason, the typical school-based suicide prevention educational program is a one-shot, less than four-hour lecture/discussion model. Do we have any reason to believe that a problem as complex as suicide can be effectively prevented in this way?

If we are to be constrained from developing either an ideal or even a relatively effective model of intervention, whatever we decide to do must be governed by the last two considerations raised in my earlier questions: Are we sufficiently aware of any iatrogenic effects? Simply put, might we be doing unintended harm by our efforts? Related to this, as well to our earlier concerns about goals, are we appropriately measuring the outcomes of our efforts in order to validate the achievement of our intended goal(s) or to revise our methods accordingly? We will return to this issue later.

AIDS PREVENTION: AN ANALOGY

Suicide and suicidal behaviors are the outcomes of a complex of interacting forces from intrapsychic to interpersonal, from genetic and biochemical to familial and sociocultural. No simple strategy of preventive education can be expected to impact significantly on these behaviors. By analogy, a brief examination of efforts at preventing another demanding social problem, AIDS, illustrates both the complexity of the problem and the difficulties inherent in its resolution.

Preventive education in the United States regarding AIDS has focused on multiple targets: The Surgeon General's office mailed an educational brochure to every postal patron in the country; specific educational programs have targeted specific high-risk groups of individuals (homosexuals and intravenous drug abusers); and condoms (and clean needles, in some cases) have been made widely and readily available. Consequently, the rate of new infections appears to be down (14) and condom use by sexually active teenagers at time of first intercourse is up (7). As well, the majority of studies support the finding that HIV antibody testing has led to a decrease in high-risk behaviors (unprotected anal intercourse) among those testing seropositive (15).

Yet all is not well. Educational efforts regarding condom use, for example, have not been effective in changing behavior among all at-risk individuals. In one study (16) only about one fourth of gay and bisexual males who reported engaging in anal intercourse "always" used a condom (and about one half "never" used a condom); and of sexually active teens only one fourth used a condom at the time of their last intercourse (7). Gay and bisexual males who practice unsafe sex generally are known to be younger, less educated, less concerned about the risk, less convinced about the efficacy of a condom, more concerned that condom use impairs pleasure, and more likely to combine sexual activity with substance use and to be ignorant of their HIV serostatus (16, 17). In addition, those maintaining high-risk behavior tend to believe that they are not capable of making necessary behavioral changes to decrease their risk (low "personal efficacy") (18). It is clear that preventive education regarding the use of a condom, only one of several target goals of AIDS prevention education, has not sufficiently impacted those most in need of behavior modification.

In a similar vein neither factual information (i.e., education) about AIDS nor knowing someone who had AIDS was found to be related to behavioral change (changed injection behavior) among intravenous drug abusers (19). In contrast, behavioral change was most correlated with the high-risk individual's belief that his or her friends were *also* changing their behavior (19) and increased feelings of personal efficacy (17). Stall, Coates, and Hoff (17) conclude that health education efforts, even if increased in quantity and duration, "may have only a modest effect within noncompliant groups" (p. 883).

SCHOOL-BASED SUICIDE PREVENTION EDUCATION

It seems reasonable to assume that only the most self-destructive and pathological of individuals would wish to contract AIDS. Therefore it would seem to follow that voluntary efforts toward known AIDS prevention behaviors would be relatively easy to accomplish and that accomplishment would be nearly universal among those at risk. Because the foregoing data do not support those assumptions, what might we extend to our thinking about high-risk suicidal youth who see suicide as a problem resolution to be sought rather than avoided?

The typical school-based suicide prevention program is not directed at the high-risk individual but, rather, the population of school-based adolescents as a whole. As surveyed and recently reported by Smith and Dyck (20), the great majority of American programs are classroom-centered (curriculum based) and use lectures, discussion and, to a lesser extent, films and/or experiential exercises to teach a variety of content areas. The most important of these involved the pragmatic skills and facts required in managing a crisis, with the one exception being teaching students to recognize and accept their feelings. Among the facts disseminated to students are signs and symptoms of suicidal risks. These, along with the skills (responding to a suicidal crisis, managing stress, solving problems, communicating, etc.), are typically taught in three to six class periods of instruction by a teacher who has received an average of 3.5 hr of training (20).

To the extent that it is presumed that this type and amount of intervention are effective, it is particularly troublesome that less than half of the programs surveyed by Smith and Dyck had any written procedures to evaluate outcomes. Among those that did, the three most important criteria measured were related to increased knowledge rather than behavioral changes (20).

Shaffer, Garland, and Whittle's (21) report of their evaluation of three New Jersey school-based programs underscores the need for adequate evaluation procedures and the concern, as raised earlier, for possible iatrogenic effects. On the positive side, they reported that students found these programs to be more "interesting" than boring, a source of "comfort" regarding their helping other students and, although behavioral outcomes went unmeasured by these programs, there was no evidence for "induced" suicidal behavior. Concurrently, they found that these programs did not change either behavioral preferences among students (e.g., what the student would do or whom the student would talk to if depressed) or attitudes about the management of a suicidal problem. Even more troubling, they documented that there was a slight *increase* in the number of students who believed drug and alcohol use was a good way to stop feeling depressed and that high-risk students, those most in need of preventive intervention, were "turned off" by these programs, with 9% of prior attempters reporting that the programs "had increased their difficulties in dealing with their problems."

To the extent that the focus of these programs will remain that of early identification of those at risk, Hoberman and Garfinkel (22) raise a different focus of concern. They note that the emphasis in these programs is often that of destigmatization, that of deemphasizing the relationship between suicide and psychopathology to make more normative the notions of problem-solving as a treatment and of peers as caregivers. As they believe, and as the research literature on youth suicide tends to document, most instances of youth suicidal behavior, particularly those of greater lethality, stem from and are preceded by episodes of diagnosable psychopathology. This attempt to normalize the experiences of suicidal youth may directly counter the goal of increasing recognition (identification) of those in need of treatment (psychotherapy).

THE PREVENTION OF YOUTH SUICIDE

Given the foregoing arguments, perhaps we may conclude that the best way to prevent youth suicide is to do nothing! After all, the rate of youth suicide generally waxes and wanes irrespective of interventive efforts; and, given the uncertainty regarding the effectiveness of any proposed interventions, there is no rational basis for implementing any particular effort, especially given the potentially large costs of such interventions (1). Doing nothing, therefore, is both considerably cheaper and potentially as effective as doing something.

But given the urgency of the problem, doing nothing about youth suicide is unconscionable. The obviously difficult question to answer is what "something" should we do? In truth, there is no hard evidence that *any* large-scale intervention works, including that of community suicide prevention centers (23).

Eddy, Wolpert, and Rosenberg's (1) survey of 15 youth suicide experts found their three most recommended strategies to be: (a) restricting access to firearms, (b) identifying high-risk youth, and (c) improving treatment. Each of these has merit, but only in combination with a number of correlated approaches. Most importantly, the school may have a pivotal role in the implementation and accomplishment of many of these interventions.

A Menu of Prevention Approaches

The following interventions focus on behavioral change through educational effort. Schools intent on promoting and advocating children's health must view their role as educators in a broad frame, to include that of teaching children skills, giving parents tools for promoting health-enhancing behavior in their families, fostering continued professional education, and lobbying their communities for legislative change.

Environmental Control

In the United States approximately two thirds of adolescent suicides are accomplished through the use of firearms, owned and made available to youth by their parents. Restricting access to immediately lethal means for self-destruction means that youth intent on suicide must use less readily available methods and, frequently, those that are less immediately lethal. Time, therefore, can allow ambivalent feelings about death to germinate and positive decisions about life to be reaffirmed. Lives thus saved may, then, have the opportunity to be redirected toward healthier futures. Parents must be taught about the deadliness of an available gun in the hands of a vulnerable (at-risk) youngster and given procedures to follow to ensure the safety of that youngster. Parents, as well, can be held accountable for the unwarranted use of a firearm by a youngster, as intended through recently enacted legislative efforts in the state of Florida (24).

Early Detection

At-risk students who are found before acting on their suicidal urges can be offered help and, if that help is accepted, treated with some hope of a positive outcome. Students and faculty can be taught to look for specific behaviors associated with suicide risk, particularly signs of psychopathology including, but not limited to, those of substance abuse and depression. A community of buddies, one where every student is paired with a fellow student, can be fostered in the schools much the way campers are taught to never be in the water alone. This practice of being attentive to another individual can go far in accomplishing the necessary mode of careful observation.

Making Referrals

Students and faculty should not be taught or expected to intervene directly, but, rather, to refer a student believed to be at risk to a professional competent to evaluate and treat that student. Often this process requires a middleman, that of a school-based adult capable of and in a position to make that referral. Schools should maximize the awareness of teachers and counselors to their roles in this system and teach these adults referral-making skills.

Resource Identification

No referral can be effective unless it is made to a competent professional. School communities can do much to investigate and evaluate the resources (agencies, private practitioners, etc.) available to its constituents to ensure that those provided in referrals are the best available. To that end, students can become part of consumer-based investigation teams, sent out with evaluative criteria to establish community resources available to meet the particular demand of dealing with at-risk youth.

Professional Education

Among those criteria to be evaluated must be that of the specific training for the local professionals who deal with suicidal youth. The typical mental health professional has surprisingly little training in this area (25). To the extent that a community's schools view as their mission the education of the community as a whole, particularly when that education impacts positively on the educability of its students by enhancing health and minimizing distress, the upgrading of professional skills falls within the province of the schools. Again, the alternative might be for the school, and its constituents, to lobby city and state legislatures for laws requiring a particular level and/or focus of professional education for those in positions to respond to youth in need.

Help-Seeking Behavior

One of the side benefits to resource identification by students is that they begin to make normative a concern for the quality of help-giving in their community, thereby increasing the likelihood that help-seeking behavior will become normative as well. One of the potentially positive outcomes to this strategy is that attention will be directed as well to increasing compliance (i.e., the likelihood that a particular referral will be followed through and acted on appropriately). Lack of compliance in families of youthful suicide attempters is notorious: It is a major problem leading to high rates of repeat suicide attempts among high-risk youth. Pilot programs to increase compliance have been conducted with some promise of success (26). Again, schools may play a significant role in developing models of parent education that lead to increased compliance with recommended treatments for their youth.

Primary Prevention

Perhaps the most effective and ultimately the most *cost*-effective program of youth suicide prevention is one that demands the long view. Schools intent on significantly impacting the health and welfare of their students need to begin early (primary grades), intervene often (annual booster shots of preventive programming), and focus essentially on teaching adaptive skills to prevent problems from developing later. Schools that can afford to encourage children to develop positive self-esteem, learn social skills, and attain coping mechanisms and problem-solving skills for dealing with anticipated stressors (life transitions) and unexpected events are likely to have fewer behavioral emergencies and residual problems that demand attention and response in later grades. The long-term cost is likely to be greatly reduced by the investment in preventive education of this kind. Note again that the goal here is not that of learning information but, rather, skills. Programs, evaluated as successful, are already available for importation to the school community (27), as are specific time-limited, structured, educational models for teaching youth to manage negative affect states related to suicidality, such as anger (28, 29) and depression (30).

The goals of primary prevention ideally, as well, involve those of eliminating or modifying factors that predispose youth to be at-risk, or at least reducing exposure to such stressors that increase vulnerability. Programs that increase student identifications with positive role models and decrease the availability or attractiveness of negative models serve substitutive parental functions when these may be insufficient for some vulnerable youth. Teachers, alumni, and concerned community members can be involved in linking vulnerable students to more appropriate role models than those that are readily available. Because many suicide-prone youngsters display their impending risk through a decreased attention to academics and an increased likelihood of dropping out of school, school-based programs that identify such youth and work toward keeping them attached positively to the academic environment will serve preventive ends.

Postvention

Schools need to develop programs to help suicide attempters reintegrate successfully into the academic/social environment of the school without increasing the risk of second attempts or subsequent completions. Schools need to attend to the bereavement of survivors after an attempt or completion in order to reduce the likelihood that survivor vulnerability (guilt, self-blame, depression, etc.) will turn into imitative or penitential (self-punishment) behavior. Attention to recommended strategies proposed by the Centers for Disease Control (31) for dealing with possible cluster phenomenon is an important component to any effective suicide prevention policy.

POSTSCRIPT

The prevention of youth suicide is the business of the entire community. Children at potential risk spend more concentrated time at school than anywhere else and with peers and teachers more than with parents. Schools, therefore, are logical sites for focusing preventive programs both for these reasons and because education, interpreted more broadly than that of information giving, is the business of the schools. When the school considers that included in its functions are fostering the attainment of skills and promoting partnerships between its students and the outside world, preventive education becomes one of its charges. These goals are equally important to the accomplishment of the school's primary charge of educating students to available information.

That the school should be in the business of preventive mental health should not be in question. What should be questioned is how best to accomplish this end. It is the primary thesis of this critique that prevention requires attention to behavioral change, not simply information processing; and that brief units of single trial learning regarding suicide will have little long-term effect in *preventing* suicide. Health education is neither an efficient nor a sufficient cause of behavioral risk reduction. Preventive education needs, instead, to focus on increasing self-efficacy, decreasing sources of distress, improving interpersonal relationships, and changing normative values toward those of behavioral change (7).

A secondary thesis is that of program evaluation. Of all places the school should be most concerned about evaluating carefully that what it is doing is, in truth, accomplishing its objectives. Integral to any program should be the measurement of outcomes and objectives, leading to program revisions where necessary. The commission of resources and personnel simply and blindly, absent significant demonstration of program effectiveness in changing desired behaviors (in contrast to typically measured outcomes of content mastery or participant satisfaction), is likely to be short-lived, only to be replaced by the demands of the next problem–crisis to be faced by the school community. The ludicrousness of the example of "nasality" used to introduce this chapter illustrates how readily a community might shift such attention in a revolving door attitude toward such issues. The problem of youth suicide is longstanding and of considerable complexity. Attempts to successfully intervene require equal attention and concern.

REFERENCES

1. Eddy, D. M., Wolpert, R. L., & Rosenberg, M. L. (1987). Estimating the effectiveness of interventions to prevent youth suicides. *Medical Care, 25,* S57–S65.
2. Fingerhut, L. A., & Kleinman, J. C. (1988). Suicide rates for young people [letter]. *Journal of the American Medical Association, 259,* 356.
3. Diekstra, R. F. W. (1989). Suicidal behavior in adolescents and young adults: The international picture. *Crisis, 10,* 16–35.
4. A brave little girl. (1987, October 26). *Newsweek,* p. 41.
5. Heroic measures for gentle giants. (1988, October 31). *U.S. News and World Report,* p. 11.
6. Mashaw, R. (1986). Children in crisis: Can sex education stem the tide of teen pregnancy? *Frontlines, 3,* 3–5.
7. Hayes, C. D. (1987). *Risking the future: Adolescent sexuality, pregnancy and childbearing.* Washington, DC: National Academy Press.
8. Kirby, D. (1984). *Sexuality education: An evaluation of programs and their effects,* Santa Cruz: Network Publications.
9. Teaching kids to say no. (1989, June 5). *Newsweek,* p. 77.
10. Mauss, A. L., Hopkins, H., Weisheit, R. A., & Kearney, K. A. (1988). The problematic prospects for prevention in the classroom: Should alcohol education programs be expected to reduce drinking by youth? *Journal of Studies on Alcohol, 49,* 51–61.
11. Koop, C. E. (1986). *The health consequences of involuntary smoking.* Washington, DC: U.S. Government Printing Office.
12. Caplan, G. (1964). *Principles of preventive psychiatry.* New York: Basic Books.
13. Jessor, R. (1982). Critical issues in research on adolescent health promotion. In T. J. Coates, A. C. Peterson, & C. Perry (Eds.), *Promoting adolescent health: A dialogue on research and practice* (pp. 447–465). San Francisco: Academic Press.
14. Bales, J. (1988, October). Sexy message needed on safe sex. *American Psychological Association Monitor, 19,* 34.
15. Coates, T. J., Stall, R. D., Kegeles, S. M., Lo, B., Morin, S. F., & McKusick, L. (1988). AIDS antibody testing. *American Psychologist, 43,* 859–864.
16. Valdisserri, R. O., Lyter, D., Leviton, L. C., Callahan, C. M., Kingsley, L. A., & Rinaldo, C. R. (1988). Variables influencing condom use in a cohort of gay and bisexual men. *American Journal of Public Health, 78,* 801–805.
17. Stall, R. D., Coates, T. J., & Hoff, C. (1988). Behavioral risk reduction for HIV infection among gay and bisexual men. *American Psychologist, 43,* 878–885.
18. Charles, K. (1985). *Factors in the primary prevention of AIDS in gay and bisexual men.* Unpublished doctoral dissertation, California School of Professional Psychology, Berkeley.
19. Friedman, S. R., DesJarlais, D. C., Sotheran, J. L., Garber, J., Cohen, H., & Smith, D. (1987). AIDS and self-organization among intravenous drug users. *International Journal of the Addictions, 22,* 201–220.
20. Smith, K., & Dyck, R. (in press). Report of a survey of school-related suicide programs. *Suicide and Life-Threatening Behavior.*
21. Shaffer, D., Garland, A., & Whittle, B. (1988, April). *An evaluation of three youth suicide prevention programs in New Jersey.* Paper presented at the Annual Meeting of the American Association of Suicidology, Washington, DC.
22. Hoberman, H. M., & Garfinkel, B. D. (1988). Completed suicide in children and adolescents. *Journal of the American Academy of Child and Adolescent Psychiatry, 27,* 689–695.
23. Dew, M. A., Bromet, E. J., Brent, D., & Greenhouse, J. B. (1987). A quantitative literature

review of the effectiveness of suicide prevention centers. *Journal of Consulting and Clinical Psychology, 55,* 239–244.

24. Governor signs gun safety bill. (1989, July 13). *Miami Herald,* p. 17-A.
25. Berman, A. L. (1983). Training committee report to the American Association of Suicidology, Denver, CO.
26. Deykin, E. Y., Hsieh, C. C., Joshi, N., & McNamarra, J. J. (1986). Adolescent suicidal and self-destructive behavior: Results of an intervention study. *Journal of Adolescent Health Care, 7,* 88–95.
27. Price, R. H., Cowen, E. L., Lorion, R. P., & McKay, J. R. (Eds.) (1988). *14 Ounces of Prevention.* Washington, DC: American Psychological Association.
28. Lochman, J. E., & Curry, J. F. (1986). Effects of social problem-solving training and self-instruction training with aggressive boys. *Journal of Clinical Psychology, 15,* 159–164.
29. Feindler, E. L., & Ecton, R. B. (1986). *Adolescent anger control: Cognitive-behavioral techniques.* New York: Pergamon Press.
30. Lewinsohn, P. M., Antonuccio, D., Steinmetz, J., & Teri, L. (1984). *The coping with depression course: A psychoeducational intervention for unipolar depression.* Eugene, OR: Castalia.
31. Centers for Disease Control (1988). CDC recommendations for a community plan for the prevention and containment of suicide clusters. *Morbidity and Mortality Weekly Report, 37* [Supplement No. S-6]: 1–12.

20

1990: Suicidology in Schools

Antoon A. Leenaars
Windsor, Ontario

(A school) should give them (students) a desire to live and should offer them support and backing at a time of life at which the conditions of their development compel them to relax their ties with their parental home and their family. It seems to me indisputable that schools fail in this, and in many respects fall short of their duty of providing a substitute for the family and of arousing interest in life from the world outside.

> S. Freud
> Vienna, June 26, 1910

Those were some of Sigmund Freud's suggestions for suicidal prevention in schools at the monumental symposium on suicide 80 years ago (1). The comment is as relevant to us today as it was then. It is within this context that I would like to reflect to the meeting in 1910 that took place in S. Freud's home in Vienna. It was the first formal statement of suicide prevention in schools. That meeting has resulted in much reflection, especially at the first annual conference of the American Association of Suicidology in Chicago in 1968 (2) and now in 1990.

There is no attempt to duplicate the points of view presented in 1910, only to highlight our development. At that meeting, David Ernest Oppenheim represented the field of education. It is his view that will be represented here:

If, since it (suicide) is the negation of the strongest of all human instincts, that of self-preservation, suicide is always anomalous, it is even more so when the suicide takes place in childhood, since we believe that youth combines an undiminished life force with an indestructible will to live. (1, p. 34)

In part, Oppenheim was reflecting on the tragic increase in suicide in 1910 in Vienna. Suicide in youth at that time was sometimes called "student suicide": A situation that repeats itself today in North America.

Oppenheim reflects whether "the school will be burdened with the blame for this sad event?" He quickly shows—even then—that suicide is a multidimensional malaise. He states that "our schools are not the only force that drives young people to suicide," rather he looks at what schools can do to help. He says "If a teacher is given the necessary clues, he may be able to do a great deal to protect an overstimulated boy from a desperate act" (p. 51).

As an example of such education, he suggests that teachers should be informed about clusters. He promotes education about contagion saying, "every suicide, no matter how it is carried out, lures others to precise imitations." Indeed, he leaves one to conclude that postvention in schools is necessary to address such a phenomenon and he even proposes something echoed today, that "newspapers confine(d) themselves to brief reports."

He proposes that fruitful cooperation be established between the school, home, and community to assist youth. "Prophylactic measures" should be avoided, rather, sound measures are needed. For example, he says "much could be gained if we tried to make suicide more difficult for the potential candidate." Oppenheim proposes that schools support the restriction of the availability of weapons (such as handguns) to prevent suicide. Such social intervention can do much! Oppenheim, in the end of his presentation, also looks to Freud, Stekel, Adler, and others to assist (intervention) with suicidal young people. Oppenheim thus advocates prevention, intervention, and postvention in schools.

What do we know now, some 80 years later, about suicide and schools? What are we doing today? These final comments are a brief summary of the views that arose from this volume, though there is no intent to be exhaustive.

INTRODUCTION

Both children and adolescents do commit suicide. An even greater number of our youth attempt and/or seriously think about suicide as *the* solution to their life's difficulties. And then there are the survivors. Something, as Oppenheim suggested, can be done. Schools especially can make major contributions toward saving lives and assisting before, during, and/or after such a dire event occurs.

Part I consisted of three chapters. The first, by J. Smith, presented some general considerations about suicide prevention in schools. She argues that in light of our problem of suicide in youth, schools provide a logical forum for suicide prevention. She introduces three strategies for such efforts, namely prevention, intervention, and postvention. She also brings forth that suicide in our schools has raised legal and legislative concerns. She concludes, "School suicide prevention programs are fledgling enterprises. They have not had experience of long term evaluation to prove their effectiveness. The need is apparent for educational involvement in the movement for youth suicide prevention."

Chapters 2 and 3, by D. Lester and G. Domino respectively, provided for the interested reader some current statistics and a research study of youth's opinions about suicide to highlight the necessity of response in our schools. Though regrettably limited by available statistics (for example, childhood is not from 5–14 nor is adolescence from 15–24; Chapter 3), Lester shows that the rate of suicide is high in the United States and that rates for youth vary from country to country. Domino shows us that beyond the rates, suicide is a concern of youth. He writes, "Suicidal concerns are no strangers to today's high school students."

Part I, thus, is preliminary to the text.

SUICIDE PREVENTION IN SCHOOLS

Prevention relates to the principles of good mental hygiene in general. In schools, this means education. This is in keeping with the general aims of schools, namely to educate our young.

Part II presented six chapters on primary prevention in our schools. The first, by R. Dyck, outlined the critical system-entry issues. There are barriers to school access; Dyck writes, "Some Departments of Education, school boards, and even individual school administrators have resisted the introduction of these programs in schools for a variety of reasons, some based more on myth than fact, and others that are legitimate and should be given serious and careful consideration." Strategies for school entry include: mandatory prevention programs through government, introduction through particular school boards, and entry through a local school. It is, however, we who wish to gain entry who must develop our skills before gaining access. Such needs include credibility, suicide prevention training, participation in educator's conferences, and research. Regrettably, there are many individuals with no expertise who are attempting to gain entry, some of whom have been suicidogenic themselves.

The next chapter, by C. Stivers, "proposes that the most effective way of preventing youth suicide is by guaranteeing each child an upbringing which is conducive to the development of a positive self-esteem." Self-esteem is vital for coping with life's difficulties. Though suicide is complex, the lack of self-esteem can lead to self-destruction. Stivers outlines self-esteem building techniques: "I'm great," instead of "I'm stupid." There is obviously much more that we can do than provide prevention programs: there is a need for *preprevention*.

In Chapter 6 L. Sattem provided a sample of a suicide prevention project for elementary schools. Based on the fact that children discuss very freely their problems with puppets, she shows us how to enter the children's world and speak their language. The program addresses death and dying (including suicide) for children who, indeed, have questions about death. She states, "A critical message of the puppet show is that when a person has experienced a loss (through death, divorce, separation, pet running away), there are many new feelings and emotions with which to deal. All of these are natural and normal. What a person does with these feelings is important." Early prevention is essential.

In the next chapter, R. Tierney, R. Ramsay, B. Tanney, and W. Lang addressed suicide prevention on a large scale. They note that most suicide prevention programs are on a small scale. Tierney et al. suggest that a program must be comprehensive, consisting of prevention, intervention, and postvention; this is, as we have seen, *the heart of this whole volume*. School programs require not only such scope and content but schools also require a system-wide policy, resources, training personnel, evaluation, and follow-up.

Chapter 8, by D. Ryerson, outlined a suicide prevention program and showed how modification is necessary for special populations and institutions. Noting that it is a mistake to educate just the young, she states that programs must address the needs of parents, teachers, and administrators. She states that "One of the most important and most challenging objectives is to encourage teenagers, as well as parents and educators, to overcome their natural reluctance to *acknowledge* that a fellow teen is in trouble and then to *take action* on the teen's behalf." Ryerson concludes that the program must be "appropriate and acceptable." Modification may be necessary because of organizational issues (such as reluctance of upper administration) and demographic issues (such as academic level of the school).

The final chapter in this section, by J. Overholser, S. Evans, and A. Spirito, addressed the need for modifications in a prevention program because of sex differences. Males kill themselves more often than females, though not in childhood. Males also respond differently to our programs; they note, "The female students were consistently found to display higher levels of knowledge, attitudes, and behavior before the curriculum and they were more likely to benefit from the curriculum when it was provided." They conclude: (a) in comparison to males, the females appeared more sensitive to suicide and its management, and (b) males may require suicide awareness curriculum that differ from the kind generally provided. In addition, it may well be that our culture needs to examine how we teach our males to be males. The findings by Overholser and his colleagues may be just one more hazard of being a male in our culture. We need to teach our males to learn about and respond to a suicidal cry, not deny it.

Not everyone favors suicide prevention in schools. Some have argued that such programs will increase the rate of suicide; that they are not cost effective. Yet, these individuals are in a minority. There is a difference between sound—and researched—education and sensationalism (as noted in some media coverage about teen suicide). And how does one place a dollar sign on young life?

SUICIDE INTERVENTION IN SCHOOLS

Intervention relates to the treatment and care of a suicidal crisis or a suicidal problem. Many people, including those in schools, can serve as lifesaving agents. Nonetheless, professionally trained people continue to play the primary roles in intervention.

Part III consisted of four chapters. The first, by L. A. Hoff, provided a model for crisis intervention in schools. Recognizing that the focus should be on prevention, Hoff notes that we need to train frontline people to respond effectively to a crisis such as a suicide attempt. She outlines an individual response as well as a social response (in those cases dealing with abuse). Once the crisis is responded to, "A general rule of thumb is that follow up psychotherapy is indicated for anyone who responds to a life crisis by a suicide attempt." We can only underscore this remark. Suicidal people are in need of treatment, often long-term. Suicidal behavior, despite some myths, is not normal. Even professionals often underestimate the need for intensive psychotherapy following a suicidal crisis.

Chapter 11, by K. Smith, outlined some guidelines for the therapeutic care of the suicidal student. Smith begins with Karl Menninger's dictate that "the patient is always right, and that it is just up to the therapist to be diligent enough to find out how." Smith shows us the complex process of how we must first accept the student's explanation (such as a rejection by a girlfriend) and then with compassion and curiosity help the person to understand the event beyond the stated reason. He notes how even slight changes in the environment can affect the therapeutic process, and highlights the problems of unfocused therapy. He argues, correctly from my view, that therapists need special preparation for such work. One special focus is the communication of hope: "It is best to indirectly communicate hope that a patient can, with the therapist's consultation, view his or her life differently."

We should also address here the growing trend toward peer counseling. Peer counseling is not therapy. There is no research to suggest that peer counselors can provide the therapeutic care that suicidal youth need. On the other hand, a peer— or a teacher, guidance counselor—may assist in identification, support, etc., in the process; yet, they must refer the young person to a professional. The fact that teens prefer to talk to teens is no justification to follow their wishes, often defensive ones. There are even liability issues for schools to consider.

Chapter 12, by J. Eyman, provided a discussion of countertransference—the feelings a therapist has toward the patient—when counseling school-aged youth. Sigmund Freud stated:

> *We have become aware of "counter-transference," which arises in him (the treater) as a result of the patient's influence on his unconscious feelings, and we are almost inclined to insist that he shall recognize this counter-transference in himself and overcome it.*

Our understanding of countertransference has developed beyond Freud's and such understanding is critical in intervening with suicidal youngsters because "suicidal individuals can evoke strong reactions in treaters." It is inevitable. Critical reactions include: conflicted dependency yearnings, ineffective management of aggressive urges, and treater's anxiety about death. Not being attuned to, and not understanding such processes can have potential deleterious consequences, including contribution to the suicidal solution.

The final chapter, by J. Richman, presented a discussion of family therapy with suicidal children. He begins with the observation that "The family is instrumental in the suicidal behavior of young people, and critical to the success of the healing process." Though individual therapy may be more appropriate for older teens, Richman argues that family therapy is the treatment of choice for children and young adolescents. In family therapy, the airing of strife, anger, and conflicts can have a positive outcome. Richman notes that all too often the schools act in isolation; yet, "Working only with the children may be leaving out those who are most concerned and who possess the greatest potential for preventing suicide."

SUICIDE POSTVENTION IN SCHOOLS

Postvention refers to those things done after the suicide has occurred. Postvention deals with the traumatic aftereffects in the survivors. School systems are an especially critical force in such endeavors with our youth.

Part IV consisted of four chapters. The first chapter, by A. Leenaars and S. Wenckstern, provided a conceptual model for postvention; posttraumatic stress disorder (PTSD). PTSD is defined as a set of conscious and unconscious behaviors and emotions associated with dealing with "a psychological traumatic event that is generally outside the range of usual human experience." The suicide of a student is one such event. Typical behaviors and emotions include the following: reexperiencing the trauma; numbing of responsiveness to a reduced involvement with the external world; and such symptoms as hyperalertness, sleep disturbance, survivor guilt. Much of this has to do with the perception that "Bill, my friend wouldn't kill himself." Leenaars and Wenckstern point out the importance of individual differences and whether the environment is supportive. Postvention in schools is designed to address PTSD and other phenomena (such as the contagion effect). They suggest that the understanding of postvention in schools must be embedded within the larger literature on PTSD (as well as the literature on grief, sudden death, and suicide in general). The program itself must be part of a larger disaster response in schools. They conclude that the most important future endeavor in postvention is research.

In Chapter 15, Wenckstern and Leenaars presented a practical model for postvention with a case illustration. They outline the generic aspects for such programs; for example, consultation, crisis intervention, community linkage, assessment and counselling, education, and liaison with the media. Postvention is not only grief counseling. They also present some principles of postvention, derived from the work of E. Shneidman. For example: Resistance may be met from survivors; some, but not all, are either willing or eager to have the opportunity to talk to professionally oriented persons. And, the postvener should play the important role of reality tester. He or she is not so much the echo of conscience as the quiet voice of reason.

Wenckstern and Leenaars address a number of important elements in postvention programs such as the importance of consultation and the academic autopsy after the program ("to aid in further refinements"), and they illustrate the program using case examples, including a negative one. They conclude the chapter by saying "The belief that suicide postvention is only temporary is a myth."

In the next chapter, B. Carter and A. Brooks addressed a critical aspect of postvention, counseling. Utilizing case illustrations they propose that, "Time-limited group therapy is an effective method for addressing the aftermath of teenage suicide." They illustrate the process, showing that survivor guilt—more accurately, pathological pressures of unresolved guilt—is a critical focus, especially because it is seen as a core element in increased risk for suicide, warning that unsound postvention itself may even create guilt in survivors. Other emotional reactions that must be addressed are anger and shame. The authors show that time and tolerance are important to develop a positive process, often to address the negative reaction of PTSD (i.e., denial, avoidance). They warn us about quick fixer-uppers, noting that "Postvention efforts can do more harm than good."

Carter and Brook's paper also raises the issue of "No Suicide" contracts in preventing suicide, which have increasingly come under professional scrutiny (4, 5). There is an overreliance on them including in schools with little, if any, evidence that they reduce the incidence of suicide. In R. Brown's review of the literature (4), he found a high usage; however, there is little research evidence for the contracts' utility. Often they are used to address defensively the therapist's own countertransference (notably anxiety). They are often alternatives for sound therapeutic plans and may result in diminishing the patient's responsibility. In a court of law, of course, there are no substitutes for sound and prudent behavior. R. Grabow (5) suggests that there are clinical alternatives; instead of contracting "if you have the impulse to kill yourself, will you promise to call," one could state "if you have the impulse to kill yourself, would you call," with nothing to be written or signed. Signing such documents with other forms during intake, according to T. Gutheil (4), renders this entire concept meaningless.

In the final chapter, F. Lamb, K. Dunne-Maxim, M. Underwood, and C. Sutton presented a discussion about postvention from the viewpoint of consultants. Common concerns are gaining entry into the schools and managing the crisis. Regarding the first, they note that there is abundant resistance from administration and other school staff, resulting in a significant challenge. Yet, they note that the greatest proportion of time spent in postvention is focusing on staffs' needs. Managing the crisis includes dealing with the media, involving the community (because no one school or agency can handle a crisis alone), intervening with parents, meeting faculty needs, and intervening with students. The consultants suggest that keys for successful postvention include establishing a positive relation before the crisis, recognizing the limits of the consultative role, and clarifying expectations.

All agree that work in postvention is stressful and offer the suggestion that the team approach may address such reactions.

CONCLUDING REMARKS

As we have seen, prevention, intervention, and postvention in our schools are important in addressing suicide in youth. Yet, at this time, as in 1910, critical reflection and research are urgently needed.

Part V consisted of three chapters (including this one). In Chapter 18, J. Kalafat and M. Elias provided a presentation on evaluation of school-based interventions. Evaluation of programs is at an early stage. Surveys indicate, however, a need for school-based prevention to address troubled youth and, perhaps more importantly, their peers who often know about the suicidal feelings. They note:

> *The overall pattern of results for students and educators showed gains in knowledge, and little or no impact on attitudes, except for reported confidence in talking to a suicidal peer. . . . these results are similar to other mental health programs (substance abuse, sexual behavior).*

Much more evaluation is needed, for example, about sex differences. They conclude:

> *. . . program improvement or program amelioration will not accelerate until there is greater systematic attention to implementation process evaluation. It is not enough to say that one has a carefully developed, published curriculum as the basis of one's program. Assessment must be a key step.*

We agree that research is essential.

In Chapter 19, A. Berman offered some important critical reflections. He begins, after the Nasalville parable, with the comments:

> *Suicide and self-destructive behaviors are outcomes of a very complex set of interactive factors and dynamics. Interventions born out of urgency rather than research, analysis and rigorous planning may lead to false impressions both about the problem and truly impactful solutions.*

Berman raises a number of questions:

Do we agree there is a problem?
Is there sufficient local (community) concern to mobilize a response?
Do we know enough about prevention in general, suicide prevention, in particular, to know what works and what doesn't work?
Can we agree on a strategy? Are there constraints to our efforts to respond effectively?
Are we sufficiently aware of iatrogenic effects?

We have many questions to ask ourselves about school programs in 1990. As an example, we agree with Berman that we must deemphasize that suicide and its aftermath are normal. It is not a normal solution to life's difficulties nor is the suicide generally inside the range of usual human experience for the survivors. The attempt to normalize the experiences of suicidal youth may directly counter our prevention, intervention, and postvention efforts. *We have a problem in our schools.*

We have come a long way since 1910. Oppenheim would, I believe, see quite a different state of the art of suicide prevention in schools. Yet, we have much more to do. Initially, I was going to call the chapter, *2010: Suicidology in Schools* (with the movie with the same name, fully implied). It was to be a discussion about suicide prevention in the future. That was impossible. We are in 1990, 80 years after the 1910 meeting. Hopefully, someone in 2010 will again look at suicide prevention in schools and write about the developing state of the art then.

REFERENCES

1. Friedman, P. (Ed.) (1967). *On Suicide.* New York: International Universities Press, Inc. (Original published in 1910)
2. Shneidman, E. (Ed.) (1973). *On the nature of suicide.* San Francisco: Jossey-Bass, Inc.
3. Leenaars, A. (1990). *Suicide across the life-span.* New York: Human Sciences (Plenum).
4. Brown, R. (Chair), Berman, A., Gutheil, T., Leenaars, A., & Moore, J. (1989, October). *Forensic Issues in Suicide.* Panel presented at American Academy of Psychiatry and The Law Annual Meeting, Washington, DC.
5. Grabow, R. (1989, April). *The no suicide contract: Adverse consequences of the "No Suicide" contract.* Paper presented at the American Association of Suicidology Conference, San Diego, CA.

Index